Dictionary of Management

Derek French and Heather Saward gained a wide knowledge of the terminology of management through editing books on management for leading British publishers. Derek French now manages the editing and production of reference books for Bowker Publishing Company Ltd; he has contributed articles on management to several publications, including the 6th edition of *Everyman's Encyclopaedia*. Heather Saward now works as a freelance editor and writer, specializing in the social sciences.

Dictionary
of Management

Derek French & Heather Saward

Pan Books London and Sydney

First published 1975 by Gower Press Ltd
This edition published 1977 by Pan Books Ltd
Cavaye Place, London SW10 9PG
© Derek French and Heather Saward 1975
ISBN 0 330 25066 3
Printed and bound in Great Britain by
Richard Clay (The Chaucer Press) Ltd, Bungay, Suffolk

Introduction

Dictionary of Management gives brief explanations of nearly 4000 terms that are likely to be encountered when reading about, or discussing, management topics. Because of the nature of management the scope of the dictionary is very wide. A management job can vary from supervision of a small group, following detailed instructions, to running successfully a large and complex organization for which the manager must set long-term objectives. Whatever the scale of a manager's job it always involves acting as an intermediary arranging the work of a group to fit in with the group's environment: the manager of part of an organization must be aware of the work of the other parts, a general manager has to act within economic, legal and social constraints. A dictionary of management must therefore include definitions of terms from numerous specialized subjects.

When deciding which subject areas to cover we looked at the books and journals in libraries specializing in management in order to find out what managers themselves feel they should know about. We were particularly helped, when listing the subjects for coverage, by research carried out at the London Business School and published in K. D. C. Vernon and Valerie Lang, *The London Classification of Business Studies* (London Graduate School of Business Studies, 1970).

Managers do not need to be experts on statistics, economics, law, psychology and the host of other subjects from which terms have been drawn for this dictionary. Only some concepts are relevant; we have chosen terms for inclusion when we have found them being used by people who write about management or for managers.

This technique for selecting terms for inclusion illustrates our method of writing the definitions. We have looked at the way in which writers about management use their special terminology and our definitions are descriptions of the meanings such writers give to words, pointing out where necessary, differences in usage.

We do not prescribe how words should be used. From time to time, it is suggested that, for example, 'stock' should mean a collection of goods in store while 'inventory' should mean a statement of the size of such a collection, or that 'management' should refer only to 'carrying out orders' while deciding on policies should be called 'direction'. Of course, people can decide to use words in special ways in their own work if they feel it helps their analysis or exposition, but a dictionary would be less than helpful if it failed to describe all contemporary (and some obsolete) uses of words. However, we have taken note of the recommendations of authoritative organizations, such as the British Standards Institution, whose job it is to lay down standard usage.

We intend the dictionary to be equally useful to American and British readers. We have carefully distinguished American and British usage, particularly of financial and accounting terminology. The dictionary gives full details of transatlantic variations in spelling.

The following paragraphs describe the conventions adopted in the dictionary.

Alphabetical order

Entry titles are in **bold** type and are listed in alphabetical order letter by letter (ignoring spaces and hyphens). For example, income bond, incomes policy, income statement are in that order.

Abbreviations

If an entry word has a commonly used abbreviation then that

is put after the entry title in parentheses. Abbreviations are also given entries of their own, grouped together under their first letters. Abbreviations are set entirely in capitals without points unless some other style (as with AIScB or c. & f.) is usual. In practice abbreviations are often written or printed with a full point after every letter (or group of letters) that represents a separate word (for example, A.I.Sc.B.) though this is now rather less common than in the past. It is quite common for abbreviations to be written or printed entirely in lower-case letters.

Function

If a word can be used with two or more different grammatical functions (for example, as a noun or as a verb) then separate entries are given for each function. The name of the part of speech defined is put in parentheses after the entry title. However, in English any word used as a noun can be used as an adjective. (Writers about management are particularly fond of piling up phrases like 'production management information system control'.) If a word is used as a noun then the dictionary gives a definition for that usage but not for the word's use as an adjective. To get the meaning as an adjective it is usually sufficient to put 'relating to' or 'characterized by' in front of the noun definition. Similarly, no distinction is drawn between transitive and intransitive uses of verbs.

Sense division

When a word can be used with more than one distinct meaning (but the same grammatical function) according to context then the definitions in this dictionary of the different meanings are preceded by arabic numerals without parentheses. There is usually no significance in the order chosen for listing the different senses although sometimes the more general meaning is given first.

Cross-references

Within an entry, a word or phrase is set in *italic* to indicate that it is defined in the dictionary. (Sometimes an inflected form—such as a plural or a participle—is italicized although the entry word to be consulted is in the uninflected form.) If the cross-reference is to only one meaning of a word with several meanings then the identifying number of the relevant meaning is given in square brackets in the cross-reference.

Geographical variation

The labels '(US.)' and '(UK.)' are used to indicate that the meaning so labelled is found almost exclusively in the USA (and countries, such as Canada, that follow US usage) or the UK, respectively. '(Chiefly US.)' and similar phrases are used where appropriate with obvious meanings. Unlabelled meanings are to be taken as common to all territories.

Spelling

If the US and UK spellings of a word differ then the dictionary gives both. The US spelling has a separate entry in its correct alphabetical position unless that would be next to the British spelling. The US spelling is always given as a variant in parentheses after the entry title in British spelling.

Words (such as organize) that end in '-ize' can be spelt either with '-ize' or '-ise' at the end (for exceptions see the next paragraph). Similarly, inflected forms (-izes, -ized, -izing, -ization) can be spelt with 'z' or with 's'. In the USA, 's' spelling is very rare; in the UK 's' spelling is sometimes adopted, especially in newspapers. In this dictionary, 'z' spelling is used. For a full explanation of the different styles of spelling, and of why 'z' spelling is preferable, see H. W. Fowler, *A Dictionary of Modern English Usage,* 2nd edition by Sir Ernest Gowers (Oxford: Clarendon Press, 1965), p. 314.

The words for which there are entries in this dictionary and which are always spelt with an 's' (both in the UK and the USA) are: advertise, demise, devise, excise, merchandise and supervise. In addition, when a body such as the International Labour Organisation, is known to adopt 's' spelling for its title consistently then that spelling is followed when referring to the body in the dictionary.

Capital letters

Entry titles are set in lower-case letters but letters that would usually be capitalized in printing regardless of the position of the word in a sentence are capitalized in the entry title. If lower-case or capital letters may be used according to personal taste then the entry title is in lower case and a note is given that capitals are used 'often' or 'sometimes' as appropriate. If capitalization is usual for only some senses of a word with several meanings then the entry title is in lower case and information about capitalization is given in the relevant sections of the definition.

Italics

An entry title is set in *bold italic* if it is usual to set the word in italic when printing English (or to underline it when typing). In fact is is quite difficult to decide whether italicization is 'usual' or not and fashions change rapidly. Therefore, most of the words italicized in this dictionary may be found printed without italicization (in some circumstances, of course, italics are not available anyway).

Synonyms

If two words or phrases have a common meaning then a full definition is given only in the entry for the word more commonly used with that meaning; the entry for the less common synonym has a cross-reference to the entry for the commoner word. If synonyms would appear next to each other in the alphabetical listing then the less common one is merely noted as a variant in the entry for the commoner word (unless this would be confusing).

In a few cases (under 'profit' for example) words with similar meanings have been grouped together and an indication given of differences in usage.

Professional associations

Whenever possible, the information about professional associations has been verified by those associations. We are very grateful to the secretaries and other officials of these organizations who have helped us in this way.

For DVF & WHF
DF
For WIMR & GJM
HS
with love

Recent changes to UK industrial-relations institutions mentioned in the Dictionary

The name of the *Conciliation and Arbitration Service* was changed in November 1974 to Advisory, Conciliation and Arbitration Service (ACAS).

The *Industrial Arbitration Board* was replaced, on 1 February 1976, by a Central Arbitration Committee (CAC) with members appointed by the Secretary of State for Employment after nomination by ACAS. Some members are experienced in representing employees and some in representing employers.

The *Terms and Conditions of Employment Act 1959* will be repealed and replaced by a new procedure in the Employment Protection Act 1975 under which claims are considered by ACAS and, if necessary, referred to the CAC. At the time of going to press, no date had been fixed for bringing this new procedure into effect.

Since 1 January 1976, *wages councils* have themselves had the power to make orders fixing minimum wages, holidays and holiday pay: *wages regulation orders* are no longer made by the Secretary of State for Employment.

a

AAIA. Abbreviation of 'associate of the Association of International Accountants' (see *Association of International Accountants*).

AB. Abbreviation of *aktiebolag*.

ABAA. Abbreviation of 'associate of the British Association of Accountants and Auditors' (see *British Association of Accountants and Auditors*).

ABC analysis/classification/method/system. See *usage-value classification*.

ACA. Abbreviation of 'associate of the Institute of Chartered Accountants in England and Wales' (see *Institute of Chartered Accountants in England and Wales*).

ACCA. Abbreviation of 'associate of the Association of Certified Accountants (see *Association of Certified Accountants*).

ACIS. Abbreviation of 'associate of the Institute of Chartered Secretaries and Administrators' (originally 'associate of the Chartered Institute of Secretaries'). See *Institute of Chartered Secretaries and Administrators*.

ACT. Abbreviation of *advance corporation tax*.

ad. Abbreviation of *advertisement*.

ADP. Abbreviation of *automatic data processing*.

ad val. Abbreviation of *ad valorem*.

AEDP. Abbreviation of 'Association européenne pour la

direction de personnel'—the French title of the *European Association for Personnel Management*.

AFL-CIO. Abbreviation of *American Federation of Labor—Congress of Industrial Organizations*.

AG. Abbreviation of *Aktiengesellschaft*.

AGM. Abbreviation of *annual general meeting*.

AIScB. Abbreviation of 'associate member of the Institute of Scientific Business' (see *Institute of Scientific Business*).

AIWM. Abbreviation of 'associate of the Institution of Works Managers' (see *Institution of Works Managers*).

AMA. Abbreviation of *American Management Association*.

AMBIM. Abbreviation of 'associate member of the British Institute of Management' (see *British Institute of Management*).

AMIEx. Abbreviation of 'associate member of the Institute of Export' (see *Institute of Export*).

AOQ. Abbreviation of *average outgoing quality*.

AOQL. Abbreviation of *average outgoing quality limit*.

AQL. Abbreviation of *acceptable quality level*.

A/S. 1. Abbreviation of *aksjeselskap*. 2. Abbreviation of *aktieselskab*.

ASCA. Abbreviation of 'associate of the Society of Company and Commercial Accountants' (see *Society of Company and Commercial Accountants*).

ATM. Abbreviation of *Association of Teachers of Management*.

abatement. An allowance or deduction.

above-the-line. 1. Taken into consideration when computing a specified kind of profit (especially *gross profit*). 2. Of, or relating to, *promotion* [1] using media whose proprietors usually pay commission to *advertising agencies*. These media are: press (newspapers, magazines, directories and annuals), television, radio, cinema, posters and public transport.

absenteeism. Failure of workers to report for work when they are scheduled to work—especially when caused by unwillingness rather than incapacity.

absolute value. The magnitude of a quantity, ignoring whether it is positive or negative. Denoted by two vertical rules: thus $|-3| = |3| = 3$.

absorption. Synonym for *overhead absorption*.

absorption costing. Computation of the cost of a unit of production as the total of all costs (*variable, semivariable* and *fixed*) associated with the manufacture of that unit.

accelerated depreciation. *Depreciation* [2] of a *fixed asset* at a faster rate than with *straightline depreciation*—e.g. by using the *declining balance* method.

accelerated vocational training. Training or (usually) *retraining* which is intended to help adult workers to acquire skills which traditionally have been acquired by *apprenticeship* in a much shorter period than is usually taken by an apprenticeship. Training programmes of this type are usually government sponsored.

accelerating premium bonus plan/scheme/system. A *preminm bonus scheme* in which the *incentive payment* per unit of time saved increases as more time is saved. (Also known as a 'progressive scheme'.)

acceleration clause. A provision in an agreement for the repayment of a loan by instalments that if a specified number of instalments are not paid then all the outstanding payments are due immediately.

accept. 1. To act as an *acceptor* of a *bill of exchange*. 2. To communicate, to an *offeror*, one's agreement to be bound by the *contract* that he proposed.

acceptable quality level (AQL). The maximum percentage of *defectives* (or number of *defects* per 100 units) that will be accepted in the output from a production process.

acceptance. An instance or the act of *accepting*.

acceptance credit. An arrangement between an importer in country A and an *accepting house* in country B by which the accepting house undertakes to *accept* [1] *bills of exchange* drawn by firms in its country who sell goods to the importer. When the accepting house pays the bills it is reimbursed by the importer. Thus the accepting house, and not the sellers of goods, takes the risk of the importer failing to pay. The importer pays a commission to the accepting house. See also, *credit* [4].

acceptance sampling. Taking a *random sample* of the units of output from a manufacturing process in order to determine whether a batch has an *acceptable quality level*.

accepting house. A firm which arranges *acceptance credits* and guarantees to pay *bills of exchange* of which it is the drawee. *Especially*, one of the 17 members of the Accepting Houses Committee in London. They are all *merchant banks* that have a particularly high reputation for granting acceptance credits (mainly to foreign importers). The bills of exchange that are drawn on one of these accepting houses are considered as having a low risk (the *Bank of England* guarantees to buy them if they are offered) and therefore are *discounted* [2] at a low rate (i.e. they may be sold for a high price).

acceptor. A drawee of a *bill of exchange* who signifies (usually by signing the bill) his agreement—either unconditionally or with qualifications—to pay the amount specified in the bill.

access time. In *computing*, the time interval between the instant the *control unit* calls for an item of data to be transferred to or from a *store* [4] and the instant when that operation is complete.

accident book. A book which almost every employer in the UK must keep at each workplace so that any employee can make a record of any personal injury suffered by him as a result of an accident at work. The legal requirements are specified in regulation 3 of the National Insurance (Industrial Injuries) (Claims and Payments) Regulations 1964 (SI 1964/73). The main purpose of the record is so that an employee can have evidence to support a claim for benefit under the industrial injuries insurance scheme.

accident frequency rate. Number of *lost-time accidents* per 100 000 man-hours worked.

accommodation bill. A *bill of exchange* that is drawn up simply to enable the payee to *discount* [2] it and thus gain money. Common arrangements are: (1) the payee (who is also the drawer) promises to reimburse the drawee after the bill is paid—on these conditions the drawee *accepts* [1] the bill; (2) the payee (again also the drawer) gives half the proceeds of discounting to the drawee and repays the rest later. (Also known as a 'kite'.)

accommodation party. Someone who signs a *bill of exchange* either as *drawer, acceptor* or *endorser,* but receives no value in exchange—i.e. he does it to lend his (presumably respected) name as a guarantor that the bill will be paid so that the payee can easily discount it. The payee is, therefore, 'accommodated'.

account. 1. A list of financial transactions relating either to a particular class of the *assets* [1] or *liabilities* [2] of a person or firm or to dealings with one other person or firm. 2. One of the 24 periods into which the year is split by the *Stock Exchange* [2]. A deal concerning *securities* [1] other than *government stocks* which is agreed at any time during one of these periods, actually takes place (i.e. the seller delivers securities and the buyer delivers money) on *account day.* 3. A continuing arrangement between a bank and a firm or individual (called a 'customer') under which the bank will provide defined services to the customer and the customer will *deposit* money with the bank: usually classified as *current accounts* [1] and *deposit accounts. Also* the *fund* [1] of money deposited by the customer (in phrases such as 'pay into an account'). *Also* a list of transactions relating to a particular account. 4. A regular client of a firm; especially of an *advertising agency.* 5. Synonym for *charge account.* 6. A *statement.*

accountability. State, or quality, of being *accountable.*

accountable. Liable to be required by a specified person (or group of people) to report on and justify actions in relation to specified matters.

accountant. One who performs, or is skilled in, *accounting.*

account day. The day on which deals made during the previous Stock Exchange *account* [2] must be settled (i.e. the buyer must pay the agreed price). It is 7 business days after the end of the account. Also known as 'settlement day' or 'settling day'.

account dealing. A transaction on the Stock Exchange which is to be completed on the next *account day.*

account executive. Employee of an *advertising agency* who is responsible for all matters relating to a specific client or clients (i.e. *accounts* [4]).

accounting. Principles and procedures of recording financial transactions. *Also* an instance of applying those principles and procedures.

5

accounting asset. See *asset* [1].

accounting period. Normal interval between the date of one *balance sheet* for a firm and the date of the next; the period covered by an *income statement*.

accounting rate of return. Synonym for *rate of return*.

accounting ratio. A *financial ratio*.

account payable. The cost of some goods or services that a firm has bought but not yet paid for.

account receivable. A sum of money owed to a firm by one of its customers.

account rendered. A statement sent by a seller to his customer of the amount that the customer owes, details of which have previously been sent.

account stated. An *account* [1] of transactions between two parties who both agree its contents.

accrual. An *accrued expense* or an *accrued revenue*.

accrual accounting. Making up accounts in which income and expense are recorded at the time when they are incurred and not when they are actually received or paid.

accrued asset. Synonym for *accrued revenue*.

accrued expense (or accrued liability). The amount incurred up to a specified date of a *liability* [1] that accumulates continually but is customarily payable at fixed times. For example, if a firm pays for electricity once a quarter then the cost of one month's consumption of electricity is an accrued expense at the end of that month.

accrued revenue. The amount accumulated, up to a specified date, of a continually increasing debt, due to one, which is customarily payable at fixed times. For example, if a person owns a *security* [1] that entitles him to a payment of £40 interest each December then in March he has an accrued revenue of £10. (Sometimes called an 'accrued asset'.)

accumulation factor. See *terminal value*.

achievement test. A test that shows the extent to which a person has acquired a specific skill. (Also known as an 'attainment test'.)

acid-test ratio. The ratio of a firm's *liquid assets* to its *current liabilities*. The ratio indicates the firm's ability to pay its debts.

(Also known as the 'quick ratio'.)

acquisition. Purchase by one firm of another. (See *merger.)*

across-the-board. Applying to everyone, or all cases, or everything. As in 'across-the-board increase': increase in wages of the same extent for every employee in an organization.

action-centred leadership. Leadership that is achieved by carrying out the actions that are expected of a leader. The phrase is associated with the work of the English management educator John Eric Adair (born 1934) who holds that leadership can be learned and is not simply a quality that certain people are born possessing. See, e.g. J. Adair, *Action-centred Leadership* (London: McGraw-Hill, 1973).

action limit. A line drawn on a *quality control chart* that indicates that if any sample goes beyond it then corrective action must be taken.

action research. Research, especially in the *behavioural sciences,* into a situation in order to bring about some practical improvement in that situation, as well as contributing to the store of academic knowledge.

action training. *Training* in which *activity learning* is emphasized.

activity. In *project network techniques,* an activity is the work required to complete a specific *event.*

activity learning. Learning by means of active participation, e.g. in *projects* [5] or discussions, as opposed to passive means such as lectures.

activity network. Synonym for *network.*

activity-on-arrow network. A *network* in which the *arrows* [2] represent *activities.* (Also known as an 'arrow diagram'.)

activity-on-node network. A *network* in which the *nodes* represent *activities.* The *arrows* [2] in an activity-on-node network are sometimes called 'sequence arrows'. (Also known as a 'node diagram'.)

activity-on-node system. Any *project network technique* that uses *activity-on-node networks* rather than *activity-on-arrow networks.*

activity ratio. A *financial ratio* that indicates how much use a

7

firm makes of its *assets* [1]—usually the ratio of total *sales revenue* over a period to the average value of a particular class of assets (such as stocks of *finished goods, cash, fixed assets*) during the period. (Also known as an 'efficiency ratio'.)

activity sampling. Recording instantaneous observations of the work or other activity that is being performed by an employee or a machine at specific points in time. The times of the observations are normally determined randomly to ensure an unbiased sample. (Also known as 'work sampling'.)

act of bankruptcy. An action committed by a debtor that an English court will recognize as justification for granting a *receiving order* (the first stage of making the debtor *bankrupt*). For example, if a debtor fails to comply with the terms of a *bankruptcy notice* then the creditor who obtained the notice can use this failure as a ground for asking a court to make a receiving order.

actuary. A person who calculates insurance *premiums* [4] on behalf of *insurers*.

adaptive control. *Control* [3] in which the standards to which the controlled behaviour must conform are altered in response to changing circumstances.

adaptive control system. A *control system* in which automatic means are used to adjust the system being controlled in a way that is intended to achieve optimum performance by the system at all times rather than a predetermined value of the controlled condition. (Also called a 'self-optimizing control system'.)

added value. Synonym for *value added*.

address. In computing, designation of a particular *location* in a *store* [4].

adjective. Procedural; of, or relating to, how tasks should be performed rather than which tasks should be performed.

adjusting entry. An entry in a firm's *accounts* [1] (in a system of *accrual accounting*) that does not record a transaction but adjusts the accounts in order to reflect more accurately the financial position of the firm at a particular date (e.g. in order to prepare a *balance sheet* and *income statement*). An adjusting entry is made, e.g., in order to apportion a *prepaid expense* (such as an insurance premium) between two accounting periods, to record *depreciation* [2], or to correct errors.

administer. To supervise some activity (especially the use of money or other assets) in accordance with established rules or in accordance with the wishes of another person. In particular, to act as *personal representative* in relation to someone's estate.

administration. 1. Synonym for *management;* especially in government or public service (public administration). 2. Activities connected with keeping records and information processing; paperwork. 3. Activities concerned with applying rules, procedures and policies determined by others. 4. The government of the day in a country—i.e. the politicians appointed by the country's political leader to take charge of particular departments. 5. The duties of an *administrator* [2].

administrative law. The law relating to the discharge of functions of a public nature in government and administration.

administrative management theory. An approach to developing general principles of management in which attention is concentrated on formal *organization structures.* The administrative-management approach dominated thinking about management in the 1930s. It replaced the *scientific-management* approach and was itself replaced by the *human relations school.* Administrative management theory was particularly influenced by the views of Henri Fayol (1841–1925) who was chief executive of the French mining and metalworking firm, Commentry-Fourchambault-Decazeville, which he rescued from the verge of bankruptcy. His article 'Administration, industrielle et générale', *Bulletin de la Société de l'industrie minérale* (1916, no. 3), was translated by J. A. Coubrough as *Industrial and General Administration* (Geneva: International Management Institute, 1929). Other important contributors to the theory were two executives of General Motors Corporation, James D. Mooney and Alan C. Reiley, whose *Onward Industry* was published in 1930, the American political and business philosopher, Mary Parker Follett (1868–1933), the American expert on public administration, Luther Halsey Gulick (born 1892) and the British management consultant, Lyndall Fownes Urwick (born 1891). The principal

9

writings of these theorists are : M. P. Follett, *Dynamic Administration*: *The Collected Papers of Mary Parker Follett,* edited by E. M. Fox and L. Urwick, 2nd edition (London : Pitman, 1973); *Papers on the Science of Administration,* edited by L. Gulick and L. Urwick (New York : Institute of Public Administration, Columbia University, 1937/reissued 1969 by Augustus M. Kelly, New York); L. Urwick, *The Elements of Administration,* 2nd edition (London : Pitman, 1947) and the second translation, by Constance Storrs, of Fayol's book, *General and Industrial Management* (London : Pitman, 1949).

The term, 'administrative management theory' was coined by James G. March and Herbert A. Simon, in *Organizations* (New York : Wiley, 1958).

administrator. 1. A person who undertakes *administration.* 2. A person appointed, by *letters of administration,* to act as *personal representative* of a deceased person.

ad referendum. For further consideration.

adult rate. See *rate-for-age scale.*

ad valorem (ad val.). According to value. Especially a tax that is proportional to the value of the goods or transaction, on which it is levied.

advance corporation tax (ACT). A tax paid by a company resident in the UK whenever it *distributes* any *profits.* If a company has paid ACT during a year then the amount is deducted from the *corporation tax* it has to pay for that year. For the *financial year* 1974, the rate of ACT is 33/67 of the amount distributed.

advanced development. Activities concerned with detailed investigation of a proposed new product or proposed solution to a problem where it has been decided that the proposal should be implemented if the advanced development study is successful.

advertise. 1. To act as an *advertiser.* 2. To put out *advertisements.*

advertisement (ad). A message, composed by, or approved by, a person, firm or other organization (called the 'advertiser'), which is presented to a number of people (often a large number) at the expense of the advertiser to persuade whoever receives it to accept an idea, buy a product or take some other action desired by the advertiser.

advertiser. See *advertisement*.

advertising. 1. *Advertisements*. 2. The activity of planning and preparing *advertisements*. Usually restricted to advertisements that are carried by media of mass communication (such as newspapers, radio, television and posters) and, sometimes, *direct-mail advertising;* other forms of advertising (e.g. by giving away calendars or pencils with an advertisement on them) are included in *sales promotion*. See *below-the-line* [2].

advertising agency. A firm which designs *advertisements* for clients who wish to advertise and arranges for the advertisements to be carried by media. Agencies receive fees for their work from their clients. Media owners customarily allow a discount (of 15%) from the price of carrying advertisements placed by recognized advertising agencies; this is a hangover from the times when the agencies acted as agents for the media owners in selling advertising space, but now the discount is passed on to the clients.

advertising manager. An employee of a firm who supervises the production of the firm's *advertisements* and decides which media will carry them.

advertising specialty. A useful article which is given away by an advertiser and which is imprinted with the advertiser's name and address and /or a sales message. The most common types of advertising specialty are calendars, writing instruments and matchbooks. (Also known as an 'advertising novelty'.)

advice note. A document sent by a seller to a buyer stating the description and quantity of goods that have been despatched to him.

affidavit. A written statement made by someone who swears that it is true to a person authorized to supervise the making of such statements (e.g., a commissioner for oaths).

affirmative action programme. ('Program' in US.) Employment practices and policies of an organization that are designed to ensure that disadvantaged sections of the community (ethnic groups, women, older workers) are encouraged to work at all levels of the organization. *Also* a statement of such a programme.

afternoon shift. A shift that is worked mainly during the afternoon—e.g.: (1) the later shift during a day in a *double day-shift system*; (2) a shift worked mainly in the afternoon in a *three-shift system*, typically worked from 14 00 to 22 00; (3) a *part-time shift* worked, for example, from 14 00 to 18 00.

after-sales service. A continuing service of maintenance, repair, supply of information on possible uses, and so on, provided to buyers of a product by the seller (or sometimes the manufacturer if the sale was made by a retailer).

agate line. (US.) A measure of advertising space in newspapers equal to a space one-fourteenth of an inch deep and one column wide. From the now obsolete system of naming type sizes after precious stones; agate type (called ruby in the UK) occupied a space one-fourteenth of an inch (5½ points) deep.

agency. 1 The powers or functions of an *agent*. 2. The relationship between an *agent* and his principal. 3. A firm that acts as an *agent* for others. 4. An administrative division of a government.

agency shop. A place of employment where all employees doing particular types of work must pay subscriptions to particular trade unions although they may refuse to actually join a union.

agenda. A list of things to be discussed at a meeting.

agent. A person or firm that acts on behalf of someone else (called the 'principal') and is capable of making the principal a party to legally binding contracts.

agreement. 1. A *contract,* especially one that is in writing. 2. The act or fact of agreeing.

aida. Mnemonic from 'attention, interest, desire, action'—a sequence of responses which, it has been suggested, a salesman should attempt to obtain from a potential buyer.

aided-recall method. Technique for assessing the effectiveness of *advertising* in which an interviewer shows someone an advertisement (or quotes from it) and asks whether he remembers having seen or heard it.

air consignment note. An *air waybill*.

air waybill. A *waybill* covering carriage by air.

aksjeselskap (A/S). (Literally, 'share company'.) A *limited company* organized according to the laws of Norway.

aktiebolag (AB). (Literally, 'share company'.) A *limited company* organized according to the laws of Sweden.

Aktiengesellschaft (AG). (Literally 'share company'.) 1. A *public limited company* organized according to the laws of the Federal Republic of Germany. An AG must have a minimum *contributed capital* of 100 000 *Deutschemarks*. An AG has two *boards of directors*: a *Vorstand*, which carries out the direction and management of the AG and an *Aufsichtsrat*, elected by *shareholders* and employees which supervises the conduct of the *Vorstand* (see *two-tier board*). 2. A *public limited company* organized according to the laws of Austria. It must have a minimum *contributed capital* of 1 million Schillings and must have a *two-tier board*. 3. A *public limited company* organized according to the laws of Switzerland. It must have a minimum *contributed capital* of 50 000 Swiss francs.

aktieselskab (A/S). A *public limited company* organized according to the laws of Denmark.

ALGOL. (Acronym from 'algorithmic language'.) A *procedure-oriented language* for computer programming. It is especially useful for describing mathematical procedures. There are three versions of increasing sophistication identified by the year of publication: ALGOL 58, ALGOL 60 and ALGOL 68. A complete specification is given in: A. van Wijngaarden, B. J. Mailloux, J. E. L. Peck and C. H. A. Koster, 'Report on the algorithmic language ALGOL 68', *Numerische Mathematik*, vol. 14 (1969), pp 79–218. Introductions for users are given in: C. H. Lindsey and S. G. van der Meulen, *Informal Introduction to ALGOL 68* (Amsterdam: North-Holland, 1971) and, referring to ALGOL 60, E. Foxley, H. R. Neave and M. C. Grayshon, *A First Course in Algol 60* (London: Addison-Wesley, 1968).

algorithm. A rule or set of rules for the solution of a particular type of problem in a finite number of steps.

alienation. 1. A *conveyance* of property to another person. 2. Loss of affection. 3. Mental illness.

allocation. 1. Reservation of something (e.g. a *stock* [1] of *materials* or an amount of money) for a particular purpose or person. *Also* the quantity reserved. 2. Identification of the process, product or *cost centre* that has incurred or benefitted from a particular *expenditure*.

allonge. A piece of paper attached to a *bill of exchange* when there is no more room on the bill for the signatures of *endorsers*.

allot. To assign newly issued *shares* to their first owners.

allotment. Acceptance, by an *issuer* of new *securities* [1] of offers by people to buy the new securities. In a *public offer*, it may happen that the total number of securities that people offer to buy is more than are being issued. If that happens then the process of allotment includes a decision on the number of securities to be issued to each applicant. The people whose offers are accepted are called 'allottees'.

allotment letter. Synonym for *letter of allotment*.

allottee. A person whose offer to buy new *securities* [1] has been accepted by the *issuer* of the securities—see *allotment*.

allowed time. The time, which, for the purposes of wage payment, is taken to be the normal time for performance of *measured work*. It consists of the *standard time* [1] for the job plus a *bonus increment* and/or a *policy allowance*.

alphameric code. Synonym for *alphanumeric code*.

alphanumeric code (or alphanumerical code, or alphameric code). A *code* [2] which makes use of both numerals and letters of the alphabet.

alternate. A person who is appointed to act as a substitute for another person in performing specified duties whenever the other person is unavailable.

alternate director. A person appointed to act as an *alternate* for a *director*.

alternating day and night. A *two-shift system* in which one group of workers work for a period (e.g. a week, fortnight, or month) on a *day shift* [1] then for the same period on a *night shift*.

amalgamation. A *merger*—especially by agreement between all concerned with the merged organizations.

American Federation of Labor—Congress of Industrial

14

Organizations (AFL—CIO). Federation of US *trade unions* formed in 1955 from the merger of the American Federation of Labor (AFL) (which was a federation of craft unions formed in 1881) and the Congress of Industrial Organizations (which was a federation of industrial unions that were expelled from the AFL in 1936).

American Management Association (AMA). An association of over 58 000 individuals and firms formed in 1923 to provide the training, research and information services needed by managers to do a better job. AMA publishes the monthly magazines, *Management Review* and *Supervisory Management* and the bimonthly *Personnel*.

Address : 135 West 50th Street, New York, NY 10020.

amortization. 1. The process or act of *amortizing*. 2. The amounts paid or set aside to *amortize* [1] a debt. 3. Systematic estimation of how much of the *cost* [1] of an *intangible asset* has expired. Also the amount of *expense* [3] determined by such an estimation.

amortize. 1. To pay off a loan gradually or to put aside money periodically in order to pay off a loan. 2. To calculate an amount of *amortization*.

analogue computer (in USA, usually spelt analog computer). A *computer* in which data are represented by measurable quantities, such as voltages, resistances, lengths or angles, rather than by digits.

analysis of variance. Techniques used in *statistical inference* to determine whether a *sample variance* can be attributed to specific causes or whether it is to be expected because of the nature of the *population* from which the sample is drawn. (Note: this is not the same as *variance analysis*.)

analytical estimating. Technique of *work measurement* in which a job (typically, a lengthy and infrequently performed task) is analysed into elements and the times for the elements are assessed either from *synthetic data* if available or from experience.

annual allowance. Obsolete name for *writing-down allowance*.

annual general meeting (AGM). A *general meeting* of the

15

members of a *registered company* at which the *directors* must present an *income statement, balance sheet, auditors' report* and *directors' report*. Every registered company must hold an annual general meeting once in each calendar year and the interval between two annual general meetings must be no more than 15 months.

annual payment. A recurrent payment, such as a payment of *interest* or an *annuity*. In UK tax law, the phrase means a recurrent payment made under a binding legal obligation (such as a contract or a court order) that is 'pure income profit' to the recipient (i.e. the recipient does not give goods or services in return).

annual profits or gains. A phrase used in UK income-tax law to cover any kind of receipt that is not a *capital receipt* but is not covered by any of the *Schedules* [3] that describe types of income.

annual report. A report which someone is obliged to make annually. Specifically, the *directors' report* of a British *registered company*.

annual return. A *return* [2] that someone is obliged to make annually. Specifically, the details of activities during the year that each British *registered company* must send to the *Registrar of Companies* who makes it available for public inspection.

annual usage value. In *stock control,* the total cost of the quantity of a particular *stock-keeping unit* used during a year.

annual value. The rent which the owner of a piece of property could get from letting it for a year to a tenant if the tenant paid *rates* and the landlord paid for repairs and insurance.

annuitant. One who receives an *annuity*.

annuity. A sum of money paid regularly (originally, annually) to a person (called the 'annuitant'), either for a fixed number of years (an 'annuity certain') or until the recipient dies (a life annuity).

annuity certain. An *annuity* that is payable for a fixed number of years (whether or not the *annuitant* lives).

anomie. 1. Lack of, or loss of, commonly held values in a social system. 2. State, of an individual, of having confused values, often accompanied by a feeling of isolation.

ante-date. To give a document a date that is earlier than the actual date of writing the document.

anthropometry. Study of human body measurements.

antifeatherbedding. Of, or relating to, moves to prevent *featherbedding* [2].

antitrust. Of, or relating to, legislation or action (especially in the USA) to curb *monopolies* and *restrictive trade practices*.

aperture card. A *punched card* (80 column) in which there is a rectangular aperture designed to contain a single frame of 35mm microfilm. Aperture cards are used to store *microcopies* of documents, engineering drawings etc. They are punched with data describing the microcopied material for use with automatic sorting processes.

a posteriori **probability.** A *probability* of an event that is estimated by observing the actual frequency of occurrence of the event.

application form. 1. A form completed by someone who applies for a job with an employer and on which he sets out basic facts about himself and his suitability for employment. (Known as an 'application blank' in the USA.) 2. A form completed by a person who wishes to buy *securities* in a *public offer* on which he states the number of securities he would like to buy.

application program. A *program* [1] of instructions for a computer to perform a particular data-processing job of value to its user. (Cf. *utility program, supervisory program*.)

apportionment. An act or result of making a proportionate division or distribution of something.

appraisal. 1. Considered judgment of the value or worth of something or someone. 2. Synonym for *performance appraisal*.

appraisal interview. An interview carried out as part of *performance appraisal*.

appraisal review. Synonym for *appraisal interview*.

appreciation. A rise in value, especially of one currency in terms of another.

apprentice (noun). An *employee* who has entered into a special contract with his employer whereby the employer will provide

17

the apprentice with training in a craft or trade for a specified number of years and the apprentice will work for that employer for that number of years.

apprentice (verb). To employ as an *apprentice*.

apprenticeship. The state or condition of being an *apprentice*.

appropriation account. A statement of how a profit shown in an *income statement* has been used or how a loss has been made good.

appropriation budget. See *budget* [2].

a priori **probability.** The actual *probability* of an event which may be estimated from its *a posteriori probability*.

aptitude. Natural ability to acquire a skill or a type of knowledge.

aptitude test. A test of a person's ability to learn a task or of potential ability to perform a task (cf. *proficiency test*).

arbitrage. Taking advantage of the existence of two or more different market prices for some commodity by entering into contracts simultaneously to buy and sell it (or to borrow money at a low rate of interest and lend it at a high rate). If only two market prices are involved the operation is called 'simple' or 'one-point' arbitrage; if three or more market prices (and contracts) are involved the operation is called 'compound' or 'two-point', 'three-point', etc., arbitrage. See also, *simple arbitrage*.

arbitrageur. Someone who practises *arbitrage*.

arbitrate. To act as an *arbitrator*.

arbitration. An instance, or the process, of acting as an *arbitrator*.

arbitrator. A person chosen by the parties to a dispute to suggest a way of settling the dispute. An arbitrator is usually chosen because he is independent of the disputants and because they think he will apply principles of fairness and practicality, rather than legal rules, in formulating his suggested solution (which is usually called an 'award'). It is usual for disputants to agree to be bound by any award their chosen arbitrator makes.

arc. Synonym for *directed edge*. 2. A sequence of connected *edges* on a *graph* [2] which includes no *vertex* more than once. When edges are *directed edges*, this is also called a *path* [1].

area sampling. Synonym for *cluster sampling*.

arithmetic mean. The arithmetic mean of n numbers, $a_1, \ldots, a_n$, is $(a_1 + \ldots + a_n)/n$.

arithmetic unit. The part of a *computer* (consisting usually of electronic devices) that carries out operations (such as addition) on data.

arrears. An unpaid or overdue debt.

arrow. 1. A *directed edge* on a *graph* [2]. 2. A line on a *network*, which connects two *nodes*, represents an *activity* or a relationship between *events* and has an arrowhead pointing toward the node that occurs later.

arrow diagram. Synonym for *activity-on-arrow network*.

articles of association. The rules governing the relationship between a British *registered company*, its *members* and its *directors*.

A company's articles of association must be sent to the *Registrar of Companies* when the company is first registered and any alterations to the articles must also be sent to the Registrar, who makes these documents available for public inspection.

(In the USA, similar rules governing the affairs of corporations are called 'bylaws'.)

articles of incorporation. Synonym for *certificate of incorporation* [2].

assemble. To carry out a process of *assembly* [1].

assembly. 1. The process of adding pieces to an item during manufacture, e.g. by welding, stapling or riveting. *Also* a piece of work that has been assembled. 2. (Capital A.) The 'European Parliament' set up on 1 January 1958 to debate all major questions of policy for the three *European Communities*. At present the Assembly consists of 198 delegates selected from the national parliaments of member states according to procedures laid down by each state. It is envisaged that members will eventually be elected directly.

assembly chart. Synonym for *gozinto chart*.

assembly line. See *production line*.

assembly sheet. A set of instructions for putting together an *assembly* [1].

assessment. 1. The process or activity or an act of determining an amount of tax to be paid. *Also* the amount of tax so determined. 2. Synonym for *appraisal*.

asset. 1. Something that: (*a*) is owned by a specified person or firm; (*b*) confers or is expected to confer an economic benefit to its owner; and (*c*) can be given a value in terms of money. (Sometimes called an 'accounting asset'.) Accounting assets of a firm are usually classified, according to their use by the firm, as *current assets* and noncurrent assets. Accounting assets are also classified, according to their form, as *intangible assets* or *tangible assets*. 2. (Plural.) The monetary value of the accounting assets of a firm. 3. A resource; something which confers an advantage but is not necessarily capable of being objectively valued.

asset stripping. Taking over a company in order to sell its *fixed assets* or use them for an entirely different purpose. The process almost always involves ending the business that the taken-over company was engaged in and making its workers redundant.

assign (noun). Synonym for *assignee*.

assign (verb). 1. To transfer to another one's rights to property (especially *intangible property*); to transfer to another one's rights and obligations as party to a *contract*. 2. To allot a task or duties to someone; to appoint someone to perform specific duties. 3. To specify.

assignee (or, sometimes, assign). Someone to whom something has been *assigned* [1, 2].

assignment. 1. The act of *assigning*. 2. A task that has been *assigned* [2] to someone—especially a task of a complex or confidential nature. 3. A piece of work to be done by a student.

assignment analysis. A method of *job evaluation* developed for professional and technical jobs in which the *assignments* [2] that the job holder carries out are graded according to complexity, experience required and so on.

assignor (sometimes spelt assigner). Someone who *assigns*.

associated company. A company, X, is said to be an associated company of a second company, Y, if Y holds a substantial proportion (more than 20%) of X's *shares* and can influence commercial and financial policy decisions relating to X (e.g., if Y can appoint a *director* of X).

Association européenne pour la direction de personnel (AEDP). French title of the *European Association for Personnel Management*.

Association of Certified Accountants. UK professional institute for accountants with over 14 000 members. An associate (designated ACCA) must have passed the association's examinations and must have had practical experience, either as an articled clerk in a firm of accountants or by employment in the finance or accounting department of a commercial or industrial company, in one of the nationalized industries or in public service.

Fellows are designated FCCA. Associates and fellows are known as 'certified accountants'.

Address: 22 Bedford Square, London WC1B 3HS (01–636 2103).

Association of International Accountants. A professional institute for accountants in all parts of the world which aims to promote international accountancy standards.

Associates (designated AAIA) must have passed the association's examinations and must have had 5 years of approved practical experience. Fellows (designated FAIA) must have passed the examinations and had 10 years experience. Associates and fellows are described as 'international accountants'.

The association was incorporated in 1932. Originally it was a branch of the International Accountants' Corporation of Australia (formed in 1928) which has now merged with the Australian Society of Accountants.

In May 1974 the association had 2000 members but 13 500 people were registered students (only registered students may sit the association's examinations).

The association publishes *The International Accountant*, holds an annual conference and seminars on matters of professional interest.

Address: Link House (P.O. Box 38), Billericay, Essex (Billericay 55988).

Association of Teachers of Management (ATM). A group of specialists in universities, technical colleges and industry which was founded in 1960. The purpose of the association is the study and appraisal of management education with a view to raising the professional standards of its members. In particular the association aims to provide means for the communication of developments in teaching, relevant research findings and the exchange of experience. The association publishes a journal, *Management Education and Development*.

Address : 4 Fitzalan Place, Cardiff CF2 1EE.

assortment. The selection of goods offered for sale by an *intermediary* or by a *retailer*.

assurance. Synonym for *insurance* (especially in *life assurance*).

assured. A person who, if he suffers loss in a specified way, will be paid compensation under a *contract of insurance*. (Also known as an 'insured'.)

at call. Lent as a *demand deposit*.

at sight. Synonym for *on demand*.

attainment test. Synonym for *achievement test*.

attendance bonus. An addition to normal wages which an employer promises to give to any of his employees who achieve a certain standard of timekeeping or lack of absence from work.

attendance time. The total time spent by an employee either working or available for work, for which payment is made over a period.

attended time. A measure of the total usage of a machine during a period. It is equal to the total length of the period minus the 'unattended time' during that period (i.e. the time when no operator, user or maintenance engineer is available to make use of the machine).

attest. To affirm the authenticity of a signature on a document by *countersigning*.

attitude. 1. Opinion, feeling or emotion concerning an event, fact or state. 2. Consistent or characteristic way of thinking about, or responding to, something.

attitude survey. 1. A *survey* (carried out among employees of a single employer) of employees' opinions about their work, working conditions and employer. 2. A *survey* of consumers' attitudes to a product or range of products.

attorney. Someone who is appointed to act on behalf of someone else, especially: (1) under a *power of attorney*; (2) as the representative of a party to a legal dispute.

attribute listing. A technique for encouraging creative thinking about something in which a list of attributes of the thing is drawn up and each is considered in turn.

auction. A method of selling goods in which a person (called an 'auctioneer') invites an assembled collection of potential buyers to compete against each other in offering money for the goods which he will sell to the person who offers most money.

auctioneer. A person who conducts the sale of goods by *auction*.

audit (noun). 1. Critical examination and analysis of the *accounts* [1] of a firm performed by an independent person in order to assess their accuracy and, often, to detect *fraud*. 2. Critical examination and analysis of an activity by an independent person performed to check the efficiency of the activity and, often, to check *security* [3].

audit (verb). To perform an *audit*.

auditor. One who performs an *audit*. Every British *registered company* must appoint at least one independent and professionally qualified person as its auditor.

auditors' report. A report by *auditors*; specifically the report which must be attached to every *income statement* and *balance sheet* prepared for the *members* of a British *registered company*. The report to members must state whether, in the auditors' opinion, the accounts present 'a true and fair view' of the company's financial affairs.

Aufsichtsrat. (Usually translated as 'supervisory board'.) A committee of not less than three people, appointed by the *shareholders* and employees of a German or Austrian public company (an *Aktiengesellschaft*) to supervise the activities of the management board (*Vorstand*). The *Aufsichtsrat* of a company appoints the directors and determines their salaries. It has power to require the directors to report to it on any aspect of the company's affairs; it can convene *general meetings* of the shareholders. The *Aufsichtsrat* of a company is limited to giving advisory opinions and requesting information; it does not directly manage the company's affairs. (See also *two-tier board*.)

autarky. Self-sufficiency; *especially* of a country with no international trade.

authoritarianism. Reliance, by a person, on unquestioning acceptance of his directives coupled with an aversion, by him, to consulting people before formulating directives that they must carry out. Authoritarianism fits naturally in an *autocracy*.

authoritarian management. A *managerial style* characterized by the practice of *authoritarianism* and, usually, belief that human relations are irrelevant to getting work done, that people are necessarily indolent, self-centred and uncooperative, and that people require strong direction and control if discipline is to be maintained. People practising authoritarian management would accept McGregor's *Theory X*, would have a '9, 1 managerial style' according to Blake and Mouton's *managerial grid*, and would be practising *System 1* management according to Likert's analysis. Authoritarian management is also very similar to *scientific management*.

Under authoritarian management. workers are *motivated* basically by fear of losing their jobs if they disobey orders or having their wages cut if their performance is inadequate.

(Also known as 'autocratic management'.)

authority. 1. A person who makes decisions, gives opinions, judgment or information or takes action that affects other people is said to have authority if the people affected believe that, if asked, he could justify his actions in terms that they are willing to accept. Authority may be acquired, for example: (1) by study and experience that make one an expert who will be able to give a rational, intellectual justification for one's opinions or a practical demonstration that what one has said is correct; (2) by *delegation* [1] from one's superior in an organization so that his authority is one's justification; (3) by being appointed in a legitimate way to take specified action, so that the method of appointment is one's justification.

Also, a person who has expertise derived from study and experience is called an 'authority'; a document appointing someone to take specified action is called an 'authority'.

2. A book that is relied on for information or opinions that are usually believed. 3. A *local authority* or a *public utility*. 4. Competence to speak on behalf of others.

authorized capital. The total *nominal value* or *stated value* of all the *shares* that a *company* is authorized by its constitution to issue. (In the UK. also known as 'nominal share capital'.)

authorized depositary. A firm that is authorized to take custody of *bearer securities,* which under the *exchange-control* regulations of many countries, must be kept by such authorized firms (on behalf of the real owners of the securities).

autocode. A *programming language* that is not a *computer instruction code.* The word is usually used to describe only *low-level languages* which do not use *macro-instructions.*

autocracy. A *power structure* in which one person (an 'autocrat') clearly has and exercises *power* over all others in his organization; in particular a power structure in which there is no means of limiting the autocrat's exercise of his power.

autocrat. One person who exercises *power* over all others in an *autocracy.*

autocratic. Of, or resembling, an *autocrat.*

autocratic management. Synonym for *authoritarian management.*

automate. To arrange a job so that part or all of the decision-making and control previously performed by humans is performed by machines.

automatic data processing (ADP). Data processing that is performed mainly by devices (e.g. *computers*) that operate automatically. In practice the devices are usually electronic and so the term 'electronic data processing' is used.

autonomy. Self-determination; especially: (1) the right of a state to organize its affairs without external interference; (2) the discretion of an individual in an organization to make decisions without consulting other people in the organization; (3) the capability of an individual to select personal values and withstand social pressures for conformity.

aval. An *endorsement* [1] on a *bill of exchange* that is not made by the *drawer.*

AVCO. (Acronym from 'average cost'.) A method of estimating the change in value, over a period, of a stock of some good. It is used in the same circumstances as *FIFO* but valuation consists of calculating the average unit cost of the stock and multiplying by the number of units remaining at the end of the period.

average. 1. Any *statistic* [1] that indicates the commonest, or middle, value of observed values of a *random variable*. For example, the *arithmetic mean, geometric mean, median* [2] or *mode* [1]. 2. In insurance and maritime law, liability, of someone who has some interest in goods that have been lost or damaged, to bear a proportion of the loss—see *general average* and *particular average*. Especially, a liability, of an *assured*, to bear a proportion of any partial loss when he has *underinsured* his goods.

average adjuster. A *loss adjuster* who is employed by an *insurer* to determine the extent of his liability to reimburse an *assured* who has had to meet a claim for a *general average contribution* or his liability to reimburse an assured when there is a *particular average loss*.

average deviation. Synonym for *mean absolute deviation*.

average outgoing quality (AOQ). The average percentage of *defectives* (or number of *defects* per 100 units) in the part of the output from a production process that has been accepted after *acceptance sampling*.

average outgoing quality limit (AOQL). The maximum percentage of *defectives* (or number of *defects* per 100 units) in the part of the output from a production process that would be accepted using a specified method of *acceptance sampling*.

b

BACIE. Abbreviation of *British Association for Commercial and Industrial Education.*
BGA. Abbreviation of *Business Graduates Association.*
BIM. Abbreviation of *British Institute of Management.*
BIS. Abbreviation of *Bank for International Settlements.*
B/L. Abbreviation of *bill of lading.*
BMT. Abbreviation of *Basic Motion Timestudy.*
BoT. Abbreviation of *Board of Trade.*
BOTB. Abbreviation of *British Overseas Trade Board.*
BPC. Abbreviation of *British Productivity Council.*
BS. 1. Abbreviation of *British Standard.* Especially as part of the identifying code of a British Standard. 2. In accordance with a British Standard. 3. In *work study*, measured on the British Standard rating (or performance) scale defined in BS 3138.
BSI. Abbreviation of *British Standards Institution.*
BWD. Abbreviation of *Basic Work Data.*
back duty. Tax which should have been paid in the past by an individual who failed to provide adequate information at the time for the *Revenue* [4] to make a correct determination of tax payable.
back-selling. Advertising *industrial goods* to the potential buyers of products that incorporate the advertised goods. The advertiser thus creates a demand which manufacturers can satisfy only by increasing their purchases of his goods.

backshift. 1. The *afternoon shift* in a *three-shift system*. 2. A *night shift*.

backwardation. 1. A fee paid to a *stockbroker*, by someone for whom the stockbroker has arranged to sell *shares*, for the privilege of delaying delivery of the shares (usually because the seller would have to buy them from someone else if the deal was to go through on the original date for delivery). 2. A state in which the *spot price* for a quantity of a *commodity* [3] is higher than the *forward price* for the same quantity. *Also* the difference between forward and spot prices in such circumstances.

backward pass. In *project network techniques*, the calculation of *latest event times*, or of *latest start times of activities* and *earliest start times of activities*.

bad debt. A debt which, it is assumed, will never be paid.

bailee. A person who takes possession over someone else's property during *bailment*.

bailment. Transfer of possession over something from one person (called the 'bailor') to another person (called the 'bailee') in order that the bailee can perform some action for which possession of the thing is necessary (e.g. store it or repair it) and return it to the bailor when the action is complete.

bailor. A person who gives possession over some of his property to another person during *bailment*.

balance. 1. The difference between the total *credit* [1] entries and total *debit* [1] entries in an *account* [1]. 2. A remainder.

balance of payments. A classified summary of payments to residents of a country by nonresidents (shown as *credit* [1] items) and payments by residents to nonresidents (shown as *debit* [1] items) over a period. Total credits must equal total debits (i.e. the two sides must 'balance') but particular classes of payments need not balance. An important classification of payments is into 'current' and 'capital' payments (see *current account* [2] and *capital account* [1]).

balance of trade. The difference between a country's exports and imports of goods. Said to be 'favourable' when exports are higher than imports and 'unfavourable' otherwise.

balance quantity. The number of *parts, subassemblies,* or other items at a specified stage in the manufacture of a finished product, that must be completed by a specified date in order to achieve a planned output of finished products.

balance sheet. A statement of the financial position of a firm at a particular time. It shows the total value of the *assets* [1] of the firm at a particular time, balanced by the sum of the firm's total *liabilities* [1] at that time and the value of the *owners' equity*.

balancing allowance. An amount that a person or company may deduct from taxable trading profits when an *asset* is sold and the *writing-down allowances* taken up to the date of sale are less than the difference between the cost of the asset and the proceeds of the sale.

balancing charge. An amount that is added to the taxable trading profits of a person or company when an *asset* is sold and the *writing-down allowances* taken up to the date of sale exceed the difference between the cost of the asset and the proceeds of the sale.

balloon note. A loan which is to be repaid by a number of small instalments and a large final payment. *Also* the *promissory note* for the final payment of such a loan.

ballot. A method of taking a vote in which each person is allowed one vote and no one else can tell which way he voted.

band chart. A chart in which the difference between two curves is emphasized by shading in or colouring the space between them.

banded pack. A form of *sales promotion* in which consumers are offered two or more packages of a product, or a package of a product plus another product from the same manufacturer, attached together (usually by a band of tape printed with details of the offer), at a reduced price.

bank account. An *account* [3] with a bank.

bank bill. A *bill of exchange* the drawee of which is a bank.

bank cheque. Synonym for *bank draft*.

bank draft. A *promissory note* made by a bank, promising to pay a stated sum on demand at a named office of the bank. (Also known as a 'bank cheque', a 'banker's draft' or a 'demand draft'.)

banker's cheque. A cheque drawn by one banker on another.

banker's draft. A *bank draft*.

banker's discount. Synonym for *simple discount*.

Bank for International Settlements (BIS). International organization established in 1930 to promote cooperation between *central banks* and to provide facilities for *international settlements*. The members are central banks from 29 countries, including all European countries (apart from the USSR), Australia, Canada and Japan. The bank has a board of directors, who are all heads of central banks and meet at least 10 times a year at the bank's offices in Basle, Switzerland (hence the popular name of 'Club of Basle' for them). These meetings have become important as occasions for discussing international financial matters.

bank note. A *promissory note* issued by a bank, which is payable to bearer on demand and is used as *money*. In England and Wales, only the Bank of England may issue bank notes.

Bank of England. A *corporation* established by a royal *charter* in 1694.

It acts as the *central bank* in the UK. Its main functions are to: (1) act as agent for the Treasury in selling *Treasury bills* [1] and maintaining an orderly *market* [1] in British *government stocks*; (2) act as banker to the government; (3) act as banker to UK commercial banks; (4) control the operation of commercial banks by requiring *special deposits*, obtaining information on operations and issuing directives on lending policy; (5) issue *bank notes* (for which it has a monopoly in England and Wales); (6) operate *exchange controls*; (7) intervene to ensure there is an orderly market for *foreign exchange*; (8) advise the government on monetary policy.

The Bank has been owned by the Treasury (through a *nominee*, the Treasury Solicitor) since 1946 when it was nationalized by the Bank of England Act 1946. The Bank is managed by a Court of Directors, which consists of a Governor and Deputy Governor (appointed for 5-year terms) and 16 directors (appointed for 4-year terms). All appointments to the Court are made by the Crown and at least 12 members must be part-time.

bank of issue. A bank that issues *bank notes* which are used as *money* in its country.

Bank rate. The minimum rate at which the *Bank of England* would *discount* [3] *bills of exchange*. For example, if Bank rate was 5% and the Bank was offered a bill of exchange for £1000 that was due for payment in 10 days' time, the Bank would pay for it a maximum of

$$£1000 \left(1 - \tfrac{5}{100} \times \tfrac{10}{365}\right) = £998.63$$

Changes in Bank rate used to cause changes in interest rates for many types of short-term borrowing. Since October 1972 the Bank of England has not set a Bank rate but has set a *minimum lending rate*.

bankrupt (adjective). Having a special status imposed by a court because of *insolvency*. A bankrupt person's property is vested in a *trustee* who must use it to pay off creditors as fairly as possible. Creditors may not take any action against a bankrupt person; they must deal with the trustee.

bankrupt (noun). A person who is *bankrupt*.

bankruptcy. State of being *bankrupt ;* status of a *bankrupt*.

bankruptcy notice. A notice requiring a *judgment debtor* to pay his debt within 7 days, or give a satisfactory guarantee that the debt will be paid. Failure by a debtor to comply with such a notice is an *act of bankruptcy*.

banque d'affaires. A firm (of which there are a number in France and Germany) which combines the businesses of a *deposit bank* and a *merchant bank* (both investing its own money and that of its clients) and which takes an active part in the management of enterprises it invests in.

bar chart. A diagram showing the expected duration and timing of tasks which are represented by rectangles ('bars') drawn alongside a scale representing time.

bargain (noun). 1. Any transaction on the *Stock Exchange* [2]. 2. An advantageous purchase. 3. An agreement between two persons on the terms of a contract between them.

bargain (verb). 1. To *negotiate* [1] the terms and conditions of a contract. 2. To engage in *collective bargaining*.

barter (noun). 1. The art or practice of carrying on trade by *bartering*. 2. The thing given in exchange in *bartering*.

barter (verb). To trade by exchanging one good for another.

Barth system. A system of *payment by results* in which: (1) a *standard time* is set for a unit of output; (2) an hourly rate of pay is set; (3) a worker's output for a period is counted and he is paid:

$$\sqrt{(\text{number of units} \times \text{standard time per unit} \times \text{number of hours actually worked})} \times \text{hourly rate}$$

Named after the American industrial engineer, Carl George Lange Barth (1860–1939).

base. See *index number*.

base rate. Synonym for *basic rate* [1, 2].

base time. Synonym for *basic time*.

BASIC. (Acronym from 'beginner's all-purpose symbolic instruction code'.) A *programming language* developed from *FORTRAN* which was designed (originally in 1963) so that it could be quickly learned and would be especially useful for computers operating in *conversational mode*. A detailed description of the language is given in G. M. Bull, W. Freeman and S. J. Garland, *Specification for Standard BASIC* (Manchester: NCC Publications, 1973). There are several books on using BASIC—see, e.g., J. G. Kemeny and T. E. Kurtz, *BASIC Programming*, 2nd edition (New York: Wiley, 1971).

Basic Motion Timestudy (BMT). A *predetermined motion-time system* developed by the staff of J. D. Woods & Gordon Ltd, a Canadian firm of management consultants. See G. B. Bailey and R. Presgrave, *Basic Motion Timestudy* (New York: McGraw-Hill, 1958).

basic product. A product that is sold almost entirely to manufacturers for incorporation in their products.

basic rate. 1. The minimum *wage rate* for a job excluding any allowances such as *overtime premium* or *bonus*. Used as a nominal rate from which other rates (e.g. overtime rates) are calculated. Also called 'base rate' or 'basic wage rate'. 2. The minimum *wage rate* for a job agreed in a national agreement but subject to local increases. Also called 'base rate' or 'basic wage rate'. 3. The rate of *income tax* in the UK tax system which applies to all income remaining after *personal reliefs* have been deducted from *net statutory income*. The rate was set by the Finance Act 1972 at 30 per cent and increased by the Finance Act 1974 to 33 per cent.

basic time. The time for carrying out an element of a job (i.e. one of the small parts into which the job has been analysed for purposes of *work measurement*) at a rate of working that would be assigned a *standard rating*. (Also known as 'converted time', 'extended time' or 'standardized time'.) *Standard time* is computed from basic time by adding allowances for relaxation, unavoidable delays etc. (Also known as 'base time'.)

Basic Work Data (BWD). A *predetermined motion-time system* developed by ICI and British Rail from *simplified PMTS*. The Production Engineering Research Association, Melton Mowbray, Leicestershire LE13 0PB is responsible for further development of the system.

basis of assessment. The items on which a tax will be charged after any adjustments allowed by law have been made. The bases of assessment of UK *income tax* are described in the *Schedules* [3] by reference to the source of the income and the period during which it was received.

basis period. The period during which income from a particular source forms the *basis of assessment* for UK *income tax*.

batch. A quantity of material, of a part or of a product, which is ordered, or produced at one time. (Also known as a 'lot'.)

batch costing. Process or activity of allocating *costs* [2] to a *batch* of identical items of production, treated as a single unit.

batch processing. Operation of a *computer* in such a way that individual jobs or *programs* [1] are dealt with one at a time: one job is not started until the previous job has been completed. (Cf. *real-time*.)

batch production. Productive activity, of which the output, over a period of time, consists of numerous small batches of different products and in which any production facility is involved, at different times, in work connected with various products. The production facilities (e.g. *machine tools*) used for batch production are usually capable of performing a wide range of work. (Also known as 'intermittent production' or 'lot production'.)

battery. A collection of *tests* which have a similar purpose or are to be administered one after another at a single session.

bear (adjective). Of, or relating to, behaviour associated with an expectation that the price of something will fall. As in 'bear market' (a stock market at a time when there is extensive selling by people who expect prices to fall).

bear (noun). Someone who anticipates that the price of something will fall. Specifically, a person who promises to sell *securities* [1] (which he does not own), for their current market value, and deliver them at some time in the future in the belief that the price of the securities will fall so that he can purchase them, near the time he has to sell them, and make a profit. (A bear is in a *short position*.)

bearer. The person who is in possession of a *financial instrument* that is 'payable to bearer' (i.e. entitles the person in possession of it to payment of a specified sum of money).

bearer bond. A *bond* [2], ownership of which is not recorded by the issuer. The owner of a bearer bond can transfer ownership simply by giving his certificate to someone else. (Cf. *registered bond*.)

bearer debenture. A *debenture* [2] that is a *bearer security*.

bearer security. A *security* [1] which can be transferred from one owner to another simply by handing over a certificate of ownership. The name of the owner is not usually recorded by the *issuer* of the security (cf. *registered security*).

bearer share. A *share*, ownership of which is evidenced by a *bearer security*. *Also* the bearer security (usually called a *share warrant* in the UK) that evidences ownership of such a share.

bear position. Synonym for *short position*.

Bedaux system. A *premium bonus scheme* in which the incentive payment per unit of time saved is less than the rate paid for the *standard time* (often it is 75 % of the rate for the standard time) and the difference is put into a fund which is divided among the *indirect workers* in the plant. Named after its inventor, Charles Eugène Bedaux (1887–1944) who was born in France but emigrated to the USA in 1908.

beggar-my-neighbour policy (in USA, beggar-my-neighbor

policy). A policy of *protectionism* at a time of world-wide economic depression. Its object is to encourage home producers to increase output (and thus employ more people and bring about economic recovery) but by denying other countries their export markets it discourages their producers and promotes their economic decline (often characterized as 'exporting unemployment').

behavioural sciences (in USA, behavioral sciences). The academic disciplines of which the field of study is the responses of living organisms (often specifically humans) to what happens around them. These disciplines include sociology, psychology and economics.

below-the-line. 1. Not taken into account when computing a specified kind of profit. 2. Of, or relating to, *promotion* [1] apart from *above-the-line* [2] advertising and *public relations*. For firms making *consumer goods*, the most common forms of below-the-line promotion are *consumer deals* and *trade deals*. For firms making *industrial goods*, below-the-line promotion is usually limited to exhibitions and giving away calendars etc.

benchmark. Originally, a mark (which looked like a bench) made on a durable surface by a surveyor to indicate a carefully measured altitude that he would use as a reference point for measuring other altitudes. Now used for any carefully described or measured object with which others are compared; in particular, in *job evaluation* a benchmark (or 'benchmark job') is a job with which others are compared.

benchmark job. See *benchmark*.

beneficiary. 1. See *documentary credit*. 2. See *trust* [1].

benefit-cost ratio. See *discounted gross benefit-cost ratio, discounted net benefit-cost ratio, undiscounted gross benefit-cost ratio* and *undiscounted net benefit-cost ratio*.

bequest. Synonym for *legacy*.

bereavement pay. Pay given to an employee while he is given leave because a close relative of his has died.

Better Business Bureau. One of about 130 local voluntary organizations in the USA that act in the interest of consumers to correct bad commercial practices and misleading advertising. All are now part of the Council of Better Business Bureaus Inc.

which was organized in 1970 (though the bureaus have existed since the 1920s).

bid (noun). 1. The price at which one is prepared to buy something. *Also* an announcement or offer of such a price (e.g. at an *auction*). 2. An offer by one company to buy all the shares of another company. (Also known as a 'takeover bid'.) 3. A *tender* [2].

bid (verb). To make a *bid*.

bid price. 1. The price at which the *management company* of a *unit trust* will buy back *units*. 2. The price at which a *jobber* [2] will buy a *security* [1].

bill. 1. Synonym for *bill of exchange*. 2. Synonym for *invoice*. 3. (Often capital B.) A draft of a statute which is presented to and discussed by a legislative body.

bill broker. A person or firm that buys *bills of exchange* and *promissory notes* at a *discount* and either *rediscounts* them or holds them in order to receive payment from *drawees*.

bill of exchange (or bill). An unconditional order, in writing, addressed by one person (the 'drawer') to another (the 'drawee') which has been signed by the drawer and requires the drawee to pay, on demand or at a fixed or determinable future time, a specified amount of money to a specified person (the 'payee').

A bill of exchange may be either a 'sight' bill, which the drawee must pay as soon as the payee presents it to him, or a 'time' bill, which cannot be paid until the 'maturity date' (typically, from one to six months after it is drawn). A payee can *discount* [2] his bill (i.e. sell it) to someone else who then becomes the payee (the first payee must *endorse* [1] the bill when he sells it). A bill is more saleable if the drawee 'accepts' it (i.e. guarantees that if the bill is presented on time he will pay it) and if the acceptor/drawee is well known as having a sound and creditworthy business.

bill of lading (B/L). A document, signed by the master of a ship and delivered by him to a person sending goods on the ship, that specifies the name of the ship, the port of departure and destination of the ship, the nature of the goods, the name of the *consignee* and the cost of carrying the goods.

At the end of the journey the goods can only be given to the consignee if he produces the bill of lading. Consequently, the person sending the goods gives the consignee the bill of lading only when he is satisfied he has received payment for the goods.

Also a similar document issued by other carriers, e.g. railway bill of lading, inland waterway bill of lading, trucking company bill of lading.

bill of material. A list of the materials and components (and their quantities) required to make a particular product.

bill of sale. A document by which the owner of goods (called the 'grantor' of the bill) transfers ownership, but not possession, of the goods to someone else. The bill may be 'conditional'—i.e., stating that ownership will be given back to the grantor on specified conditions (usually, if he repays a loan) or 'absolute'—i.e. ownership will not revert to the grantor.

binary digit. See *binary system.*

binary number. A number written in the *binary system.*

binary system. A system for the representation of numbers using only two different characters, 0 and 1, called 'binary digits' or 'bits'. A number is represented by an ordered sequence of binary digits and a point. The contribution of any digit to the representation of a number depends on its position in the sequence relative to the point; if it is in the nth place to the left of the point its contribution is the value of the digit (zero or one) multiplied by 2^n; if it is in the nth place to the right of the point its contribution is the value of the digit multiplied by 2^{-n}. The number represented by the whole sequence is then the sum of the contributions of the individual digits.

Note, the representation usually employed for writing numbers is the 'denary system' using ten characters in which the contribution of a digit is its own value multiplied by 10^n or 10^{-n}. 2 is called the 'base' or 'radix' of the binary system, while 10 is the base of the denary system. Systems with any other base are possible but the only systems in widespread use are the denary (for normal writing) and binary (in *computing*).

bin card. A record of usage of a *stock-keeping unit* that is kept near the place of storage. It normally records the quantity and date of each movement of stock in or out of the store.

binomial coefficient. The binomial coefficient, usually denoted by $\binom{n}{r}$ is the numerical coefficient of $a^r b^{n-r}$ when $(a+b)^n$ is 'expanded' (i.e. the n multiplications are performed). It is equal to:

$$\frac{n!}{r!(n-r)!}$$

where ! means *factorial*.

binomial density function. The *frequency function* of the *binomial distribution*.

binomial distribution. The *probability distribution* of a *discrete random variable* of which the *frequency function* is:

$$f(x) = \binom{n}{x} p^x (1-p)^{n-x}$$

where n and x are positive whole numbers and

$$\binom{n}{x} = \frac{n!}{(n-x)!\,x!}$$

If p is the *probability* that an event will occur and there are n opportunities for it to occur then $f(x)$ is the probability that it will occur exactly x times. The *mean* [1] of the binomial distribution is np and its *variance* [2] is $np(1-p)$.

biotechnology. Synonym for *ergonomics*.

bit. Abbreviation of 'binary digit'—see *binary system*.

black (adjective). Having been *blacked*.

black (verb). To declare that one will not handle certain goods —especially as part of a union campaign against a firm that used, manufactured, processed or transported the goods.

blackleg. A worker who does not support union action; for example, by working when others are on strike, by refusing to join a union, by accepting employment in place of a union member who is on strike, or by working for less than union rates. (Also called a 'scab'.)

blacklist (noun). List (especially one circulated among a group of people or firms) of people who are not to be employed or of people or firms who are not to be given credit.

blacklist (verb). To put a name on a *blacklist*.

blind advertisement. An *advertisement* in which the advertiser's identity is not revealed (e.g. an advertisement using a box number).

blind test. A technique for evaluating consumers' reactions to products, especially food, in which a group of people are given unidentified samples and asked for their comments.

block diagram. A diagram which shows relationships between major components of a system (e.g. the connections between parts of an electronic device, or the logical relationship between parts of a *program* [1] for a computer) but which does not analyse each component in great detail.

block diagramming. The process or activity of preparing *block diagrams* as a first stage of analysing something or of preparing a *program* [1] for a computer.

block release. An arrangement under which employers give their employees a period off work (averaging about 18 weeks in a year) in one or more continuous 'blocks' (cf. *day release*) without loss of pay in order that the employees can attend a course of further education.

blue book. 1. Any UK government publication with a blue cover (cf. *white paper, green paper*). Specifically the annual report, *National Income and Expenditure*, prepared by the Central Statistical Office and published by HMSO. 2. Colloquial name for the second (1969) edition of the *City Code on Takeovers and Mergers* (cf. *red book*).

blue chip. A *listed company* which, because of its large size, long history of profitable trading and good management, commands a high level of confidence from stock-market investors. *Also* an *ordinary share* of such a company. (High-value chips for gambling —e.g. in poker—are coloured blue.)

blue-collar. Of, relating to, or performing manual work with no (or very few) supervisory responsibilities. (From the traditional blue colour of overalls—cf. *white-collar*.)

blueprint. A detailed, precise plan or specification, especially in the form of an engineering drawing. (Originally a copy of an engineering drawing made by a process that produced a photographic print in which the drawing was white on a blue background.)

blue-sky laws. (US.) Legislation designed to protect people from being persuaded to invest in *securities* [1] which are actually worthless. (From a remark by a US judge that a certain security seemed to 'have about the same value as a patch of blue sky'.)

board. 1. Synonym for *committee*. 2. Synonym for *board of directors*.

Board of Customs and Excise. Collective title for the *Commissioners of Customs and Excise*.

board of directors. The *directors* of a *company*, considered as a group.

Board of Inland Revenue. Collective name for the *Commissioners of Inland Revenue*.

Board of Trade (BoT). A committee of members of the *Privy Council* established in 1786 as the 'committee appointed for the consideration of matters relating to trade and foreign plantations'. The BoT gradually became a large central-government department responsible for a wide range of matters concerning government relations with commercial and industrial activity. The committee ceased to meet and its functions were exercised by its President. In 1970, the *Department of Trade and Industry* was formed and its Secretary of State became President of the Board of Trade; since April 1974 the functions have been transferred to the *Department of Trade*.

body-punched card. Synonym for *centre-punched card*.

Bolton report. The report, *Small Firms,* Cmnd 4811 (London: HMSO, 1971), of a committee appointed in 1969 by the President of the Board of Trade to consider the role of small firms in the national economy, the facilities available to them and the problems confronting them. 'Small firms' were regarded as those employing fewer than 200 people. The chairman of the committee was John Eveleigh Bolton (born 1920), chairman and managing director of Growth Capital Limited.

bond. 1. A *deed* by which one person (called the 'obligor') promises ('binds' himself) to do or not to do some act in order to benefit a second person (called the 'obligee'). (Also known as a 'single bond'—see *double bond*.)

2. A *security* [1] that has a *nominal value* and which entitles its holder to payment of interest (calculated as a percentage of the nominal value) by the *issuer* at regular intervals (typically, twice a year) until the issuer *redeems* the bond. At redemption the issuer pays the nominal value of the bond to its holder (occasionally, more than the nominal value is paid—either as a *call premium* or as a *redemption premium*). In the UK, 'bond' is used to describe securities of this type only when they are issued by the government or by local authorities; when they are issued by private-enterprise firms they are called 'debentures'. In the USA, 'bond' is used if the issuer is a private-enterprise firm except when the issuer gives no *security* [2] (e.g. in the form of a *mortgage* or *floating charge*) in which case 'debenture' is used. (See also, *callable bond, serial bond*.)

3. A *contract of insurance* in which the *insurer* undertakes to compensate the *assured* if the assured should suffer loss from failure by a specified person to carry out a promise made to the assured.

bonded goods. Goods on which *excise duty* or *customs duty* must be paid and which are kept in a *bonded warehouse* pending payment.

bonded warehouse. A *warehouse* in which goods may be stored without *customs duty* or *excise duty* being paid until they are withdrawn from the warehouse. The proprietors of the warehouse enter into a *bond* [1] to guarantee that duty will be paid to the *Revenue* [4] when necessary on the goods they store.

bondholder. One who owns a *bond* [2].

bond rating. (US.) An estimate of the ability of a corporation to pay the interest on and to *redeem bonds* [2] that it issues.

bonus. Part of an employee's remuneration that is related in some way to the value, quantity or quality of work done. Especially a payment that is made at the discretion of management rather than according to a set formula (cf. *incentive payment*). Also used to describe any kind of incentive payment.

bonus increment. An addition (other than a *policy allowance*) to *standard time* [1] as a basis for an *incentive payment system*.

bonus issue. Synonym for *capitalization issue*.

bonus-size package. A package that contains more of a *product* [2] than is normally sold at the price being charged. (A form of *consumer deal*.)

book. As recorded in the *books of account* of a firm. See *book value*.

bookkeeping. Recording the financial transactions of a firm.

books of account. The records of a firm's financial transactions.

book value. The amount that is recorded in the *accounts* [1] of a firm as the value of an *asset* [1] of the firm. (From the phrase, *books of account*.)

boom. A period of rapid increase in the output of producers in an economy, resulting in low unemployment and high prices for *primary products*.

booster training. Synonym for *refresher training*.

bought. Recording purchases. As in 'bought ledger' (the section of a firm's *ledger* that records purchases by the firm).

bought-out. Purchased from outside a specified firm.

Boulwarism. The attitude toward *collective bargaining* and industrial relations adopted by Lemuel Ricketts Boulware (born 1895), vice-president for employee, community and union relations of the US General Electric Company from 1947 to 1956. Especially, a tactic, often employed by Boulware in negotiations about pay, of making an offer believed to be fair and then refusing to amend it unless it could be demonstrated to be unfair. Boulware wished to avoid the usual situation in which the employer makes a low offer and only increases it after, basically emotional, argument.

bound-in insert. An *insert* that is attached to a publication.

bourse. A European *stock exchange*.

brainstorming. A technique for encouraging creative thinking. A problem is presented to a small group of people who spend a few minutes formulating alternative statements of it and then some time stating their ideas as rapidly as possible (the ideas may be tape-recorded but are commonly written, often on flipcharts so that the group can see them). During the production of ideas, four principles are observed: (1) quantity is important—the more ideas that are produced the more likely it is that they will include a good one; (2) cross-fertilization should take place—people should try to build on the ideas produced by others; (3) there must be no criticism of others' ideas—this would dampen their enthusiasm; (4) individuals must also suspend judgment and not evaluate their own ideas—an idea may seem extraordinary to one person but may, through the principle of cross-fertilization, get the group to generate useful ideas.

branch register. A *dominion register*.

brand (noun). A name, term, sign, symbol or design, or combination of them, which is intended to identify the goods or services of one seller and to differentiate them from those of competitors. (Sometimes also called a 'label'.)

brand (verb). To assign a *brand* to a product.

branded goods. Goods that are normally sold under the *brands* of their suppliers.

brand leader. A *branded* product which has the largest *market share* for all products of its type.

brand loyalty. Continual purchasing by a consumer of the same *brand* of goods.

brand manager. Synonym for *product manager*.

brand name. A word or group of words used as a *brand*.

brand share. Synonym for *market share;* used when referring to *branded goods*.

break-even analysis. Computing *costs* [2] and *revenues* [2] for different volumes of production in order to determine the *break-even point*.

break-even chart. A chart on which two curves are plotted: the expected *sales revenues* from the production of various quantities of a product and the *costs* (*fixed* and *variable*) of producing those quantities. The curves intersect at the *break-even point*.

break-even point. The volume of production at which the producer's *revenues* [2] are the same as his *costs* [2] so that he makes neither a profit nor a loss.

break-up value. The amount of money which could be obtained for the *assets* [1] of a firm if the firm ceased its production or business activities and the assets were sold as quickly as possible to the highest bidder. (Also known as 'liquidating value'.)

British Association for Commercial and Industrial Education (BACIE). A non-profit-making association of business enterprises and other bodies concerned to promote education and training in commerce and industry. BACIE was established in 1919. It publishes the monthly *BACIE Journal* and handbooks, training manuals and reports. It conducts courses on training methods and runs a purpose-built training centre. Each corporate member is entitled to nominate a number of 'representatives' depending on the size of its organization. About 5000 representatives have been nominated.

Address : 16 Park Crescent, London W1N 4AP (01–636 5351).

British Association of Accountants and Auditors. Professional institute founded in 1923. Associates (designated ABAA) must have passed the association's examination and must have had not less than 5 years accountancy experience. A fellow (designated FBAA) must have been an associate (or an associate of another approved body of accountants) for 5 years and must have held a senior accountancy position for 5 years. Associates and fellows are described as 'registered accountants'. A licentiate (designated LicBAA) must be at least 25 and must have been an accountant for 7 years.

The association publishes a quarterly journal, *The Registered Accountant,* and local societies organize professional meetings.

Address : Stamford House, 2/4 Chiswick High Road, London W4 1TP (01–994 3477).

British Business Graduates Society. An association, formed in 1973, of individuals who have successfully completed a degree course in business studies at a British educational establishment.

The objectives of the society, as stated in its constitution, are: (1) to 'promote and assist the integration of British business graduates as a necessary and essential part of industry, commerce and the public sector'; (2) to 'secure the British business graduate . . . as the leading professional manager and executive throughout the UK and overseas'; (3) to 'stimulate the need for, and acceptance of business education . . .'; (4) to 'contribute to the advancement of all types of business education . . .'; (5) to 'liaise with representative bodies of, and include at associate and affiliate status, all other graduates of business courses at home and overseas'.

Membership is in 5 categories: (1) members who must be graduates of a British degree course in business studies; (2) associates who must be graduates of a British degree course containing a substantial element of business studies; (3) fellows who are elected for outstanding service to the society; (4) affiliates who may be either students of business at British educational establishments or business graduates of foreign educational establishments; (5) honorary members.

Address: 9 Constance Road, Bush Hill Park, Enfield, Middlesex EN1 2HR.

British Employers' Confederation. Federation, formed in 1919, of British *employers' associations*. Until 1939, it was called the National Confederation of Employers' Organizations. It became part of the *Confederation of British Industry* in August 1965.

British Institute of Management (BIM). Professional institute established in 1947 (as a *guarantee company*) to promote the art and science of management.

Associate members (designated AMBIM) must possess the *Diploma in Management Studies* or an approved equivalent qualification and must have held a management job for at least one year. Members (designated MBIM) must have held a *general-management* job for at least two years. People who have achieved eminence in the practice of management or, in a few cases, have made outstanding and original contributions to management knowledge or theory may be invited to become fellows (designated FBIM). In March 1974 there were 32303 associate members, 6844 members and 809 fellows.

The BIM issued a 'Code of Best Practice' for its members in July 1974.

BIM publishes the quarterly *Management Review and Digest* and cooperates in the publication of *Management Today*. It also publishes a wide range of reports and books, runs courses and provides information services.

Address : Management House, Parker Street, London WC2B 5PT (01–405 3456).

British Overseas Trade Board (BOTB). A committee of businessmen and representatives of the *Department of Trade* and the Foreign and Commonwealth Office formed in 1971 (as the British Export Board—the name was changed as from 1 March 1972). Its objectives are to ensure that official export promotion activities are conducted with due regard to the needs of industry and commerce, and to utilize available government export promotion resources to the best advantage. The President of the BOTB is the Secretary of State for Trade.

Address : 1 Victoria Street, London SW1H 0ET (01–222 7877).

British Productivity Council (BPC). An organization supported by the *Confederation of British Industry,* the *Trades Union Congress,* the Association of British Chambers of Commerce and nationalized industries to promote higher *productivity* by spreading knowledge, to management and workers, of better methods and encouraging acceptance of necessary change. It was founded in 1952 and received government assistance until 1973. BPC works through 54 Local Productivity Associations (LPAs) which arrange activities suited to the industry in their area—including information and advisory services; seminars, conferences and courses; interfirm visits; and study groups.

Address: 1st floor, 16 South Molton Street, London W1Y 1DE (01–629 4254).

British Standard (BS). A specification of, e.g., quality or dimensions of materials that has been formulated by the *British Standards Institution.*

British Standards Institution (BSI). A non-profit-making organization incorporated by royal charter in 1929 (though its origins go back to 1901) to coordinate the work of establishing standard specifications of quality and dimensions for materials used in industry. The institution endeavours to ensure that its published standards have the widest possible support by carrying out extensive consultations during the drafting of standards. BSI is financed by subscriptions from its members (individuals, companies, technical and trade associations), by a government grant and by the sale of its publications.

Address: British Standards House, 2 Park Street, London W1Y 4AA (01–629 9000).

broadening. The process of preparing a *middle manager* for a *top-management* position by means of *job rotation* so that he acquires a broader outlook.

broad-line strategy. Strategy of offering a wide range of variants within a single *product line*. (Also known as a 'full-line strategy'.)

broker. A person who arranges transactions between other people, receives a *commission* [1] (usually a percentage of the value of the transaction) for doing so, and is usually an *agent* of one of the parties to the transaction. E.g. a *commodity broker*, an *insurance broker*, a *money broker*, a *shipbroker* or a *stockbroker*.

brokerage. 1. *Commission* [1] charged by a *broker*. 2. Synonym for *broking*.

broking. Acting as a *broker*.

bucket shop. A firm which sells *securities* [1] or *futures contracts* for *commodities* [3] but which is not a member of an *organized market* and is not regulated by government or other agencies and usually swindles its customers. (In the late nineteenth century, 'bucket shop' was used in the USA to describe a low-class bar— either because the drink was concocted in buckets or because it could be bought in buckets. The phrase was transferred to low-class share-dealers.)

budget. 1. A *plan* expressed in financial terms; a summary of planned financial expenditures and receipts over a period or related to an activity. 2. A list of permitted, or authorized expenditures. (Also known as an 'appropriation budget'.) 3. (Usually capital B.) A plan for the public expenditure of a country and the way it will be financed by taxes (e.g. that presented by the British Chancellor of the Exchequer to the House of Commons in March or April each year).

budgetary control. *Control* [1] which is based on the use of *budgets* [1] for various activities and comparison of actual performance with budgeted performance.

budget centre (spelt budget center in USA). The smallest section of a firm for which a *budget* [1] is prepared in a system of *budgetary control*.

budgeting. The process or activity of preparing *budgets*.

buffer stock. Synonym for *safety stock*.

building society. A non-profit-making society that raises money from some of its members (and pays interest on it) in order to loan money to other members for the purchase of houses, taking *mortgages* on the houses as *security* [2] for its loans.

bull (adjective). Of, or relating to, behaviour associated with an expectation that the price of something will rise.

bull (noun). Someone who anticipates that the price of something will rise. Specifically, a person who buys, or promises to buy, *securities* [1] (especially if he does not have sufficient money to pay for them) in the belief that the price of the securities will rise so that he can sell them and make a profit. (A bull is in a *long position*.)

bulletin board. 1. A notice board. 2. An outdoor *advertisement* consisting of a large painted board, sometimes with mechanically operated louvres which can move to display changing advertisements.

bullion. Gold or silver in a form (e.g. ingots or dust) in which it has intrinsic value only. The term usually excludes gold or silver coins that are in circulation in a specified country.

bull position. Synonym for *long position*.

bumping. *Downgrading* or dismissing a junior employee because his job is to be taken by an employee with longer service who has had to be demoted because of a contraction of business.

burden (or burden cost). Synonym for *indirect cost*.

Burnham committee. A permanent committee of representatives of employers and employees in the teaching profession which reviews teachers' salaries. There are three Burnham committees covering different types of educational establishment. Named after Sir Harry Lawson Webster Levy-Lawson, Viscount Burnham (1862–1933), proprietor of the *Daily Telegraph* and described by the *Dictionary of National Biography* as 'the ideal chairman for public assemblies of every kind'. He was chairman of a joint committee representing teachers and local education authorities in 1920.

business. 1. The activities of buying and selling goods, manufacturing goods or providing services in order to make a profit. *Also* a *firm* [1] engaged in such activities. The term usually excludes activities relating only to *primary production,* operation of *nationalized* industries and the activities of non-profit-making organizations. 2. An *industry* [2]; a particular type of economic activity.

business agent. A full-time, paid official of an American trade union who represents members of a *local* in negotiations and acts as treasurer to the local.

business cycle. A *trade cycle.*

business enterprise. A *firm* [1] engaged in *business* [1] activities.

business game. Synonym for *management game.*

Business Graduates Association (BGA). A non-profit-making organization formed in 1967 to advance business education at postgraduate level.

Individual members of the BGA must have successfully completed an approved postgraduate course in business studies in the UK or elsewhere. Corporate membership is open to any company that subscribes to the association's funds.

The BGA's activities are intended: (1) to increase the numbers of suitably qualified people seeking graduate business education; (2) to contribute to the development of graduate business schools; (3) to assist industry, commerce and the public sector in making the most effective use of business graduates; (4) to provide information for management in every field on the role of graduate business education in the development of professional managers; (5) to improve the opportunities for the further education of business graduates throughout their careers.

In 1974 there were 1700 individual members and 200 corporate members.

Address: Rutland House, Rutland Gardens, London SW7 1BY (01–584 1436).

business interruption insurance. *Insurance* against losses to a firm that are indirectly caused by specified perils. For example, fire insurance will usually cover the cost of buildings destroyed by fire but not the loss of earnings during rebuilding, this 'consequential loss' would be covered by business interruption insurance.

business logistics. Synonym for *industrial logistics*.

Business Monitors. A series of more than 150 periodicals published by HMSO which are compiled by the government's Business Statistics Office and give information about the performance of individual industries.

business ratio. A *ratio* used in analysing activities of a firm. (Also known as a 'management ratio'.)

business risk. The *risk* [1] that a firm's *profits* will decrease because of the nature of its activities—e.g. because there is a decline in the demand for its product or an increase in the cost of its materials.

buyers' market. A situation in which the supply of a good is high so that a seller finds it difficult to sell his entire stock at a price that yields him a good profit.

buying in. Purchase on the *Stock Exchange* [2], by a *stockbroker* appointed for the purpose by the Stock Exchange Council, of *securities* [1] that another stockbroker has failed to deliver in accordance with a contract he has entered into.

buzz group. A *syndicate* [1]; a small group formed for discussion of a specific matter.

bylaw. 1. (UK.) *Delegated legislation* made by a *local authority*—typically for regulating the conduct of people within its area—or by a *statutory corporation* [1]—typically to regulate the conduct of people visiting premises owned by the corporation. **2.** (US.) A regulation made by a *corporation* dealing with the rights and duties of *stockholders* [1] and *directors*. The bylaws of a US corporation are equivalent to the *articles of association* of a UK company.

by-product. A product made by a manufacturer or processor on a much smaller scale than another product of his but using the same materials and, initially at least, with the same operations or processes.

byte. A sequence of 8 *bits* that is operated on as a single unit in many types of *computer*.

C

CA. Abbreviation of 'chartered accountant' used to designate membership of the *Institute of Chartered Accountants of Scotland*.

c. & f. (abbreviation of cost and freight). A type of contract for the sale of goods in which the seller supplies goods and pays for them to be shipped to a foreign port. The seller does not insure the sea journey (cf. *c.i.f.*) and the buyer bears all risks relating to the goods as soon as they are on the ship at the port of shipment.

If the terms of sale are 'cost and freight landed' then the seller also pays all the costs of unloading the goods at the foreign port.

CAS. Abbreviation of *Conciliation and Arbitration Service*.

CBA. Abbreviation of *cost-benefit analysis*.

CBD. Abbreviation of *cash before delivery*.

CBI. Abbreviation of *Confederation of British Industry*.

CCT. Abbreviation of *Common Customs Tariff*.

CES. Abbreviation of 'Confédération européenne des syndicats' (French title of the *European Trade Union Confederation*).

CET. Abbreviation of 'Common External Tariff' (see *Common Customs Tariff*).

c.i.f. (abbreviation of cost, insurance, freight). A type of contract for the sale of goods in which the seller supplies goods, pays for them to be shipped to a foreign port and insures them for the journey.

CII. 1. Abbreviation of *collective investment institution*. 2. Abbreviation of *Confederation of Irish Industry*.

CIOS. Abbreviation of *Conseil international pour l'organisation scientifique*.

CIR. 1. Abbreviation of *Commissioners of Inland Revenue*. 2. Abbreviation of *Commission on Industrial Relations*.

COD. Abbreviation of *cash on delivery*.

COI. Abbreviation of *Central Office of Information*.

CPA. 1. Abbreviation of *critical path analysis*. 2. Abbreviation of *certified public accountant*.

CPFF. Abbreviation of 'cost plus fixed fee' (see *cost-plus contract*).

CPIF. Abbreviation of 'cost plus incentive fee' (see *cost-plus contract*).

CPM. 1. Abbreviation of *critical path method*. 2. Abbreviation of *cost per thousand*.

CPT. Abbreviation of *cost per thousand*.

CPU. Abbreviation of *central processing unit*.

Cr. Abbreviation of *creditor* [1]. Used in accounts to mark a column of *credits* [1].

CTC. Abbreviation of *Central Training Council*.

CWO. Abbreviation of *cash with order*.

call (noun). 1. A demand by a *company* [1] for payment of part or all of the amount outstanding on a *partly paid share*. 2. A *call option*. 3. A claim; a demand for the payment of money.

call (verb). 1. To announce that a *security* must be presented for *redemption*. 2. To exercise a *call option*.

callable. *Redeemable*.

callable bond. A *bond* [2] that is issued subject to a condition that the issuer may, at any time, demand that the bond be presented for *redemption*. (Also known as a 'redeemable bond'.)

call-back pay. Synonym for *call-in pay*.

call-in pay. A guaranteed minimum payment for being specially called in to work. (Also known as 'call-back pay'.)

call off. To request delivery of a quantity of parts made according to the *call-off system*.

call-off system. Arrangement for buying manufactured parts for use in *assemblies* [1] by which the purchaser places a firm order for a specific quantity of the parts to be manufactured over, say, the next year on the basis that required quantities will be delivered as and when the manufacturer needs them.

call option. An *option* under which the option holder may, at any time within a set period, decide to buy, from the other party to the arrangement, a specified quantity of something (e.g. *securities* [1] at a specified price. The holder may decide to do nothing but, whether he buys or not, he has to pay a fee ('option money') to the other party.

call premium. An addition to the *nominal value* of a *callable bond* which is paid to the bondholder by the issuer if the issuer exercises its right to demand *redemption* before a specified date. The call premium compensates bondholders for losing the future payments of interest that they would have received if the bonds had not been redeemed.

call up. To make a *call* [1] for part of the *nominal value* of issued shares.

capacity. 1. The maximum amount of work that can, in theory, be performed using a particular machine or production facility. Expressed either in terms of *machine-hours* or in terms of the number of units of output over a period. 2. A biologically inherited, innate potentiality of an individual for learning. 3. A *job* [1] or *position* occupied by someone.

capital. A stock of money, possessed by a person or firm, which may be invested from time to time in *assets* [1] in order to earn *income* [1] but which is intended not to be diminished.

capital account. 1. The section of the statement of a country's *balance of payments* that records all payments not in the *current account* [2]. 2. An *account* [1] recording the contributions by a partner to the *capital* of a *partnership*.

capital allowance. An amount that may be deducted from a UK taxpayer's income, when computing liability to *income tax* or *corporation tax*, to allow for expenditure on *fixed assets* such as plant, machinery and buildings.

Capital Allowances Act 1968. UK statute which consolidates the law on *capital allowances*.

capital budget. A document showing the extent and timing of a firm's proposed *capital expenditure* over a future period, the *revenue* [1] that the expenditure is expected to produce, the *cost of capital* to be used for the expenditure and the *net profit* [1] that will result. (Also known as a 'capital expenditure budget'.)

capital budgeting. The process of choosing from possible *investment projects* the ones that a firm will invest money in.

capital duty. A tax charged in the UK when a *limited company* is formed or its *contributed capital* is increased. The tax is 1% of the contributed capital. See also, the Finance Act 1973, part 5.

capital employed. A measurement of the total value of the *operating assets* of a firm.

capital expenditure. Expenditure on *fixed assets* (i.e. on *capital goods*).

capital expenditure budget. Synonym for *capital budget*.

capital gain. Profit from the sale of an *asset* [1] other than a *current asset*. (Also known as a 'capital profit'.)

capital gains tax. A tax levied on *capital gains*. In the UK, a capital gains tax was introduced by the Finance Act 1965. The UK tax applies only to gains made by individuals (gains made by corporations are subject to *corporation tax*). The tax is 30% of the gain but if an individual has a gain less than £5000 then he can have half tax-free and the other half treated as *investment income* if this is to his advantage. Losses from the sale of assets may be offset against gains made in the same year of assessment. Gains from the sale of some assets are not chargeable (and losses from their sale may not be offset against chargeable gains): the exemptions include private cars, a dwelling-house that was the seller's main place of residence, *tangible property* (apart from *real property*) sold for less than £1000 and British *government stock*.

capital goods. Manufactured or constructed objects that have a long useful life and are used to assist in the production of (but are not incorporated in) other goods. Capital goods include machinery, tools and factory buildings.

capital investment. *Investment* in *capital goods*.

capitalism. Private or corporate ownership and control of the means of production and distribution of goods and services.

capital issue. An issue of *securities* [1] made in order to acquire *capital* for a firm.

Capital Issues Committee. A committee that advises the *Treasury* on whether applicants should be granted permission to raise large sums of money (since 1972, more than £3 million at a time) by issuing *securities* [1].

capitalist (adjective). 1. Advocating or supporting *capitalism*. 2. Marked by the presence of *capitalism* (as in 'capitalist economy').

capitalist (noun). Someone who possesses *capital*; especially, someone who *invests* his capital in firms (e.g. by buying *shares*) but takes little part in the direction or management of the firms.

capitalization issue. An issue of *shares* in a *company* [1] which are given free to existing *shareholders* in the company in proportion to the size of their holdings. The total *nominal value* of the capitalization issue is transferred from the *account* [1] recording the company's *retained earnings* to the account recording its *contributed capital* (thus the retained earnings are 'capitalized'). (Also known as a 'bonus issue'.)

capitalization rate. 1. The ratio of the *returns* [1] from an investment over a specified period to the price of the investment at a particular time. 2. Synonym for *market capitalization rate*.

capitalize. 1. To exchange (actually or conceptually) a stream of future receipts for a lump sum. Specifically, to compute the *present value* of future receipts. 2. To convert *retained earnings* into *contributed capital* by means of a *capitalization issue*. 3. To turn to one's advantage.

capital market. The *market* [1] or [4] for the supply of *capital* to firms.

capital profit. Synonym for *capital gain*.

capital rationing. A situation in which a firm has only a limited amount of money available for *capital expenditure*.

capital receipt. A receipt of money for the sale of an *asset* [1] other than a *current asset*.

capital redemption reserve fund. If a British *company limited by shares* has issued *redeemable preference shares* and redeems any of them for cash, then an amount of money equal to the *nominal value* of the redeemed shares must be set aside in a 'capital redemption reserve fund'. This fund is regarded as part of the *contributed capital* of the company and cannot be used to pay *dividends* [2]. It is not necessary to transfer money to the fund if the redeemable preference shares are redeemed with money acquired from issuing new shares.

capital reserve. A sum of money which a *company* has received (apart from *contributed capital*) but which it decides cannot be distributed to its *shareholders* as *dividends* [2]. This may simply be a policy decision or there may be a legal prohibition on using the money in that way.

capital stock. Actual or potential *contributed capital* of a company (especially of a corporation in the USA) measured in various ways—e.g. (1) *authorized capital*; (2) the total *nominal value* or *stated value* of *outstanding stock*; (3) present *contributed capital*.

capital structure. The way in which the *capital* of a firm is divided among various sources.

capital surplus. Money (or a measurement in monetary terms of the value of assets) received by a *company* [1] in exchange for issuing its *shares* and which is in excess of the *nominal value* or *stated value* of those shares. The term is regarded as being misleading and should be avoided because it suggests that the money is surplus to requirements and can be quickly distributed to shareholders. Also known as 'paid-in surplus'. In the UK, the term, *share premium*, is normal. See also, *contributed capital*.

capital transaction. A transaction between a resident of one country and a nonresident in which payment is made for a future benefit.

capital transfer tax. A tax on gifts of money or other valuable assets made by a person during his lifetime or, by his will, on death. In the UK, a capital transfer tax is levied on all gifts made after 26 March 1974. The tax was introduced by the Finance Act 1975 and replaced *estate duty*.

car card. 1. (US.) An *advertisement* on a card that is attached to the inside of a bus or railway carriage. 2. (UK.) An *advertisement* on a card that is attached to the inside of a carriage of a London Transport underground train. (Advertisements in other kinds of trains are called 'train spots'.)

card. 1. A *punched card*. 2. A document showing that its holder is a member of a trade union.

career. A sequence of *occupational roles* undertaken by a person.

career curve. Synonym for *maturity curve*.

carry back. To have an entitlement to a reduction of tax that relates to one *accounting period* and use it to reduce the tax that relates to an earlier period.

car tax. An *indirect tax* [1] paid when a firm sells a car that it has manufactured in the UK or imported into the UK. The tax is 10% of the wholesale value of the car.

cartel. A group of independent commercial enterprises that have agreed to limit competition (e.g. by charging identical prices) between themselves.

case history. An account of events, especially those relating to a particular business problem. (Also known as a 'case study'.)

case method. A method of training in which trainees (usually in groups) study an account of a business situation (the 'case') and decide how they would have solved the problem presented by the situation.

case study. 1. Synonym for *case history*. 2. The process or an instance of using the *case method* of training.

cash. *Money* in an immediately usable form. In practice, coins and *currency notes*.

cash and carry warehouse. An establishment where a *wholesaler* sells *consumer goods* (mainly food) to retailers who pay cash and collect the goods themselves.

cash before delivery (CBD). A condition made by a seller of goods that he will not despatch goods to a buyer until after he has received payment for them.

cash-book. A record of payments and receipts.

cash budget. A statement of the estimated totals of cash that will be received and payed by a firm during each of a number of

57

future periods (months, weeks, etc.). If a significant surplus is forecast for a month then plans can be made to invest it; if a deficit is forecast then arrangements must be made to borrow the necessary cash.

cash discount. A deduction that a firm will allow from the total value of an *invoice* sent out if payment is made within a short time. (Also called a 'settlement discount'.)

cash flow. 1. A *cash inflow* or a *cash outflow*. 2. The pattern and extent of payments and receipts of cash by a firm over a period. 3. The difference between total *cash inflows* and total *cash outflows* relating to a specified activity (especially, an *investment project*) over a specified period. (Sometimes called 'net cash flow'.) 4. Synonym for *gross cash flow*.

cash-flow statement. A statement of a firm's actual or projected *cash inflows* and *cash outflows* measured at suitable intervals (weekly, monthly, etc.) over a period.

cash inflow. A receipt, by a firm, of money from outside the firm.

cash on delivery (COD). A condition made by a seller of goods that the person delivering them will not release them to the buyer until he is paid for them.

cash outflow. A payment, by a firm, of money to someone outside the firm.

cash tender offer. See *tender offer*.

cash with order (CWO). A requirement by a seller that any order for his goods must be accompanied by payment for them.

casual (adjective). 1. Occurring by chance; unpredictable. 2. Occurring irregularly or intermittently. See *casual work*.

casual (noun). Synonym for *casual worker*.

casual work. Work, or opportunity for employment, that occurs intermittently. (Also known as 'daywork'.)

casual worker. Someone who is employed temporarily to perform *casual work*. (Also known as a 'casual' or a 'dayworker'.)

catalogue store. A retail establishment in which few goods are displayed to the public who choose what they want from printed catalogues and tell assistants who get the goods from storerooms. Like *discount stores*, catalogue stores specialize in selling *consumer durables* at low prices but only small shops are required and so they can be sited in main shopping areas.

caveat emptor. (Latin for 'let the buyer beware'.) The doctrine that when a person buys goods he takes the risk that there is something wrong with them. The doctrine cannot so often be invoked now in the UK because various statutes make the seller responsible for guaranteeing the quality of what he is selling.

Census of Production. An annual detailed enquiry conducted by the UK government's Business Statistics Office to provide information on the structure of industry. All establishments with more than 25 employees in orders 2–19 and 21 of the *Standard Industrial Classification* (i.e. mining and quarrying, manufacturing, and gas, electricity and water supply) provide information. This is published in separate reports (155 for the 1971 census) for individual industries in the series of *Business Monitors*. For more information, see Department of Trade and Industry Business Statistics Office, *Report on the Census of Production 1971 : Introductory Notes* (Business Monitor PA 1001) (London: HMSO, 1973).

central bank. A bank set up by a government to transact government business (for example, raising and repaying loans, acting as banker to the government), and to advise on and implement the government's monetary policy (for example, by controlling the *money stock* of an economy).

centralize. 1. To give control over something, or transfer some operation, to the headquarters of an organization. 2. To make an organization *centralized*.

centralized. (Of an organization) consisting of a number of distinct units (e.g. units that are geographically dispersed) that are all directed and controlled by one small group of managers from a headquarters.

Central Office of Information (COI). Department of the British government that produces information (including newspaper stories, radio programmes, films, books, magazines and photographs for press and display purposes) about Britain for overseas, and publicizes government activities and decisions in the UK.

central processing unit (CPU) (or central processor or processor). The principal data-processing devices within a *computer*; consisting of an *arithmetic unit,* a *control unit* and a *store* [4]. The store in the CPU is normally an *immediate-access store.* (Also known as the 'main frame'.)

Central Training Council (CTC). A committee of up to 32 people representing employers, employees, nationalized industries and *industrial training boards* which advised the Secretary of State for Employment on industrial and commercial training. The Council was set up under the *Industrial Training Act 1964* and was disbanded on 31 December 1973 when the *Manpower Services Commission* was established.

centre-punched card (or centre-slotted card). A card used for recording data and enabling *information retrieval.* The card has a number of holes. When dealing with a particular *file* of data the space between each pair of holes (one above the other) is allotted to a particular attribute of the items of data. When an attribute is present in a particular item the pair of holes representing the attribute on the card for that item is made into a slot by cutting away the material between the holes. All cards in a pack that record a particular attribute can be found by passing a needle through the lower hole for that attribute and lifting it; slotted cards then drop down and can be identified. (Also known as a 'body-punched card'.)

certificate of deposit. A certificate that a specified amount of money (in the UK a minimum of £50 000) has been deposited with the bank that issued the certificate. The certificate states the interest that the bank will pay on the deposit and the length of time for which the deposit is made (from 3 months to 5 years). Certificates of deposit are *negotiable instruments*.

certificate of incorporation. 1. A document issued by the *Registrar of Companies* to a *registered company* certifying that the company is *incorporated* and that all the requirements of the *Companies Acts* relating to the formation of a company have been complied with. 2. A document, given by people who wish to form a *corporation* in a state of the USA, to a state official, which sets out details of the proposed corporation and corresponds approximately to a *memorandum of association* in the UK. (Also known

60

as 'articles of incorporation'.)

certificate of origin. A statement that specified goods were produced or manufactured in a named country. The certificate is usually countersigned by an official of a *chamber of commerce* and is used when exporting goods to countries that charge lower *tariffs* [1] for goods originating from particular countries.

certificate of value. A statement in a *transfer* [2] or *conveyance* that the *consideration* being received is less than a certain amount so that *conveyance duty* is either not payable or is payable at a reduced rate.

certification mark. An identifying mark which is applied to goods that satisfy specific criteria of quality, method of manufacture or place of manufacture but which does not identify the manufacturer or distributor of the goods. Typically, use of a certification mark is administered by a trade association that specifies the quality criteria and authorizes use of the mark. In the UK a certification mark may be registered as a *registered trademark*.

certified accountant. An associate or a fellow of the *Association of Certified Accountants*.

certified cheque. Synonym for *marked cheque*.

certified public accountant (CPA). A person who has been certified (after examination), according to state laws in the USA, as being qualified to practise accountancy. In particular a CPA is qualified to carry out an *audit* [1].

certified transfer. A *transfer* [2] made out by a *shareholder* who is selling some of his shares and on which there is a statement by an official of the company which issued the shares that the transferor's *share certificate* has been lodged with the company. The transferor does not give his certificate to the transferee (usually because the transferor is selling him only some of the shares covered by the certificate), but the certification proves that a valid certificate exists and that the company will issue new certificates in due course.

chain. 1. Synonym for *multiple*. 2. A sequence of connected *directed edges* in a *graph* [2] in which each directed edge occurs only once. Also known as a 'path'.

chain of command. Synonym for *line of command*.

chain store. A retail establishment that is one of a group of two or more establishments with a single owner.

chairman. A person chosen to carry out specific tasks at a formal meeting of a group of people (e.g. a *committee* or *board of directors*) that usually include regulating discussion by determining who should speak and what subjects should be discussed, and ensuring adherence to any rules governing proceedings of the meeting.

chamber of commerce (or chamber of commerce and industry): An association of businessmen in a particular geographical area which is formed to promote commerce and industry in the area.

channel of distribution (or distribution channel). A series of enterprises, or types of enterprises, involved in transferring ownership of goods from producer to ultimate consumer.

characteristics of easy movement. A set of basic principles that are observed in *method study* concerning the way in which human movements should be arranged for easiest working. *Especially* those listed in: British Standards Institution, *Glossary of Terms used in Work Study* (BS 3138: 1969). The characteristics were first stated, as 'rules of human motions', by the American industrial engineer, Frank Bunker Gilbreth (1868–1924). Gilbreth's rules were rearranged and amplified by the American industrial engineer, Ralph M. Barnes (born 1900) and called 'principles of motion economy'. For a full discussion, see R. M. Barnes, *Motion and Time Study: Design and Measurement of Work*, 6th edition (New York: Wiley, 1968). The name 'characteristics of easy movement' was adopted by the British Standards Institution to emphasize that they led to ease rather than speed of working.

character reader. A device, used in *electronic data processing*, which produces a transcription, into a form that can be used by a computer, of written or printed data.

charge. 1. An obligation (especially to pay a debt) that is attached to property so that anyone who owns the property must fulfil the obligation. 2. The price demanded for services or goods.

chargeable gain. A *capital gain* on which *capital gains tax* must be paid.

charge account. An arrangement between a retailer and one of his customers that the price of any purchases made by the customer will be recorded by the retailer and the customer will periodically pay the outstanding total. (Also called an 'account'.)

chargehand. An employee who, to some extent, does the same work as others in a group of workers but is given some supervisory duties as well.

charisma. Capability, of a person, to influence a wide range of the behaviour of other people (or to persuade the people to accept a wide range of his views), especially when the capability seems to be an innate capacity.

charismatic (adjective). Of, or relating to, or possessing, *charisma*.

charismatic (noun). A person who has *charisma*.

charm price. Synonym for *psychological price*.

charter (noun). A document recording a grant of rights, property, powers, privileges or immunities.

charter (verb). 1. To give a *charter* to someone, or establish something by means of a charter. 2. To obtain the use of a ship or aircraft from its owner by means of a *charterparty*.

chartered accountant. An associate or a fellow of the *Institute of Chartered Accountants* in England and Wales.

chartered company. A British *corporation* formed for the purpose of carrying out a business and incorporated by a *charter* given by the Crown. At one time, a royal charter was the only means of creating any kind of corporation and some chartered companies from that period still exist (e.g. the Peninsular and Oriental Steam Navigation Company, chartered in 1840, and The London Assurance, chartered in 1720 but now a subsidiary of Sun Alliance and London Insurance Ltd).

charterer. A person or firm that obtains the use of a ship or aircraft from its owner under the terms of a *charterparty*.

charterparty. A contract by which the owner of a ship leases his ship, or part of it, to the *charterer* for the conveyance of goods for an agreed time or for a particular voyage. The owner promises to take the goods to a particular place in return for money paid by the charterer.

chartist. Someone who makes or recommends investments in *securities* [1] or *commodities* [3] according to an assessment of future prices that is based on his study of past prices. It is convenient to plot prices of a security or a commodity on a chart in order to make these assessments—hence the name.

chattel. Obsolete term for *personal property*.

check. US spelling of *cheque*.

checking account. Equivalent in the USA of a *current account* [1] at a British bank.

checking copy. Copy of a publication sent to an advertiser or an *advertising agency* to show that an *advertisement* appeared as specified. (Also known as a 'voucher copy'.)

check-off. Deduction of trade union subscriptions from wages by an employer who makes a lump-sum repayment of them to the union.

check time. A time interval used to check the accuracy of observations when conducting *time study* [1] by *flyback timing*. Before commencement of the first element of the job to be timed, the stopwatch is started at a known time as shown by a clock or wristwatch. After completion of the last element of the job the stopwatch is allowed to run on until a definite time by the same timepiece. The interval between starting the stopwatch and starting to time the job (the 'time elapsed before starting') plus the interval between finishing the job timing and stopping the stopwatch (the 'time elapsed after finishing') is the check time. Check time plus the total of the recorded times for all elements of the job should equal the interval shown by the other timepiece.

cheque (check in the USA). A written order, addressed to a bank by one of its customers, requiring the bank to pay on demand a fixed sum of money to a specified person (or to the bearer of the cheque). The person signing the cheque is called the 'drawer', the person who is to be paid the money is called the 'payee'. A cheque is a special kind of *bill of exchange* and may be *endorsed* [1] by a payee in favour of someone else, but the procedure for *accepting* [1] does not apply to cheques.

chief executive. A member of an organization who has *authority* [1] over all other members in determining the conduct of the organization.

The chief executive of a *company* (usually called 'managing director' in the UK, 'president' in the USA) is invariably a *director* of the company and, in small companies, is usually permanent *chairman* of the board of directors. He is elected as a director by the *shareholders* and appointed chief executive by the board. In practice, the chief executive of a small company is usually the founder and majority shareholder of the company. In a large, long-established company he is likely to have been appointed to his position. He is responsible to the shareholders of the company—who may dismiss him—for the successful conduct of the company.

Chief Registrar of Trade Unions and Employers' Associations. Office created by the *Industrial Relations Act 1971* and abolished by the *Trade Union and Labour Relations Act 1974*. The registrar's main functions were: (1) to maintain a public register of *trade unions* [1] and *employers' associations* and determine the eligibility of organizations for entry in the register; (2) to see that the rules of registered organizations conformed with the Industrial Relations Act; (3) to investigate complaints against registered organizations; (4) to examine *annual returns* submitted by registered organizations; (5) to examine the affairs of insolvent organizations.

chi-square distribution (or χ^2 distribution). The *probability distribution* of a *random variable* that is the sum of the squares of n random variables that each have a *normal distribution* of which the *mean* [1] is 0 and the *standard deviation* [1] is 1. n is called the number of 'degrees of freedom' of the distribution.

The *frequency function* is:

$$f(x) = \frac{(\frac{1}{2})^{\frac{1}{2}n}}{\Gamma(\frac{1}{2}n)} x^{\frac{1}{2}n-1} e^{-\frac{1}{2}x} \qquad (x > 0)$$

(See *gamma distribution*.) The *mean* [1] of the chi-square distribution is n and its *variance* [2] is $2n$.

65

chi-square test. Any of a number of *nonparametric tests* that use the *chi-square distribution*.

chose in action. An item of *intangible property*.

chose in possession. An item of *tangible property*.

chronocyclegraph. A composite photograph of how a worker performs a job. Light bulbs which produce a pear-shaped flash of light at regular intervals are attached to each of the worker's hands. A long-exposure photograph is taken which shows the path of the hands (and also the direction—from the shape of the flashes—and speed—from the distance between successive flashes). This is superimposed on a conventional photograph of the worker so as to show the path of movement in relation to the layout of the workplace.

circuit. In a *graph* [2], a sequence of connected *edges* which begins and ends at the same *vertex*.

circular letter of credit. A *letter of credit* addressed to a large number of banks (e.g. all branches of a bank in a particular country).

circular note. Precursor of the modern *travellers cheque*.

circulating assets. See *current assets*.

City Code on Takeovers and Mergers. A set of principles and rules to be observed during *takeover bids* for companies that are *listed* on the *Stock Exchange* [2]. The object of the Code is to ensure that all shareholders of the offeree company are treated fairly. The Code was first issued (under the title of 'Notes on Amalgamations of British Businesses' in October 1959) and is revised periodically. It is compiled by the City Working Party, which consists of representatives of the *Stock Exchange* [2] and a number of associations of financial institutions. Provisions of the Code are enforced by the *Panel on Takeovers and Mergers*. (See *blue book* [2], *red book*.)

class. A type of *share* issued by a British *registered company* (e.g. *ordinary shares, preference shares*).

classification. 1. Systematic arrangement in groups or categories according to established rules. 2. A category.

classification method. A method of *job evaluation* in which descriptions of a small number of classes of jobs are established and the classes *ranked* in order of value. The jobs to be evaluated are then assigned to a class by comparing their *job descriptions* with the descriptions of the classes. (Also known as the 'grade method' or 'grading method'.)

classified advertisement. An *advertisement* in a section of a newspaper or magazine that contains many advertisements, all set in the same simple style, grouped according to a classification scheme devised by the publisher.

class meeting. A meeting of *shareholders* of a British *registered company* who hold shares of a particular *class*.

clawback. An amount (£52 when this book went to press) that is deducted from a man's *personal reliefs* if he receives a *family allowance*. The deduction was introduced in 1968 when the family allowance was increased by 50p with the object of recovering this increase from people whose income was high enough to pay income tax.

Clayton Act 1914. US statute which clarifies and strengthens the *Sherman Act 1890*. In particular a manufacturer may not: (1) make contracts with retailers under which they cannot sell the products of the manufacturer's competitors; (2) charge different prices to different buyers of the same goods. Named after its promoter in the House of Representatives, Henry De Lamar Clayton (1857–1929).

clearing bank. A bank that is represented on the Committee of London Clearing Bankers which runs a national *clearing house* (the London Bankers' Clearing House) for *cheques* and *credit transfers* [2]. There are now 6 clearing banks: Barclays Bank Ltd, National Westminster Bank Ltd, Midland Bank Ltd and Lloyds Bank Ltd (known as the 'Big Four'), Coutts & Co (which is a subsidiary of National Westminster), and Williams & Glyn's Bank Ltd.

clearing house. An organization set up by a number of banks to accumulate and offset financial claims against each other (in the form of *cheques* or *credit transfers*) so that they can periodically settle by single payments.

clock card. A card on which a particular employee's starting and finishing times are stamped, by a device connected to a clock, each day or each shift. (Also known as a 'time card'.)

close company. For the purposes of UK *corporation tax*, a close company is, roughly, a company that is resident in the UK and is controlled by five or fewer *participators* or by participators who are *directors*.

In this context, 'company' means a corporation or an *unincorporated association* but not a *partnership*, a *local authority* or an association of local authorities; 'director' includes a person 'in accordance with whose directions or instructions the directors are accustomed to act'.

A person has 'control' if he exercises, or is able to exercise or is entitled to acquire, control over the company's affairs.

There are special provisions with regard to *shortfall* to ensure that close companies are not used for tax avoidance. Certain companies are exempt from these provisions—for example, building societies, registered industrial and provident societies and companies controlled by the Crown.

The full definition of the term is given in the Income and Corporation Taxes Act 1970, sections 282, 283, 302 and 303 as amended by the Finance Act 1972, Schedule 17, paragraphs 1, 5 and 6.

close corporation. In the USA, a *corporation* of which *shares* are held by only a few people and are rarely if ever bought and sold. Close corporations correspond to *private companies* in other countries but there are no separate legal rules in the USA covering them so the term is descriptive only.

closed-loop control system. A *control system* in which there is *monitoring feedback* and the information about the deviation (e.g. the difference between actual and desired states of the controlled condition) is used within the control system to change the controlled condition in a way that reduces the deviation. If no human beings are involved in the process of feedback and interpretation of the feedback information, the system is said to be 'automatic'; if human beings are involved it is said to be 'manual'. (Also known as a 'monitored control system'.)

closed shop. An area of employment where all workers must belong to a union. There are two types: *pre-entry closed shop* and *post-entry closed shop.*

close out. To arrange a *forward contract* or a *future contract* that has precisely the opposite effect of one that has already been arranged so that it is not necessary to take possession of the goods to which the contracts refer.

cluster sampling. A *sampling procedure* used when the *population* [1] is widely dispersed geographically but where representative groups ('clusters') can be identified. A *random sample* is taken from each cluster. For example, if the population is 'all households in Scotland' it may be adequate to sample households in some large towns in Scotland. (Also known as 'area of sampling'.)

coaching. A form of training, in which the trainee undertakes practical exercises (or actually performs his job) and there is continuous appraisal, discussion, and counselling from the trainer.

COBOL. Acronym from COmmon Business Oriented Language. A widely used *procedure-oriented language* for programming computers which is designed for general use in commercial applications. A COBOL program is written in a stylized but easily understandable version of English.

code. 1. A systematic statement of principles or laws. 2. A system of symbols used for representing data for purposes of communication or for storage or processing of information. (Specifically, a *programming language.*)

Code of Industrial Relations Practice. See *Industrial Relations Code of Practice.*

codetermination. Joint decision-making by management and workers in a firm—especially when carried out by formally elected committees (usually called *works councils*). See also, *employee participation.*

codification. 1. Systematic arrangement (e.g. of descriptions of the materials used by a firm) in groups or categories according to established rules; especially when accompanied by *coding*. 2. An act of *codifying*.

codify. To restate a set of principles or laws as a *code* [1].

coding. Assignment of symbols according to established rules for the purposes of communication, identification or for storage or processing of information.

CODOT. (Acronym from 'Classification of Occupations and Directory of Occupational Titles'.) A systematic classification of *occupations* [1] that are followed in the UK with descriptions of the principal tasks involved in each occupation and the common *job titles* applied to each. CODOT was prepared by the Department of Employment and published by HMSO in 1972. It covers 3500 occupations.

coefficient of correlation. A measure of the degree of *correlation* between two quantities, i.e. how far variation in one quantity can be completely predicted from knowledge of the variation of a second quantity.

The coefficient of correlation between two *random variables* is usually represented by ρ and estimates of it by *r*. One commonly used coefficient is the 'Pearson coefficient of correlation' (named after the English statistician, Karl Pearson, 1857–1936) defined by:

$$\rho_{12} = \sigma_{12}/\sigma_1 \sigma_2$$

where σ_{12} is the *covariance*, σ_1 and σ_2 are the *standard deviations* [1] of the two random variables. (Also known as a 'correlation coefficient'.)

coefficient of variation. 1. Ratio of *standard deviation* [1] to *mean* [1]. 2. Ratio of *standard deviation* [2 or 3] to *mean* [2].

cognitive dissonance. State of an individual of having conflicting or inconsistent items of knowledge, beliefs or perceptions about some subject.

collate. Synonym for *merge* [2].

collateral security. 1. *Security* [2] for a debt given by someone other than the debtor. 2. An extra *security* [2] for a debt given by a debtor in addition to a major security that in some circumstances might be considered sufficient. 3. (Chiefly US.) A *security* [2] for a debt that consists of rights over property, as opposed to personal *guarantees* [1].

collective agreement. An agreement between one or more trade unions and one or more employers or employers' associations about terms and conditions of work.

collective bargaining. A process by which terms and conditions of employment for a group of employees are negotiated on their behalf by their representatives who may conduct the negotiations with a single employer or manager or with a representative of a number of employers.

collective investment institution (CII) (or institution for collective investment). An organization for investing a fund of money (provided by a large number of individuals) in a wide variety of *securities* [1] so that the individuals who provided the fund can share in the returns from the investments and the diversity of the investments reduces the overall risks.

There are two basic forms of CII: (1) the CII is a *company* [1] and the fund for investment is the *contributed capital* of the CII; (2) the fund is used by one company (called the 'management company') to buy and sell securities as it thinks fit and the securities are held in *trust* [1] by a second company (called the 'trustee company') for the benefit of the contributors of the fund. The first type is called an 'investment company' or *investment trust* (though it is not a trust) or *mutual fund*; the second type is called a *unit trust*.

collector of taxes. Person appointed by the *Commissioners of Inland Revenue* to collect taxes as notified by *Her Majesty's inspectors of taxes*.

column-inch. Unit of measurement of advertising space in newspapers. It is a space one inch deep and one column wide.

commerce. The activities of buying and selling goods and commodities on a large scale, and connected activities such as the provision of finance and insurance for transactions in goods and commodities.

commercial (adjective). Of, or relating to, *commerce*.

commercial (noun). An *advertisement* that is broadcast by radio or television.

Commercial Court. Section of the *High Court* established in 1970 to deal with commercial disputes.

commercial paper. *Promissory notes* issued by industrial firms, bought and sold in a *money market*.

commission (noun). 1. Payment to someone in return for obtaining work, orders or sales for others; especially a payment that is a fixed percentage of the value of the business transacted. For example (*a*) payment to a salesman of a percentage of the value of the sales he makes, (*b*) payment to an *agent* of a percentage of the value of work he procures for others. 2. An action or a document that confers authority (especially legal authority) to perform specified duties. *Also* duties specified in such a way. 3. A task entrusted to someone who is to act as an *agent* in performing it. 4. A body of people given authority to perform a specific task. Especially a government agency with investigative or administrative duties. 5. A task given to an artist or designer to create something according to outline instructions in return for a fee fixed in advance.

commission (verb). 1. To give someone a *commission* [2, 3, 4 or 5] to do something. 2. To put a piece of machinery into service.

commissioner. A person specially authorized by the Crown or by Parliament to carry out specified duties.

commissioner for oaths. A person (usually a solicitor) given a *commission* [2] by the Lord Chancellor empowering him to take *affidavits* and similar sworn statements.

Commissioner of Customs and Excise. One of the civil servants responsible to the Treasury for managing the collection of *car tax, customs duties, excise duties* and *value added tax* in the UK. There are at present 11 commissioners who are known collectively as the Board of Customs and Excise. One commissioner is chairman of the Board.

Commissioner of Inland Revenue. A person appointed by the Crown to manage the collection of *income tax, corporation tax* and *estate duty* in the UK. There are now 11 commissioners (including a chairman and 2 deputy chairmen) known collectively as the Board of Inland Revenue. The commissioners are responsible to the Chancellor of the Exchequer and manage the Inland Revenue Department.

Commission of the European Communities. Body set up on 1 July 1967 to formulate the detailed policy of the three *European Communities*. There are 13 commissioners appointed for four-year terms by agreement among the member states with at least 1 but not more than 2 commissioners from each member state. The commissioners must act entirely independently of national considerations. Each is responsible for coordinating work on a particular topic. The Commission has a staff of international civil servants in Brussels.

Commission on Industrial Relations (CIR). A *commission* [4], originally established in March 1969 following a recommendation in the *Donovan report*. It produced several reports on aspects of industrial relations in the UK. Its status was altered, from 1 November 1971, by the *Industrial Relations Act 1971,* which gave it the function of investigating and reporting on matters referred to it by the *National Industrial Relations Court,* principally questions of recognition of unions by employers. Under the *Trade Union and Labour Relations Act 1974* the CIR was abolished on 16 September 1974. Its investigatory functions have been taken over by the *Conciliation and Arbitration Service.*

commitment. 1. State of being obliged to do something. *Also* the extent of what has to be done. 2. State of having predominantly positive feelings towards something (opposite to *alienation* [2]).

committee. A group of people who consider together specific matters that have been assigned to them for consideration by other people (i.e. the matters have been 'committed' to them).

committee of inspection. 1. A committee appointed by the *contributories* and *creditors* [1] of a British *registered company* that is being *wound up.* The committee's function is to assist the company's *liquidator* and supervise his proceedings. 2. A committee appointed by the *creditors* of a *bankrupt* to supervise the work of the bankrupt's trustee.

committee of investigation. A body appointed by the Secretary of State for Employment to investigate an industrial dispute.

Committee of Twenty. A committee, consisting of members of the board of governors of the *International Monetary Fund* (IMF), which was asked by the IMF to consider ways of reforming the international monetary system. It first met on 28 September 1972. It made recommendations on 13 June 1974.

commodity. 1. Synonym for *good.* 2. Synonym for *economic good.*

3. Synonym for *primary product*, especially a primary product for which an *organized market* exists.

commodity broker. A person who arranges deals, on behalf of his clients, on *organized markets* for *commodities* [3].

commodity exchange. An *organized market* for buying and selling *primary products* or *futures contracts* relating to primary products.

commonality. Use of the same component or components in a number of different final products.

common carrier. Someone who will transport for a payment the goods of anyone who asks him—so long as he has the necessary carrying capacity.

common cost. A measurement, for the purposes of accounting, of the cash value of whatever a firm has parted with (or is liable to part with) in making an *expenditure* on goods, services or labour which have been used by or have benefited several different departments, activities or products of the firm although it is not possible to identify the precise proportions used by each. A common cost may be apportioned between individual activities according to some arbitrary rule.

Common Customs Tariff (CCT). The list of *import duties* charged by members of the *European Economic Community* (EEC) on goods originating from countries outside the Community. The original six members of the EEC adjusted their individual tariffs over a 9-year period between 1 January 1959 and 1 July 1968 until they were eventually all the same. The 3 new members of the EEC are altering their individual tariffs progressively until 1 July 1977 when all 9 members will apply the CCT. The CCT can be altered by the *Council of the European Communities*. (The CCT is sometimes known as the 'Common External Tariff' or 'CET'.)

Common External Tariff (CET). Name sometimes applied to the *Common Customs Tariff*.

common law. The body of law that has been developed by judges when deciding cases and which was originally based on unwritten customs that were believed to have been established by long use.

common market. A *customs union* in which: (1) there are no

74

restrictions on individuals moving from one country to another in order to establish business enterprises, perform services or be employed; (2) efforts are made to ensure that there is no distortion of competition throughout the market; and (3) the member countries coordinate their economic policies.

common ownership. Principle that everyone who works permanently for an enterprise should have a proprietary share in it.

common stock. A part of the *authorized capital* of a US *corporation* received in exchange for *securities* [1] (called 'shares of common stock' or, simply, 'common stock') that give rights of ownership and control over the corporation, including: (1) a right to vote in appointing *directors*; (2) a right to a *dividend* [2] if the directors recommend one should be paid; (3) a right to share in any surplus the corporation has after it has been *liquidated* [3].

common stockholder. Someone who owns one or more shares of *common stock* of a particular corporation.

communication. Transmission of information, ideas, attitudes or emotions from one person or group to another person or group.

communications mix. Synonym for *promotional mix* [1].

Companies Act. One of a series of British statutes which regulate the formation and operation of *registered companies*. The most important Companies Acts (each of which superseded previous ones) were passed in 1862, 1908, 1929 and 1948. The 1948 Act, which is currently in force, was extensively amended by the Companies Act 1967. The phrase 'Companies Acts 1948 to 1967' means the Companies Act 1948 together with sections 1–57 (part 1) and Schedules 1–4 of the Companies Act 1967 and the Companies (Floating Charges and Receivers) (Scotland) Act 1972.

Companies House. The building at 55 City Road, London EC1, where the *Registrar of Companies* and his staff keep records of the affairs of *registered companies* available for public inspection.

company. 1. A *corporation* formed for a limited and specific purpose according to simple procedures set out in the laws of the country of incorporation. The incorporation procedure typically involves registering, with an official, a constitution for the company and details of its *members*. A company usually has *contributed capital* that is supplied by members in exchange for *securities* [1] (called *shares*) that entitle them to a share of any profits the company makes (or to a share of any surplus left over when the company is dissolved) in proportion to the capital they contributed. However, in many companies, a member may sell his shares (i.e. his entitlement to profits and surplus) to someone else who then replaces him as a member. Members of companies are commonly referred to as *shareholders*. It is usual for the law to require members to appoint *directors* who are regarded by the law as the principal representatives of the company. To encourage people to buy shares, shareholders (members) are usually given *limited liability*. In most countries (but not in the USA) there are two types of company: *private companies* and *public companies* [1]. (See also *chartered company, guarantee company, statutory company, unlimited company*.)

Note. In the USA, the word 'corporation' is used when referring to any kind of corporation and 'company' is not used in the specialized sense described above.

2. A *partnership*. 3. *Partners* or business associates (especially in the name of a firm).

company law. The law relating to the formation, operation and dissolution of *companies* [1].

company limited by guarantee. Synonym for *guarantee company*.

company limited by shares. A British *registered company* that is a *limited company* in which the limit of a member's liability is the *nominal value* of his *shares*.

company secretary. Official of a British *registered company* who has certain legal and administrative responsibilities laid down by the *Companies Acts*. The basic functions of a company secretary are to arrange meetings of the *board of directors* and act as secretary to those meetings, deal with correspondence to the company, sign company documents—notably the *annual return* required by the Companies Acts—and attend to all matters relating to *shareholders*. The company secretary is often responsible for considering the legal aspects of company activities and for general administrative work.

company union. A trade union membership of which is limited to employees of a single firm.

comparative management. Study of the practice of *management* in different cultures or countries in order to determine widely observed basic principles as well as cultural differences.

compensating balance. An amount of money that a bank requires a borrower to *deposit* with the bank while the bank lends money to the borrower.

compensation. 1. (Chiefly US.) *Remuneration* of employees. 2. Payment which is made to somebody who has suffered loss or harm to his person, or to his property or reputation, and which is intended to put him back in the position he was in before his loss.

competence. 1. State or quality of being able to take specified action without referring to other people, or without gaining special authorization, or without violating rules about who may take that action. 2. Quality of having the necessary ability, training or experience to undertake a specified task.

compiler (or compiling routine). A *translating routine,* especially one that converts a *program* [1] written in a *high-level language* into *computer instruction code.*

composition. A partial payment, or promise of partial payment, of debts made by an *insolvent* debtor and accepted by his creditors as a complete discharge of his liability to them.

compound. 1. Periodically to add interest, of $r\%$ per period, to an amount owing, in such a way that, at the end of each period the interest added is $r\%$ of the sum of the *principal* [1] and the interest added in previous periods. If the principal is £P then at the end of n periods the total of principal and interest is:

$$£P\left(1+\frac{r}{100}\right)^n$$

2. To agree with one's creditors to pay them a *composition.*

compound arbitrage. *Arbitrage* that is achieved by carrying out more than two transactions.

compound discount. A *discount* calculated by *compound discounting*. (Sometimes called 'true discount'.)

compound discounting. Computing a *discount* according to the formula:

$$d = P\{1 - (1+i)^{-n}\}$$

where P is the amount from which the discount, d, is to be subtracted, i is the 'discount rate' per unit of time and n is the number of units of time. $P - d$ is called the 'present value' of P and is equal to:

$$\frac{P}{(1+i)^n}$$

compound interest. Interest that is *compounded* [1].

Comptroller and Auditor General. UK public official responsible for auditing the accounts of government departments, presenting an annual report to the Public Accounts Committee of the House of Commons, and for ensuring that no money leaves the *Consolidated Fund* without proper authority. He is head of the Exchequer and Audit Department, is appointed by *letters patent* and can be removed from office only after a formal request from both houses of Parliament.

compulsory licence (in USA, compulsory license). A *licence* [2] of *patent rights* which the *patentee* is compelled to grant by a court—usually on the grounds that the patentee has not used his invention, that the person applying to be the *licensee* [2] is willing to use it, and that it is in the public interest that the invention should be used.

computer. A device which can automatically perform *data-processing* tasks according to instructions (*programs* [1]) that are stored and can be altered within the device.

computer bureau. An enterprise that hires the use of its *computer* to people for individual jobs.

computer instruction code. A *code* [2] used to represent the basic instructions that a *computer* has been built to execute. (Also known as 'computer code', 'machine code' or 'machine instruction code'.)

computer science. Synonym for *computing.*

computing. The theory and practice of using *computers.* (Also known as 'computer science'.)

concentration ratio. The percentage of the total business (measured in a specified way) of a specified industry that is done by a specified number of the largest firms in that industry. For example, the percentage of the total sales revenue of an industry that is received by the 4 largest firms in that industry. Several different forms of concentration ratio are in use.

Conciliation and Advisory Service. Branch of the Department of Employment that sought to promote better management/employee relationships in industry, to provide conciliators in industrial disputes and to provide advice to individual firms on industrial relations, personnel and management problems. Because it was a branch of a government department its independence was thought to be threatened. In 1974 it was reconstituted as the independent *Conciliation and Arbitration Service.*

Conciliation and Arbitration Service (CAS). An independent body set up by the British government in September 1974 to provide conciliation and arbitration as a means of avoiding and resolving industrial disputes, to make facilities available for arbitration, to provide advisory services for industry on industrial relations, and to undertake investigations as a means of promoting the improvement and extension of collective bargaining. The CAS has a governing council with ten members, one of whom is chairman. It has taken over most of the tasks of the Department of Employment's *Conciliation and Advisory Service,* and of the *Commission on Industrial Relations.*

conditional probability. The *probability* that an outcome will occur if some other event (which is itself unpredictable) occurs. The conditional probability $P(A|B)$ of A occurring when B has occurred is $P(A|B) = P(A \text{ and } B)/P(B)$.

Confédération européenne des syndicats (CES). French title of the *European Trade Union Confederation.*

Confederation of British Industry (CBI). An organization (incorporated by Royal charter) formed in 1965 as a 'spokesman for British industry and commerce'. The CBI is an amalgamation of a number of older organizations, including the *British Employers' Confederation, Federation of British Industries* and *National Association of British Manufacturers.* Its members are commercial and industrial firms (about 12 000), *employers' associations* (about 200), *trade associations* and nationalized industries. Its principal objective is to promote the growth and success of British industry. The CBI has a permanent staff of about 400 in London and in 11 regional offices headed by a director-general. It is governed by a council of 400 which meets monthly.

Although maintaining strict political neutrality, the CBI continuously advises, consults and where necessary takes issue with the government of the day on all aspects of its policies likely to affect either directly or indirectly the interests of British business both now and in the future. It is in constant day-to-day touch with the government and countless other organizations—including the EEC and various bodies overseas—for this purpose. Detailed formulation of policy is carried out by its many committees and working parties which submit their recommendations to the CBI central council. Regional councils and regional and area offices cover every part of the UK including Northern Ireland, Scotland and Wales and deal with both national and local issues. Special attention is paid to the interests of smaller firms, comprising about one third of the individual companies in membership. Regular meetings held both in London and the regions are supplemented as necessary by numerous special meetings and conferences on particular subjects. The CBI issues a wide range of regular and *ad hoc* booklets and reports on overseas, economic, commercial, technical and employment questions. An important part of the Confederation's task is to promote and publicize the viewpoints of industry and business as widely as possible at home and overseas.

Address: 21 Tothill Street, London SW1H 9LP (01–930 6711).

Confederation of Irish Industry (CII). An organization founded in 1932 to represent business interests in Ireland. In

June 1974 the CII had 1500 individual firms and 65 *trade associations* as members.

Address: 28 Fitzwilliam Place, Dublin 2, Irish Republic (0001–760366).

conference. A meeting of people to solve particular problems, take specific decisions or discuss specific matters.

confidence interval. A range of numbers which, according to *statistical inference,* has a specified *probability* of including a particular *population parameter.* The two ends of the range are called 'confidence limits'.

For example, if a statistician says, 'the 95% confidence interval for the mean is 401–405', he is saying that, on the basis of the samples that have been analysed, he asserts, with a 95% probability of being correct, that the *mean* [1] is between 401 and 405. In other words there is a 5% chance that the interval has been calculated wrongly and does not really include the mean.

confidence limits. See *confidence interval.*

confirming house. An enterprise in one country that will confirm orders for goods made by buyers in other countries to exporters in the confirming house's country. The confirming house undertakes to pay exporters for the goods and will collect the money from the foreign buyer. The buyer pays a fee to the confirming house.

conglomerate. A firm that has many unrelated business activities or a *holding company* [2] whose *subsidiaries* are engaged in a diverse range of activities; especially one that has been built up by *conglomerate mergers.*

conglomerate merger. A *merger* of firms with unrelated activities.

Conseil international pour l'organisation scientifique (CIOS). International association of national management institutes (at present 40) founded in 1926 to promote modern management methods and techniques. It aims to foster a permanent exchange of experience and know-how among managers in order to increase the standard of living in countries where it is represented.

CIOS organizes an international management congress once every 3 years to discuss problems of paramount importance to management. CIOS has three regional organizations: Asian Association of Management Organizations of CIOS (AAMO CIOS), European Council of Management (CECIOS) and the Pan-American Committee of CIOS (PACCIOS).

Also known by its English title 'International Council for Scientific Management'.

Address: 1 rue de Varembé, 1211 Genève 20, Switzerland (34 14 30).

consensus. General agreement by a number of people; especially on fundamental principles by people who hold differing views on related matters.

consideration. A benefit which one party to a *contract* receives for performing his obligation under the contract. Under English law, a contract that does not give consideration to one of the parties cannot be enforced in a court of law unless it is contained in a *deed*. *Specifically*, the price paid by a buyer to a seller.

consign. 1. To send goods to someone; to *despatch* [1] goods. 2. To send goods to an agent or a manufacturer under a *consignment* [2, 3] arrangement.

consignee. Someone to whom something is *consigned* or shipped.

consignment. 1. The act or process of sending goods to someone. 2. An arrangement whereby goods are sent to an *agent* who tries to sell them on behalf of the sender. 3. An arrangement whereby goods are sent to a manufacturer for use by him as *materials* but he does not take ownership of them until he uses them (and can usually return any he does not use). 4. A batch of goods that have been *consigned* to someone.

consignment stocks. *Stocks* [1] of goods sent to or held by an *agent* or a manufacturer under a *consignment* [2, 3] arrangement.

consignor. A person who has *consigned* goods.

consolidated accounts. Accounts which treat a *holding company* and its subsidiaries as though they were a single firm.

Consolidated Fund. The fund of money held in an *account* [3] at the *Bank of England* into which all UK government revenues must be paid. The full title of the account is the 'Account of Her Majesty's Exchequer'—see *Exchequer*. A withdrawal from the account can be made only if Parliament has authorized it (e.g. if it is in accordance with legislation). The *Comptroller and Auditor General* is responsible for checking that withdrawals are authorized. If there is a surplus in the fund at the end of a day that surplus is transferred to the *National Loans Fund;* if there is a deficit at the end of a day it is made up from the National Loans Fund.

Until the eighteenth century, government revenues were kept in separate funds according to the source of the revenue but this became too cumbersome and so, in 1787, all funds were 'consolidated'.

consolidation. 1. Preparation of *consolidated accounts* of a group of companies. 2. Replacement of *shares* of low *nominal value* by an equivalent number of shares of higher nominal value (for example, replacement of 20 5p shares by 1 £1 share). (Also known as a 'reverse split'—see *stock split*.) 3. Merging of two distinct companies to form a single new company—see *merger*.

consortium. 1. A number of companies associated together for a particular purpose, e.g. to carry out the work of constructing a factory. Especially an international association. 2. See *group relief*.

conspiracy. Agreement by two or more persons to do something which will harm a particular person. The person who is likely to be harmed may be able to take legal action to prevent the conspirers carrying out their plan (or may be able to claim *damages* if they do harm him) even if the plan would not be actionable if carried out by only one person. Similarly it may be possible to take criminal action against the conspirers if their plan harms the public interest even if no criminal action would be possible if only one person carried out the plan. The idea is that a combination of people is particularly menacing whereas it ought to be possible to stand up to one person doing something that is unfair though not actually illegal. See also *Conspiracy and Protection of Property Act 1875*.

Conspiracy and Protection of Property Act 1875. An English statute concerning industrial relations. Under the 'conspiracy' part a *conspiracy* to perform some harmful act in contemplation or furtherance of a *trade dispute* cannot be the subject of a criminal action unless the act would be punishable as a crime if it were performed by one person alone. The 'protection of property' part makes it a criminal offence to break a *contract of employment* knowing that the probable consequence would be to endanger human life or cause bodily injury or expose valuable property to destruction or serious injury.

constructed-response programmed instruction. Synonym for *linear programmed instruction*.

consular invoice. An *invoice* prepared by an exporter which is certified by the importer's consul in the exporter's country, usually on payment of a fee.

consultative management. A *managerial style* which is characterized by consulting subordinates about decisions that will affect them while making it clear that their views are for information only and will not necessarily influence the decision. Often forms part of the *paternalistic management* style.

consumer. 1. Someone who, or a firm that, consumes specified goods—i.e. buys them but does not directly use them for manufacturing other goods or for resale at a profit. 2. Someone who usually buys goods for consumption by himself or by members of his *household* and not for use in manufacturing other goods or for resale at a profit.

consumer contest. A *sales-promotion* activity in which *consumers* [1] of a *product* [2] are entitled to enter a contest for prizes. (Also known as a 'promotional game' or 'game'.)

consumer credit. Facilities which enable *consumers* [2] to obtain *consumer goods* and delay paying all or most of the price for them for some time after acquiring possession of them. The term includes credit facilities given by retailers (e.g. *charge accounts*), loans by *finance companies* for the purchase of specific goods and *hire-purchase* arrangements.

consumer deal. A reduction in the price that *consumers* [1] are asked to pay for a specified *product* [2] (or a reduction in the *recommended retail price*) which is made for a limited period by the manufacturer of the product as an inducement to consumers to buy more of it.

consumer durable. A *consumer good* that is expected to last for considerably more than a year. (Land and dwellings are usually not considered to be consumer durables.)

consumer expendables. *Consumer goods* that are not *consumer durables*.

consumer goods. *Goods* that are usually bought by individuals (often after purchase and resale by *intermediaries*) for consumption or personal use by themselves or by members of their *households* but not for incorporation in, or assistance in manufacturing, other goods.

consumerism. The view that efforts should be made by or on behalf of *consumers* [2] in order to secure improvement in *consumer products*, in the methods of marketing and distributing *consumer goods* and in *after-sales service* for *consumer durables*. The alternative view is that such improvements will be made automatically by the suppliers of goods and services, if there is *free enterprise*, because an improvement made by one supplier of a good would increase his sales at the expense of his competitors. However, there is great ignorance among consumers (and even among the producers of goods) about what features are desirable in particular goods and about the relative merits of the goods of different producers. An important aspect of consumerism is, therefore, a belief that much more information about and evaluation of consumer goods and marketing practices should be made available.

consumer jury. A group of people, forming a representative cross-section of consumers, who are asked for their opinions during *market research*. They may, for example, be asked to comment on proposals for new products, or to taste new food products, or to state their reactions to proposed advertisements.

consumer loyalty. *Customer loyalty* in the purchase of *consumer goods*.

consumer market. The *market* [1, 3] for *consumer goods*.

consumer panel. Synonym for *consumer purchase panel*.

Consumer Price Index. An *index number* computed monthly by the US Bureau of Labor Statistics. It reflects changes in the prices of about 300 goods and services purchased by the families of urban wage earners and clerical workers. The index was first published in 1918 and its current base period is 1967. (The UK equivalent is the *General Index of Retail Prices*.)

consumer product. A *product* [2] of a firm that is a *consumer good*.

Consumer Protection Advisory Committee. A permanent body, of not less than 10 nor more than 15 members, established by the Fair Trading Act 1973. The members are appointed (as either full-time or part-time members) by the Secretary of State for three-year terms. The Secretary of State appoints one of the members as chairman and one as deputy chairman. The *Director General of Fair Trading* or the Secretary of State or any Minister can ask the Committee to report on whether any 'consumer trade practice' adversely affects the interests of consumers in the UK. A consumer trade practice is any practice carried on in connection with the supply of goods or services and which relates to: (1) terms and conditions on which the goods or services are to be supplied; (2) the manner in which terms and conditions are communicated to potential buyers; (3) *promotion* [1]; (4) methods of salesmanship; (5) methods of packaging; (6) methods of demanding or securing payment.

consumer purchase panel. A representative group of *consumers* [2] who record their purchases and periodically report them to an information-gathering organization (e.g. for purposes of *market research*). (Also known as a 'consumer panel'.)

contango. 1. A fee paid to a *stockbroker* by someone who has arranged to buy *securities* [1], for the privilege of delaying payment for those securities. 2. A state in which the *spot price* for a quantity of a *commodity* [3] is lower than the *forward price* for the same quantity. *Also* the difference between the spot and forward prices in such circumstances.

continental shift system. A *rapidly rotating shift system* in which each group of workers changes from working one type of shift to another three times each week (3 days of one type, 2 of a second and 2 of a third) with a 24-hour break at each change. For example, one group would work 3 consecutive *morning shifts* then 2 consecutive *afternoon shifts* and then 2 consecutive *night shifts*, usually followed by 3 rest days. (Also known as the '3-2-2 shift system'.)

contingency allowance. When calculating the *standard time* for a job in *work study*, it is usual to add to the *basic time* a small allowance (typically, no more than 5% of the basic time) to represent time that the worker has to spend, while working on the job being measured, on matters other than that job (such as adjusting tools, answering the telephone, or consulting with a superior).

contingent liability. A *liability* [1] that will arise if some event (which is itself unpredictable) occurs.

continuation day. The first day of a Stock Exchange *account* [2].

continuous production. Productive activity, of which the output is large quantities of a small number of different products and in which most production facilities are always involved with work connected with a single product. Production facilities (e.g. tools and equipment) in continuous production are often designed specifically to make one product and are often laid out as a *production line*. (Also known as 'flow production'.)

continuous random variable. A *random variable*, the possible values of which are all possible real numbers in a particular range. (See *discrete random variable*.)

continuous shiftwork (or continuous shift system). A system of *shiftwork* [1] in which work is carried on all day every day of the week.

continuous stocktaking. System of checking records of *stocks* [1] held by a firm in which the actual quantities of goods in stock are physically counted very frequently.

continuous timing. Synonym for *cumulative timing*.

contract. A legally enforceable agreement between two or more individuals (or *corporations*) that they will do or not do something.

contract for services. A *contract* under which one party (usually called the 'contractor') promises to perform, personally, defined services for the other party (usually called the 'employer') but not as an *employee*. A contractor working under a contract for services usually does not form part of his employer's organization and/or does not work under the direct control of his employer and/or usually works for a number of different employers over a short period of time. Conversely an employee working under a *contract of employment* usually forms part of his employer's organization and works under the direct control of the employer and usually works for one employer continuously for a long period.

contract in. To give notice that one wishes to incur a minor obligation under a *contracting-in* arrangement.

contracting-in. Arrangement with an effect opposite to that of *contracting-out ;* in other words, an individual must give formal notice of his intention to incur the minor obligation.

contracting-out. Arrangement by which a minor obligation is automatically linked to a principal obligation and an individual has to give formal notice if he wishes to cease having the minor obligation. For example, members of trade unions in the UK are usually required to pay contributions to a political fund unless they give notice that they do not wish to.

contract note. A document sent by a *broker* to his client immediately the broker has carried out a transaction for him. It gives details of what the client will have to pay or what he can expect to receive for the deal.

contract of employment. A *contract* by which one party agrees to be an *employee* of the other party. A contract of employment may be oral or in writing but, in Britain, an employer must give every one of his employees a statement of certain terms and conditions related to the employment, under the *Contracts of Employment Act*. (Also known as 'contract of service'.)

contract of insurance. A contract between an 'insurer' and an 'assured' under which the insurer promises that if a specified peril causes a loss to the assured or if a specified event occurs then the insurer will pay the assured a specified sum of money. Most contracts of insurance require the insurer only to *indemnify* the assured. The *consideration* paid to the insurer by the assured is called a 'premium'.

contract of service. Synonym for *contract of employment*.

contractor. A person or firm that performs work according to a *contract*.

contract out. To give notice that one does not wish to incur a minor obligation under a *contracting-out* arrangement.

contract research. Research (especially scientific or technological) carried out by an organization, the results of which are to be used by another organization which commissioned the research.

Contracts of Employment Act. British legislation requiring every employer to provide every employee with certain details of his *contract of employment*. The legislation also prescribes minimum periods of *notice* [2] which must be observed when either employer or employee wishes to end a contract of employment. The first Contracts of Employment Act was passed in 1963; a revised version was passed in 1972.

contributed capital (or paid-in capital). Money that has been received by a *company* [1] in exchange for the issue by the company of its *shares* (or a measurement in monetary terms of the value of property received by or services performed for the company in exchange for shares). Contributed capital represents the money that is regarded as permanently available for the use of the company. In most countries, companies are forbidden to decrease their contributed capital by returning it to the shareholders as dividends or by cancelling their shares. (A company may, of course, lose its contributed capital if it is not successful in its activities.) In this respect, contributed capital is different from *debt capital* which is regarded as a loan to the company that may be repaid according to circumstances. Contributed capital is usually divided into two amounts: (1) the total *nominal value* (or *stated value*) of the shares that have been issued; (2) money (or a measurement of the value of other assets or services) received in excess of nominal or stated value. In the UK, item (2) is usually called 'share premium'; in the USA, the terms 'capital surplus' and 'paid-in surplus' have been used in the past but are now regarded as misleading.

contribution. The difference between the *sales revenues* received for a specified quantity of a product and the *variable expenses* associated with producing and selling that quantity. (Also known as 'contribution margin'.)

contribution margin. Synonymous with *contribution*.

contributory. A person who is liable to contribute towards paying the debts of a British *registered company* when it is being *wound up*.

contributory pension scheme. A scheme for providing pensions to employees the cost of which is contributed to by employees.

control (noun). 1. A means or method, or the process, of *controlling*. 2. A capability of a person successfully to *control* the behaviour of others. 3. An act or instance of *controlling*. 4. The state of being *controlled*. 5. The state of *controlling* something.

control (verb). 1. To affect the behaviour of someone or of a group so that it conforms with one's wishes. See, e.g., A. S. Tannenbaum (editor), *Control in Organizations* (New York: McGraw-Hill, 1968). 2. To affect the activities of an *open system* so that they conform to a standard or to a plan. (See also *control system*.) Controlling activities is usually thought to be one of the principal tasks of management. Henri Fayol (see *administrative management theory*), in *General and Industrial Management* (translated by Constance Storrs) (London: Pitman, 1949), said that: 'control consists in verifying whether everything occurs in conformity with the plan adopted, the instructions issued and principles established. Its object is to point out weaknesses and errors in order to rectify them and prevent recurrence.' (p. 107.) The link between planning and controlling is stressed in R. N. Anthony, *Planning and Control Systems: A Framework for Analysis* (Boston: Division of Research, Graduate School of Business Administration, Harvard University, 1965): 'although planning and control are definable abstractions and are easily understood as calling for different types of mental activity, they do not relate to separable major categories of activities actually carried on in an organization, either at different times, or by different people, or for different situations' (pp 10–11). Anthony and others stress that it is usually necessary to control adaptively—i.e. it must be possible to revise plans in the light of new information.

control account (or controlling account, or total account). An account that records periodical totals of debits and credits to all ledger accounts within a particular division of a *ledger*. The *balance* [1] on a control account should be the same as the total of the balances on the individual ledger accounts.

control chart. Synonym for *quality control chart*.

controllable cost. A *cost* [2], the extent of which can be controlled by a person holding a particular job in a firm.

controlled-circulation journal/magazine. A periodical publication that is sent free of charge to individuals selected because of their job title, business or profession and which consists largely of *advertisements*. (Also known as a 'qualified-circulation journal' or magazine.)

controlled condition. The parameter of a system that is affected by a *control system*.

controller (or comptroller). The chief *accountant* in a US *corporation*.

control limit. See *quality control chart*.

control system. A *subsystem,* of an *open system,* in which activity is directed towards maintaining, or affecting in a prescribed way, the value of some parameter of the output of the system. The parameter affected is called the 'controlled condition'.

convener. A senior *shop steward* in a factory; usually elected by the other shop stewards.

control unit. The part of a *computer* that directs the sequence and timing of the computer's operations. It interprets the instructions in a *program* [1], activates the relevant circuits to feed data into the *arithmetic unit*, activates the arithmetic unit to perform the required operations and activates circuits to remove the results of the operations to a required position.

convenience goods. Low-priced, standardized *consumer goods* which consumers will usually buy from the most convenient seller who offers them at a reasonable price. (Cf. *shopping goods.*)

conversational mode. A method of operating a *computer* in which an individual person gives instructions directly to the computer and receives an immediate response from it.

conversion. 1. An act of exchanging for an equivalent; especially, exchanging a *convertible security*. 2. An act of wrongfully depriving someone of the use and possession of his property.

conversion cost. The *direct costs* of, and the proportion of *indirect costs* associated with, one or more stages of a production process excluding the cost of the materials involved.

converted time. Synonym for *basic time*.

convertibility. The degree to which something is convertible—*especially* the extent to which the holder of a specified currency is permitted to convert it into other currencies.

convertible. Capable of being converted. Specifically: (1) When referring to *securities* [1] of any kind, exchangeable for a different security at the owner's option (for example, convertible *unsecured loan stock* may be issued by a company which promises that any *stockholder* [1] may exchange his stock five years after issue for *ordinary shares* of the company with a specified *nominal value*); (2) when referring to a foreign currency, exchangeable for another currency; (3) when referring to a *bank note*, or other form of currency, exchangeable for gold.

convertible debt. *Debt capital* obtained by selling *securities* [1] which may be exchanged by their holders at a future date for *equity shares*. Also securities issued with these conditions.

convertible security. A *security* [1] which, after a specified date, may be exchanged (usually within specified time-limits) for a different security according to a known formula. Typically, the convertible security is a *bond* [2] or *debenture* [2] which may be exchanged for *equity shares* after a set date.

conveyance. Formal process of transferring ownership of property (especially land) from one person to another. *Also* a document recording such a transfer.

conveyance duty. A *stamp duty* payable in the UK on any document that is a *conveyance* or *transfer* [2] of property. The rate fixed by the Finance Act 1974 is 2% of the purchase price but a transfer of any property except *securities* [1] is exempt if the price is below £15 000 and liable to reduced rates if the price is between £15 000 and £30 000. Transfers of British *government stock* are always exempt.

conveyancing. Art, practice or techniques of transferring and creating rights over land.

cooling-off period. A period during which a trade union is forbidden to call a *strike* or an employer is forbidden to enforce a *lockout*. A cooling-off period may be ordered by the President in the USA. In the UK the *National Industrial Relations Court* had the power to order a cooling-off period but did so only once.

cooperative advertising. *Advertisements* that advertise the products or services of two or more separate advertisers who share the cost.

cooperative relationship. Relationship between people characterized by: (1) a willingness to engage in *teamwork*, (2) a feeling of having a common purpose, and (3) a sense of membership of a larger group or organization.

co-opt. To invite someone to join an established group of people (e.g. a committee) in order, for example, for the group to benefit from his special experience or to attempt to silence his criticism of the group.

co-optation. The process or an act of *co-opting*.

coordinate. To plan, or take action to improve, the inter-relationships (especially of timing and methods of communication) between a number of various activities, which contribute to the achievement of a single objective, so that they do not conflict and the objective is achieved with a minimal expenditure of time and effort.

coordination. The action of *coordinating*.

co-ownership. Synonym for *copartnership*.

copartnership. An arrangement by which all those who work in a firm share to some extent in the profits, capital and control of the firm. The share of profits or capital is in addition to the normal wages paid in the firm's industry. Copartnership was quite widespread in the UK coal-gas industry before it was nationalized and is practised at present by the John Lewis

Partnership—see A. Flanders, Ruth Pomeranz and Joan Woodward, *Experiment in Industrial Democracy: A Study of the John Lewis Partnership* (London: Faber & Faber, 1968). (Also known as 'co-ownership'.)

copy. 1. The text (as opposed to drawings, illustrations or decorations) of a printed *advertisement*. 2. Matter to be set for printing.

copyright. The right to control the use (including making copies) of an artistic or literary creation.

copywriter. Someone who writes *copy* [1] for *advertisements*.

core. A small piece of magnetic material (usually shaped like a ring) used for storing data in a *computer*. (Also known as a 'magnetic core'.)

core time. The period of each day during which employees must be at work when working *flexible working hours*.

corner. To gain control (either actual ownership or the right to delivery under *futures contracts*) of most of the supply of a *commodity* for a period of time and thus be able to fix high prices for resale.

corporate advertising. Synonym for *institutional advertising*.

corporate goal. Synonym for *corporate objective*.

corporate identity. Characteristic, or uniform, style of design adopted by an organization in all forms of visual communication with the public—e.g. for packaging, letterheads, delivery vehicles, advertising. (Also known as 'house style'.)

corporate image. The *image* that people usually have of a particular *corporation*.

corporate income tax. A tax levied on the *income* of *corporations*. E.g., in the UK, *corporation tax*.

corporate objective. An objective which is to be achieved by a firm or other organization. (Also known as a 'corporate goal'.)

corporate planning. The activity, process or study of planning changes in the *corporate strategy* of a firm over a future period of time. (Also known as 'strategic planning'.)

corporate secretary. Equivalent in a US *corporation* to the *company secretary* in a British *registered company*.

corporate strategy. The general nature of a firm's relation-

94

ships (at present and planned for the future) with its environment (especially, its competitors and customers). A firm's corporate strategy may be described in terms of the *products* [2] it offers, the *markets* [2] for these products, the *market share* it has, its *profitability*, its size, its rate of growth, and the way in which its resources are allocated to its various activities.

corporation. An entity, created in accordance with the laws of a particular country, which can own property, can be made a party to contracts, can be sued in a court and which continues in existence until it is dissolved according to the laws by which it was created. A corporation is, in effect, an artificial person created by law (corporations are sometimes said to have 'legal personality'). Only certain persons permitted by law may take action in the name of a corporation (e.g. making it a party to a contract or making it the owner of property). These persons are in three groups: (1) the 'members' of the corporation (qualifications for membership are usually set out in the corporation's constitution); (2) people who are appointed by the members to conduct the day-to-day affairs of the corporation—usually called *directors* or governors or *managers;* (3) *agents* and *employees* of the corporation.

English law distinguishes between 'corporations sole' (which have only one member) and 'corporations aggregate' (with more than one member). Some corporations aggregate are created by a royal *charter* but the vast majority are created (or 'incorporated') by an Act of Parliament, which can be either an Act specifically creating one corporation (see *statutory company, public corporation*) or one of the *Companies Acts* which allow people to create a particular type of corporation (called a *registered company*) simply by delivering certain documents and paying a fee to the *Registrar of Companies*.

See also, *company*.

corporation tax. Tax charged on the *income* (including *capital gains*) of any *corporation* resident in the UK. The rate of tax for the *financial year* 1973 is 52%. There are provisions for a lower 'small companies rate' and for a lower rate for registered industrial and provident societies, housing associations and building societies.

The law on corporation tax is contained in the Income and Corporation Taxes Act 1970 as amended, in particular, by the Finance Act 1972.

correlation. Attribute (of two quantities) of being related so that variation in one is accompanied by a predictable variation in the other.

correlation coefficient. Synonym for *coefficient of correlation.*

cost. 1. A measurement, for the purposes of accounting, of the cash value of whatever a firm has parted with (or is liable to part with) when making an *expenditure.* 2. A measurement, for the purposes of *cost accounting,* of the cash value of whatever a firm has parted with (or is liable to part with) in making an *expenditure* in exchange for specified goods, services or labour used for a specified purpose. *Also* an estimate of the value of such an expenditure that is to be made in the future or is hypothetical. It is conventional to divide the cost associated with a specified purpose into: *expenses* [4], *labour cost* and *materials cost.* In *financial accounting,* a cost that has been incurred is usually called an *expense* [3]. 3. Synonym for *opportunity cost.*

cost accounting. Systematic measurement, analysis and recording of the *costs* [2] incurred by a firm or by particular activities, processes, or departments of a firm and estimation of costs to be incurred in the future or the costs that would be incurred in given circumstances.

cost and freight. See *c. & f.*

cost-benefit analysis (CBA). Providing a basis for choosing between two or more *investment projects* by assigning monetary values to benefits that would arise from the projects but would not be in the form of cash. See, e.g., R. F. J. Dewhurst, *Business Cost-Benefit Analysis* (Maidenhead: McGraw-Hill, 1972).

cost centre (spelt cost center in USA). A location, person, item of equipment or other division of an enterprise for which *costs* [2] may be ascertained and which is used for purposes of cost control.

cost estimating. Estimating the *costs* [2] of producing an item —usually in order to fix its price.

cost hammock. An *arrow* [2] that represents a sequence of activities, in an *activity-on-arrow network,* that have been grouped together for the purpose of allocating *costs* [2].

costing. Activities or techniques of ascertaining *costs* [2].

cost, insurance, freight. See *c.i.f.*

cost of capital. The minimum *rate of return* which a firm must give to the suppliers of its *capital.* The capital of a *company* is supplied from three main sources: the purchasers of *shares, retained earnings* and the suppliers of *debt capital.* It is usual to take a *weighted arithmetic mean* of the costs of the three types of capital.

cost of living. The amount of money that an individual or a family in a specified geographical area must spend in order to maintain a specified standard of living.

cost-of-living increase. An increase in an employee's remuneration that is intended to compensate for an increase in his *cost of living.*

cost-of-living index. 1. An *index number* that reflects the *cost of living* of specified people or families. In the UK, the *General Index of Retail Prices* is often regarded as a cost-of-living index. 2. (Usually capital C, L and I.) An *index number* which was published regularly between 1914 and 1947, and which represented the average percentage increase (compared with July 1914) in the cost of maintaining unchanged the standard of living prevailing in UK working-class families in 1914. It was replaced by an 'Interim Index of Retail Prices' which was published from 1947 until 1956 when publication began of the present *General Index of Retail Prices.*

cost of sales. The *expenses* [3] incurred in producing or acquiring goods that have been sold.

cost per thousand (CPT or CPM). Ratio of the price charged by the owner of a communication medium for carrying a specified advertisement to the number of thousands of people in the audience for the medium.

cost-plus contract. A contract for the performance of specified work under which the firm performing the work is reimbursed the amount of specified *costs* [2] and is also paid a fee. The fee may be calculated in two main ways: an amount fixed when the contract is signed (a cost-plus-fixed-fee, or CPFF, contract); or an amount that is related to how well the work is performed in terms of total cost, timing and so on (a cost-plus-incentive-fee, or CPIF, contract).

cost-plus pricing. Activity or practice of determining the selling price of a manufactured product by calculating the cost to the manufacturer of producing it (almost always by *absorption costing*) and adding a standard percentage of this cost to represent profit.

cost-price squeeze. A situation in which the *costs* [2] that a firm must incur to make its products are rising but the prices it can charge for the products cannot be increased.

cost-push inflation. *Inflation* that is caused by workers putting up wages (without increasing *productivity*) and manufacturers putting up prices but not following an increase in demand for goods or labour. Sometimes called 'wage-push inflation'. Many governments have tried various forms of controls over prices and incomes to cure this kind of inflation.

cost variance. The difference between a *standard cost* and the comparable actual cost incurred during a period.

cost-volume-profit analysis. Analysis of the relationships between actual or potential *sales revenue* from a product and the *costs* [2] of producing and selling it for different volumes of production and different selling prices.

Council of the European Communities. A body set up on 1 July 1967 to be the principal governing body of the three *European Communities*. Each member state is entitled to send one delegate to the Council (normally a minister—hence its popular name of 'Council of Ministers'). Each member state holds the presidency of the Council in turn for a period of 6 months. The Council takes all basic decisions concerning the activities of the Communities.

Council on Prices, Productivity and Incomes. Committee of three people (hence its popular name of 'The Three Wise Men') appointed by the UK government, initially in 1957, to keep under review movements in prices and incomes. It had no powers, the members were unpaid, and its only activity was to publish some analytical reports. It was disbanded in 1962 when the *National Incomes Commission* was established.

counselling. Giving one's friendship, experience and knowledge to someone so as to help him solve his problems.

countersign. To add one's own signature to a document that has been signed by someone else, usually as a guarantee of authenticity.

countervailing duty. An *import duty* imposed by a country on the import of specific goods from a specific country of origin in order to offset the effects of a *subsidy* given by the country of origin to producers of those goods.

county court. One of about 375 courts in England and Wales which have jurisdiction over civil cases, in general when the amount of money involved is less than £750. The courts have nothing to do with counties—there were county courts in Anglo-Saxon times that were related to counties and the name was resurrected when the present system was set up in the nineteenth century.

coupon. 1. Part of a *share warrant* which is cut off by the owner of the warrant and sent to the company (at times announced by the company), which, in exchange, pays the *dividend* [2] due on the shares that the warrant refers to. *Also* part of similar *bearer securities* which are exchanged for *dividend* [2, 3] or *interest* payments. 2. The rate of interest to be paid on a debt that is raised by selling *securities* [1] (such as *debentures* [2] or *bonds* [2]). Also known as the 'coupon rate'. 3. Part of an *advertisement* which is cut off, completed with an enquirer's name and address and sent to the advertiser as a request for more information or as an order form for goods. 4. A certificate authorizing the purchase of rationed goods. 5. A certificate entitling its holder to a reduction in the price of specified goods. 6. Part of an advertisement or of the wrapping of a product that is to be cut out and: (*a*) exchanged for a *premium* [3] or (*b*) used as an entry form for a *consumer contest*.

coupon advertising. A form of *direct-response advertising* using *space advertising* or *inserts* that include *coupons* [3].

coupon pack. A package of a *consumer product* which includes a *coupon* [5] (as part of the wrapping or container or inside the package) which can be used to buy the same or another product at a reduced price.

coupon rate. Synonym for *coupon* [2].

court of inquiry. A body appointed by the Secretary of State for Employment under the *Industrial Courts Act 1919* to inquire into the circumstances of an industrial dispute and present a report to Parliament. A court usually consists of equal numbers of representatives of employers and employees from outside the industry in which the dispute is taking place, plus an independent chairman.

Court of Justice of the European Communities. The court set up on 1 January 1958 to decide legal disputes in the framework of the treaties establishing the three *European Communities*. There are 9 judges appointed for 6-year terms by agreement among the member states. There are also 4 advocates-general whose duty is to present impartial legal argument on cases being heard by the court.

cousins group. In *group training*, a group that consists of people who work in the same organization and have roughly the same status but do not normally work closely together.

covariance. The covariance of two *random variables*, X_1 and X_2, which have *means* [1] μ_1 and μ_2 is:

$$\sigma_{12} = E\{(X_1 - \mu_1)(X_2 - \mu_2)\}$$

where E is the *expectation*. If the covariance of two random variables is zero they are said to be 'uncorrelated'.

cover (noun). Synonym for *margin* [2].

cover (verb). To buy goods that one has contracted to sell when in a *short position*.

Coverdale training. A form of *group training* in which groups are given tasks to perform and analyse their performance. The technique is intended to develop people's ability to work in teams and to form teams in order to plan projects or carry out plans made by others. Named after the English behavioural scientist, Ralph Coverdale (1918–75).

cover note. A *contract of insurance* which gives insurance temporarily while negotiations about a permanent contract continue or while administrative work connected with preparation of the final contract is in progress.

coworker. Someone that a person works with who is neither his superior nor a subordinate.

craftsman. A worker in a particular occupation who possesses a whole range of manual skills and knowledge and who uses his own initiative and judgment to decide how to carry out his work, which is usually non-repetitive and unsupervised. Especially one who has acquired his skills and knowledge during a period of *apprenticeship*.

craft union. A *trade union* [1] that will admit as members only workers who are skilled in a particular craft.

crash cost. Cost of doing something in the minimum possible time.

crawling peg. A system of controlling *exchange rates* in which an official parity is set which can change by a small amount (say 7% per year) and market rates are allowed to vary over a fairly wide 'band' either side of the parity rate (up to $2\frac{1}{4}\%$).

credit (noun). 1. An entry in an *account* [1] that represents a decrease in the value of *assets* [2] or an increase in the amount of *liabilities* [2]. It is conventional to make credit entries on the right-hand side of an account. (Cf. *debit* [1].) 2. An increase in the amount that a banker's client has deposited with the banker (which is a liability—see meaning 1—from the banker's point of view). 3. An allowance of time during which a debt may be repaid. 4. An arrangement between a bank, or an *accepting house*, and one of its customers by which the bank undertakes to pay specified *bills of exchange* on behalf of the customer. The usual situation is that the customer wishes to buy goods; the seller draws a bill of exchange with the bank, instead of the buyer, as *drawee* and sends it to the bank for *acceptance*. Because the bank is a well-known and respected institution the seller will be able to *discount* [2] the accepted bill for a higher price than if the buyer had been the drawee. The bank is reimbursed by the buyer and charges him a fee. The bank sends a letter to the seller informing him that the arrangement exists; such a letter is also

101

called a 'credit' or, sometimes, a 'letter of credit'. A letter of credit usually states that the promise to pay the bills is 'irrevocable'—hence the terms 'irrevocable credit' and 'irrevocable letter of credit'. The letter may stipulate that the bank will accept a bill only if it is accompanied by documents (usually a *bill of lading* and a certificate of insurance) to prove that goods have been despatched. Such a letter is known as a 'documentary letter of credit' or 'documentary credit'.

credit (verb). To make a *credit* [1] entry in an *account* [1].

credit agency. Synonym for *credit-reporting agency*.

credit bureau. A *credit reporting agency*; especially one that supplies information about private individuals.

credit card. A card issued by an organization that embosses the card with a code to identify its holder who writes a specimen of his signature on his card. A credit card is used to pay for goods and services as follows: a supplier transfers details from a buyer's card to an invoice which the card holder must sign. The supplier sends a copy of the invoice to the organization that issued the card; it pays him (often deducting a *commission* [1]) and asks the card holder for reimbursement.

credit control. The activity of: (1) deciding whether a firm should grant *credit* [3] to a customer and how much credit (i.e. for what amount of money and length of time) should be granted; (2) ensuring that customers who have been granted credit are paying on time.

credit controller. An employee who carries out *credit control* in a firm.

credit insurance. *Insurance* designed to compensate a seller if a buyer who has been granted *credit* [3] fails to pay.

credit line. An arrangement between a person or firm and a bank that the bank will be willing to loan up to a specified amount if required. *Also* the maximum amount available under such an arrangement. (Also known as a 'line of credit'.)

credit note. A document stating that a *credit* [1] has been made in an *account* [1] and why. It usually records a situation in which a seller reduces the amount owed by a buyer because of some mistake on the seller's part.

creditor. 1. Someone to whom money is owed. 2. (In plural.) The total amount that a firm owes to others.

credit rating. An assessment of how freely *credit* [3] should be allowed to someone or to a firm.

credit-reporting agency. An organization that will supply information about the *creditworthiness* of individuals or firms. (Also known as a 'credit agency' or 'credit bureau'.)

credit sale. A transaction for the sale of goods or services where the buyer is allowed by the seller to pay some time after delivery of the goods or performance of the services.

credit slip. A form completed by a customer of a bank when *depositing* money into his *account* [3] which gives details of the deposit.

credit squeeze. Restriction by a government of (*a*) the availability of loans from banks (either by forbidding certain loans or by ensuring that there are high rates of interest) or (*b*) retail sales on *credit* or by *hire-purchase*.

credit transfer. 1. A *giro* system. 2. An instance of paying money by a *giro* system. *Also* an amount of money so paid.

credit union. (US.) An organization, financed by members' subscriptions, of which the principal objectives are to make loans (often at favourable interest rates) to members and to pay dividends (out of the interest received) to subscribers. Membership of a credit union is open only to people in a category defined in the union's charter (usually employees of a particular company). Officials are unpaid.

creditworthiness. Degree to which it is prudent to grant *credit* [3] to someone or to a firm.

critical activity. An *activity* or a *dummy* on a *critical path*.

critical event. An *event* on a *critical path*.

critical-incident. Of, or relating to, concentration of attention or effort on a few important occurrences. As in 'critical-incident approach' (to *group training*) in which the trainer pays particular attention to handling events that could contribute to the development of his group.

critical path. An unbroken sequence of *arrows* [2] (a 'path') in a *network*, going from the *start event* to the *end event* and having a lower *total float* than any other path between those points.

critical path analysis (CPA). Activity or process of finding the *critical path* in a *network*, finding ways of reducing the time taken by the critical path and using the critical path for control purposes.

critical path method (CPM). A *project network technique* developed, about 1957, by employees of the American chemical producer, E. I. du Pont de Nemours & Co. It is similar to *PERT* except that only two time estimates (called 'normal' and 'crash') are made for each activity. Costs are calculated for performing activities in 'normal' and 'crash' times. If some crash costs are higher than the normal costs, CPM enables the analyst to see how to reduce the overall time of the project in the most economical way. For more details, see Jerome D. Wiest and Ferdinand K. Levy, *A Management Guide to PERT/CPM* (Englewood Cliffs, NJ: Prentice-Hall, 1969).

crossed cheque. A *cheque* with a *crossing*.

cross-firing. Operating two or (usually) more *current accounts* [1] at different banks to obtain money fraudulently. The simplest type of cross-firing is as follows: the holder of the accounts goes to bank A and draws out cash from his account there, though there is no cash in it. He covers his withdrawal by paying in a cheque drawn on his account at bank B which also has no money in it. It takes several days for the cheque to reach bank B and during that time the operator can pay a cheque (drawn on bank A or on a third bank) into the account at bank B. The process can be carried on for some time with enough bank accounts.

crossing. 1. Two parallel lines drawn or printed across a *cheque* (or a similar order to pay money on demand) as an instruction to the *drawee* that he must pay the money specified in the cheque only to a banker. 2. The name of a banker written or stamped across a cheque (or a similar order to pay money on demand) as an instruction to the *drawee* that he must pay the money specified in the cheque only to the named banker.

Note. The first type of crossing is called a 'general crossing'; the second type is called a 'special crossing'. A special crossing can be added to a general crossing. The words 'and company' or '& co' are often written between the lines of a general crossing because when the practice of crossing started in the eighteenth century every bank was a partnership and had 'and company' as the last words of its name (see *company* [2]): therefore, 'and company' meant 'any bank'. The practice of crossing is unknown outside the UK. See James Milnes Holden, *The History of Negotiable Instruments in English Law* (London: Athlone Press/ New York: Oxford University Press, 1955).

cross-rate. 1. The *exchange rate* between the currencies of two foreign countries. 2. The effective exchange rate between two currencies, A and B, achieved by (or which could be achieved by) an *arbitrage* deal in which currency A is sold for a third currency, C, which is used to buy currency B.

crosswalk. A diagram showing the relationship between items in *programme budgets* and those in budgets that have been prepared for departments or other *budget centres* of an organization.

cum. With. Used in the opposite sense to *ex* [1].

cumulative-part method. A method of training in which the operation to be learned is divided into small parts and the trainee practises the first part on its own, then the first part plus the second part, then the first two parts plus the third part, and so on.

cumulative preference share. A *preference share* that carries the right that, if in one year the company cannot pay a *dividend* [2] it must be paid in the next year in which sufficient profits are made together with the dividend for that year.

cumulative timing. A method of timing a job using a stopwatch in *time study* [1] in which the hands of the stopwatch are allowed to continue to move without returning them to zero at the end of each element of the job. The time for each element is obtained subsequently by subtraction.

currency. The coins, *bank notes* or other objects that are in general use in a particular country for settling debts.

currency note. A piece of paper that is used as *currency* in a particular country (usually a *bank note*).

currency rate. Synonym for *indirect rate*.

current account. 1. An *account* [3] with a bank where the customer makes *demand deposits* and asks for repayment of the deposits by drawing *cheques*. (Known as a 'checking account' in the USA.) 2. The section of the statement of a country's *balance of payments* that records all payments made to purchase goods and services. Payments made to residents for exports are *credited* to the account and payments made by residents for imports are *debited*. A deficit in the current account must be matched by a surplus in the *capital account* [1] (i.e. there must be an increase in foreign investment or a foreign loan or a decrease in the country's *official reserves*). The current account is usually sub-divided into accounts for *visibles* (i.e. goods) and *invisibles* (i.e. services).

current asset. Something owned by a firm which is either a *liquid asset* available for use in current operations or is owned by the firm with the intention of selling it for cash (as part of its normal operations) within a short period (usually, either one year or one of the firm's *operating cycles* if its operating cycle is longer than one year). A firm's current assets consist of its *stocks* [1]—either of finished goods, work-in-progress and materials or of its stock-in-trade—plus its *accounts receivable,* temporary investments and cash. (Current assets are sometimes called 'circulating' or 'floating assets' in contrast to *fixed assets.* The total value of a firm's current assets is known as 'gross working capital'—see *working capital.*)

current liability. An amount of money that must be paid by a firm in the near future (for most purposes, within one year or within the *operating cycle* of the firm).

current ratio. Ratio of the total value of the *current assets* of a firm to its total *current liabilities.*

current transaction. A transaction between a resident of a country and a nonresident in which a payment is made for goods or services. Payments for such transactions are recorded in the *current account* [2] of a country's *balance of payments.*

current yield. Synonym for *running yield.*

curriculum vitae. A summary of a person's life given by him when applying for a job. It usually contains date of birth, education, qualifications and previous jobs.

customer loyalty. Pattern of repeated purchasing—by a person, household or firm—from one supplier, or of repeated purchasing of the goods of one producer (*brand loyalty*, or *institutional brand preference*).

customs duty (or duty of customs). A tax payable on goods exported or imported from a country. See *import duty*. There are now no export duties in the UK.

customs union. A *free trade area* in which all countries apply the same *customs duties* and other restrictions on trade with territories outside the area.

cybernetics. The scientific study of communication and control, often concentrating on comparative studies of *control systems*.

cyclegraph. A photograph similar to a *chronocyclegraph* except that the lights are on continuously so that only the path of movement is shown.

d

D/A. Abbreviation of 'documents on [or against] acceptance'—i.e. the *drawee* of a *bill of exchange* that pays for goods is to be given documents proving the despatch of the goods (usually a *bill of lading*) before he will *accept* [1] the bill. Usually, a D/A bill is to be paid some time after it has been accepted—cf. *D/P*.

DCF. Abbreviation of *discounted cash flow*.

DD (or D/D). Abbreviation of 'demand draft'—see *bank draft*.

DE. Abbreviation of *Department of Employment*.

DEP. Abbreviation of *Department of Employment and Productivity*.

DF. Abbreviation of *degrees of freedom*.

disc. Abbreviation of *discount*.

DMS. Abbreviation of *Diploma in Management Studies*.

DP. Abbreviation of *data processing*.

D/P. Abbreviation of 'documents on [or against] payment'—i.e. the *drawee* of a *bill of exchange* that pays for goods is to be given documents proving the despatch of the goods (usually a *bill of lading*) before he will pay the bill. The bill is usually payable at sight—cf. *D/A*.

Dr. Abbreviation of *debtor*. Used in accounts to mark a column of *debits* or a debit entry.

DTI. Abbreviation of *Department of Trade and Industry*.

damages. A sum of money claimed or awarded as *compensation* [2] for loss or harm suffered by a person or by his property or reputation. *Also* a sum of money (often called 'exemplary

108

damages') which a court orders a person who has caused another loss or harm, to pay to the other and which is intended to show distaste for the action which caused the loss.

dangle. An *arrow* [2], in an *activity-on-arrow network*, that has no preceding or succeeding *event* or *activity* at one end.

data base (sometimes spelt database). A large, comprehensive, central or otherwise significant collection of data; especially when carefully organized and recorded so that information may be derived from it by using *electronic data processing*.

data flow chart. A diagram of the sequence of operations, both manual and automatic, involved in processing data. A data flow chart identifies the particular items of data at each stage and is normally used to describe a complete *data processing system*. (Also known as a 'flow chart', 'procedure flow chart', 'procedure chart', 'system chart' or 'systems flow chart'.)

data processing (DP). Systematically operating on data (e.g. by transcription, filing, sorting or computing) in order to produce new data according to established rules (e.g. by addition) or to extract information or to revise the data.

data processing system. A group of machines and of procedures for using them in order to carry out some task of data processing.

Datel. The service of transmitting coded data over telephone or telegraph circuits.

dawn shift. A *shift* that is worked early in the morning.

daybook. Synonym for *journal*.

day rate. A *time rate*.

day release. Arrangement under which employers give their employees a period off work (typically one day a week) without loss of pay in order that they can attend a course of further education. (Cf. *block release*.)

day shift. 1. A *shift* that is worked mainly during the hours of daylight. 2. The *morning shift* in a *three-shift system*.

days of grace. A period for which, by custom, payment of a debt may be delayed without any adverse consequences.

daywork. 1. Synonym for *time work*. 2. Work that is performed mainly during the hours of daylight. 3. Synonym for *casual work*.

dayworker. 1. Synonym for *timeworker*. 2. An employee who always works on a *day shift* or who works mainly during the hours of daylight. 3. Synonym for *casual worker*.

dead rent. A minimum amount payable, for example, on a lease of a mine (where rent is usually charged as a *royalty* on the quantity mined).

dead stock. *Stock* [1] of goods for which no further demand can be foreseen.

deal. 1. A transaction; especially a large-scale transaction in *securities* [1]. 2. A form of *promotion* [1] in which a price reduction is given for a limited period. See *consumer deal*; *trade deal*.

death duty. Synonym for *estate duty*.

debenture. 1. A document acknowledging a debt. (Now rarely used in this general sense.) 2. (UK.) A *security* [1], which is one of a large number of identical securities with a *nominal value* (from which the price of the security is computed), issued by a *company* [1] and entitling its holder to a regular payment of interest that is computed as a percentage of the nominal value. Now nearly always refers to a security of this type for which the company gives a *floating charge* over its *assets* [1] as a guarantee that interest will be paid. (Cf. *mortgage debenture* and *naked debenture.*) Debentures are usually *redeemable* (i.e. the issuing company can demand surrender of the debentures, on paying a fixed sum of money, at its option) and often specify a latest date by which they must be redeemed (called a 'maturity'). If no latest date is specified the debentures are called 'perpetual debentures'. If the issuer has no option to redeem then the debentures are said to be 'irredeemable'. The securities are usually issued in the form of *stock* [4] and called 'debenture stock'. 3. (US.) Synonym for *debenture bond*.

debenture bond. (US.) A *bond* [2] for which the issuer gives no *security* [2], e.g. in the form of a *floating charge* or a *mortgage*. (Equivalent to *unsecured loan stock* in the UK.)

debenture capital. 1. Synonym for *debt capital*. 2. The money that a company has received from selling *debentures* [2].

debenture holder. Someone who owns one or more *debentures* [2] (or some debenture stock).

110

debenture stock. See *debenture* [2].

debenture trust deed. A *deed* in which a *trustee* is appointed for the holders of *debentures* [2] (or debenture stock) of a company. The trustee is given the right to take steps to protect the debenture holders if there is default in paying their interest, or in redeeming their debentures, on time. He may be entitled to appoint a *receiver* and is usually given a *floating charge* on the *assets* [1].

debit (noun). 1. An entry in an *account* [1] that represents an increase in the value of *assets* or a decrease in the amount of *liabilities*. It is conventional to make debit entries on the left-hand side of an account. (Cf. *credit* [1].) 2. A decrease in the amount that a banker's client has *deposited* with the banker.

debit (verb). To make a *debit* entry in an *account* [1].

debt. 1. Something which someone is under an obligation to give to someone else; especially an amount of money that has to be paid to someone else as repayment of a loan or in payment for goods or services. *Also* the state of owing a debt. 2. Synonym for *debt capital*. 3. A *security* [1] (e.g. a *bond* [2] or *debenture* [2] issued when *debt capital* is raised.

debt capital. Money that has been loaned to a *company* for more than a short time (conventionally, more than one year). If a company is *liquidated* [3] it must repay debt capital before it can repay *contributed capital*. A company pays fixed annual *interest* on debt capital but distributes profits when possible to the holders of *equity shares*. The most common form of debt capital is that obtained by issuing *bonds* [2] or *debentures* [2]. (Also known as 'loan capital'.)

debt collection. The activity or process of getting *debtors* [1] to pay their debts.

debtor. 1. A person who owes money. 2. (In plural.) The total amount of debts owed to an enterprise.

debt ratio. The ratio of a company's *debt capital* to the sum of its debt capital and its *contributed capital*.

debug. To trace and eliminate faults; especially errors in a *program* [1] for a computer.

decelerating premium bonus plan/scheme/system. A *premium bonus scheme* in which the incentive payment per unit

111

of time saved decreases as more time is saved. (See *gain-sharing*. Also known as a 'regressive scheme'.)

decile. The first, second, third etc. deciles of a *probability distribution* or of a *frequency distribution* are the tenth, twentieth, thirtieth etc. *percentiles*. The fifth decile is also called the *median*. The deciles divide a distribution into ten equal parts.

decision-making. The process or activity of selecting, from among possible alternatives, a future course of action.

decision theory. The part of mathematics that deals with ways of analysing decision-making problems and provides methods for making optimum decisions.

decision tree. A diagram of a sequence of decisions, each of which involves choosing between a known number of alternatives and depends on the results of the previous decisions.

declaration of solvency. A sworn statement, made by a majority of the *directors* of a British *registered company* which is to be *wound up*, that all the debts of the company will be paid within a specified period (not longer than 12 months).

declining balance. A method of calculating *depreciation* [2] of a *fixed asset* in which the amount of depreciation is a fixed percentage of the previous year's depreciated value. (Also known as 'diminishing balance'.)

dedicated. Used for one purpose or product only. As in 'dedicated machine' (machine, which could be used for many purposes but is used for one purpose only in a particular factory).

deductible. Synonym for *excess*.

deduction at source. An arrangement for the collection of an *income tax* under which a person who pays, to another person, money that is taxable income of that other person deducts the income tax before making the payment and sends the tax to the tax collector.

deed. A written document containing a promise by a person to do or refrain from doing something, which is signed by him and has a *seal* attached. The promise constitutes a particular form of *contract* (called a 'specialty contract'). If a contract is made in a deed then no *consideration* is necessary to make the contract enforceable in a court.

In the past, if there were two parties to a deed then two copies were made on the same sheet of paper which were then separated by a zigzag tear so that they could be identified by matching the indentations (see *indenture*). If only one person was party to a deed this was unnecessary and the edge of the paper would be 'poll' (i.e. cut even)—hence the name 'deed poll' for a deed which concerned only its maker (e.g. one announcing a change of name).

deed of arrangement. A *deed* by which a person, who is *insolvent, assigns* [1] his property to a *trustee* who uses it to pay the person's creditors as best he can.

default (noun). 1. A failure to pay a debt, or an instalment of a debt repayment. 2. A failure to appear at a court hearing of one's case.

default (verb). 1. To fail to pay a debt or an instalment of a debt repayment. 2. To fail to fulfil an obligation.

defect. A point of nonconformance with specified requirements that causes a unit of production to be classed as a *defective*.

defective. A unit of production which in some way does not conform with specified requirements.

deferred. Put off; withheld for or until a stated time (as in 'deferred payment').

deferred annuity. An *annuity*, payment of which will commence some time in the future.

deferred charge. See *prepaid expense*.

deferred creditor. A creditor of a *bankrupt* whose debt cannot be paid until all creditors who are not deferred creditors have been paid in full. The most important debts of this type are: (*a*) loans by a woman to her husband (or a man to his wife) for business purposes and (*b*) interest in excess of 5% on loans.

deferred revenue expenditure. Expenditure by an enterprise which it is hoped will produce *revenue* [1] at some time in the future.

deferred share. A *share* in a *company* [1] that carries rights which are in some way inferior to those carried by *ordinary shares* in the company. Typically a *dividend* [2] is payable only if there is any money left after a specified dividend has been paid to ordinary shareholders. However, deferred shares often carry

113

other rights that may become extremely valuable—such as the right to a share of *all* profits left after paying ordinary shareholders' dividends. Because they are often issued to founders or managers of a company, deferred shares are sometimes called 'founders' shares' or 'management shares'.

deficiency. Excess of *liabilities* [2] over *assets* [2].

deficiency account. A statement of the changes in the *assets* [2] and *liabilities* [2] of a *bankrupt* over the twelve months preceding the date on which a *receiving order* was made against him. It forms part of the bankrupt's *statement of affairs*.

deflation. A general fall of prices and costs in an economy.

deflationary. Tending to induce *deflation*.

degrees of freedom (DF). Name given to certain *parameters* used to describe particular types of *probability distribution*. (See, e.g., *chi-square distribution*.)

del credere agent. An *agent* who *indemnifies* his *principal* [2] against loss incurred on the transactions the agent enters into on behalf of the principal.

delegate (noun). Someone who represents other people at a conference or convention.

delegate (verb). 1. To entrust to another. 2. To entrust part of one's *authority* [1] to another while retaining responsibility for that person's exercise of authority.

delegated legislation. Legislation that is composed and promulgated by a person or organization other than the supreme legislative body in a country but in accordance with *authority* [1] that has been *delegated* [2] by that body.

delegation. 1. The act of *delegating*. 2. One or more persons who have been authorized to represent other people.

delivery. Transfer of possession over something from one person to another.

delivery period. 1. (From a buyer's point of view.) The interval between sending an order for goods and receiving them. 2. (From a seller's point of view.) The interval between receiving an order for goods and despatching them.

Delphi method. A method of obtaining forecasts of future developments (e.g. for *market research*) in which a number of experts are asked to give their individual forecasts; these are collected, and summarized; a summary of all forecasts is sent to each expert and each is asked whether he would reconsider his views in the light of what others have said; the process is repeated until the predictions are satisfactorily uniform. (Named after the ancient Greek religious site at which the gods were believed to communicate answers to humans' questions about the future.)

demand. The quantity of something that a particular group of people is willing to buy (usually, at a particular price).

demand curve. A *demand schedule* presented as a graph.

demand deposit. A sum of money *deposited* by someone with a bank on condition that he can withdraw it *on demand*.

demand draft (DD). Synonym for *bank draft*.

demand-pull inflation. *Inflation* caused by an excess of *demand* for goods in an economy over the economy's ability to supply the goods. The prices of goods tend to go up because of unsatisfied demand by consumers. Manufacturers wish to increase output and so have a high demand for labour, which becomes scarce so wage rates go up. Increased wages give people more money to spend and this increases demand for goods again. Governments usually try to cure demand-pull inflation by reducing consumers' ability to spend (by increasing taxes, reducing the rate of growth of the *money stock,* or reducing government expenditure).

demand schedule. A list of the *demands* for something when it is offered for sale at various prices.

demarcation dispute. A dispute between trade unions over which union's members should perform a job.

demise (noun). Synonym for *lease*.

demise (verb). To grant possession over one's property to someone else by means of a *lease*.

democratic management. Synonym for *participative management*.

DEMON. Acronym from 'decision mapping via optimum networks'. A procedure for systematically evaluating whether it will be worth while marketing a new product on a national scale, taking account of, among other things, the results of *test marketing* and *promotion* [1]. The 'networks' involved are *stochastic decision trees*. A description is given in A. Charnes, W. W. Cooper, J. K. DeVoe and D. B. Learner, 'DEMON: decision mapping via optimum go-no networks—a model for new products', *Management Science*, vol. 12 (1966), pp 865–87.

denary system. See *binary system*.

density (or density function). See *probability density*.

department. One of a number of distinct parts of an *organization*; usually recognizably distinct because its activities are the responsibility of a single manager.

departmentation (or departmentalization). The aspect of *organizing* [1] which consists of specifying that parts of the organization are to be *departments*.

department head. The *manager* of a *department* of an organization.

Department of Employment (DE). UK central-government department responsible for policy and practice concerning employment throughout the country. In particular the DE is concerned with formulating manpower policy and collecting statistics on employment, promotion of good race relations in employment, promotion of equality of opportunity for women, payment of unemployment benefit, and administration of redundancy payments.

Address: 8 St James's Square, London SW1 (01–214 6000).

Department of Employment and Productivity (DEP). The name given to the *Department of Employment* from 15 May 1968 to 20 October 1970.

Department of Industry. UK central-government department responsible for general industrial policy and for the industrial component of regional policy, including financial assistance to industry. The department sponsors individual manufacturing industries, including iron and steel, aircraft and shipbuilding; it is responsible for two nationalized industries—the British Steel Corporation and the Post Office.

Address: 1 Victoria Street, London SW1H 0ET (01–215 7877).

Department of Prices and Consumer Protection. UK central-government department responsible for policy on retail prices and food subsidies. The Department deals with consumer affairs generally and is responsible for policy on fair trading, consumer credit, standards, weights and measures, monopolies, mergers and restrictive trade practices. The *Office of Fair Trading* and the *Price Commission* are associated with the Department.

Address: 1 Victoria Street, London SW1H 0ET (01–215 7877).

Department of Trade. UK central-government department responsible for commercial policy and relations with overseas countries. It promotes UK commercial interests overseas, negotiates on trade and commercial matters, and administers *protective duties*. The Secretary of State for Trade is President of the *Board of Trade* and of the *British Overseas Trade Board*. He is also responsible for the *Export Credits Guarantee Department*. The Department of Trade is responsible in general for the basic legal framework for the regulation of industrial and commercial enterprises, including the law relating to *companies, copyright* and *patents*.

Address: 1 Victoria Street, London SW1H 0ET (01–215 7877).

Department of Trade and Industry (DTI). UK central-government department set up on 20 October 1970 to deal with all aspects of government's relations with commercial and industrial activity. The DTI was split up into the Departments of Energy, Industry, Trade, and Prices and Consumer Protection as from 16 April 1974.

department store. A large retail establishment offering a wide range of goods and organized in departments that sell specific types of goods.

dependency arrow. Synonym for *sequence arrow*.

dependent relative allowance (or dependent relative relief). A *personal relief* given to a taxpayer who proves he maintains, at his own expense, a relative who is: (1) not self-sufficient because of old age or infirmity and; (2) has an income less than a certain amount.

depletion. Systematic estimation of how much of the *cost* [1] of a *fixed asset* has expired—especially when the asset consists of natural resources such as minerals. *Also* the amount of *expense* [3] determined by such an estimation.

deposit (noun). 1. A sum of money entrusted to an organization (e.g. to a bank, finance house, local authority) and repayable on known conditions. A 'demand deposit' is repayable when the depositor asks for it—the most common example is a deposit of money in a *current account* [1] at a bank. A 'time deposit' is repayable if the depositor gives a specified period of notice. Normally the organization taking the deposit pays *interest* on it. 2. A sum of money given as *security* for the performance of a promise or obligation.

deposit (verb). To entrust a sum of money to some organization as a *deposit* [1].

deposit account. An *account* [3] with a bank where the customer makes *time deposits* with the bank.

deposit bank. A firm which: (1) takes *demand deposits* of money from a large number of people who are regular customers; (2) makes loans to customers; and (3) makes short-term loans to other people. In the UK the term is used to refer to the firms (at present there are 18 including the *clearing banks*) that are identified as deposit banks by the Bank of England.

deposit banking. Carrying on the type of business performed by *deposit banks*.

deposit ticket. (US.) A *credit slip*.

depreciation. 1. A fall in value especially of one currency in terms of another. 2. Systematic estimation of how much of the *cost* [1] of a *fixed asset* has expired. *Also* the amount of *expense* [3] determined by such an estimation. (Sometimes called 'amortization' when the asset is *intangible* or 'depletion' when the asset consists of natural resources such as minerals.)

depreciation expense (or depreciation). The amount of *expense* [3] determined by *depreciation* [2].

desk research. Research, especially *market research*, that consists of analysing published or previously collected data (almost literally at the researcher's desk). (Cf. *field research*.)

despatch. 1. To send something one has sold to its buyer. 2. To give an instruction to a particular department to perform a specified manufacturing process on a particular piece of work.

detail man. A salesman, employed by a manufacturer, whose

118

principal task is to give detailed information about a product to potential buyers who will usually order the product through an *intermediary*.

devaluation. Action by the government of country A to change a *peg* for its currency in terms of the currency of country B so that in future a unit of currency A will be exchanged for fewer units of currency B.

development area. An area of the UK which has been designated by the Secretary of State and in which industry is given government assistance in order to reduce unemployment. In particular, *regional employment premiums* are paid and enterprises may apply for a *regional development grant* of 20% of the cost of new buildings and machinery. The areas (first designated in 1966) are the Scottish Development Area (almost the whole of Scotland), Northern DA, Merseyside DA, Welsh DA and South Western DA.

devise (noun). A gift of *real property* made by someone in his will.

devise (verb). 1. To make a gift of *real property* in a will. 2. To use mental processes to formulate a novel method of doing something.

diagnostic program (or diagnostic routine). A *program* [1] for a computer that is designed to identify faults in the computer or errors in other programs.

diary method. Technique used in social research in which people are asked to keep records of what they do. Used, for example, to assess the size of audience for television programmes where viewers are asked to write down the names of the programmes they watch.

diazo process. A process for producing copies, on specially coated paper, of an image that has been written, printed or typed on a transparent sheet (called a 'master'). The copy paper is coated with a transparent emulsion of diazonium salts (from which the name is derived). These salts decompose rapidly when exposed to strong ultraviolet light. However, when exposed to ammonia they form a new compound that dyes the paper under-neath (hence the alternative name of 'dyeline' for the process).

To produce a copy, the copy paper is placed underneath the transparent master and exposed to ultraviolet light which decomposes the diazonium salts everywhere on the copy paper except underneath the opaque matter to be reproduced which is left as an image on the copy paper. This image is developed by exposure to ammonia (or, with some types of copy paper, to heat).

dies non. A day on which no business is transacted.

differential. A difference between wage rates or total remuneration of different individuals or groups of employees, which is part of a planned or negotiated *pay structure*.

digital computer. A *computer* in which data are represented by sets of digits.

diminishing balance. Synonym for *declining balance*.

Diploma in Management Studies (DMS). A national academic award designed for students with graduate or equivalent qualification and some experience in industry or commerce who follow a course of study which is given at many polytechnics and colleges of technology and lasts from 6 months (full-time study) to 3 years. The award is administered by two committees (one for Scotland and one for the rest of the UK) consisting of representatives of government departments of education and of the *British Institute of Management*.

direct. A *direct worker*.

direct advertising. *Advertisements* that are distributed to their audience as individual items and not as part of a publication containing other material. The most common examples are leaflets, brochures and catalogues distributed by retailers, by post (*direct-mail advertising*) or by door-to-door distribution. *Also* the use of such advertisements.

direct cost. A measurement, for the purposes of *cost accounting*, of the cash value of whatever a firm has parted with (or is liable to part with) in making an *expenditure* on goods, services or labour which can reasonably be said to have been directly used by, or to have directly benefited, only a specified activity, product or *cost centre* of the firm. *Also* the total direct costs incurred in manufacturing an item.

direct costing. Computation of the *cost* [2] of a unit of production as the total of all *direct costs* associated with the production and sale of that unit.

direct debiting. System by which a regular customer of a firm can pay regularly occurring but variable bills. The customer authorizes his bank to pay whatever amounts are requested by the seller. Thus the seller obtains immediate payment of his invoices instead of having to wait for the customer to deal with them.

directed edge. An *edge* on a *graph* [2] that is assigned a direction which is usually indicated by drawing an arrowhead on the line. (Also known as an 'arc' or 'arrow'.)

direct expense. A *direct cost* that relates to an *expenditure* by a firm on services (or to the extent of *depreciation* [2] of *fixed assets*). (See *expense* [4].) *Also* the total of such expenses incurred for a specified purpose or over a specified period.

direct labour. Building workers who are employed for maintenance or construction work directly by the organization for which the work is done instead of by a contractor.

direct labour cost. A *labour cost* that relates to payment of a *direct worker*. *Also* the total of such labour costs associated with a particular activity, product or *cost centre*, or over a particular period. (Also known as 'direct wages'.)

direct-mail advertising. 1. Sending *advertisements* to people by post (mail). 2. *Advertisements* sent to people by post (mail).

direct materials cost. A *direct cost* that relates to *expenditure* on *materials* or *supplies*. (See *materials cost*.) *Also* the total of such costs incurred for a specified purpose or over a specified period.

director. A person appointed by the *shareholders* (or *members*) of a *company* [1] to ensure that the company's affairs are conducted to the advantage of the shareholders. The directors of a company are known collectively as the 'board of directors' or 'board'. *Also* a member of the board of directors appointed to represent the interests of employees of the company (usually called a 'worker director').

It is usual for some directors to be full-time employees of the company (the *chief executive* is invariably a director) and such

121

directors are usually responsible for particular parts of the company's operations; they are called 'executive directors' or 'inside directors'. Directors who are not also employees are called 'nonexecutive directors' or 'outside directors'. The precise powers of a company's directors are defined in its constitution (e.g. in the *articles of association* of a British *registered company* or the *bylaws* [2] of a US *corporation*) and they are also usually given duties and powers by the laws of the country in which the company is incorporated.

In some countries, notably the Federal Republic of Germany, it is common for the executive and nonexecutive directors to meet separately—see *two-tier board*.

Every British *public company* [1] registered after 1 November 1929 must have at least 2 directors. Other British companies must have at least 1 director. There have been several recent proposals for changing these rules, including proposals: (1) that all companies should have at least 2 directors; (2) that all public companies should have some nonexecutive directors; (3) that companies should have some worker directors.

Director General of Fair Trading. Office created by the Fair Trading Act 1973. The Director General is appointed by the Secretary of State for a five-year term. The Director General's main functions are: (1) to keep under review and collect information on all commercial activities in the UK that are connected with supplying goods or services to the general public; (2) to ascertain whether any activity could adversely affect consumers' interests; (3) to make recommendations to the Secretary of State on measures to be taken to mitigate the adverse effects of particular trading practices; (4) to investigate whether particular situations should be referred to the *Monopolies and Mergers Commission* and to assist that Commission in its work.

directors' report. A report, on the state of the company's affairs, which must be attached to every *balance sheet* submitted by the directors of a British *registered company* to the *members* of the company. The *Companies Acts* 1948 and 1967 specify the information that must be included in a director's report.

direct profit. The difference between *sales revenue* for a particular product and the total *direct costs* associated with the production and sale of that product.

direct rate. An *exchange rate* between the currencies of countries A and B is stated in 'direct' form in country A if it is expressed as the number of units of country A's currency that are exchanged for 1 (or, usually, 100) units of B's currency. When two direct rates are given as a *quotation,* the lower is the rate at which the foreign currency will be bought by the person making the quotation; the higher rate is the one at which he will sell the foreign currency. The direct rate in country A is equivalent to an *indirect rate* in country B.

direct-response advertising. *Advertising* that is intended to persuade people to communicate directly with the advertiser (as opposed to, e.g., advertising intended to persuade people to go to a retailer to buy the advertiser's product). The most important form (apart from the special case of *recruitment advertising*) is *mail-order advertising*.

direct sale. A sale made by a manufacturer direct to a consumer and not through a retailer or other intermediary.

direct tax. 1. A tax levied in such a way that the wealth of the person who pays the tax is reduced by the amount paid (as opposed to an *indirect tax* [1] which is such that the person who pays it subsequently recovers the amount from someone else). In the UK *corporation tax* is a direct tax. UK *income tax* is traditionally classified as a direct tax although the majority of people have their income tax paid by their employer under *Pay as You Earn.* 2. Synonym for *income tax.*

direct wages. Synonym for *direct labour cost.*

direct worker. An employee whose work is directly concerned with the production of his employer's products. (Also known as a 'direct'.)

discharge. 1. Action by an *employer* to end an *employee's contract of employment.* 2. Release from an obligation or contract.

discontinuous shiftwork (or discontinuous shift system). A system of *shiftwork* [1] in which, for one or more days a week, work is not carried on all day.

discount (noun). A deduction from a standard or nominal price or value of something that is made to arrive at the price of that thing in a specified transaction. For example, (1) a deduction from a *recommended retail price* to give the price at which a particular retailer will sell; (2) a deduction from the *nominal value* of a *security* [1] to give the price at which it is sold in a particular transaction; (3) a deduction from the amount of a debt due to be repaid at some time in the future to give the amount that (*a*) the debtor will pay before the due date to discharge the debt or (*b*) the amount a third party will pay the creditor, before the due date, to take over his right to receive the money; (4) an addition, which is to be made to the number of units of a foreign currency that will be obtained in a *spot* purchase for one unit of a currency, in order to arrive at the number of units to be obtained in a *forward purchase* (cf. *premium* [1]).

discount(verb). 1. To reduce the price of something; to give a *discount* to a purchaser. 2. To sell to someone else the right to receive, at a future date, payment of a debt. The debt may be an *account receivable* by a firm (see *factor* [2]) or a *bill of exchange* or *promissory note*. The amount received, by the seller, for the debt is normally less than the amount of the debt and the difference is known as the 'discount'. Such a discount is often expressed as a percentage of the amount of the debt per year of the period until the debt is due for payment (a 'discount rate'). 3. To buy the right to receive payment of a debt (e.g. an *account receivable*, a *bill of exchange* or a *promissory note*) for a price that includes a *discount*. 4. To calculate a *present value*.

discount company. A *discount house* [1] that is a *registered company*. All the 11 discount houses are now companies though most were originally *partnerships*.

discounted cash flow (DCF). The *present value* of a sequence of *cash flows* [3].

discounted cash flow method/technique. Any method for evaluating *investment projects* involving the calculation of a *present value* or *terminal value*.

discounted gross benefit-cost ratio. The ratio of the *present value* of the total forecast *cash inflows* of a project to the present value of the *cash outflows* for the project. (Also known as the 'profitability index'.)

discounted net benefit-cost ratio. The same as the *undiscounted net benefit-cost ratio* except that the *present value* of annual *cash inflows* minus depreciation is compared to the present value of annual *cash outflows*.

discounter. A retailer who specializes in selling goods (especially *consumer durables*) at low prices.

discount house. 1. (UK.) A firm of which the principal business is to buy and sell *securities* [1] that have a high *liquidity* [2]—notably *Treasury bills* [1], government and local authority *bonds* that are due for repayment in a short time (less than 12 months), and *trade bills* that are due for payment in a short time.

The term is usually restricted to 11 firms which are members of the London Discount Market Association. The name, discount house, is used because the firms were originally established as *bill brokers* to *discount* [3] *bills of exchange*.

2. (US.) Synonym for *discount store*.

discount market. A *market* [4] in *bills of exchange, Treasury bills* [1]. short-dated *bonds* [2], and short-term loans from banks. A specialist market in these items has developed only in London.

discount rate. A number (usually a percentage) used to determine *discounts*. See *compound discounting* and *simple discounting*. In particular, a discount rate (as used in simple discounting) quoted by a bank for *discounting* [3] *bills of exchange*.

discount store. A retail establishment, usually very large and situated outside traditional shopping areas, that offers goods—especially *consumer durables*—at lower prices than other shops. Low prices are achieved mainly by having cheap accommodation and by negotiating *quantity discounts* with manufacturers. (Also known as a 'discount house'.)

discrete random variable. A *random variable*, the possible values of which are distinct numbers, e.g. only whole numbers, rather than all possible real numbers within a particular range (a *continuous random variable*). For example, the number of complete letters dictated by a manager in a day is a discrete random variable whereas the time taken up by dictation is a continuous random variable.

discretion. 1. Competence of a person to make a specified decision according to his own judgment alone. 2. Cautious reserve in speech.

discretionary content. The discretionary content of a task that has been assigned to someone consists of the aspects of the task that are expected to be carried out according to plans or decisions made by that person using his own judgment.

dishonour. To fail to pay a *bill of exchange* or *cheque* when it is properly presented for payment.

dismiss. To carry out the *dismissal* of an *employee*.

dismissal. Action by an *employer* to end an *employee's contract of employment*.

dispersion measure. A *statistic* [1] which indicates the degree to which a *frequency distribution* or a *probability distribution* spreads out around its *mean*. The most frequently used dispersion measure is the *standard deviation*.

display advertisement. A printed *advertisement* which forms part of a newspaper, magazine, book or similar publication and which has been especially designed with the intention of attracting the attention of readers. (Cf. *classified advertisement*.)

display board. A board to which prepared material may be attached for display to an audience. There are five basic types classified according to the method by which the material is attached for display: (1) pin-up boards (made of hardboard, chipboard, cork, etc.) to which material is normally attached by a drawing pin; (2) pegboards (boards with holes to take fittings which carry the display material); (3) flannelgraph boards (covered with rough material, to which items that are backed with or made from a similar rough material will adhere); (4) plastigraph boards (surface of plastic; items made from plastic will adhere under atmospheric pressure); (5) magnet boards (ferrous material to which magnetized items will adhere).

dissatisfaction. See *grievance*.

dissaving. Diminution of the amount of one's savings.

dissolution. Ending of the existence of a *company*. In the UK, dissolution normally occurs three months after the end of the process of *winding up* the company's affairs.

distrain. To seize a debtor's goods and sell them to recover the debt.

distrainor. A creditor who *distrains* his debtor's goods.

distraint. An action of *distraining*.

distress. Seizure of a debtor's goods and sale of them to recover the debt.

distribute. To pay a portion of the profits of a firm to its owners.

distribution. 1. The activity, business, or industry concerned with bringing about a change of ownership of goods between the producers of the goods and the consumers or users of them. The term excludes the activity of transporting goods. 2. An instance of *distributing* the profits of a firm to its owners.

distribution channel. Synonym for *channel of distribution*.

distribution cost. 1. The *cost* [2] of transporting a firm's products to customers. 2. (Often plural.) The *cost* [2] of *marketing* a firm's products (including the cost of transporting the products to customers). See also, *selling cost*.

distribution curve. The *graph* [1] of a *distribution function*.

distribution function. A mathematical *function* [2] that gives, for each possible value, x, of a *random variable,* the *probability* that the random variable will actually occur with a value less than or equal to x.

distribution mix. The *channels of distribution* used by a firm.

distribution network. The *wholesalers, retailers* and other firms in an economy that do not manufacture or produce goods but participate in the process of changing the ownership of goods from producer to consumer.

distributive bargaining. *Collective bargaining* in which the principal objective of each side is to obtain the most favourable distribution of limited resources.

distributive trades. The *industry* [2] concerned with *distribution* [1].

distributor. An *intermediary*, especially a *wholesaler*.

diversification. An act or the process of *diversifying*.

diversify. 1. To invest money in several different *securities* [1]. 2. To increase the range of a firm's *products* [2] or operations.

divestment. Action or process, undertaken by a firm, of transferring ownership and control of part of its activities to another firm.

dividend. 1. A quantity to be divided. 2. The amount of a firm's profits paid to the proprietors of the firm (e.g. to the *shareholders* of a *company*). Originally, the total amount to be paid; now usually either the amount paid to a specified individual or the rate at which the profits are to be divided among proprietors (e.g. 'a final dividend of 1.3727p per share'). 3. An instalment of interest to be paid on a loan, especially a *government stock*. Originally, the total amount to be paid out to the *stockholders* [1]; now usually either the amount paid to a specified individual or the rate at which the interest is paid. 4. The proportion of the debts, of a *bankrupt* or of a company which is being *liquidated,* that will be paid to creditors. ('A dividend of 25p in the £ has been declared.')

dividend cover. The ratio of *EPS* to the *dividend* [2] paid per share by a company.

dividend mandate. Document by which a *shareholder* authorizes a British *registered company* to pay the *dividends* [2] due to him into his bank account by *credit transfer* [2].

dividend payout ratio (or payout ratio). The ratio of the *dividend* [2] paid, or expected to be paid, by a *company* per share, over a period, to the *EPS* over that period.

dividend-stripping. Taking control of a company with large *retained earnings* and declaring a large *dividend* [2] to *shareholders* in such a way that tax is avoided.

dividend warrant. A form of *cheque* used to pay a *dividend* [2]. (See *warrant* [2].)

dividend yield. The *rate of return* from purchasing a *security* [1] when the returns are in the form of *dividends* [2, 3]. It is the ratio of the dividends that are paid, or expected to be paid, over a period (usually a year) to the price of the security.

division. A *department* of an organization; especially a large department.

division of labour. Allocation of different parts of a task to different people.

docket. An abstract or summary of a document.

dock warrant. A *warrant* [4].

documentary bill. A *bill of exchange* to which the *payee* (who is also the *drawer*) has attached documents to show that he has sent goods, to the value of the bill, to the *drawee* who will then be willing at least to *accept* [1] the bill (if not actually pay it) before receiving his goods. The documents involved are usually a copy of an *invoice* and a *bill of lading*.

documentary credit (or documentary letter of credit or credit). An undertaking by a bank given at the request of one of its customers that the bank will make payments to someone (the 'beneficiary') if the beneficiary produces specific documents (principally a *bill of lading*). Documentary credits are usually 'irrevocable'—i.e. the bank cannot fail to make payments according to the terms of the undertaking. If the bank is in one country and the payments are to be made in another country the bank will usually arrange for the payments to be made by an associate bank in that country. It is customary for the second bank to 'confirm' the documentary credit (which is then known as a 'confirmed credit').

domicile. The country in which a person has a permanent home (though he may not be a national of that country).

dominion register. A *register of members* that contains only the names of members living in a particular country of the British Commonwealth and is kept in that country. (Also known as a 'branch register'.)

donor. Someone who makes a gift or grants some power such as a *power of attorney* or *trust* [1].

Donovan report. The report of the Royal Commision on Trade Unions and Employers' Associations (Cmnd 3623) (London: HMSO, 1968). The Commission was appointed in 1965 to consider relations between managements and employees and the role of trade unions and employers' associations in promoting the interests of their members and in accelerating the social and economic advance of the nation. The chairman of the Commission was a judge, Terence Norbert Donovan, Baron Donovan (1898–1971), and the Commission was supposed to pay particular attention to the law on industrial relations. However, its recom-

mendations in this area were ignored and the *Ind*
Act 1971 was produced instead.

double bond. A *bond* [1] in which the obligor p
not to do some act and also that if he fails to
promise he will pay a penalty to the obligee.
provision for penalty is sometimes called a 'singl*e*

double day-shift system (or double-day syste
shiftwork [1] in which two shifts are worked eac
0600–1400 and 1400–2200.

double daywork. A type of *payment by res*
standard level of output is set and two *time rates*
who do not achieve the standard are paid the
workers who reach or exceed the standard receiv

double-entry bookkeeping. A method of
actions (almost universally applied in busines
which each transaction is recorded as a *credit*
[1] and a *debit* [1] in another account.

double jobbing. Synonym for *moonlighting*.

double option. A combination of a *call option*
so that the option holder may buy or sell—wh
advantageous to him.

double taxation. Taxation of an item of inc
example, before 1973 (when the law was chang
resident in the UK made a profit of £100 000 t
paid to the Inland Revenue as *corporation tax*
£60 000 was distributed as *dividends* [2] to s
£23 250 of that was taken by the Inland Reven
Thus the shareholders received only 36.75 per
their company had made.

double taxation agreement. A treaty betwe
designed to avoid *double taxation* occurring if
one country but earns money in the other. Th
which government should tax such earnings.

downgrading. Movement of an employee to a j
responsibilities and/or involves less skill and/or
or, especially, has a lower rate of pay.

downtime. Period when a machine could be

not work because of a fault or because of planned maintenance operations.

downtime pay. Payment to a machine-operator while he is prevented from working because his machine is not functioning.

draft. A document by which one person (the 'drawer') gives an instruction to a second person (the 'drawee') to pay money to a third person. Often used to describe such a document when drawer and drawee are different branches of a bank (a *bank draft*) so that the document is more like a *promissory note* than a bill of exchange. (Also called a 'warrant'.)

drawback. 1. Repayment of *customs duty* that has been paid on imported goods when those goods are exported again or when they are incorporated in articles that are exported. 2. Repayment of *excise duty* that has been paid on goods manufactured in the UK when those goods are exported.

drawee. The person or firm that is instructed by the *drawer* of a *bill of exchange,* a *cheque* or a *draft,* to make a payment.

drawer. The person who signs a *bill of exchange, cheque* or *draft* and thereby instructs the *drawee* to pay money to the *payee.*

dual-purpose trust. Synonym for *split-level investment trust.*

dummy. An arrow in an *activity-on-arrow network* that is inserted only to show that two *events* must take place simultaneously. (Also known as a 'zero-time activity'.)

dummy activity. A node in an *activity-on-node network* that does not represent an activity but is put in to aid visualization.

dump bin. A container for displaying goods in a retail establishment which consists of an open-topped box or bin in which goods are piled in an unarranged jumble.

dumping. 1. Selling by a firm of a surplus production of something to people who are not the firm's usual customers and at very much lower prices than the usual customers are charged. In particular, selling abroad at very much lower prices than are charged at home. 2. Severe price-cutting in order to discourage competitors.

duopoly. An *oligopoly* limited to two sellers.

duopsony. An *oligopsony* limited to two buyers.

Dutch auction. An *auction* at which the auctioneer announces a high price and then successively lower prices until someone calls out that he will buy at the most recently announced price (i.e. he accepts the auctioneer's offer to sell at that price).

duty. 1. A task, especially a recurring one, which a specific person is obliged to perform as part of his job. 2. A tax other than an *income tax*.

duty of customs. Synonym for *customs duty*.

duty of excise. Synonym for *excise duty*.

dyeline process. Synonym for *diazo process*.

dynamic programming. Mathematical or logical techniques for dealing with multistage decision processes—i.e. problems that involve deciding an *optimum* sequence of decisions where each decision in the sequence depends on the ones before it.

e

EAPM. Abbreviation of *European Association for Personnel Management*.

EBIAT. Abbreviation of 'earnings before interest and after taxes' —that is, *EBIT* minus payments of *corporate income tax*.

EBIT. Abbreviation of 'earnings before interest and tax'—that is, the *net income* of a company over a period without deducting payments of interest on *debt capital* and *corporate income tax*.

EBQ. Abbreviation of *economic batch quantity*.

ECGD. Abbreviation of *Export Credits Guarantee Department*.

ECSC. Abbreviation of *European Coal and Steel Community*.

EDC. Abbreviation of *economic development committee*.

EDP. Abbreviation of *electronic data processing*.

EEC. Abbreviation of *European Economic Community*.

EFMD. Abbreviation of *European Foundation for Management Development*.

EFTA. Abbreviation of *European Free Trade Association*.

EIB. Abbreviation of *European Investment Bank*.

ELS. Abbreviation of *economic lot size*.

EMV. Abbreviation of *expected monetary value*.

EOQ. Abbreviation of 'economic order quantity' (see *economic lot size*).

EPS. Abbreviation of 'earnings per share'—that is, the *net profit* [1] of a *company* [1] over a period (after deducting payments of interest on *debt capital*, payments of *corporate income tax* and payments of *preference dividends*) divided by the number of issued *ordinary shares* (or the number of outstanding shares of *common stock*).

ETUC. Abbreviation of *European Trade Union Confederation.*

Eur. Abbreviation of 'unit of account of the European Communities' (see *unit of account*) which is 0.88867088 grammes of fine gold.

EVP. Abbreviation of 'Europäische Vereinigung für Personalfragen'—the German title of the *European Association for Personnel Management.*

EWMA. Abbreviation of 'exponentially weighted moving average' (see *exponential smoothing*).

EWS. Abbreviation of *experienced-worker standard.*

earliest event time. The earliest possible time at which an *event* in an *activity-on-arrow network* can occur.

earliest finish time of an activity (or earliest finish date of an activity or earliest finish). The earliest possible time at which an *activity* in an *activity-on-node network* can be completed.

earliest start time of an activity (or earliest start date of an activity or earliest start). The earliest possible time at which an *activity* in an *activity-on-node network* can be started.

early shift. 1. The earlier *shift* during a day in a *double day-shift system.* 2. The *morning shift* in a *three-shift system.*

earned for ordinary. The amount of the *earnings* [2] of a *company* [1] for a period that could be distributed to its *ordinary shareholders*; in other words, *net profits* [1] after deducting *corporate income tax*, payments of interest on *debt capital* and payments of *preference dividends.*

earned income. Defined in the *Income Tax Acts* as remuneration from an *office* [1] or employment, pensions given in respect of past service in an office or employment, payments made on termination of an office or employment, income 'immediately derived' (a phrase that can cause much dispute) by the recipient from carrying on his trade, profession or vocation, and income from *patent rights* where the recipient was the original inventor.

earned income relief. A *personal relief* (now abolished) which was equal to two-ninths of an individual's *earned income*.

earned surplus. Synonym for *retained earnings*.

earning power. 1. The ratio of the *net operating income* of a firm over a period to its *operating assets*. 2. Synonym for *internal rate of return*.

earnings. 1. Money received by a person from being employed. 2. *Net profit* [1] of a firm measured either with or without deducting payments of *corporate income tax*, interest on *debt capital* and *preference dividends*.

earnings before interest and after tax. See *EBIAT*.

earnings before interest and tax. See *EBIT*.

earnings per share. See *EPS*.

earnings yield. Ratio of the *EPS* of a *company* [1] over a period to the price at a specified time of one share in the company (i.e. the reciprocal of the *P/E ratio*).

easement. A right, which is automatically acquired by whoever owns a specified piece of land, to use a second piece of land in a specific manner (apart from a right to take something from that land—e.g. by mining or fishing). The most important easements are rights of way, a right to light and a right to have a building supported by an adjoining building.

econometrics. The study or practice of making quantitative studies of economic activity; especially in order to determine the relationship between economic variables.

Economic and Social Committee. A body established on 1 January 1958 to ensure consultation by the *Council of the European Communities* and by the *Commission of the European Communities* (until 1 July 1967, the separate councils and commissions of the Communities) with representatives of 'the various categories of economic and social activity, in particular, representatives of producers, farmers, carriers, workers, dealers, craftsmen, professional occupations and representatives of the general public'. (Article 193 of the Treaty establishing the EEC.) There are 144 members appointed, by the Council from lists submitted by the member states, for four-year terms.

economic development committee (EDC or little Neddy). A committee of representatives of government, management and unions in a particular industry in the UK which considers the prospects and performance of the industry and organizes research into those matters. Nine EDCs were set up in 1964 and there are now 16. Research and other services for the EDCs are provided by the *National Economic Development Office*.

economic good. A *good* [1] which is scarce and is usually supplied to those who want it in exchange for some other good. Economic goods command a price and are the concern of *economics*.

economic life. The period for which an *investment project* will yield *returns* [1].

economic lot size (ELS). The quantity of a *stock-keeping unit*, which is regularly used, that should be ordered at regular intervals so as to minimize the costs of stockholding and of ordering. (Also known as 'economic order quantity' or 'optimum order quantity'.)

economic man. Idealization of a human being that is used in *economics*. Economic man is assumed to be rational, and well-informed, and to act so that he will maximize *utility* [1, 2] as he defines it.

economic order quantity (EOQ). Synonym for *economic lot size*.

economic rent. Synonym for *rent* [2].

economics. A social science concerned with describing and analysing the use of scarce resources in the production and distribution of goods and services for consumption by individuals and groups.

economies of scale. Reduction of the cost of producing something achieved by increasing the quantity produced. Increasing the scale of production enables the producer to: (1) use non-human power; (2) automate the production process; (3) divide his organization into specialist functions; (4) use *production-line* techniques. All of these factors can lead to lower unit costs.

edge. A line connecting two vertices on a *graph* [2]. (Also known as a 'link'.) If the two joined vertices are the same then the edge is known as a 'loop'.

edge-notched card. Synonym for *edge-punched card* [1].

edge-punched card. 1. A card, used in recording and analysing data, which has holes near to the edge of one or more sides. Each hole position represents a particular aspect of the data to be recorded and the piece of a particular card between the edge and a hole is removed to represent the presence of that aspect in the piece of data recorded on that card. Cards can be selected from a pack by passing a long needle through all holes in a selected position and then lifting so that the cards that have been notched in that position are left behind. (Also known as an 'edge-notched card'.) 2. Synonym for *verge-punched card*.

effectiveness. The extent to which an action or activity achieves its stated purpose. (See also, *managerial effectiveness*.)

efficiency ratio. Synonym for *activity ratio*.

eighty-twenty law/rule. A widely observed phenomenon that if a firm has a large number of products then 80% (in number) of the products account for only 20% of its *sales revenue* from all products; or that 80% of a firm's *stock-keeping units* that are *materials* account for 20% of the total *usage value* of the firm's stocks of materials.

electronic data processing (EDP). *Automatic data processing* that is carried out largely by electronic devices (i.e. devices whose action depends on the controlled motion of electrons, as in transistors).

element. A distinct part of a specified job that is separately identified, especially for purposes of *work study* or training.

embargo. 1. A prohibition, either general or particular, of commerce. 2. A request, made to newspaper editors and broadcast news editors, not to publish specified information before a specified time.

embezzle. To take for one's own use property that has been entrusted to one's care.

emoluments. The total payment in money, or in goods or services that have a monetary value, for services or work done. (See *remuneration*.)

employ. 1. To make use of. 2. To be an *employer*.

employee. Person who enters into a *contract* with another (the employer) to perform work—(1) under the control of the employer, or another of that employer's employees, and (2) as part of the organization run by the employer—in return for wages or salary or some other valuable *consideration*.

employee benefit. Something of value, apart from agreed regular monetary payments of salary or wage, given by an employer to an employee—e.g. sick pay or subsidized meals. The term 'employee benefit' has largely replaced 'fringe benefit' as it has been realized that such benefits are regarded as usual components of compensation rather than as fringe elements.

employee handbook. A book, given by an employer to all his employees, that gives information on employer-employee relations. A company's employee handbook usually contains descriptions of the history of the company and its products, regulations on such matters as lateness, notification of illness, car parking, details of union recognition and grievance procedures, and descriptions of employee benefits, such as sick pay, pension schemes, canteens and recreational facilities.

employee participation. Participation by the employees of a firm in the process of taking decisions concerning the firm's activities.

Terms with similar meanings include: 'codetermination', 'co-partnership', 'co-ownership', 'democratic management', 'industrial democracy', 'joint consultation', 'participative management' and 'workers' control'.

'Participative management' and 'democratic management' are used only to refer to the *managerial style* of an individual manager; the other terms refer to methods of influencing the running of a whole firm.

'Employee participation' and 'industrial democracy' have the most general meaning: both refer to any arrangement by which the opinions of the employees of a firm are automatically considered during decision-making.

'Copartnership' and 'co-ownership' are used to describe schemes in which employees acquire a significant proportion of the ownership of the firms they work in. However, their influence on the running of the firms is often as limited as that of non-employed shareholders.

'Joint consultation' and 'codetermination' usually do not involve any ownership of the firm by its employees: 'codetermination' implies that certain decisions can be taken only by a joint committee of workers and management; 'joint consultation' implies only that there is a formal system by which management can obtain the opinions of workers.

'Workers' control' may or may not involve actual ownership of the firm by its workers but does imply that employees must approve all managerial decisions.

employee relations. Relations between an employer and his employees regarded as individuals rather than as members of unions.

employer. 1. Person or organization that enters into a *contract* with someone who thereby becomes an *employee*. 2. Person or organization that has *employees*.

employers' association. A body whose members are employers and whose principal activities include regulating relations between employers and employees. *Also* a federation of such bodies.

employers' organization. The term used in the *Industrial Relations Act 1971* to describe an *employers' association* that was not registered with the *Chief Registrar of Trade Unions and Employers' Associations*.

employment. 1. Act of *employing*. 2. State of being an *employee*. 3. Use. 4. State of being *employed*. 5. The job someone is *employed* [2] to perform. 6. The use to which something is put.

employment agency. A firm which finds people to work for other firms. An employment agency usually receives fees from the firms to which it supplies workers. (Also called a 'personnel agency'.)

employment exchange. (Now obsolete.) Synonym for *employment office*.

employment medical adviser. A registered medical practitioner appointed by the Secretary of State to undertake duties defined in the Employment Medical Advisory Service Act 1972. These are, principally, to carry out medical examinations of workers in dangerous trades and to advise young people

139

(especially those with a known health problem) on medical aspects of their chosen careers.

Employment Medical Advisory Service. An organization within the Department of Employment which was set up on 1 February 1973 under the Employment Medical Advisory Service Act 1972. Its objectives are to provide a full service of advice and information, both to employers and to the Department of Employment, on matters concerning the health of employed persons. The doctors working in the Service are called *employment medical advisers.*

employment office. An office run by a government agency (e.g. *Employment Service Agency* in UK, Department of Labor in USA) where people seeking employment are given information about existing vacancies.

Employment of Women, Young Persons, and Children Act 1920. Statute applying to England and Scotland which implements conventions formulated by the *International Labour Organisation.* The Act makes it illegal to employ a child (i.e. someone under compulsory school age) in an 'industrial undertaking' (which includes factories, mines, quarries and transportation); and illegal to employ anyone under 18 in an industrial undertaking at night (except in certain industries where processes must be operated continuously). The sections of the Act relating to the employment of women have been replaced by the *Hours of Employment (Conventions) Act 1936.*

Employment Service Agency. Body responsible for helping people to find jobs, and employers to recruit, in the UK. Set up as a departmental agency of the Department of Employment it was reconstituted on 1 October 1974 as a *corporation* (under the Employment and Training Act 1973) with three members appointed by the *Manpower Services Commission.* One of these members is appointed as director by the Manpower Services Commission with the approval of the Secretary of State for Employment.

employment test. Set of questions or exercises or other means of measuring a person's suitability for a particular job, or for working in a particular *occupation* [1] or a particular organization.

end event. An *event* in a *network* with no succeeding *activities*. (Also known as a 'network-ending event'.)

endogenous. 1. Originating inside a system. 2. Determined by factors that are predicted by a specified model.

endorse. 1. (Sometimes spelt indorse.) To make an *endorsement* [1] on a *negotiable instrument*. 2. To give one's *endorsement* [2] to a product. 3. To write an *endorsement* [4] on a licence.

endorsee (sometimes spelt indorsee). A person who is designated in an *endorsement* [1] as the person to whom the endorser is transferring the right to receive money.

endorsement. 1. (Sometimes spelt indorsement.) A statement written on the back of a *negotiable instrument* (e.g. a *bill of exchange* or a *cheque*) by its *payee* and which transfers to someone else all rights to receive payment of the amount specified in the bill or cheque. The person who makes an endorsement is called the 'endorser' and the person to whom the rights are transferred is called the 'endorsee'. If a *drawee* refused to pay an endorsee the money due on a bill then the endorsee could sue the endorser for the money. An endorsement consists of the endorser's signature with other words as necessary.

There are three kinds of endorsement: (*a*) 'endorsement in blank' which consists of the endorser's signature only and makes the negotiable instrument payable to *bearer*; (*b*) 'special endorsement', which specifies who is to be the endorsee; (*c*) 'restrictive endorsement' which is like a special endorsement but which prohibits the endorsee from himself endorsing the instrument.

2. A statement, by a well-known person, used in *advertisements* for a *product* [2], that he uses the product or believes it to be good value.

3. A new clause added to a standard printed *contract of insurance,* usually on a piece of paper attached to the printed form, which restricts or extends the insurance.

4. A record written on a *licence* [1], e.g. a driving licence, of an offence committed by the licensee.

endorser. 1. (Sometimes spelt indorser.) Someone who makes an *endorsement* [1]. 2. Someone who makes an *endorsement* [2].

endowment policy. A *contract of insurance* by which the insurer promises to pay the assured a fixed sum of money either when he reaches a specified age, or if he should die at a younger age.

Engel curve. A graph of the relationship between the quantity of a good purchased by households over some period and the incomes of the households. Named after the German statistician, Ernst Engel (1821–1896).

Engel's law. Widely observed phenomenon that the proportion of a household's budget that is spent on food tends to decline as the household's income increases. First proposed in 1857 by the German statistician, Ernst Engel (1821–1896).

engineering development. Activities concerned with solving detailed practical problems of implementing a proposal for a new product for a firm. (Also known as 'product development'— see also *production planning*.)

engineering psychology. Branch of psychology that concerns the contributions made by psychology to *ergonomics*.

entrepreneur. A person who is skilled at identifying new products (or, sometimes, new methods of production), setting up operations to provide new products, *marketing* the products and arranging the financing of the operations.

entrepreneurial. Of, relating to or characteristic of *entrepreneurs*.

equal pay. Pay that is the same for men and women who perform the same or similar work.

Equal Pay Act 1970. UK statute stipulating that, from 29 December 1975, men and women who do the same or similar work must have the same pay and conditions of employment.

equifinality. A characteristic, possessed by some *systems*, of always evolving towards the same final state whatever the initial conditions.

equilibrium price. The price at which the *supply* curve for a good and its *demand curve* intersect.

equipment-type flow process chart. See *flow process chart*.

equitable payment. The remuneration which would be generally considered fair (at a particular time and in a particular country) for employees with a particular *time-span of discretion*. Evidence that people do have common views on what represents equitable payment for particular jobs was collected by Elliott Jaques (born 1917, now Director of the Institute of Organization and Social Studies, Brunel University, England) while working on the *Glacier Project*. See E. Jaques, *Equitable Payment : A General Theory of Work, Differential Payment, and Individual Progress* (London: Heinemann Educational Books/Carbondale, Ill: Southern Illinois University Press, 1961).

equity. 1. A collection of legal doctrines which a court may use to override the rules of *common law* in order to achieve a fairer decision in a case than if common-law principles only were applied. *Also* a right which is recognized by the doctrines of equity. E.g. 'equity of redemption' (the right of a *mortgagor* to *redeem* his mortgage at any time by repaying the relevant debt). 2. The residual rights that belong to the owner of something (as distinct from the rights that other people have over the thing). *Also* the value of such rights. 3. Residual rights of ownership over the *assets* [1] of a firm—rights that can be enforced only when everyone else (e.g. *creditors* [1]) has been paid. *Specifically* the *ordinary shares* (which usually entitle owners to the equity) of a *company* [1].

equity capital. *Capital* that has been obtained in exchange for issuing *equity shares*—i.e. *contributed capital* apart from *preference share capital*.

equity dilution. Reduction of existing *shareholders'* control of a company by issuing new *shares*.

equity share. A *share* that gives its owner a right to the *equity* [3] of a *company* [1]; especially a share that confers no other rights over the company's *assets* [1].

equity share capital. The total *nominal value* of all *shares* in a *company* [1] that have been issued and which carry unlimited opportunities to receive *dividends* [2] and to share in the distribution of a surplus when the company is dissolved. The nominal value of *preference shares*, for example, is not included in equity share capital because preference shareholders are entitled to receive no more than a fixed amount of dividend.

ergonomics. Activity or branch of study concerned with ways of designing machines, operations and work environments so that they match human capacities and limitations. (Also known as 'biotechnology', 'human factors engineering' or 'human engineering'.)

escalation clause. A clause in a contract for the performance of work by a firm under which the firm is allowed to increase its charge for the work if there is an increase in the *costs* [2] of materials, labour, etc. associated with the work.

escalator clause. A clause in a *collective agreement* [1] which states that wages should increase at the same rate as a specified *cost-of-living index* [1].

escape clause. A clause in a *contract* which enables one party to escape an obligation he would normally have under contracts with similar subject matter.

establishment expense. Synonym for *indirect cost*.

estate. 1. The set of rights that a person has over a piece of *real property*. 2. The total *assets* [1] of a person (especially at the time of his death).

estate duty. A tax charged in the UK on the value of the *estate* [2] of a dead person. The tax has to be deducted, by the dead person's *personal representative*, from the estate before heirs receive their legacies. (Popularly known as 'death duty'.) Estate duty is not payable in respect of a death which occurred after 13 March 1975. Under the Finance Act 1975, estate duty was replaced by *capital transfer tax.*

estimate (noun). A statement of size, extent, duration, cost, price, value, worth or significance that has been *estimated.* Especially, a statement sent to a prospective customer of the likely cost of doing some work that he has enquired about.

estimate (verb). 1. To determine roughly the size, extent or duration of something. 2. To state what one judges to be the likely cost or price of something. 3. To judge tentatively the value, worth or significance of something.

estimated work. Work for which *standard times* [2] have been set without using *work measurement* (i.e. they have been based on practical experience or previous production records).

estop. To prohibit by *estoppel.*

Europäische Vereinigung für Personalfragen (EVP).

European Atomic Energy Community (Euratom). An international organization established, by a treaty signed at Rome on 25 March 1957, in order to create the conditions necessary for the speedy establishment and growth of nuclear industries in the member states. The members are the same as those of the *European Coal and Steel Community* (ECSC) and, like the ECSC, Euratom is run by the institutions of the three *European Communities*.

European Coal and Steel Community (ECSC). A *common market* for coal, iron and steel only which was established by a treaty signed in Paris on 18 April 1951. The treaty came into force on 23 July 1952. The original signatories of the treaty were Belgium, France, Federal Republic of Germany, Italy, Luxembourg and the Netherlands. Denmark, the Republic of Ireland and the UK became members on 1 January 1973. The ECSC is now run by the institutions of the three *European Communities*.

European Communities. The *European Atomic Energy Community,* the *European Coal and Steel Community* and the *European Economic Community.* Administration of the three organizations is now performed by institutions that are common to all three. Since 1 January 1958 they have had a common *Assembly, Court of Justice of the European Communities* and *Economic and Social Committee.* Since 1 July 1967 they have had a common *Council of the European Communities* and *Commission of the European Communities.*

European Communities Act 1972. UK statute by which the UK joined the *European Communities.* The Act alters several aspects of UK law to accord with Community requirements. In particular, section 9 affects the *Companies Act* 1948.

European company. See *societas europaea.*

European Court. Title given in UK statutes to the *Court of Justice of the European Communities.*

European Economic Community (EEC). A *common market* for all products except those covered by the *European Coal and Steel Community* (ECSC). EEC was established by a treaty signed in Rome on 25 March 1957 which came into force on 1 January 1958. Its membership is the same as that of ECSC and, like ECSC, it is run by the institutions of the three *European Communities*.

European Foundation for Management Development (EFMD). Association of individuals who are professionally interested in *management development* (303 in June 1974) and of organizations professionally engaged in management development in Europe (157 in June 1974). EFMD was founded in 1971 to help to improve the quality of management development within the economic, social and cultural context of Europe. It conducts surveys, runs conferences and seminars and acts as a clearing house for information on management development in Europe. It sponsors a quarterly journal, *Management International Review* and publishes *Documentation Bulletin* (monthly) and *International Management Development* (5 times a year).

Address: rue de la Concorde 51, B–1050 Bruxelles, Belgium (Bruxelles 512 16 92).

European Free Trade Association (EFTA). A *free trade area* established in 1960 consisting of Austria, Iceland (since March 1970), Norway, Portugal, Sweden and Switzerland. Finland has been an 'associate member' of EFTA since June 1961. Denmark and the UK were members until January 1973 when they became members of the *European Economic Community*. All *import duties* imposed by members of EFTA on imports from other members were abolished by 31 December 1966; there are also no export restrictions between members.

European Investment Bank (EIB). An international organization established in 1958. Its members are now the 9 members of the *European Economic Community*. The Bank's task is to contribute to the balanced and steady development of the EEC's common market. It is empowered to grant loans and guarantees for projects to develop less-developed regions and projects which are too large to be undertaken by one member state alone. It operates on a non-profit-making basis. It has a board of governors (a minister designated by each member state) which determines general policy, a board of directors (18 appointed by the board of governors for 5-year terms following nomination by the member states) which is responsible for supervising the running of the Bank and for fixing the terms of loans, and a management committee (appointed by the board of governors on a proposal from the board of directors) which is responsible for the day-to-day operation of the Bank.

European Parliament. Alternative name for the *Assembly* [2].

European Trade Union Confederation (ETUC). Association formed in 1973 of national federations of trade unions from European countries (30 federations from 17 countries in May 1974). The objectives of the ETUC are to represent and promote the social, economic and cultural interests of workers throughout Europe, in particular to the institutions of the *European Communities*. A congress of representatives of each national federation meets once every 3 years and elects the members of the executive committee which meets 6 times a year.

Also known as Confédération européenne des syndicats (CES), Europäischer Gewerkschaftsbund and den Europeiske Faglige Samorganisasjon.

Address : rue Montagne aux Herbes Potagères 37, 1000 Bruxelles, Belgium (Bruxelles 2179141).

Europeiske Faglige Samorganisasjon. Norwegian title of the *European Trade Union Confederation*.

evening shift. A *shift* that is worked mainly in the evening— e.g. from 16 00 to 24 00.

event. In *project network techniques,* an event is a specific accomplishment that occurs at a recognizable point of time.

ex. 1. Without an indicated benefit. When a company is to distribute some benefit (such as a *dividend* [2]) to holders of its *shares* it sets a date for 'closing the register'. Everyone who is on the *register of members* on that date will receive the benefit. Because there is usually a long delay between selling a share and registering the transfer, it is necessary to make clear whether buyer or seller is to receive a benefit that is distributed in the meantime. If a share is sold 'ex' some benefit then the seller

148

retains that benefit. Thus 'ex all' (seller retains all the specified benefits), 'ex dividend' (seller receives the next dividend to be paid), 'ex rights' (seller receives the *rights* in a forthcoming *rights issue*), 'ex scrip' (seller receives forthcoming *capitalization issue*). Also used in similar circumstances for other securities, e.g. 'ex interest' (seller receives the next payment of interest). The opposite of 'ex' is 'cum'. 2. Without the buyer being responsible for goods up to a specified point; e.g. 'ex ship' (buyer takes on responsibility and pays for transport and handling when the goods leave a specified ship).

exception report. A report on a deviation from a plan that is presented to someone practising *management by exception*.

excess. An amount that *insurer* and *assured* agree will be deducted from any claim made by the assured under his *contract of insurance*. (Also known as a 'deductible'.)

exchange. 1. An arrangement by which two people transfer property to each other. Sometimes one person pays some money in addition (part-exchange) and this money is known as 'payment for equality'. 2. Action of giving money of one currency for that of another. 3. A place where business is transacted, especially an *organized market*.

exchange control. Action taken by the government of a country to regulate or restrict *international settlements* by residents of the country.

Exchange Equalisation Account. An *account* [3] of the British *Treasury* at the *Bank of England* established by the Finance Act 1932. Money, of unlimited amount, may be transferred from the *National Loans Fund* to the Exchange Equalisation Account, which is to be used to check undue fluctuations in the *exchange rate* for sterling. In addition the UK's *official reserves* are held in this account.

exchange rate. The number of units of one *currency* which may be bought or sold for one unit (or, often, 100 units) of another currency.

exchange reserves. Synonym for *official reserves*.

exchange risk. The risk that *exchange rates* will vary and that a future payment will therefore be more expensive, or a future receipt less valuable, than is expected.

Exchequer. The fund of revenue acquired by the British government—now the *Consolidated Fund*. From the medieval practice of accounting by means of counters on a chequered cloth.

excise duty (or duty of excise). A tax charged in the UK: (1) on goods produced or manufactured in the UK (at present, on beer, British wine, hydrocarbon oils, matches, mechanical lighters, petrol substitutes, power methylated spirits, spirits, tobacco, and gas used as fuel for road vehicles); (2) on licences (see *excise licence duty*); or (3) on betting and gaming (at present, general betting duty, bingo duty, gaming licence duty, gaming machine licence duty, and pool betting duty).

excise licence. A licence which is issued on payment of an *excise licence duty*.

excise licence duty (UK). A tax charged in the UK when a *licence* [1] is issued to someone permitting him to: (1) use a particular mechanically propelled vehicle; (2) manufacture or produce particular goods (at present, chiefly, beer, spirits, tobacco, mechanical lighters and matches); or (3) carry on a particular trade or business (now very few and at a nominal rate of duty). The object of imposing the duties of types (2) and (3) is to ensure that an authoritative register is kept of manufacturers and distributors in particular trades (mainly those dealing in goods on which *excise duty* is charged); only vehicle licence duty (type (1)) is intended to raise significant amounts of money.

exclusive licence (in USA, exclusive license). A *licence* [2] of *patent rights* under which only the licensee may exercise the rights (i.e. the licensor cannot exercise them).

execution. Legal process to enforce the payment of a *judgment debt*.

executive director. A *director* of a *company* [1] who is also a full-time employee of the company. (Also known as an 'inside director'.)

executive routine. Synonym for *supervisory program*.

executor. 1. A *personal representative* appointed in a will. 2. Synonym for *supervisory program*.

ex gratia. Voluntary; not obligatory.

Eximbank. Abbreviation of *Export-Import Bank of the United States.*

ex officio. By virtue of holding a particular *office* [1].

exit interview. *Interview* of an employee who has given notice to end his employment in order to gain information about his reasons for leaving.

exogenous. 1. Originating from outside a system. 2. Determined by factors that are not predicted by a specified model.

expectation. The expectation of a *random variable* is the *weighted arithmetic mean* of all its possible values weighted by the *probability* of occurrence of each value. If X is a *discrete random variable* then its expectation $E(X)$ is:

$$\sum_i x_i p_i$$

where p_i is the probability of X taking the value x_i. If X is a *continuous random variable* having $f(x)$ as *frequency function* then:

$$E(X) = \int_{-\infty}^{\infty} x f(x) \, dx$$

(Also known as the 'mean' of the probability distribution.)

expected monetary value (EMV). The EMV of an action is the *weighted arithmetic mean* of the possible *payoffs* [1] of the action weighted by their *probabilities*. Thus, if the payoffs of an action are $v_1, \ldots, v_n$ with probabilities $p_1, \ldots, p_n$, then the EMV of the action is:

$$\sum p_i v_i$$

(Also known as 'expected payoff' or 'expected value'.)

expenditure. A relinquishment by a firm of money or some other *asset* [1] or an incurrence of a *liability* [1] in exchange for a benefit received or to be received.

expenditure tax. A tax of which the effects on individuals depend only on the way they spend money. E.g., in the UK, *value added tax*. (Also known as an 'indirect tax', or 'outlay tax'.)

expense. 1. A disbursement or outlay of cash. 2. (Plural.) Money paid out by an employee in connection with his job and reimbursed by his employer. 3. A measurement, for the purposes of accounting, of the cash value of whatever a firm has parted with (or is liable to part with) in making an *expenditure* in exchange for specified goods, services or labour that have been used by the firm in any way that has assisted the firm in acquiring *revenue* [1]. (Also known as an 'expired cost'.) *Also* (often plural) a measurement of the expenditure on all goods, services and labour that have been used for a specified purpose—e.g. *selling expenses*. 4. (UK.) A *cost* [2] that relates to the provision of services (as opposed to *labour cost* and *materials cost*) or the *depreciation* [2] incurred through the use of *fixed assets*. *Also* (often plural) the total of such costs that relate to a particular purpose.

experienced-worker standard (EWS). The quantity and quality of output from a particular type of work that a person who is experienced in doing that type of work would produce during a specified period (e.g. during one working day).

expired cost. A measurement, for the purposes of accounting, of the cash value of whatever a firm has parted with (or is liable to part with) when making an *expenditure* on goods or services that are no longer available for use within the firm (e.g. because they have been used in manufacturing something that the firm has sold).

exploratory development. Activity that is directed towards investigating proposed solutions to problems or proposed new products for a firm before any decision is taken on whether to implement the proposal.

explosion. Analysis of an *assembly* [1] into its constituent parts.

exponential distribution. A *probability distribution* of which the *frequency function* is:

$$f(x) = \beta e^{-\beta x}$$

where β is a positive number (a *parameter*). The *mean* [1] of the exponential distribution is $1/\beta$ and its *variance* [2] is $1/\beta^2$.

exponentially weighted moving average (EWMA). See *exponential smoothing*.

exponential smoothing. A method of predicting the next observation in a *time series* from a knowledge of the previous observations. The idea is to take a *weighted arithmetic mean* of previous observations and assign greater weights to the most recent observations. A 'smoothing constant' (usually denoted by α) is chosen, between 0 and 1. If the most recent observation is x_0, the one before that is x_1 and so on, then the estimate of the next observation is:

$$\alpha x_0 + \alpha(1-\alpha)x_1 + \alpha(1-\alpha)^2 x_2 + \ldots$$

i.e.

$$\alpha \sum_i (1-\alpha)^i x_i$$

The estimate is sometimes known as an 'exponentially weighted moving average' or 'EWMA'.

Export Credits Guarantee Department (ECGD). A department of the British government that provides *credit insurance* for British exporters.

export house. An enterprise specializing in selling goods to foreign buyers. An export house may act: (1) as a *merchant* [1] buying a manufacturer's products and attempting to sell them abroad; (2) as an *agent* for a manufacturer, promoting and arranging the sale of his products abroad; (3) as an agent for a foreign buyer, seeking sources of supply in the export houses's country and arranging purchases there.

Export-Import Bank of the United States (Eximbank). An independent agency of the US government established in 1934 to finance and otherwise facilitate the foreign trade of the USA. Eximbank has 5 directors all appointed by the President of the USA. It finances, guarantees and insures payment for goods and services of US origin. It was originally called the Export-Import Bank of Washington and its name was changed in 1968.

extended time. Synonym for *basic time.*

external currency market. The *market* [4] for lending, to firms outside of a particular country, *deposits* [1] (at banks) of the currency of that country. A market of this type first developed when firms outside the USA that had become owners of bank deposits (in US dollars) in the USA (e.g. because they had sold goods to American importers who paid by cheque) began to lend these deposits to other nonresidents instead of converting them into non-US currency. These loans were arranged by banks mainly in London and the money was called 'Euro-dollars'. Gradually other currencies were loaned in the same way and were called 'Euro-francs', 'Euro-sterling' and so on.

extraordinary general meeting. A *general meeting* that is not a *statutory meeting* and is not an *annual general meeting.*

extraordinary resolution. A *resolution* taken by a *general meeting* of a British *registered company* which is binding if more than three-quarters of the votes cast at the meeting are in favour of it.

ex-works. A type of contract for sale of goods in which the seller supplies the goods at a delivery point specified by him and the buyer bears all the costs of transporting the goods from that point.

f

FAIA. Abbreviation of 'fellow of the Association of International Accountants' (see *Association of International Accountants*).

f.a.s. (Abbreviation of 'free alongside ship'.) A type of contract for international sale of goods which is similar to an *f.o.b.* contract except that the buyer pays for the goods to be loaded onto the ship.

FBAA. Abbreviation of 'fellow of the British Association of Accountants and Auditors' (see *British Association of Accountants and Auditors*).

FBI. Abbreviation of *Federation of British Industries*.

FBIM. Abbreviation of 'fellow of the British Institute of Management' (see *British Institute of Management*).

FCA. Abbreviation of 'fellow of the Institute of Chartered Accountants in England and Wales' (see *Institute of Chartered Accountants in England and Wales*).

FCCA. Abbreviation of 'fellow of the Association of Certified Accountants' (see *Association of Certified Accountants*).

FCIS. Abbreviation of 'fellow of the Institute of Chartered Secretaries and Administrators' (originally 'fellow of the Chartered Institute of Secretaries). See *Institute of Chartered Secretaries and Administrators*.

FIEx. Abbreviation of 'fellow of the Institute of Export' (see *Institute of Export*).

FIMC. Abbreviation of 'fellow of the Institute of Management Consultants' (see *Institute of Management Consultants*).

FISB. Abbreviation of 'fellow of the Institute of Scientific Business' (see *Institute of Scientific Business*).

FIWM. Abbreviation of 'fellow of the Institution of Works Managers' (see *Institution of Works Managers*).

f.o.b. (Abbreviation of 'free on board'.) A type of contract for international sale of goods in which the seller supplies goods and pays for them to be taken to a ship named by the buyer and loaded onto that ship.

f.o.r. (Abbreviation of 'free on rail'.) A type of contract for the sale of goods in which the seller supplies goods and pays all the costs of loading them into a railway wagon at a place selected by the seller.

FSCA. Abbreviation of 'fellow of the Society of Company and Commercial Accountants' (see *Society of Company and Commercial Accountants*).

FWH. Abbreviation of *flexible working hours*.

FWT. Abbreviation of *flexible working time*.

fabrication line. See *production line*.

face value. A *nominal value* printed on a *security* [1] or other document.

facilities management. Planning, installation and operation of a firm's *electronic data processing* equipment by another, specialist, firm.

factor (noun). 1. An *agent* who is provided by his principal with a stock of goods which he sells; the principal receives the proceeds of the sale, less the agent's *commission* [1], but bears the risk of the goods not selling. 2. A firm that lends money to firms on the *security* [2] of their *accounts receivable*. Many factors also take over the collection of the accounts.

factor (verb). To work or act as a *factor*.

factor-comparison job-evaluation system. System of *job evaluation* in which: (1) a number of *benchmark jobs* are carefully described and analysed; (2) a number of factors (such as: skill, effort, responsibility, working conditions) are chosen; (3) for each factor, the benchmark jobs are *ranked* according to the degree to which the factor is involved in the jobs; (4) numerical values are assigned to each ranking position for each factor; (5) each job to be evaluated is compared with the benchmark jobs, factor by factor, and a total numerical value for each job calculated by adding the numerical values of its individual jobfactor rankings.

factorial. The factorial of a positive whole number (an 'integer') n is the product of all the integers less than or equal to n. It is usually written $n!$ Thus:
$$5! = 5 \times 4 \times 3 \times 2 \times 1 = 120$$
The factorial of zero $(0!)$ is taken to be 1.

Factories Act 1961. UK statute which consolidated the law concerning health, safety and welfare of workers in factories. The operation of the Act was criticized by the *Robens report* and it will be gradually replaced by health and safety regulations and by codes of practice recommended by the *Health and Safety Commission*.

factor of production. A resource used in the production of goods; traditionally classified as land, labour and capital or as land, labour, capital and entrepreneurship.

facultative reinsurance. *Reinsurance* on an *ad hoc* basis.

Fair Labor Standards Act. US federal law (1938) regulating hours of work and wages in industries engaged in commerce or the production of goods for commerce.

fair trade law. A state law in the USA that permits *resale price maintenance*.

Fair Wages Resolution. A resolution passed by the House of Commons in 1946 instructing government departments to include a term in all their contracts with private firms requiring the firms to provide workers with terms and conditions not less favourable than those agreed by *collective bargaining* in which the firm was represented or those 'observed by other employers whose general circumstances in the trade or industry in which the contractor is engaged are similar'.

false market. A *market* [1] for goods in which either buyers or sellers are acting on false information (e.g. buyers are paying high prices because they believe the goods are scarce but in fact they are not).

family allowance. A *social-security* benefit of a periodic (usually weekly) payment to people who have children to support. In the UK a family allowance is given to families with two or more children under 16 (or under 19 but receiving full-time education).

Family Expenditure Survey. A continuous survey of the expenditure of households in the UK which is carried out by the Department of Employment. The results are published annually and are used, among other things, in calculating the *General Index of Retail Prices*.

family group. In *group training*, a group that consists of people who work together for most of the time.

favourable variance. A *variance* [1] in which actual results are better than budgeted results (e.g. actual costs are less than *standard costs*).

F distribution. A *probability distribution* of a *continuous random variable* of which the *frequency function* is:

$$f(x) = \frac{\alpha^{\frac{1}{2}\alpha} \beta^{\frac{1}{2}\beta} \Gamma[\frac{1}{2}(\alpha+\beta)] x^{\frac{1}{2}\alpha-1}}{\Gamma(\frac{1}{2}\alpha) \Gamma(\frac{1}{2}\beta)(\alpha+\beta x)^{\frac{1}{2}(\alpha+\beta)}}$$

for $x > 0$ where α and β are positive integers and Γ is the gamma function (see *gamma distribution*). α and β are called the 'degrees of freedom' of the distribution. The distribution is important in statistical theory because it is the distribution of the *variance ratio* of samples of sizes $\alpha+1$ and $\beta+1$. The letter F is used in honour of the English statistician, Sir Ronald Aylmer Fisher (1890–1962).

featherbedding. 1. A term used by opponents of government assistance to industry to describe any assistance they do not like. (Assistance that they do like is known as an 'incentive'.) 2. Provision of more jobs, or employment of more workers, than is necessary—usually as a result of union pressure.

feature card. A card used for recording data and enabling *information retrieval*. When used for recording a *file* of data, one card is allotted to each attribute (or 'feature') that has to be recorded. All the cards are then divided into squares and each item in the file is allotted one square on each card (in the same

158

position on each). If an item possesses an attribute then a hole is made in its square on the card for that attribute. The cards are used to identify all items that have a required combination of attributes: the cards for the particular combination of attributes are held up to the light which shines through any hole that is punched in all of those cards.

Federal Reserve System. 12 banks (Federal Reserve Banks) in the USA which are coordinated by a 7-member Federal Reserve Board and which form the USA's *central bank*.

federated firm. A firm that is a member of an *employers' association*.

Federation of British Industries (FBI). Body founded, in 1916, for the encouragement, promotion and protection of British industries of all kinds. It became part of the *Confederation of British Industry* in August 1965. Its members were individual firms engaged in productive industry (but not the nationalized industries) and *trade associations*.

feedback. Part of the *output* of a *system* that is used to evaluate the performance of the system.

felt-fair pay. Term used by Elliott Jaques for the rate of pay that the holder of a job thinks would be fair for that job—see *equitable payment*.

fiche. Synonym for *microfiche*.

fidelity policy. A contract of *guarantee insurance* under which the *insurer indemnifies* the *assured* against losses caused by dishonesty of one or more of the assured's employees.

fiduciary. Involving or depending on confidence or trust.

field research. *Market research* that involves observing or questioning (e.g. by interviewing or by sending a questionnaire) the people, or representatives of the firms, in a *market* [2, 3]. (Cf. *desk research*.)

field warehouse. A section of the premises of a firm on which it stores its products and which is cordoned off and put under the control of a *warehouse company*. In effect the warehouse is brought to the goods rather than the goods to the warehouse.

FIFO. (Acronym from 'first in first out'.) A method of estimating the change in value, over a period, of a stock of some good when batches of the stock have been purchased at varying prices during the period and withdrawals have been made from the stock during the period but there is no way of distinguishing the batch from which any withdrawal was made. It is assumed that the oldest stock is withdrawn first so that the stock remaining at the end of the period is that which was purchased most recently.

file. A collection of related *records*.

film loop. An 8 mm movie film, not more than 50 feet long, of which the ends are joined. Film loops are shown continuously on specialized projection equipment, showing the same piece of action again and again, for example in training or as part of an exhibition. (Also known as a 'single-concept film'.)

final dividend. The final payment of *dividend* [2] paid by a company in respect of its profits for a financial year.

Finance Act. Any of the UK statutes called by that name that impose taxes and amend the law relating to taxation. At least one Finance Act is passed by Parliament each year usually receiving the royal assent at the end of July.

finance bill. 1. An *accommodation bill*. 2. (Usually capital F and B.) A *Bill* [3] that is a draft of a *Finance Act*.

finance company. A firm of which the main activity is lending money, usually to enable the borrower to make a specific purchase.

finance house (chiefly UK). A *finance company*.

financial accounting. Activity or process of systematically recording and analysing information in monetary terms, relating to the transactions of a firm, primarily in order to provide information to people other than the management of the firm—e.g. the owners (*stockholders* [1] or *shareholders*) of the firm, its creditors, government agencies, or members of the public who might be persuaded to buy the firm's *securities* [1]. *Also* the body of knowledge concerning such work.

financial gearing. The use of *debt capital* by a firm. When a *company* [1] has debt capital, any change in its *net profit* [1] (measured without deducting payments of interest on debt capital, payment of *corporate income tax* and payments of *preference dividends*) is magnified (or 'geared') and produces a larger

160

change in the *EPS* of the company. The owners of the *equity* [3] of any other kind of firm benefit in a similar way from the use of debt capital. (Also known as 'financial leverage' or 'gearing'.)

financial instrument. A written or printed document of which the main effect is to entitle a specified person to a sum of money; especially such a document in a commonly used, standardized form such as a *certificate of deposit* or a *bill of exchange*.

financial leverage. Synonym for *financial gearing*.

financial management. Activities concerned with acquiring funds for a firm and assessing the best uses for those funds.

financial ratio. A *ratio* of two quantities that have been measured in monetary terms which is used in analysing the activities of a firm. (Also known as an 'accounting ratio'.)

financial risk. The *risk* [1] that the returns to the owners of the *equity* of a firm will decrease because of the necessity to pay interest to suppliers of *debt capital*.

financial year. An *accounting period* that is 12 months long. Specifically that ending 31 March which is used for computing liability to UK *corporation tax* (e.g. the 'financial year 1975' means the year ending 31 March 1976).

financing. Act, process, or an instance of raising or providing funds. *Also* the funds raised or provided.

fine paper. *Securities* [1] for which there is practically no risk that the issuer will not pay interest or *redeem* them at the due time.

finger dexterity. Ability of a person to make controlled skilful movements with his fingers.

finished goods. The goods that a manufacturer has ready for sale. *Also* the value of a stock of such goods.

firm. 1. Any organization or individual person engaged in any form of activity of which an important aim is the production of goods or services for sale to others. Used as an all-inclusive term for units of economic activity. 2. A *partnership*.

first-day premium. Difference between the price at which new *shares* are *issued* [2] and the price at which they are sold on a *stock exchange* [1] on the first day after they have been issued.

161

first in first out. See *FIFO*.

first-line supervisor. A manager who is responsible for the activities of a number of subordinates, none of whom manage anyone else. (Sometimes known as a 'front-line supervisor'.)

first-year allowance. A *capital allowance* given to a trader who purchases machinery or plant. The allowance is equal to the amount of expenditure incurred (rate fixed by Finance Act 1972— previously the rate was 80% of the expenditure incurred). First-year allowances were introduced by the Finance Act 1971.

fiscal. Of, or relating to, taxation or government expenditure.

fiscal year. 1. Synonym for *year of assessment*. 2. (Chiefly US.) An *accounting period* that is 12 months long.

Fisher's ideal index. An *index number* that is computed as the *geometric mean* of a *Laspeyres index* and a *Paasche index*. Named after the American economist, Irving Fisher (1867–1947).

fixed asset. An *asset* [1] of a firm that is not a *current asset* and is intended to be used by the firm for some time (usually, longer than a year or longer than one *operating cycle*). Fixed assets are often described as 'property, plant and equipment' as these are the main types of fixed asset.

fixed charge. 1. A recurring *liability* [1] that a firm has (e.g. to pay rent or loan interest) the size of which does not depend on the scale of operations of the firm. (Also known as a 'fixed expense'.) 2. Synonym for *mortgage*.

fixed cost. A *cost* [2] that is incurred during the production of goods by a firm and is the same whatever quantity is produced over a wide range of quantities (for example the rent paid for a factory).

fixed expense. Synonym for *fixed charge* [1].

fixed shift system. A system of *shiftwork* [1] in which one group of workers always works the same *shift*.

fixtures and fittings. Items attached to the structure of a building but not forming part of it.

flannel board (or flannelgraph board). A *display board* with a surface of a rough material (such as flannel or felt) to which objects backed with a similar material will adhere.

flash pack. A package of a particular *product* [2] with a 'flash' giving details of a price reduction (as part of a *consumer deal*) printed on its wrapping or container. (Also known as a 'money-off pack'.)

flat yield. Synonym for *running yield*.

flexible budget. A *budget* [1] in which costs are estimated for various levels of activity.

flexible working hours (FWH). An arrangement under which each employee in an organization may choose the times at which he starts and finishes work each day to suit himself. In most arrangements of this kind, an employee must be at work during one or more periods of 'core time' (e.g. 1000 to 1600) and must work for a minimum number of hours in each week or month. In some arrangements it is possible to carry forward an excess or deficit in the number of hours worked from one week (or month) to the next. (Also known as 'flexible working time' or FWT.)

flexible working time (FWT). Synonymous with *flexible working hours*.

flipchart. A device for presenting information to an audience, which consists of a number of large sheets of paper. Each sheet can be flipped over or torn off to reveal the next.

float (noun). 1. The amount of time that can be added to the duration of an *activity* in a *network* without affecting the overall duration of the project. 2. A small quantity of cash from which change can be given.

float (verb). 1. (Transitive.) To make no attempt (as a *central bank*) to keep the *exchange rates* for a country's currency fixed over a period of time. (Intransitive.) To be free (as a currency) from action by central banks to maintain a particular exchange rate. 2. To invite the public to buy particular *securities* [1] or the securities of a particular company, for the first time.

floating asset. Synonym for *current asset*.

floating charge. Rights over a company's property that it grants to lenders (or their *trustee*) as *security* [2] for a loan. If the company fails to repay its debts on time, then the lenders may convert the floating charge into a *mortgage* over the specific property that the company owns when default occurs. Until that time, the company can deal with its property as it wishes.

163

floating labour (spelt floating labor in USA). Workers who are unskilled and move from job to job and, sometimes, from place to place without acquiring stable employment.

flotation. An act or instance of *floating*.

flow chart (sometimes spelt flowchart). 1. A *data flow chart*. 2. A *program flow chart*. 3. Synonym for *flow diagram*.

flow-chart form of network. An *activity-on-node network* in which the arrows are used solely to represent the sequence and logical relationship of activities. (Also known as a 'logic network'.)

flow diagram. A diagram or model, to scale, showing the location of specific activities carried out in a workplace and either: (1) the routes followed by workers; or (2) the routes along which materials or equipment are moved. (Also called a 'route diagram' or a 'flow chart'.)

flow process chart. A *process chart* which shows all operations (including transport, delay and temporary delay—unlike an *outline process chart*) involved in a process. There are three types according to the subject of the chart: (1) man-type flow process chart (or 'process chart—man analysis') which records what one worker does; (2) material-type flow process chart (or 'process chart—product analysis') which records what happens to the materials that go into the final product; (3) equipment-type flow process chart, which shows how an item of equipment is used.

flow production. Synonym for *continuous production*.

flyback timing. A method of timing a job using a stopwatch in *time study* [1] in which the hands of the stopwatch are returned to zero at the end of each element of the job. (Also called 'snapback timing'.)

folio. A piece of paper; used to describe the individual sheets or pages of a book in which *accounts* [1] are written. Specifically: (1) the page of a *journal* from which a particular *ledger* entry was *posted*; (2) the page of a *ledger* to which a particular *journal* entry has been *posted*.

Foras Bainistíochta na hÉireann. Irish title of the *Irish Management Institute*.

forced-choice question. A question that must be answered by choosing from a small number of statements supplied with the

164

question.

forced-distribution method. Assigning (to people, projects etc.) a *rating* (according to a *rating scale*) in such a way that the *frequency distribution* of ratings is a *normal distribution*. Especially in *performance appraisal* where the appraiser is asked to give 10% of his subordinates the top rating, 20% the next highest rating, 40% the middle rating, 20% the next rating and 10% the lowest rating.

forecast (noun). A result of *forecasting*.

forecast (verb). To give a statement of what is likely to happen in the future, based on considered judgment and analysis.

foreclose. To carry out a *foreclosure*.

foreclosure. Action by a *mortgagee* to acquire complete ownership of property that has been *mortgaged* to him.

foreign exchange. 1. *Currencies* of foreign countries. 2. Methods of exchanging one *currency* for another.

foreign-exchange market. The *market* [4] for buying and selling different countries' *currencies*. In practice, nearly all deals in this market are conducted by telephone, and buyers and sellers rarely meet.

foreman. A *first-line supervisor* who is responsible for planning and supervising the work (usually manual work) of others but does not usually perform work himself (apart perhaps from demonstrating methods). Cf. *chargehand*.

foreshift. The *morning shift* in a *three-shift system*.

formation expenses. Synonym for *preliminary expenses*. (Although the phrase 'preliminary and formation expenses' is often used.)

formboard. Synonym for *pegboard*.

FORTRAN. Acronym from FORmula TRANslation. A widely used *procedure-oriented language* designed for use in scientific and mathematical applications. A FORTRAN program is written in a combination of stylized English and algebraic formulae. Several versions of increasing sophistication have been developed. FORTRAN IV is now the standard version.

forward. Of, or relating to, *delivery* at a fixed time in the future.

forward contract. A contract for the delivery of goods at a

165

specified future date (an 'outright' forward contract) or at a date to be chosen by either the buyer or the seller within specified limits (an 'option' forward contract). A forward contract that is entered into with no intention of making or taking delivery is often called a *futures contract*.

forward cover. An amount of foreign currency bought *forward* to settle a known future obligation (i.e. to cover it).

forward pass. In *project network techniques*, the calculation of *earliest event times*, or of *earliest start times of activities* and *earliest finish times of activities*.

forward price. The price at which someone is willing to buy or sell something for delivery at some specified future time.

forward rate. An *exchange rate* at which someone promises to buy or sell foreign currency at some date in the future.

founders' shares. See *deferred shares*.

four-day week. 1. An arrangement under which employees in an organization work for only four days each week especially because of *short-time working*. 2. An arrangement under which employees in an organization work for only four days each week but work the same number of hours that were previously spread over five days. Also known as 'four-day, forty-hour week' because the number of hours worked is commonly 40 a week.

fractile. A value of a *random variable* (e.g. a *decile, percentile* or *quartile*) that measures off a specified fraction of a *frequency distribution* or a *probability distribution*. (Also called a 'quantile'.)

frame. 1. See *programmed instruction*. 2. Synonym for *sampling frame*.

franchise. 1. An arrangement by which a retailer is given an exclusive right to sell specified goods, or use a particular trading name, within a specified area. 2. A condition in a *contract of insurance* that claims for less than a specified amount will not be paid by the *insurer ;* however, claims for more than that amount will be paid in full (if they are valid). Cf. *excess*.

franked investment income. An item of income paid to a company resident in the UK which is a *dividend* [2] of another company and in respect of which *advance corporation tax* has been paid.

If a company that has received franked investment income then distributes the money as a dividend, the company does not itself pay advance corporation tax on it (as the tax has already been paid).

fraud. Illegal practice of deception to induce someone to give up something of value.

free alongside ship. See *f.a.s.*

free enterprise. Production of goods and provision of services only by private individuals (and *corporations* owned by private individuals) for profit in which individual producers act according to their own judgment and not under the direction or influence of government (thus the government provides no *subsidies* or price controls).

free float. The length of time for which an *activity* in a *network* may be delayed or extended without delaying the start of any succeeding activity.

free good. A *good* [1] which, at a given time and place, is either in such abundance that anyone can obtain it without cost (e.g. air) or is incapable of being sold (e.g. sunshine).

free issue materials. Materials supplied to a manufacturer free of charge by a customer for conversion into goods to be supplied to the customer.

free on board. See *f.o.b.*

free on rail. See *f.o.r.*

free trade. Unrestricted international trade either with no *customs duties* or with customs duties that are used only to create revenue and not to exclude imports.

free trade area. An area consisting of several independent countries in which no *customs duties* are imposed on goods going from one of those countries to another. Unlike a *customs union,* each country in a free trade area sets its own customs duties for trade with countries outside the area.

frequency curve. The *graph* [1] of a *frequency function.*

frequency diagram. The *graph* [1] of the *frequency distribution* of observations of a *discrete random variable*. At each value of the random variable an ordinate is drawn with a length that indicates the number of occurrences of the value.

frequency distribution. The pattern of occurrence of the values of a *random variable* as shown by observing a *sample* [1] of its actual occurrences. A frequency distribution consists of a list giving the number of observed occurrences of each value of the random variable, either tabulated or presented graphically as a *frequency diagram* or *histogram*. A frequency distribution is an approximation to the *probability distribution* of the random variable.

frequency function. A mathematical *function* [2] that indicates the *probability distribution* of a *random variable*. The frequency function of a *discrete random variable* gives, for each possible value, x, of the random variable, the *probability* that it will actually occur with that value.

If the random variable is a *continuous random variable* then the *graph* [1] of its frequency function gives the following information: the section of the area between the graph and the x-axis that is included between the ordinates $x = a$ and $x = b$ is equal to the probability that the random variable will occur with a value between a and b.

The frequency function of a continuous random variable is sometimes called a 'probability density function'.

frequency polygon. A *graph* [1] of a *frequency distribution* obtained by drawing straight lines joining the mid-points of the tops of the rectangles in a *histogram*.

friendly society. A society formed mainly in order to collect money from its members to be invested in a fund that will provide for members in sickness or old age or for the relief of widows and children of deceased members.

fringe benefit. Something of value, apart from agreed regular monetary payments of salary or wage, given by an employer to an employee—e.g. sick pay or subsidized meals. The term 'employee benefit' is now often used instead of 'fringe benefit' to emphasize that such benefits are regarded as usual components of compensation rather than as fringe elements.

front-line supervisor. Synonym for *first-line supervisor*.

F test. A *statistical test* used to decide whether two *samples* [1] with different sample *variances* [3, 4] may be presumed to come from *normal populations* with the same population *variance* [2]. The *F distribution* is used for the test.

full cost. The *cost* [2] of manufacturing a particular item as determined by *absorption costing* (i.e. the sum of *direct costs* and a proportion of *indirect costs*).

full-line strategy. Synonym for *broad-line strategy*.

fully paid share. A *share* in a company, the full *nominal value* of which has been received by the company.

Fulton Committee. A committee appointed by the British government on 8 February 1966 to examine the structure, recruitment and management, including training, of the Home Civil Service. The committee's report and recommendations were published in June 1968 (*The Civil Service*, Cmnd 3638, HMSO). Named after the chairman, Sir John Fulton, Baron Fulton of Falmer (born 1902, created a life peer 1966).

function. 1. A group of related activities that contribute to the performance of work by an organization (such as, the 'purchasing function', i.e. all activities related to purchasing materials for use by an organization). *Also* the part of an organization that performs such a group of activities.

2. (Mathematics.) Something that assigns, to each element of a *set*, at least one element of the same or another set.

functional organization. Organization into departments according to *function* [1].

fund (noun). 1. A stock or sum of money, especially one set aside for a particular purpose. 2. (Plural.) British *government stocks*. (Originally, the name for the sums set aside by Parliament for payment of interest on loans to the government.) 3. (Plural.) Financial resources. 4. (Plural.) *Working capital*.

fund (verb). 1. To provide for a financial obligation by borrowing money for a specific period. 2. To provide for a future financial obligation by setting aside money and lending it to earn interest; to create a *sinking fund*.

funded debt. A debt that does not have to be repaid—especially one represented by an *irredeemable* security.

funds-flow statement. A summary of the way in which the *net current assets* of a firm have changed over a period. (Also

169

called a 'statement of source and application of funds'.)

futures contract. A contract, arranged on an *organized market,* by which a seller promises to deliver a fixed standard quantity of a *commodity* [3] of a standard quality to the buyer on a fixed future date. Futures contracts are normally entered into for purposes of *hedging* and speculation; less than 5% of futures contracts actually result in delivery of the material. A typical use of futures contracts is as follows: one person, A, buys a futures contract for delivery of goods to him by B in 3 months' time at a fixed price; A hopes that, before the delivery date, the price of the goods will rise so that he can 'close out' by selling a contract to a third person, C, for delivery to C at exactly the same time as A was to take delivery. A, who has acted as a *bull,* can then stand aside with his profit and leave B to deliver the goods to C. To facilitate deals of this kind organized markets usually specify a few standard dates each year for use as delivery dates in contracts (these dates are called 'positions'). A contract for delivery in the future that is bought with the intention of taking delivery is usually called a *forward contract.*

futures market. An *organized market* for buying and selling *futures contracts.*

g

GATB. Abbreviation of *General Aptitude Test Battery*.
GATT. Abbreviation of *General Agreement on Tariffs and Trade*.
GDP. Abbreviation of *gross domestic product*.
GIGO. Acronym from 'garbage in, garbage out'—a phrase used to emphasize the fact that a computer cannot correct mistakes in the data supplied to it and will produce erroneous results if it is given erroneous data to work on.
GInstM. Abbreviation of 'graduate of the Institute of Marketing' (see *Institute of Marketing*).
GmbH. Abbreviation of *Gesellschaft mit beschränkter Haftung*.
GNP. Abbreviation of *gross national product*.
GTC. Abbreviation of *government training centre*.
gain-sharing. Operation of a *premium bonus scheme* in which the *incentive payment* per unit of time saved decreases as the time saved increases. It is argued that gains from producing at more than the standard rate of performance should be shared between the worker and his employer.
game. 1. A situation of conflict or competition that can be studied using *game theory*. 2. Synonym for *management game*. 3. Synonym for *consumer contest*.
game theory (or theory of games). A mathematical theory that applies to certain situations in which there are conflicts of interest between two or more individuals or groups.

Game theory deals with situations, called 'games', that can be represented by the following model: (1) there are n 'players' (individuals, corporations, groups) each of whom is required to make one choice from a specified set of possible choices; (2) when every player has made a choice the particular combination of choices they have made determines an 'outcome' which, in some way, affects or interests all players; (3) each player knows what outcome results from each possible combination of choices; (4) each player has an order of preference for the possible outcomes (often each player assigns to each outcome a numerical value called a 'payoff' which can be thought of as representing the number of points, or dollars, etc., that he gains or loses from the outcome); (5) each player knows the preferences of the other players (i.e. he knows what their payoffs are) and all players are assumed to act so as to gain the most they can from the game; but (6) each player makes his choice without knowing what choice the other players are making.

The theory attempts to answer the question: In a situation of this kind, what choice should a player make? A simple version of the problem is when there are only two players (a 'two-person game'). The payoffs for each player can then be arranged as a *matrix*. The simplest form of the two-person game is a 'two-person zero-sum game' in which, for each outcome, the payoff for one player is exactly opposite to the payoff for the other player (e.g. if one player gains 5 points the other loses 5 points). For further deatils, see, e.g., R. D. Luce and H. Raiffa, *Games and Decisions: Introduction and Critical Survey* (New York: Wiley, 1957).

gamma distribution. A *probability distribution* of a *continuous random variable* of which the *frequency function* is:

$$f(x) = \frac{\beta^{\alpha}}{\Gamma(\alpha)} x^{\alpha-1} e^{-\beta x} \qquad (x > 0)$$

where α and β are positive numbers (*parameters*) and Γ is the 'gamma function' defined by:

$$\Gamma(\alpha) = \int_0^{\infty} u^{\alpha-1} e^{-u} du \qquad (\alpha > 0)$$

The *mean* [1] of the gamma distribution is α/β and its *variance* [2] is α/β^2. If $\alpha = 1$ the distribution is called the *exponential distribution;* if $\alpha = \frac{1}{2}n$ and $\beta = \frac{1}{2}$ (where n is a positive integer) the distribution is called a *chi-square distribution.*

Gantt chart. A graphic representation on a timescale of the current relationship between actual and planned performance; especially, one which uses a standard set of symbols invented by the American industrial engineer, Henry Laurence Gantt (1861–1919).

Gantt task-and-bonus payment system. A system of *payment by results* in which a *standard time* is set for the production of one unit of output by a worker. From this a standard number of units per week (= hours worked per week ÷ standard time per unit) can be calculated. Any worker producing this standard output or less is paid a guaranteed minimum wage. Anyone producing more than the standard is paid according to the formula:

120% of number of units produced × standard time per unit × rate per hour.

Named after the American industrial engineer, Henry Laurence Gantt (1861–1919), who used the system and published a description of it in 1901.

garnishee. See *garnishee order.*

garnishee order. An order, obtained by a *judgment creditor* from a court, which requires a specified person (called the 'garnishee') who owes money to the *judgment debtor* not to pay the money to him but to the creditor instead.

gearing. See *financial gearing.*

General Agreement on Tariffs and Trade (GATT). An international treaty signed at Geneva on 30 October 1947. The GATT has never come into force because it must be accepted by the governments of territories which account for 85% of the international trade of the 33 signatories but the USA (which has 20·6% of the trade according to the agreed method of computation) has never accepted the GATT. However, all the signatories have agreed to apply the GATT 'provisionally' and this arrangement has been in force since 1 January 1948.

The object of the GATT is to reduce controls on international trade, particularly in the form of *import duties* and *exchange controls* on payments for imports. The contracting parties meet periodically to negotiate reductions of controls product by product and country by country. The result of a set of negotiations is then a vast list of bilateral agreements between pairs of countries on trade in particular items. Under article 2 of the GATT, if country A agrees a particular set of conditions for trade in a product originating from country B then country A must extend the same treatment to the same product when it comes from any other party to the GATT (most-favoured-nation treatment).

Part 1 of the GATT contains the agreement to give most-favoured-nation treatment. Part 2 contains detailed rules on the conduct of international trade, Part 3 deals with procedural matters and Part 4 (which was added in 1966) contains special provisions for increasing trade with less-developed countries.

There is a permanent secretariat headed by an Executive Secretary in Geneva.

General Aptitude Test Battery (GATB). A set of *aptitude tests* devised for the United States Employment Service and used for vocational guidance.

general average. 1. The system of reimbursing people for *general average loss*. 2. A liability (e.g. of an insurer) to pay a *general average contribution*.

general average contribution. A proportion of a *general average loss* paid to the person whose interest was sacrificed by someone whose interests were protected.

general average loss. The extent (measured in monetary terms) of a loss suffered by someone who voluntarily sacrificed his property during a sea voyage in order to save the ship or its cargo from greater loss. All the parties interested in the voyage (i.e. shipowner, person to whom freight charges are due and cargo owners) must pay a proportion (called a 'general average contribution') of the loss to the owner of the property that was sacrificed.

General Commissioner. A person appointed by the Lord

Chancellor to be a *commissioner* for the general purposes of the *income tax*. General Commissioners who are unpaid, are appointed to 'divisions' which cover particular geographical areas and hear the simpler appeals by taxpayers against *assessments* [1].

general crossing. See *crossing*.

General Index of Retail Prices (or Index of Retail Prices). An *index number* computed monthly by the Department of Employment and showing changes in the cost of purchasing standard quantities of a wide range of goods and services that are bought by households in the UK. The present base date is 15 January 1974. Earlier series used the base dates 16 January 1962 and 17 January 1956.

Extensive sampling is undertaken by the Department to obtain prices each month (including visits by 200 local officers to food shops). The index number is a *Laspeyres index*; the quantities of each item used in calculating it are determined from the *Family Expenditure Survey* (ignoring households in which 75% or more of the income is from pensions or in which the head of the household earns more than a certain amount—£75 a week in 1973). Full details of the calculation methods are given in: Department of Employment, *Method of Construction and Calculation of the Index of Retail Prices*, 4th edition (London: HMSO, 1967). The index is published each month in the *Department of Employment Gazette*.

Until 1969, only one index was published (called the Index of Retail Prices). Then the Department of Employment started to publish indexes based on the expenditure patterns of one-person pensioner households and two-person pensioner households. The name, General Index of Retail Prices, was adopted for the principal index.

general manager. A manager who determines and influences the broad objectives of a whole organization, determines the resources to be made available for attaining those objectives and has significant responsibilities in more than one major field of activity (usually working through managers who specialize in single fields of activity). A general manager is especially concerned with the formulation and interpretation of policy and with long-term planning.

general management. 1. The work performed by *general managers*. 2. The *general managers* within an organization.

general meeting. A meeting which may be attended by all the *members* of a *company* [1] and which gives them some opportunity to control the company's affairs. See *annual general meeting, extraordinary general meeting, statutory meeting.*

general strike. Simultaneous strikes by all members of several trade unions over a wide area; in particular the strike from 4 to 12 May 1926 of transport workers, printers, building workers and workers in the iron and steel, heavy chemical and power industries which was called by the *Trades Union Congress* to support striking miners.

general union. A *trade union* [1] that will accept workers of any kind as members.

geometric mean. The geometric mean of n numbers is the nth root of their product. Thus if the numbers are $x_1, \ldots, x_n$ then the geometric mean is $(x_1.x_2\ldots x_n)^{1/n}$.

Gesellschaft mit beschränkter Haftung (GmbH). (Literally 'company with limited liability'.) 1. A *private limited company* organized according to the laws of the Federal Republic of Germany. A GmbH must have a minimum *contributed capital* of 20 000 Deutschemarks. Unlike an *Aktiengesellschaft* [1], it does not have an *Aufsichtsrat* unless it has more than 500 employees or its constitution (*Gesellschaftsvertrag*) calls for one. 2. A *private limited company* organized according to the laws of Austria. It must have a minimum *contributed capital* of 100 000 Schillings. 3. A *private limited company* organized according to the laws of Switzerland.

gilt-edged. Of unquestionable safety. As in 'gilt-edged stock' (*stock* [4] issued by a government, especially the British government, so that it is inconceivable that interest payments would not be made).

gilts. *Government stocks* (from shortening of *gilt-edged* stocks).

giro. System of paying money in which the payer instructs a bank to credit the payee's account and does not himself have to inform the payee (that is done by the bank). (Also known as 'credit transfer'.)

Glacier Project. Research into managerial and organizational problems undertaken at the Glacier Metal Company Limited, a large British engineering firm, and led by the firm's chairman and managing director (from 1939 to 1965), Wilfred Banks Duncan Brown, Baron Brown (born 1908, created a life peer 1964) and by Elliott Jaques (born 1917). The research was initially undertaken in 1948 by a team, led by Jaques, from the Tavistock Institute of Human Relations and was government financed. The results of this stage of the work were published in: E. Jaques, *The Changing Culture of a Factory* (London: Tavistock Publications, 1951). From 1952 to 1965 Jaques continued working with Glacier as a 'social-analytic consultant' —this term is explained in: E. Jaques, 'Social-analysis and the Glacier Project', *Human Relations,* vol. 17 (1964), pp. 361–75; reprinted in *Glacier Project Papers,* edited by W. Brown and E. Jaques (London: Heinemann Educational Books/Carbondale, Ill: Southern Illinois University Press, 1965).

Brown developed the view that a manager can exercise authority only so far as he is supported by the people he has authority over. This support was provided in Glacier by an elaborate system of committees representing all employees for deciding policy which managers were to execute within guidelines approved by shareholders. This system is described in: W. Brown, *Exploration in Management* (London: Heinemann Educational Books/Carbondale, Ill: Southern Illinois University Press, 1960/Harmondsworth: Penguin, 1965). The theory of organizations that Brown developed from the Glacier Project is described in: W. Brown, *Organization* (London: Heinemann Educational Books, 1971/Harmondsworth: Penguin, 1974). See also, *equitable payment.*

gnome (or gnome of Zurich). An unidentified person who is alleged to speculate in international money markets.

goal. 1. A desired result of activity by an individual or an organization. 2. The end-result of a plan. 3. A state which an individual, consciously or unconsciously, strives to achieve.

goal setting. Process of establishing what a person or an organization should achieve at some time in the future.

go-go. Involving *speculation* and offering high but risky rewards. As in 'go-go fund' (a *mutual fund* specializing in speculative investments). (From the French, *à gogo* = abundant, galore.)

gold standard. System of controlling the *foreign-exchange market* by specifying an amount of gold for which a country's *central bank* will always exchange a unit of its currency if required. The amount of gold is called the 'gold content' of the currency.

Gompertz curve. A curve with an equation of the form:

$$y = ka^{b^x}$$

where *a*, *b* and *k* are constants and where $0 < a < 1, 0 < b < 1$. Gompertz curves are used to describe growth processes where the rate of growth is small at first, increases over a period and then slows down as a limit (*k*) is approached. Named after the English actuary and mathematician, Benjamin Gompertz (1779–1865).

go/no-go gauge (spelt gage in USA). A device used in *inspection* to test the size of an article that has been cut from a larger piece of material and which accepts the article if enough has been cut off but rejects it if too much has been cut off. Such a gauge does not measure the size of the article — only whether it falls within acceptable limits. (A typical go/no-go gauge for testing the diameter of a cylindrical piece has a hole into which the cylinder should 'go' if it is small enough and a second hole into which the cylinder should 'not go' unless it is too small.)

good. 1. Any object, substance, action or service that is capable of satisfying a human want. Usually classified as *free goods* and *economic goods*. 2. Any object or substance that is capable of satisfying a human want.

goods-in-process. Synonym for *work-in-process* [2].

goods received note. Document prepared when goods are delivered to a firm, giving a description of the goods and the quantity delivered. Used within the firm for purposes of *stock control*, checking that suppliers' invoices are correct and so on.

goods returned note. A document similar to a *goods received*

178

note but used to record *returns* [3] of the firm's own goods.

goodwill. The likelihood that customers will return to the same supplier. *Also* an estimate of the value of goodwill to the supplier.

go public. To become a *listed company* on a *stock exchange* [1] for the first time—usually by making a *public offer* of *securities* [1].

go-slow. Action by employees, involving doing less work than normal without actually stopping work, which is taken to bring pressure on their employers in a dispute.

government stock. *Securities* [1] issued by a government in the form of *stock* [4].

government training centre (GTC). An establishment, run by the Department of Employment, that provides *accelerated vocational training.*

gozinto chart. A chart showing, for a product, the sequence in which individual fabricated parts are made up into *subassemblies* and subassemblies are made up into complete *assemblies* [1]. (Also known as an 'assembly chart'.)

grade. A recognized standard specification of quality—especially for *commodities* [3].

graded hourly rates. A *payment system* in which each worker is paid according to his *merit rating.*

grade method (or grading method). Synonym for *classification method.*

grant. 1. A bestowal of a right by authority (as in 'grant of a *patent*'). *Also* the right that is bestowed. 2. An allocation of money from a *fund* [1]. Also the amount that is allocated. 3. *Conveyance* of property by means of a *deed.*

graph. 1. A diagram that represents the way in which one quantity varies as another quantity does. 2. A diagram consisting of points (called 'vertices', or 'nodes') and lines (called 'edges', or 'links') in which each edge has a vertex at each end. (Also called a 'network'.)

gratuity. A gift, especially of a small sum of money, made in response to service received or anticipated.

graveyard shift. Synonym for *night shift.*

green paper. A publication of the British government with a green cover—usually a proposal to which the government is not committed but would like public comment on.

grievance. An aspect of conditions of employment that is thought by an employee to hurt him or cause him injustice and which he complains about. (Sometimes distinguished from a 'dissatisfaction' which is an aspect of conditions that an employee feels hurt by but does not complain about.) *Also* the complaint made by an employee about such a state of affairs. *Also* the feeling of distress caused by such a state of affairs.

grievance interview. An *interview* which is intended to provide an opportunity for an employee to state fully the nature of a *grievance* to someone who is responsible for attempting to remove the grievance.

grievance procedure. The way in which an employee who has a *grievance* can seek to redress it. In Great Britain under the *Contracts of Employment Act* 1972, every employee must be given a written statement of the grievance procedure to be followed in his employment.

gross annual value. The rent that could be obtained for a year for a piece of land if it were let, on the open market, with the conditions that the landlord would pay for all repairs and the tenant would pay all rates.

gross cash flow. The sum of *net profits* [1] (after tax has been paid) and the amount of *expense* [3] determined as *depreciation* [2] of a firm over a period. (Sometimes also known as 'cash flow'.)

gross domestic product (GDP). The total value of goods and services that are produced within a specified country (including those produced by nonresidents) over a period (usually one year) excluding all goods and services used during that period to produce further goods and services.

Like *gross national product,* GDP may be measured at 'market prices' or at 'factor cost'.

gross income. The amount of *revenue* [1] received by a firm over a period.

gross margin. Synonym for *gross profit.*

gross national product (GNP). The total value of all goods and services that are produced by the residents of a specified country over a period (usually one year) excluding all goods and services used during that period to produce further goods and services.

Unlike *gross domestic product*, GNP includes income that a country's own residents derive from assets owned abroad but not the income of foreigners within the country.

GNP consists of three components: (1) consumption—i.e. the value of goods and services actually used during the period; (2) investment—i.e. the value of goods produced during one period that will be used to produce goods in future periods (*capital goods*) and goods produced for sale in future periods (*stocks* [1]); (3) the value of exports minus the value of imports. 'Net national product' is GNP minus an estimate of the *depreciation* [2] of the country's capital goods during the period.

GNP may be measured either at 'market prices' (i.e. at the prices that the consumers of goods and services actually paid for them, including *expenditure taxes*) or at 'factor cost' (i.e. after deducting expenditure taxes and adding the value of *subsidies*).

gross profit. *Sales revenue* (or *net sales*) from selling specified goods over a period minus the *expenses* [3] incurred in acquiring or manufacturing the goods. The expenses incurred in selling the goods and any *indirect costs* are not subtracted from revenues when calculating gross profit. *Also* this figure expressed as a percentage of sales revenue. (Also known as 'gross margin'.)

gross profit margin. The ratio of the *gross profit* acquired by a firm over a specified period from the sale of a specified *product* [2] to its *sales revenue* for that product during the same period. (Usually expressed as a percentage.)

gross working capital. The total value of the *current assets* of a firm. (See also, *working capital*.)

group. 1. Two or more persons who perceive themselves as forming a distinguishable entity because they interact fairly regularly over a period of time in pursuit of goals or interests that they have in common. A group need not be *organized* [1] although, if it exists for a long time, people will tend to adopt set *roles* and rules of conduct will emerge.

2. Two or more persons who meet together and, while they are meeting, interact with each other to such an extent that every

181

single person can at least take personal cognizance of the activities of every other member.

Note. The first definition of group tends to be used by sociologists who are interested in the continuing interaction of people (as in a *work group*) while the second tends to be adopted by psychologists who are interested in individual reactions to what happens when a group meets (see *group dynamics*).

3. A number of *companies* which are all under common ownership or control; particularly, a *holding company* [2] and its subsidiaries.

group appraisal. *Performance appraisal* of a person carried out by a group of three or more of his superiors working as a team.

group-decision method (or group decision-making or group problem-solving). A method of solving a problem affecting a manager and some or all of the group of people he manages, in which the manager states the problem to a meeting of the group and asks the group to decide on a solution. The manager's task is, then, not to present his own solution but to draw the best possible solution from the group. The American psychologist, Norman Raymond Frederick Maier (born 1900), is a leading proponent of the method—see, e.g., N. R. F. Maier, *Problem-solving Discussions and Conferences : Leadership Methods and Skills* (New York: McGraw-Hill, 1963).

group dynamics. Area of study concerned with the nature of groups of people, their patterns of development and their relationships with individuals and other groups.

group dynamics training. Activity that is intended to teach individuals about *group dynamics*. (Sometimes called 'laboratory training'.)

group incentive payment. *Incentive payment* that is related to the value or quantity of work done by a group of workers within a factory or other production unit.

group income. In the *Corporation Tax Acts,* a *dividend* [2] paid by a company to another company in the same 'group of companies', which is paid at a time when the paying and the receiving companies have jointly decided that, for such dividends, the paying company will not pay *advance corporation tax* and the receiving company will not receive a *tax credit*.

Section 256 of the *Income and Corporation Taxes Act 1970* as amended by Schedule 15 to the Finance Act 1972, gives a lengthy definition of what constitutes membership of a 'group of companies'.

group insurance. *Insurance* of a group of people (especially *life assurance*, accident and sickness insurance) by a single *contract of insurance* covering all members of the group.

group interview. A *selection interview* at which two or more applicants for a job are interviewed simultaneously—often conducted as an informal conversation.

Group of Ten. The richest and most influential members of the *International Monetary Fund*: Belgium, Canada, France, Federal Republic of Germany, Italy, Japan, Netherlands, Sweden, UK and USA. These countries signed the 'General Arrangements to Borrow' in 1962 by which they agreed to lend each other (through the IMF) up to US dollars 6000 million to forestall or cope with an impairment of the international monetary system. Representatives of the countries meet frequently to discuss monetary matters.

group process. A method by which or the manner in which a group of people interact.

group production. Synonym for *group technology*.

group relief. A reduction in the amount of *corporation tax* payable by one member of a 'group of companies' made by transferring a right to reduce tax liability from another company in the group (called the 'surrendering company').

Broadly, two companies are members of a 'group of companies' if one is a 75% *subsidiary* of the other or both are 75% subsidiaries of a third company.

For example, if companies X and Y are both members of a group, X makes a £5000 profit one year and Y makes a £5000 loss, then Y's loss can be offset against X's profit so that X pays no tax. However, Y loses the right to offset its loss against profits in future years.

Group relief can also be claimed by a member of a 'consortium' that either owns the surrendering company or controls it through a *holding company*. A consortium consists of five or fewer companies that directly and beneficially own all the *share capital* of a company.

group selection. Selection of persons for employment by observing a group of candidates performing an exercise in, for example, problem-solving.

group technology. Arranging *batch production* so that some of the economies of *continuous production* can be obtained. Groups of items are identified that require similar operations and the machines for these are grouped together. (Also known as 'group production'.)

group training. Form of *group dynamics training* in which the trainees meet in small groups and each trainee studies the behaviour and *group processes* that take place in his own group.

The groups may be given special tasks to perform (as in *Coverdale training*) or there may be very few rules about what it should do (as with a *T-group*). (See also, *cousins group, family group* and *stranger group.*)

group training scheme. An arrangement whereby two or more firms have common facilities for training.

guarantee (in USA, often spelt guaranty). 1. A promise by one person (usually called the 'guarantor') that he will be responsible for the discharge of a second person's liability (sometimes up to a specified limit) to a third person. 2. A promise, given by a manufacturer of goods which are sold by retailers, that the manufacturer will correct any defects in the goods found by a purchaser within a certain time. (In theory, it is the retailer's duty to correct defects and so the manufacturer is acting as guarantor of the retailer.) 3. Loosely, a *warranty*. 4. A *guarantor*.

guarantee company. A British *registered company* that has *members* (called 'guarantors') who guarantee that if the company is *liquidated* [3] and has insufficient funds to pay off its debts then they will each contribute up to a stated amount. The guarantors have *limited liability* because they cannot be asked to pay more than that amount. At present a guarantee company may also issue *shares* if it requires *contributed capital*. (Also known as a 'company limited by guarantee'.)

guaranteed bond. A *bond* [2] issued by one company with another company (e.g. the *parent company*) guaranteeing that interest will be paid.

guaranteed stock. *Stock* [4] issued by one body with some other body (usually a government) guaranteeing that *dividends* [3] will be paid.

guaranteed week. A minimum number of hours for which an employer agrees to pay a *timeworker* each week, so long as he is available for work, whether he actually works or not.

guarantee insurance. An arrangement by which an *insurer* promises to *indemnify* an *assured* if a specified person fails to carry out a specified obligation to the assured.

guarantor. A person who promises that if a second person fails to fulfil some obligation then he will fulfil it instead or pay money (up to a specified limit) to compensate for any loss caused by the second person's failure. (Also called a 'guarantee'.)

guaranty. US spelling of *guarantee*.

guesstimate (noun). An *estimate* made with little belief or pretence that it is accurate (i.e. it is just a guess).

guesstimate (verb). To make a *guesstimate*.

h

halo effect. Phenomenon found during *performance appraisal* in which a person's impression of one characteristic of someone is so strong that it affects his impressions of that person's other characteristics. (Also known as 'horns effect'.)

Halsey constant sharing scheme (or Halsey sharing plan or Halsey system). A *premium bonus scheme* in which time saved is paid for at half the basic time rate. Named after the Canadian mechanical engineer, Frederick Arthur Halsey (1856–1935).

hammering. Public announcement at the *Stock Exchange* [2] that a member cannot pay his debts. In the past attention was drawn to the announcements by an attendant striking a rostrum three times with a mallet.

hard copy. A permanent, immediately readable record of some data—as opposed to, e.g., a record on microfilm or on a magnetic tape.

hardening price. A price that is increasing.

hardware. Physical apparatus used for some purpose (especially *computers*) as opposed to 'software'—i.e. the instructions for using the apparatus.

harmonic mean. The reciprocal of the *arithmetic mean* of a set of numbers.

hash total. A sum of a set of numbers, each of which refers to a single item of data, which has no significance in itself but is

186

used to check that every item of data has been dealt with.

Hawthorne experiments. A long series of observations of people at work carried out at the Hawthorne factory, near Chicago, of the Western Electric Company from 1927 until 1932. The Hawthorne plant was very large, employing about 29 000 workers and producing telephone apparatus. The original aim of the experiments was to continue some earlier research on the effect of levels of lighting on productivity. The experiments were carried out jointly by the company's Employee Relations Research Department and the Harvard Graduate School of Business Administration. They showed that changes in working conditions (lighting, hours of work and timing of rest breaks) and incentive payment systems had little or no effect on productivity but that the interpersonal relationships of the workers had a very great influence. The complete experiments are described in F. J. Roethlisberger and William J. Dickson, *Management and the Worker* (Cambridge, Mass: Harvard University Press, 1939).

Health and Safety Commission. A statutory corporation set up on 1 October 1974 under the Health and Safety at Work, etc, Act 1974. It has a chairman and between 6 and 9 other members appointed by the Secretary of State. The Commission supervises the work of the *Health and Safety Executive*, assists and encourages research, training and distribution of information about health and safety at work, and makes proposals for safety regulations to be issued by the Secretary of State.

Health and Safety Executive. A statutory corporation set up on 1 January 1975 under the Health and Safety at Work, etc, Act 1974. It has three members (one of which is the director) appointed by the *Health and Safety Commission*. The Executive's job is to enforce statutory requirements concerning health and safety at work. It has a large staff of inspectors formed by amalgamating previous inspectorates that covered factories, mines and quarries, explosives, nuclear installations and alkali works.

hectographic process (or hectography). A process for making copies of an image that has been typed, printed or drawn on a master. The image on the master is formed of carbon and this is transferred to copy paper (which has been slightly dampened with a solvent) when the copy paper is pressed against the master. Because the carbon on the master is slowly removed by successive copies there is a limit to the number of copies; in early versions this limit was about 100 and the name derives from the Greek hekaton = hundred. (Also known as 'spirit duplicating' because the solvent used is known as 'industrial spirit'.)

hedge. To protect oneself against financial loss; *especially* to make a transaction in a *futures market* for a commodity or for foreign currency which reduces the *risk* [1] of loss from a commitment one already has in connection with that commodity.

hereditament. An item of *property* [1] which, if it had been owned by a person who died *intestate* in England before 1926 would have been inherited by his heir. For all practical purposes it means an item of *real property*. (Before 1926 an intestate person's *personal property* was divided up amongst his next of kin but real property—principally land—was kept intact and inherited by one person. Now all property is divided up after intestacy.)

Hereditaments are classified as: (*a*) 'corporeal hereditaments' —that is, anything which is part of or affixed to land; (*b*) 'incorporeal hereditaments'—that is, rights over land such as rights of way and *easements*.

Her Majesty's Inspector of Taxes. An official who supervises the *assessment* [1] (but not collection) of *income tax* and *corporation tax* in one of about 700 'tax districts' in the UK.

hidden agenda. The matters that are important to an individual at a meeting (e.g. of a committee) but which he cannot discuss or deal with, either because the matters are not on a formal *agenda* for the meeting or because they are personal emotional matters relating to the meeting (e.g. intense dislike of another member of a committee).

hierarchy. An arrangement of the *positions* in an *organization* into *ranks* such that the holder of a position in one rank is *responsible* [2] to the holder of a position in the next higher rank for the performance of his job.

hierarchy of needs. It has been proposed by the American psychologist, Abraham H. Maslow that the *needs* which dominate human behaviour may be grouped into five main classes and that these classes fall into a 'hierarchy' in the sense that needs belonging to one class became apparent (and set up drives) only when needs of 'lower' classes have largely been satisfied. The classes that Maslow distinguishes are: (1) physiological needs (e.g. for food); (2) safety needs (e.g. for security, stability, protection); (3) belongingness and love needs (e.g. for friendship and a position in a group or family); (4) esteem needs (e.g. for a constant high evaluation of oneself and for the esteem of others); (5) need for *self-actualization*.

More information is given in A. H. Maslow, *Motivation and Personality*, second edition (New York: Harper & Row, 1970).

High Court. The principal institution for settling civil legal claims in England and Wales. It is organized in three 'divisions': Queen's Bench Division (which includes two special sections: the Commercial Court and the Admiralty Court), the Chancery Division and the Family Division. Each division has jurisdiction over a particular class of cases. The judges of the High Court (the Lord Chief Justice, the Vice-Chancellor, the President of the Family Division and 'puisne'—pronounced as puny and meaning junior—judges) are assigned to particular divisions and hear cases (sitting alone) in London. There are also judges of the High Court who hear cases in 24 'circuit courts' in provincial centres.

high-level language. A *programming language* that makes considerable use of *macro-instructions,* is designed to be used easily by programmers and is not designed specifically for use on a particular type of computer. It is necessary to use a *compiler* to translate a program written in a high-level language into the particular *computer instruction code* used in the computer by which the program is to be executed.

hire purchase. An arrangement by which one person (called the 'hirer') is lent goods (and pays *rent* [1] for them) and has an option to purchase the goods outright, usually after paying a specified number of instalments of rent.

histogram. A diagram that represents the *frequency distribution* of a *continuous random variable*. Rectangles are drawn with heights proportional to the number of times that the random variable was observed to take a value within the interval represented by the base of the rectangle.

historical cost. The actual *cost* [2] that has been incurred in producing something.

holding company. 1. Synonym for *parent company*. 2. A *company* whose business consists wholly or mainly in holding the *shares* or *securities* [1] of other companies. In particular (for UK tax purposes) one that holds shares or securities principally in companies that are 90% *subsidiaries* of itself.

holding out. Pretending that a partner who has in fact left a *partnership* is still a member of it and obtaining credit on the strength of his name. (An ex-partner who is 'held out' in this way is liable for all debts thus incurred: hence the practice of widely advertising the departure of a partner.)

holiday pay. Payment by an employer to an employee who does not work because he is on holiday.

homeostatis. Capability, of a *system*, of automatically counter-ing external efforts to change certain of its properties, qualities, internal relationships or other attributes.

horizontal merger. A *merger* of two firms with very similar activities in the same industry.

horns effect. Synonym for *halo effect*.

hour-for-hour plan. Synonym for *standard-time payment system*.

Hours of Employment (Conventions) Act 1936. UK statute which forbids the employment of women in any industrial under-taking at night (see *nightwork*). It implements a convention drawn up by the *International Labour Organisation*.

hours of work. The time during which an employee should be doing his job.

household. A group of people who all live regularly at the same address and can be treated as a unit. There are two basic methods of identifying households: (1) by defining 'housing units' (indi-vidual houses, flats etc.) and treating all the people living in one housing unit as a household; (2) by identifying groups of people who regularly live together as a family—usually defined as a group who are all catered for by one person for at least one meal a day.

house journal. A regular publication, in the form of a newspaper or magazine, that is distributed to all employees of an organization and contains information of common interest.

house mark. A *brand* used by a firm or by a group of firms on all products.

house style. 1. Synonym for *corporate identity*. 2. Custom or system of spelling, capitalization and punctuation adopted by a printer or publisher for printing material or by an organization for typing letters, memoranda and so on.

house union. Synonym for *company union*.

human asset accounting. Attempts to measure, in monetary terms, the value to a firm of its employees. See, e.g., R. Likert, *The Human Organization: Its Management and Value* (New York: McGraw-Hill, 1967), chapter 9.

human engineering (or human factors engineering). (Chiefly US.) Synonym for *ergonomics*.

human relations school. An approach to the theory of management and of organizations that emphasizes the individual worker's need for satisfactory relationship with other members of his work group and his need to participate in decisions that affect his work (i.e. a requirement for *participative management*). This approach developed from the *Hawthorne Experiments*.

hurdle rate. A figure, set by the management of a firm, for the minimum *internal rate of return* that an *investment project* must have if it is to be accepted.

hygiene factor. An aspect of a job that can contribute to the dissatisfaction but not the satisfaction of the job holder according to the *motivation-hygiene theory*. (Also known as a 'maintenance factor'.)

hygienic management. A *managerial style* characterized by provision of high wages, employee benefits, good working conditions and good supervision in the belief that workers will therefore have high morale and will work harder. In terms of Herzberg's *motivation-hygiene theory*, managers with this style concentrate on ensuring that *hygiene factors* are right, so that there is no dissatisfaction. Herzberg suggests that this approach does not *motivate* employees to work harder. Hygienic management is sometimes seen as a sophisticated version of *paternalistic management*.

hyperinflation. Extreme *inflation*. For example, in Hungary, between August 1945 and July 1946, prices rose by $3.81 \times 10^{29}\%$.

hypothecation. Putting up goods as a *security* [2] for a loan from someone without giving him possession of the goods.

i

IBRD. Abbreviation of *International Bank for Reconstruction and Development.*

ICFTU. Abbreviation of *International Confederation of Free Trade Unions.*

IDA. Abbreviation of *International Development Association.*

IFC. Abbreviation of *International Finance Corporation.*

ILO. 1. Abbreviation of *International Labour Office.* 2. Abbreviation of *International Labour Organisation.*

IM. Abbreviation of *Institute of Marketing.*

IMF. Abbreviation of *International Monetary Fund.*

IMI. Abbreviation of *Irish Management Institute.*

IOE. Abbreviation of *International Organisation of Employers.*

I.O.U. A document acknowledging a debt but usually not specifying a time for repayment (so that it is not a *promissory note*) and not transferable.

IPM. Abbreviation of *Institute of Personnel Management.*

IRC. Abbreviation of *Industrial Reorganisation Corporation.*

IRR. Abbreviation of *internal rate of return.*

ISB. Abbreviation of *Institute of Scientific Business.*

ISCO. Abbreviation of *International Standard Classification of Occupations.*

ITB. 1. Abbreviation of *industrial training board.* 2. When the names of *industrial training boards* are abbreviated, ITB stands for 'industry training board'.

ITS. Abbreviation of *international trade secretariat*.

idle time. 1. Part of *attendance time* when a worker has work available but does not do it. 2. Synonym for *machine idle time*.

image. In psychology, a sensory experience that occurs without corresponding stimulation. Used to mean the mental picture that someone, or people in general, have of a person, company, organization, product, etc.

immediate-access store. A *store* [4] in a computer which is constructed so that the *access time* for any location in the store is the same and is very small.

impact day. The day on which the terms of a *public offer* of *securities* [1] are first made generally known.

impersonal account. An *account* [1] that records all transactions of a particular type (e.g. all receipts or payments of cash) as they affect a firm.

import duty. A tax imposed on the importation of goods into a country. In the UK, the term is usually restricted to cover *protective duties* rather than *revenue duties* (but both are called customs duties).

import licence (spelt import license in USA). A licence given by a government to a trader which permits him to import specified goods into his country.

imposed date. In *project network techniques,* a time at which some activity must occur and which is determined by external circumstances.

impressed stamp. Mark made on a document by pressing it between two dies, especially as evidence that a tax has been paid.

imprest. A sum of money given to someone by a firm (originally by a government) to spend on its behalf for specified purposes. Hence 'imprest system'—a system of controlling *petty cash* in which the person responsible for petty cash is given an initial sum of cash; each time he disburses cash he must take a properly authorized voucher for the amount disbursed; at regular intervals he exchanges the vouchers for an amount of cash equal to their total value so that, in theory, his fund is restored to its initial sum. *Also* a similar system of *stock control*.

impulse goods. *Consumer goods* that are normally bought by consumers without any previous planning (i.e. on impulse).

in-basket test. Synonym for *in-tray exercise*.

incentive. Something that urges a person on to achieve some goal. Especially something external (such as a financial reward) to the person who is urged on (cf. *motivation* [1]).

incentive payment. Part of an employee's remuneration that is related (according to a known rule) to the degree to which he has achieved an objective desired by his employer (such as an increase in the quantity or quality of output or an improvement in timekeeping).

incentive payment system. A *payment system* of which *incentive payment* is a principal feature.

incident process. A method of training in which: (1) the trainer gives trainees an account of a business situation (the 'incident') which describes a problem and calls for a decision although not enough information is given for a decision to be made; (2) each trainee is given an opportunity to discover the extra information he needs by asking the trainer; (3) trainees come to independent decisions that they write down with their reasons; (4) the trainer uses the written decisions to put the trainees into groups each of which contains people who have come to the same decision; (5) each group debates and formulates a group decision with supporting reasons; (6) the groups come together to evaluate the various decisions and reasonings with the trainer. (Cf. *case method*.)

income. 1. *Revenues* [1] of a person or firm over a period. (Sometimes called 'gross income'.) 2. Synonym for *profit*.

Income and Corporation Taxes Act 1970. UK statute that consolidates the law relating to *income tax* and *corporation tax*.

income and expenditure account. An *income statement* for a non-trading organization, such as an *investment trust* or a professional firm. The final balance is known as the 'excess of income over expenditure' or 'excess of expenditure over income' instead of 'net profit' or 'net loss'.

income bond. A corporate *bond* [2] on which interest is payable only if sufficient profit is made by the issuing corporation. (With normal bonds nonpayment of interest would lead to action, by the *trustee* for the *bondholders*, to sell some of the corporation's *assets* [1] to raise money to pay the interest.) In effect an income bond is the same as a share of *preferred stock* except that the money received by the corporation for issuing the bond is part of its *debt capital* rather than its *contributed capital*.

incomes policy. A set of rules or guidelines, determined by a government, on increases in wages and salaries.

income statement. A statement of the *revenues* [1] and *expenses* [3] (and, hence, profit or loss) of a firm for a period. (Also known as a 'profit and loss account'.)

income tax. A tax that is related to the income of a tax-payer.

In the UK (i.e. England, Wales, Scotland and Northern Ireland, but not the Isle of Man or the Channel Isles) income tax was introduced in 1799. The system is now managed by the *Board of Inland Revenue* and is governed by the *Income and Corporation Taxes Act 1970* and the *Taxes Management Act 1970* as amended by the *Finance Acts* which are produced each year.

The tax is based on an individual's *net statutory income* for each *year of assessment*. Any person who knows he is liable to income tax must inform the Board of Inland Revenue of that fact; inspectors (appointed by the Board) may require a person to complete a *tax return*. An individual's *personal reliefs* are deducted from his net statutory income. Tax is charged on the remainder which is divided into bands or 'slices' that are taxed at progressively increasing rates, which for 1974–75 were:

First £4500	33%	Next £2000	58%
Next £500	38%	Next £2000	63%
Next £1000	43%	Next £3000	68%
Next £1000	48%	Next £5000	73%
Next £1000	53%	The remainder	83%

In addition, an individual's *investment income* above £1000 is subject to an additional tax of 10% on the first £1000 and 15% on the remainder.

Income Tax Act 1952. UK statute which has been replaced by the *Income and Corporation Taxes Act 1970*.

Income Tax Acts. Legally, 'all enactments relating to income tax'. Practically, this means the *Taxes Management Act 1970, Income and Corporation Taxes Act 1970,* Income and Corporation Taxes (No. 2) Act 1970 and the annual *Finance Acts* from 1970 onwards.

incorporate. 1. To form into a *corporation.* 2. To make one object or substance a part of another—e.g. as part of a mixture or as one of a number of components or as a material that is changed in form.

incorporator (US). A person who signs a *certificate of incorporation* [2] as one of the first owners of a new corporation. (The UK equivalent is a subscriber to a company's *memorandum of association.*)

incoterms. A set of international rules for the interpretation of the chief terms used in foreign trade contracts drawn up by the International Chamber of Commerce. The terms defined are: *c. & f., c.i.f.,* carriage paid to..., ex-quay, ex-ship, *ex-works, f.a.s., f.o.b* and *f.o.r.*

incremental pricing. The practice of setting two prices for a manufactured product: (1) a higher price to be charged for a specified quantity of the product and which is intended to cover the *full cost* of the product; and (2) a lower price to be charged for any further units of the product and which is intended to cover only the *variable costs* of producing the further units. Usually the two prices are charged to entirely separate groups of buyers (e.g. buyers in different countries).

indemnify. To promise to someone that if he should suffer loss as a result of some specified event then he will be reimbursed (but he cannot claim more than he loses).

indemnity. A promise to *indemnify.*

indent (noun). An order for goods; originally, from an *agent* abroad.

indent (verb). To make out an *indent.*

indenture. A formal legal document, originally drawn up in duplicate on the same sheet of paper and the two copies separated by a zigzag tear to prevent forgery. Now especially: (1) a contract of *apprenticeship*; (2) (USA) a contract between a *corporation* and a *trustee* for *bondholders* concerning the terms of an issue of *bonds* [2] (equivalent to a *debenture trust deed* in the UK).

index (verb). To arrange that the size of cash payments to be made in the future (e.g. payments of pensions or of interest on a loan) should be in proportion to a specified *index number* especially, a *cost-of-living index*).

indexation. The practice, or an instance, of *indexing*.

index number. A number which shows the degree to which the quantities observed in a *time series* vary. One of the times for which observations were taken is selected as the 'base'. The simplest form of index number is then the observation for a particular date or period expressed as a percentage of the observation for the base. (This type of index number is called a 'relative'.) For example if a time series is:

year	1968	1969	1970	1971	1972	1973
observation	2000	2100	2200	2300	2400	2800

and 1968 is chosen as base then the relatives for the subsequent years are:

year	1969	1970	1971	1972	1973
relative	105	110	115	120	140

The percentage signs are usually omitted when writing index numbers and it is customary to indicate that 1968 is the base by writing '1968 = 100'.

More complicated forms of index number are needed to express the way the *average* [1] of a group of observations varies relative to a base. See *Laspeyres index*, *Paasche index*, *Fisher's ideal index*.

Index of Retail Prices. See *General Index of Retail Prices*.

indifference curve. A graph, all points on which represent combinations of quantities that are all considered equally valuable by a specified person.

indirect. An *indirect worker*.

indirect cost. A *cost* [2] of an expenditure on goods, services or labour used by, or benefiting, a number of activities, products or *cost centres* where the extent of the use for each individual purpose cannot easily be measured. *Also* a portion of such a cost that is associated with a particular activity, process or cost centre by means of *overhead absorption. Also* the total amount of such apportioned costs associated with a particular activity, product or cost centre. (Also called 'burden', 'burden cost', 'establishment expense', 'oncost' or 'overhead'.)

indirect expense. An *indirect cost* that relates to an *expenditure* by a firm on services or to the extent of *depreciation* [2] of *fixed assets*. (See *expense* [4].) *Also* a portion of such an expense that is associated with a particular activity, product or *cost centre* by means of *overhead absorption. Also* the total amount of such apportioned expense associated with a particular activity, product or cost centre.

indirect labour cost (spelt indirect labor cost in USA). A *labour cost* that relates to payment of an *indirect worker. Also* a portion of such a cost that is associated with a particular activity, product or *cost centre* by means of *overhead absorption. Also* the total amount of such apportioned costs associated with a particular activity, product or cost centre. (Also known as 'indirect wages'.)

indirect materials cost. An *indirect cost* that relates to an expenditure by a firm on *materials* or *supplies. Also* a portion of such a cost that is associated with a particular activity, product or *cost centre* by means of *overhead absorption. Also* the total amount of such apportioned costs associated with a particular activity, product or cost centre.

indirect rate. An *exchange rate* between the currencies of countries A and B is stated in 'indirect' form in country A if it is expressed as the number of units of country B's currency that are exchanged for 1 unit of A's currency. When two indirect rates are given in a quotation, the higher is the rate at which the foreign currency will be bought by the person making the quotation; the lower rate is the one at which he will sell the foreign currency. See also *direct rate.* (Also known as a 'currency rate'.)

indirect tax. 1. A tax levied in such a way that the person who pays it can subsequently recover the amount from someone else (the payer is said to 'shift' the tax). In the UK, the *excise duties* on the production of beer and spirits are examples of indirect taxes. 2. Synonym for *expenditure tax*.

indirect wages. Synonym for *indirect labour cost*.

indirect worker. An employee of a firm whose work does not directly contribute to the manufacture of one of the firm's products. (Also known as an 'indirect'.)

indorse. Variant spelling of *endorse* [1].

indorsee. Variant spelling of *endorsee*.

indorsement. Variant spelling of *endorsement* [1].

indorser. Variant spelling of *endorser* [1].

induction procedure (or induction programme or, in USA, induction program). Activities taking place when a new employee joins an organization of which the objectives are to acquaint the individual with the organization and his colleagues and to ensure that all the organization's records concerning the employee are complete.

industrial action. Action by employees that is intended to impede the activities of the firm they work for, or of another firm, as part of an *industrial dispute*.

Industrial Arbitration Board. A permanent body set up in 1919 as the Industrial Court and given its present name on 1 December 1971. Members of the Board are appointed by the Secretary of State for Employment and form three panels: one representing employers, one representing employees and a panel of independent persons. One of the independent persons is appointed President of the Board with the status of a High Court judge. The Secretary of State may refer an industrial dispute to the Board for settlement if both sides to the dispute agree and if any existing arrangements for settling disputes in their industry have failed. When hearing disputes the Board may co-opt expert assessors. The Board also hears claims reported to it by the Secretary of State under section 8 of the *Terms and Conditions of Employment Act 1959* and determines what amendments need to be made to collective agreements and wage structures for them to comply with the *Equal Pay Act 1970*.

Industrial Court. 1. Permanent court set up by the Industrial Courts Act 1919 and renamed *Industrial Arbitration Board* on 1

December 1971. 2. Synonym for *National Industrial Relations Court*.

Industrial Courts Act 1919. UK statute which made arrangements for settling industrial disputes. The Act: (1) established a permanent Industrial Court (now renamed the *Industrial Arbitration Board*); (2) authorizes the Secretary of State for Employment to appoint a court of inquiry to report to Parliament on any dispute; (3) authorizes the Secretary of State to appoint an arbitrator in any dispute so long as both sides to the dispute agree and the existing procedures for settling disputes in the industry concerned have failed.

industrial democracy. See *employee participation*.

industrial dispute. A dispute between, on one side, one or more employers or organizations of employers and, on the other side, one or more employees or organizations of employees. In British law the term *trade dispute* is used to describe such a dispute when it concerns certain matters defined by statute. 'Trade dispute' is also used to describe disputes between groups of employees, such as *demarcation disputes*.

industrial distributor. An *intermediary* that buys *industrial goods* from their manufacturers and sells them to users.

industrial engineering. Activity, process, or study of designing means of production (from whole factories to individual jobs) taking account of men, materials, tools and plant, in order to produce required quantities of a product to a specified design in the most satisfactory manner.

industrial goods. Goods that are normally bought for incorporation in, or to aid the production of, other goods or services. (Also known as 'producer goods'.)

industrial logistics. Study or management of all parts of an enterprise that are concerned with or directly affect the movement of *materials* and *work-in-progress* [2] and the distribution of *finished goods* to customers.

industrial market. The *market* [3] for goods and services that are bought by firms for incorporation in, or to aid the production of, other goods and services. (Also known as the 'producer market'.)

industrial market research. *Market research* concerned with the *market* [3] for *industrial goods*.

Industrial Participation Association. A voluntary non-profit-making association of individuals and firms concerned with research into, and practice of, *employee participation,* involvement and *motivation* at work. The association was founded in 1884 as the Labour Co-partnership Association (see *copartnership*), changed its name to Industrial Co-partnership Association in 1927 and adopted the present title in 1972. It offers an advisory service to firms that wish to introduce or extend participative practices and publishes the quarterly journal, *Industrial Participation.*

Address : 25/28 Buckingham Gate, London SW1 (01-828 8754).

industrial psychology. Synonym for *occupational psychology.*

industrial relations. 1. (Chiefly UK.) Relations between *trade unions* [1] and employers or between an employer and the unions representing his employees. 2. (Chiefly US.) Relations between employers and employees both as individuals ('employee relations') and as members of organized unions ('labor relations').

Industrial Relations Act 1971. A British statute which was intended to provide a comprehensive framework of law governing industrial relations. In particular it set up the *National Industrial Relations Court* and established a list of *unfair industrial practices* for which trade unions or employers could be sued for compensation. Most of the Act was brought into force between 1 October 1971 and 28 February 1972 but provoked bitter opposition from trade unions. It was eventually repealed by the *Trade Union and Labour Relations Act 1974* although some sections of the 1971 Act were never brought into use.

Industrial Relations Code of Practice. A document setting out practical advice for promoting good industrial relations, issued by the Secretary of State with the approval of Parliament initially under the *Industrial Relations Act 1971* and subsequently under the *Trade Union and Labour Relations Act 1974.* The code is not a set of laws that must be obeyed. However, evidence about whether or not the code was followed may be important in a legal dispute. The first version of the code came into effect on 28 February 1972.

Industrial Reorganisation Corporation (IRC). A *statutory corporation* [1] established in 1966 by the Industrial Reorganisation Corporation Act 1966 and dissolved in 1971 by the Industry Act 1971. Its objects were to promote or assist the reorganization or development of any industry in the UK and to establish, develop, promote or assist the establishment or development of any industrial enterprise. It acted rather like a *merchant bank*.

Industrial Society, The. An association of over 11 000 industrial and commercial companies, trade unions, employers' associations and nationalized industries which provides training and advice on industrial relations and personnel management. It organizes about 300 courses each year and has a wide range of advisory services backed up by exchanging information between members. It specializes in five fields: leadership, industrial relations, communication and involvement, conditions of employment and the development of young employees.

The society was founded in 1918 by Sir Robert Hyde and was originally called the Industrial Welfare Society.

Address : Robert Hyde House, 48 Bryanston Square, London W1H 8AH (01-262 2401).

Industrial Training Act 1964. UK statute which aims to provide industrial and commercial training for persons over the age of fifteen through the medium of *industrial training boards*.

industrial training board (ITB). One of the bodies set up by the Secretary of State for Employment to implement the *Industrial Training Act 1964*. Each board covers a particular industry (e.g. engineering). A board consists of an independent chairman and equal numbers of members representing employers and employees. An ITB has wide powers to establish whatever training facilities it feels necessary for its industry but must submit its plans for approval by the *Training Services Agency*. An ITB can raise money to provide training by means of a *training levy* on employers in its industry.

industrial tribunal. A tribunal—consisting of one member each from panels of lawyers, of persons representing employers' associations and of persons representing employees—that has

203

jurisdiction over a variety of disputes between employers and employees. Industrial tribunals hear disputes about: (1) the operation of the *Redundancy Payments Act 1965*; (2) *unfair dismissal*; (3) the operation of the *Contracts of Employment Act*; (4) the operation of the *Equal Pay Act 1970*; (5) the registration system for work in docks; (6) *training levy*.

In the past the tribunals have also dealt with disputes about *selective employment tax*.

An appeal from a decision of an industrial tribunal is usually heard by the High Court in England or the Court of Session in Scotland.

industrial union. A *trade union* [1] that will admit as members anyone who works in a particular *industry* [2].

industry. 1. The activities of processing or manufacturing goods on a large scale using extensive plant and equipment. 2. A class of firms that are sufficiently similar in their main activities or products to be grouped together for purposes of description, analysis or classification. (Sometimes called a 'trade'.)

inertia selling. Practice of delivering goods to people who have not ordered them and inviting them either to pay for the goods or to return them within a specified time. Unscrupulous practitioners hope that natural inertia will stop people from returning the goods within the imposed time-limit (whether they really want the goods or not) and will make threatening demands for payment. There are now severe legal controls on the practice in most countries.

in-firm training. Training that takes place on the premises of the employer of the trainees. (Also known as 'in-plant training'.)

inflation. A continuing increase in the general level of prices in an economy.

information retrieval. Activity or process of obtaining specific required information from a store of data.

information theory. The general mathematical theory of the transmission of information.

injunction. An order issued by a court that forbids a specified person from taking specified action.

in-plant training. Synonym for *in-firm training*.

input-output matrix (or table, or tableau). A table of figures describing the interdependence of industries in an economy. Each industry has a row and a column in the table and there is also a column for final consumption. An entry in the table, which is in the row for industry A and the column for industry B, represents the value of the part of industry A's output that is used as an input by industry B.

input tax. See *value added tax*.

inscribed stock. *Stock* [4] for which no certificate of ownership is issued; instead, the names of *stockholders* [1] are recorded (inscribed) on a register kept by the issuer.

insert. A printed *advertisement* that is included in a publication but is printed separately (often not by the printer of the rest of the publication) at the expense of the advertiser. It may be a 'bound-in insert' which is secured to the rest of the publication or a 'loose insert' which is not. (Also called a 'supplement'.)

insertion order. A formal order from an advertiser or an *advertising agency* to a publisher that the publisher should include a specified *advertisement* in a publication at a specified time.

in-service training. Training that is related to the trainee's current employment and takes place while the trainee is employed.

inside director. Synonym for *executive director*.

insider deal. A transaction in *securities* [1] of a company, carried out by someone (an 'insider') who has acquired information about the company, by virtue of his connection with the company (e.g. by being a senior employee or *director*), which is not generally available and will affect the price of the securities when it is generally known. For example, a sale by a director of his shares when he knows (but the general public does not) that his company has not achieved anticipated profits. Insider deals are generally regarded unfavourably. In the USA they are illegal; in the UK it is likely they will be soon.

insolvency. State of being *insolvent*.

insolvent. Unable, or having ceased, to pay debts as they fall due.

inspection. Comparison with a specification.

inspector of taxes. See *Her Majesty's inspector of taxes.*

Institute of Chartered Accountants in England and Wales.
A professional institute for accountants, formed in 1880 and incorporated by royal charter.

Associates (designated ACA) must have passed the institute's examinations and must have served under a training contract with a member of the institute who is practising as a public accountant in the UK. The duration of a training contract is 3 years for graduates but 4 years for trainees who have either 3 'A' level and 1 'O' level GCE passes or 2 'A' level and 3 'O' level passes.

A fellow (designated FCA) must have practised for 5 years as a public accountant or have been an associate of the institute for 10 years.

Fellows and associates are described as 'chartered accountants'. In March 1974 there were 27 820 fellows, 22 563 associates and 4291 retired members.

The institute enforces a strict code of professional conduct, provides technical guidance for members, conducts courses and conferences, and publishes books.

Address: Chartered Accountants' Hall, Moorgate Place, London EC2R 6EQ (01-628 7060).

Institute of Chartered Accountants of Scotland. Professional institute for accountants in Scotland founded in 1854. Members of the institute (designated CA) must have served under a training contract with a member of the institute in practice in the UK, must have attended the institute's training course and must have passed the institute's professional examination. Intending members who hold a Scottish Higher National Diploma in accounting must undertake a four-year training contract. Graduates must undertake a three-year training contract but may be required to follow a one-year full-time course in relevant subjects in addition.

The institute had 9095 members in December 1974. It publishes a monthly journal, *The Accountant's Magazine.*

Address: 27 Queen Street, Edinburgh EH2 1LA (031-225 3687).

Institute of Chartered Secretaries and Administrators.
A professional institute representing administrators in commerce, industry and the public service, including *company secretaries*, in the UK and the Commonwealth. The institute was founded in 1891 and granted a royal charter in 1902. It was called the Chartered Institute of Secretaries until 1970 when it took over the Corporation of Secretaries.

Associates of the institute (designated ACIS) must have passed the relevant examinations of the institute and have had 6 years (less in the case of graduates) practical experience.

Fellows of the institute (designated FCIS) must have passed the institute's examinations, have had at least 8 years experience and must have been, for at least 3 years, a company secretary or assistant secretary of a 'substantial company' or have held a position of equivalent status.

The institute holds an annual conference and organizes an extensive programme of meetings. It publishes a monthly journal, *Professional Administration*.

On 31 July 1973 there were 33 633 associates, 10 599 fellows and 698 licentiates (who have passed examinations but have not had the required experience).

Address: 16 Park Crescent, London W1N 4AH (01-580 4741).

Institute of Cost and Management Accountants. Professional institute founded in 1919, with 14 600 members in 1974.

Address: 63 Portland Place, London W1N 4AB (01-637 2311).

Institute of Export. British professional institute founded in 1935 (out of the British Export Society which was set up in 1924) to promote the study of activities concerned with exporting and international trade. The institute is a *guarantee company*.

Associate members (designated AMIEx) must be (or have been) rendering services to export. Members (designated MIEx) must hold positions of responsibility for management of some aspect of international trade. Graduate members (designated MIEX (Grad)) must have passed an examination set by the institute. Fellows (designated FIEx) must have published a thesis on some aspect of exporting or must have been graduate

207

members for 15 years.

The institute has nearly 5000 members. It publishes the monthly journal, *Export*, and organizes courses, conferences and meetings on exporting.

Address : World Trade Centre, London E1 9AA (01-790 7979).

Institute of Management Consultants. UK professional body for *management consultants* founded in 1962. It sets ethical standards for the practice of management consulting including a 'code of professional conduct'.

Associates of the institute must be at least 25 and have served satisfactorily for not less than 6 months in the public practice of management consulting. Members (designated MIMC) must be at least 30, have been an associate for at least 3 years and practised management consulting during that time, and must demonstrate satisfactory knowledge. Fellows (designated FIMC) must have served with distinction or gained a position of considerable responsibility in the public practice of management consulting after at least 7 years as a member of the institute. In December 1974 there were 256 associates, 1957 members and 158 fellows.

The institute publishes a quarterly journal and a newsletter, and holds professional meetings.

Address : 23/24 Cromwell Place, London SW7 2LG (01-584 7285).

Institute of Management Sciences, The. See *The Institute of Management Sciences.*

Institute of Marketing (IM). British professional institute for marketers founded in 1911 to develop the body of knowledge about marketing and to make the principles and practices of marketing more widely known and effectively used throughout industry.

Graduate members (designated GInstM) must have passed the institute's examination for the Diploma in Marketing or have an equivalent qualification.

Members (designated MInstM) must have had two years' practical experience of marketing in a senior-management position or must be graduate members with one year's experience.

In November 1974 the institute had 2190 graduate members and a total of 17 700 members in all grades.

The institute provides marketing information and professional services to members, runs residential courses and seminars and administers the examinations for the Diploma in Marketing (for which 16 000 people were studying in 1974).

Address : Moor Hall, Cookham, Berkshire SL6 9QH (Bourne End 24922).

Institute of Personnel Management (IPM). British professional institute for personnel managers founded in 1913. Since 1 January 1975, membership is by experience and examination only.

The development of formal training for personnel specialists has always been an important part of the institute's work. A network of personnel management training facilities has been built up in conjunction with universities and polytechnics. IPM sponsors the monthly magazine, *Personnel Management,* organizes a comprehensive programme of courses and conferences and publishes a regular series of books, reports and surveys.

The institute has over 17 000 members.

Address: Central House, Upper Woburn Place, London WC1H 0HX (01-387 2844).

Institute of Scientific Business (ISB). A British professional institute founded in 1963 which aims to assist in the development of management as a recognized profession with a scientific foundation and accepted standards of qualifications and ethics.

Associate members (designated AIScB) must have a degree in management studies or a degree plus a postgraduate qualification in management. Fellows (designated FIScB) must be at least 28 and have submitted a dissertation, or have a higher degree in management research, or have rendered outstanding service to the profession of management or the advancement of management science. Other grades of membership are affiliates and companions.

The institute sponsors a quarterly journal, *Management Decision,* and organizes conferences on management science.

Address: 200 Keighley Road, Bradford, Yorkshire, BD9 4JZ (Bradford 43823).

institutional advertising. *Advertising* that is intended to create a favourable estimation of the advertiser rather than of any particular product of the advertiser. (Also called 'corporate advertising'.)

institutional brand preference. Regular choice by a consumer of differing products carrying the same *house mark*.

institutionalization. The establishment of unvarying or standard rules of social behaviour.

institution for collective investment. Synonym for *collective investment institution*.

Institution of Works Managers. A British professional institute of which the objectives are: (1) to increase industrial productivity by developing and raising the standards of industrial management; (2) to promote management education in industry by the provision of training and examination facilities, and by awarding certificates and diplomas of competence in industrial management; (3) to encourage and conduct research into the application of industrial management techniques.

Membership of the institution is in four grades: student, associate (designated AIWM), member (designated MIWM), fellow (designated FIWM).

The institution organizes conferences, seminars and training courses. It publishes a journal, *Works Management*, 12 times a year.

Membership of the institution in April 1974 was: 6029 students, 4823 associates, 5761 members and 1401 fellows.

The institution was founded in 1947 by the amalgamation of the British Works Management Association (founded 1931) and the Institute of Factory Managers (founded 1938).

Address: 45 Cardiff Road, Luton, Bedfordshire LU1 1RQ (Luton 37071).

in-store promotion. A form of *sales promotion* in which a special display or facilities for sampling or demonstrating a product are arranged in a particular retail establishment.

instrument. 1. A document intended to have a specific legal effect, e.g. a written *contract*, a *financial instrument* or a *Statutory Instrument*. 2. A device for measuring or testing either physical or mental attributes (e.g. a *questionnaire* or an *achievement test*).

instrumental. Serving as a means, or tool, for achieving some objective.

instrumentality. 1. The quality or state of serving as a means, or tool for achieving some objective. 2. The degree to which something may be used as a means or tool for achieving some objective.

insurance. Transference of risk to someone else, especially by means of a *contract of insurance*. (Sometimes called 'assurance'.)

insurance broker. A person who finds *insurers* for his clients and attempts to negotiate *contracts of insurance* for clients on the best possible terms.

insurance policy. A document setting out the terms of a *contract of insurance*.

insured. Synonym for *assured*.

insurer. A person (usually a *corporation*) that promises to pay compensation to an *assured*, under the terms of a *contract of insurance*, if a specified event occurs.

intangible asset. Something that is owned by a specified person or firm, is useful and will be useful for some time, can be assigned a value on the basis of its usefulness, but has no physical form. E.g., *patent rights, know-how, goodwill*.

intangible property. A right to ownership of a specified benefit that is not a right to possession of an item of *tangible property*. E.g. a debt, a *share* in a company, *patent rights*. (Also known as a 'chose in action' or a 'thing in action'.) *Also* a collection of such property.

integer programming. Techniques of *mathematical programming* that are applied when only whole numbers ('integers') can be given as solutions (i.e. the decision variables can have only integer values).

inter-bank loan. A loan from one bank to another for a fixed period, from overnight to 12 months.

intercompany comparison. Synonym for *interfirm comparison*.

interest. Payment made for borrowing or using someone else's money that is related to the amount of money and the time for

estoppel. An absolute prohibition, imposed by law, on a person denying the truth of a particular statement he made.

Euratom. Abbreviated title of the *European Atomic Energy Community*.

Eurco. An artificial *unit of account* used occasionally for representing the nominal value of securities. 1 Eurco is equal to DM0.90 + FF1.20 + £0.075 + L80 + Fl0.3 + FB4.50 + DKr0.20 + I£0.006 + FLux0.50. Officials of the Luxembourg stock exchange calculate the value of the Eurco daily in terms of the ingredient currencies, and also in terms of the US dollar, by using the exchange rates at specified times of the day.

Euro- (prefix). Of, or relating to the *external currency market*. As in 'Euro-currency' (a currency which is lent and borrowed in the external currency market), 'Euro-dollar' (a US dollar lent and borrowed in the external currency market) and 'Euro-bank' (a bank that takes *deposits* [1] reckoned in Euro-currencies).

Europäische Vereinigung für Personalfragen (EVP). German title of the *European Association for Personnel Management*.

Europäischer Gewerkschaftsbund. German title of the *European Trade Union Confederation*.

European Association for Personnel Management (EAPM). An international association of national societies of personnel managers in Europe. EAPM was founded in 1962 and now has 14 national societies as members. Among its objectives are: (1) to disseminate knowledge and information concerning the personnel function of management; (2) to establish and maintain professional standards; (3) to establish an organization representative of personnel management in Europe. It holds an international conference once every two years.

The UK member of EAPM is the *Institute of Personnel Management*.

Address: c/o D. Perret, Directeur du Personnel, Clin-Byla, 20 rue des Fossés-St-Jacques, Paris 5, France.

Also known by its French and German titles: Association européenne pour la direction de personnel (AEDP) and

145

which it is borrowed.

interest arbitrage. *Arbitrage* that consists of taking advantage of discrepancies in interest rates by borrowing at a low rate and lending at a higher rate.

interface activity. An *activity* that is common to two or more *activity-on-node networks*.

interface event. An *event* that is common to two or more *activity-on-arrow networks*.

interfirm comparison. Comparison, usually by means of *ratio analysis*, of the performance of several similar firms. The comparison is made by an independent organization (e.g. a *trade association* or an *economic development committee*) to ensure that confidential information about one firm is not revealed to others. (Also known as 'intercompany comparison'.)

interim dividend. A *dividend* [2] paid by a company before its *financial year* has ended with the intention that another dividend will be paid at the end of the financial year (*a final dividend*).

intermediary. A firm that is engaged in the *distribution* [1] of goods. An intermediary may take possession and ownership of a product (as most *retailers* and *wholesalers* do) or possession only (as an *agent* does) or may simply arrange transactions (as a *broker* does). The term is not used to refer to firms concerned only with transporting goods. (Also known as a 'middleman'.)

intermediate area. An area of the UK designated by the Secretary of State in which enterprises may be given government assistance but not to the same extent as in *development areas*. *Regional development grants* are given only for buildings in intermediate areas.

intermittent production. Synonym for *batch production*.

internal audit. An *audit* (of its accounts or of one of its activities) performed by employees of a firm who report to senior management.

internal rate of return (IRR). The 'discount rate' (see *present value*) at which the *net present value* of a project is zero. (Sometimes called the 'yield', or 'yield rate' or 'investment rate' or 'earning power' of the project.)

internal relativity. A *relativity* between the remuneration of different groups of workers with the same employer.

international accountant. An associate or fellow of the *Association of International Accountants*.

International Bank for Reconstruction and Development (IBRD). An international organization established on 27 December 1945 in accordance with an agreement reached by the Bretton Woods conference (see *International Monetary Fund*). IBRD's objective is to assist the economic development of member nations by making loans, in cases where private capital is not available, to finance productive investment. Loans are made only to governments or to private firms with government guarantee. IBRD has obtained most of its funds by issuing *securities* [1] but it also uses *contributed capital* from member nations. A country can be a member of IBRD only if it is a member of the International Monetary Fund. Membership reached 123 in July 1973 when the Bahamas joined. The only socialist countries that have joined are Romania and Yugoslavia. (Also known as the 'World Bank'. The word 'reconstruction' is in the title because its primary objective at first was the reconstruction of industry following the Second World War.)

international company. Synonym for *multinational company*.

International Confederation of Free Trade Unions (ICFTU). An international association, formed in 1949, of national federations of trade unions. ICFTU has 119 member organizations (in 88 countries) to which 48 million workers are affiliated. Member organizations must be free from outside domination and must have democratically elected leaders. The ICFTU supreme authority is its congress, which meets every 3 years and elects an executive board, which meets at least twice a year and elects the president and vice-presidents.

The 8 basic aims of ICFTU are: (1) to promote the interests of working people everywhere; (2) to work for rising living standards and full employment; (3) to reduce the gap between rich and poor, within and between nations; (4) to work for international understanding, disarmament and the establishment of peace; (5) to help to organize the workers and secure union negotiation as free bargaining agents; (6) to support the right to

213

democratic elections; (7) to fight against oppression and discrimination; (8) to defend human and trade-union rights.

Address: 37–41 rue Montagne aux Herbes Potagères, Bruxelles 1000, Belgium (217.80.85).

International Council for Scientific Management. English title of *Conseil international pour l'organisation scientifique.*

International Development Association (IDA). An international organization established in 1960 to supplement the work of the *International Bank for Reconstruction and Development* by providing finance on generous terms to the poorest countries of the world. Membership reached 112 in February 1973 when Oman joined.

International Finance Corporation (IFC). An international organization established in 1956 to supplement the work of the *International Bank for Reconstruction and Development.* IFC invests in private firms without government guarantees. Its membership reached 98 in February 1973 when Oman joined.

International Labour Office (ILO). Permanent establishment in Geneva, run by the *International Labour Organisation.* The office is responsible for running a very large programme of assistance—particularly technical and vocational training—for developing countries. It is also the most important source of information and statistics on worldwide working conditions.

International Labour Organisation (ILO). International organization established in 1919, along with the League of Nations, at the end of the First World War to be an instrument for promoting peace by improving the conditions of working life throughout the world.

In January 1972 membership of ILO consisted of 120 nations. Each nation is represented by 6 delegates to an annual general conference. 2 delegates represent government, 2 represent employers and 2 represent employees. (The employers' and employees' representatives are nominated by governments, which promise to consult representative organizations before making the appointments.) Each delegate has 1 vote. This tripartite structure is repeated in the 'governing body' of 48 (24 represent government—10 of them appointed by the 10

214

'members of chief industrial importance'— 12 represent employers and are elected by the employers' delegates to the general conference—12 represent employees and are elected by the workers' delegates).

The governing body appoints a director-general to run the *International Labour Office* in Geneva. The organization's formal method of securing improved working conditions is to prepare draft international conventions. When these are approved by the annual conference they must, in theory, be ratified and acted on by member states within 18 months. The educational and informative work of the International Labour Office is also of great importance in furthering the ILO's objectives.

International Monetary Fund (IMF). An organization established by an international treaty drafted at the United Nations Monetary and Finance Conference held at Bretton Woods, New Hampshire in 1944. The treaty came into force on 27 December 1945 when the IMF had 22 member countries; membership reached 126 in July 1973 when the Bahamas joined. The most important nonmembers are socialist countries (except Romania and Yugoslavia) which regard the Fund as a puppet of the US government, and Switzerland. The Fund's objective is to facilitate *international settlements* by: (1) stabilizing *exchange rates*; (2) reducing *exchange controls* on payments for *current transactions*; (3) making foreign currency or gold available to any member country to enable it to finance a temporary deficit on the *current account* [2] of its *balance of payments*. The currency and gold that the Fund can supply to members is obtained from them as subscriptions; the size of a member's subscription is determined by its 'quota' which depends on the size of its *reserve assets*, volume of foreign trade and national income. The Fund has a board of governors (one appointed by each member) which meets annually. Day-to-day management is entrusted to executive directors (some appointed by members with large quotas, others elected by the members) who appoint a managing director. (See also *special drawing right.*)

International Organisation of Employers (IOE). An international association of national employers' federations. A member of the IOE must be a free and independent voluntary association of employers in one country which: (1) is not subject to control or interference of any kind from any governmental authority or any outside body; (2) stands for and defends the principles of free enterprise. The most important work of the IOE is in connection with the *International Labour Organisation*. It acts as secretariat to the employer groups at almost all ILO meetings. IOE acts as a permanent liasion body for the exchange of views and experience among employers throughout the world. It was founded in 1920 and now has 90 members representing 81 countries. The UK member is the *Confederation of British Industry*.

Address: 98 rue de Saint-Jean, 1201 Genève, Switzerland (31 73 50).

international settlement. A payment of money by one country to another or by a resident of one country to a nonresident.

International Standard Classification of Occupations (ISCO). A systematic classification of *occupations* [1] followed throughout the world which has been prepared by the *International Labour Office*. Each occupation is described and given a number. The *occupational titles* are claimed to be 'those in common English use'. The current version of ISCO was published by the ILO in 1968.

international trade federation. An international association of national trade unions within a specific industry or occupation formed under the auspices of the *World Confederation of Labour* (cf. *international trade secretariat, trade union international*). There are 12 such federations.

International Trade Organization. An international organization which was to have been set up, under the auspices of the United Nations, in accordance with an international treaty, called the Havana Charter, signed in 1948. The organization was to have regulated international trade and would have complemented the work of the *International Monetary Fund.* However, it became clear that the USA would not join and the proposal was eventually abandoned. The *General Agreement on Tariffs and Trade* was signed as an interim measure pending agreement on

216

the International Trade Organization. (See also, *Organization for Trade Cooperation.*)

international trade secretariat (ITS). An international organization representing national trade unions in a particular industry and associated with the *International Confederation of Free Trade Unions.*

international union. An American union that has members in countries other than the USA (usually Canada, Mexico or Central America).

interquartile range. The difference between the first and third *quartiles* [2] of a *frequency distribution.*

interview (noun). Formal face-to-face meeting between people in which one person supplies information to another or others. Especially: (1) so that a person's suitability for a job can be assessed (*selection interview*); (2) so that one person can present a complaint (*grievance interview*); (3) so that a person's progress can be assessed (*appraisal interview*).

interview (verb). To meet with someone and ask him questions in an *interview.*

intestacy. Condition or state of dying without having made a will.

intestate (adjective). Of a person: not having made a will. Of things: not disposed of by will.

intestate (noun). A person who died *intestate.*

in transitu. On the way.

in-tray exercise. A training exercise in which the trainee is given a bundle of correspondence and asked to deal with it as if he were the person to whom it is addressed. The bundle represents the in-tray of a fictitious manager whose duties and position in a fictitious organization are explained to the trainee. The trainee is expected to take whatever action he considers appropriate, such as immediate reply, request for further information, or delegation. A time-limit is usually set for the exercise which is followed by discussion and evaluation with a trainer. (Also known as an 'in-basket test'.)

introduction. *Listing* of a *company* on a *stock exchange* [1] without the company issuing new shares (as in a *prospectus*

217

issue or *offer by tender*) and without an *offer for sale* of a large block of existing shares. Usually the company is already listed on another stock exchange and the new listing simply provides an opportunity for its shares to be traded in a different centre.

inventory. 1. (Chiefly US.) A quantity of something that is kept or stored for use as the need arises; especially quantities of *materials, goods-in-process, finished goods* and *supplies*. (In the UK, *stock* [1] is used in this sense.) 2. A detailed list of goods or articles in a particular place or of the *assets* [1] of someone. 3. A *stocktaking*.

inventory control. (Chiefly US.) *Stock control*.

inventory level. Synonym for *stock level*.

inventory turnover. Synonym for *stock turnover*.

invest. To make an *investment*; or habitually to make investments.

investment. An act, or the activity of, giving up a benefit presently enjoyed (usually, handing over cash) in order to gain a benefit in the future. *Specifically*: (1) purchasing *securities* [1]; (2) purchasing *capital goods* or *fixed assets*. *Also* the thing acquired (e.g. a security or a fixed asset) during this process. *Also* the value of the benefit given up (e.g. the amount of cash paid for a security or fixed asset).

investment bank (chiefly US). An *issuing house*.

investment company. Synonym for *investment trust*.

investment currency. Foreign currency that has been acquired by a UK resident by selling foreign-currency *securities* [1] (i.e. securities that were originally issued in exchange for foreign currency). Under *exchange-control* regulations UK residents may use only investment currency for purchasing foreign-currency securities. For convenience, the value of investment currency is always expressed in US dollars.

investment grant. A cash sum, which it was possible for a UK firm to receive from the Department of Trade and Industry, to help pay for new machinery and equipment. Investment grants of between 20 and 45% of the cost of the equipment were given in respect of expenditure incurred between 17 January 1966 and 26 October 1970.

investment income. For the purposes of UK *income tax*,

investment income is any income that is not *earned income*. Investment income beyond a certain amount (fixed at £2000 a year by the Finance Act 1972) is subject to an additional tax (currently 15%).

investment project (or project). An opportunity or proposal for *investment* (i.e. for giving up a presently enjoyed benefit in order to receive a future benefit).

investment rate. Synonym for *internal rate of return*.

investment surcharge. An additional charge of *income tax* (set by the Finance Act 1972 at 15%) on *investment income* above a certain figure (fixed at £2000 by the 1972 act).

investment trust. A *collective investment institution* organized as a *limited company*. Only a few of the earliest investment trusts were organized as *trusts* [1] (like a modern *unit trust*) but the name survived because it implied a prudence and solidity that attracted small investors. (Also known as an 'investment company'.)

invisible (or invisible transaction). A sale, by a resident of one country to a nonresident, of services (rather than goods)—e.g., insurance, carriage of goods, accommodation for tourists—or *intangible assets*—e.g. patent *licences* [2]. For the buyer's country, such a transaction is an 'invisible import'; for the seller's country it is an 'invisible export'.

invoice (noun). A detailed list of goods supplied or services performed with a statement of their value or the charge made for them.

invoice (verb). To prepare an *invoice* relating to some transaction.

Irish Management Institute (IMI). An institute founded in 1952 with the objective of raising the general level of management in Ireland. It is owned by its members and governed by them through an elected executive committee and council.

There are three categories of membership: personal, associate and corporate. Personal membership is open to practising managers. Associate membership is open to individuals who have an interest in management development but are not practising managers. Corporate membership is for corporations.

The activities of the IMI include: (1) management development programmes; (2) consultancy; (3) training; (4) research and

219

development; (5) membership services. It publishes a monthly magazine, *Management*.

In 1974 the institute had 1465 personal members, 110 associate members and 1012 corporate members.

Also known by its Irish title 'Foras Bainistíochta na hÉireann.

Address : Sandyford Road, Dublin 14, Irish Republic (Dublin 983911).

ironclad. Synonym for *yellow-dog contract*.

irredeemable. Not *redeemable*. Used to describe a *security* [1] when the *issuer* has no right to require the holder to surrender the security—either at a fixed time or at the issuer's option— and the holder has no right to require redemption of the security apart from exceptional circumstances—e.g. if the issuer goes into *liquidation* [2].

irrevocable credit. See *documentary credit*.

island. 1. A separate display of particular goods in a shop. 2. A *display advertisement* that is completely surrounded by the text of the publication in which it is printed.

issue (noun). A block of *securities* [1] that were *issued* [2] at the same time and all carry the same rights.

issue (verb). 1. To be an *issuer* of a *security* [1]. 2. To come into existence as a *security* [1].

issued share capital (or issued capital). The *nominal value* of all the *shares* in a *company* [1] that are in existence. (Note that this may not be the same as the *paid-up capital*.)

issue price. The price at which a *security* [1] is sold by its *issuer*.

issuer. The *corporation,* or government or individual, over which rights are given (in exchange for money or other valuable consideration) by a *security* [1].

issuing house (chiefly UK). A firm of which the main activity is to arrange *public offers* of *securities* [1]. An issuing house normally buys the securities from their *issuer* and then resells them at a profit. (Usually called an 'investment bank' in the USA.)

j

JIC. Abbreviation of *joint industrial council.*

JIT. Abbreviation of *job instruction training.*

JMT. Abbreviation of *job method training.*

job (noun). 1. The collection of tasks, duties and assignments that an employee is employed to perform. 2. A piece of work. A single item of work, complete in itself, performed by a person, or by an organization or by a machine (especially, a computer); especially, a piece of work that is separately identified for purposes of accounting, costing, *work study* or paying wages.

job (verb). 1. To do small pieces of work for a variety of customers. 2. To buy and sell *securities* [1] as a *jobber* [2].

job analysis. Activity or process of examining a *job* [1] in order to prepare a *job description* and/or a *job specification.*

jobber. 1. A *wholesaler.* 2. A person or firm that buys and sells *securities* [1] (especially on the *Stock Exchange* [2]) taking ownership and possession of them as opposed to a stockbroker who arranges purchases and sales as an *agent* for others and never takes ownership. (Also called a 'stockjobber'.)

jobber's turn. The difference between the prices quoted by a *jobber* [2] for buying and for selling *securities* [1]; it represents the jobber's possible gross profit if his prices are accepted by buyers and sellers.

221

Jobcentre. Name given to some of its *employment offices* by the *Employment Service Agency*.

job costing. Practice or activity of allocating *costs* [2] to specific *jobs* [2] or items of production.

job cycle. The complete sequence of operations that a worker has to perform in order to complete a unit of his output.

job description. A statement of the purpose, scope, organizational relationships, responsibilities and tasks which constitute a particular *job* [1].

job design. Process, or activity, of deciding on the tasks and responsibilities to be included in a particular job and of deciding on the methods to be used for carrying out those tasks.

job enlargement. 1. Training and encouraging employees to perform a range of jobs related to the ones they hold so that manpower can be used more flexibly. 2. Assigning additional tasks to an employee in order to make his job more varied and interesting.

job enrichment. Changing features of a job other than *compensation* [1], physical working conditions and the essential tasks of the job in order to increase the *job satisfaction* of the person performing it.

job evaluation. Establishment of the relative worth of a number of *jobs* [1] (not employees) in an organization by considering, for example, their complexity, the amount of training or experience required, how much the organization would suffer if they were done badly and so on.

job factor. An identifiable, measurable requirement that a *job holder* must contribute, assume or endure in a specified job (e.g. skill, responsibility, effort, working conditions).

job holder. The person who is employed in a specified *position* in an organization.

job improvement plan. Part of a *management guide* which lists the tasks a manager has agreed with his boss that he will carry out by a stated date.

job instruction training (JIT). A training programme, originally developed as part of *training within industry* (TWI), in which trainees are taught how to instruct other people to perform simple industrial tasks. In the current UK version of TWI, this programme is known as 'job instruction and communication'.

job method. Method of performing a piece of work.

job method training (JMT). A training programme, orginally developed as part of *training within industry* (TWI), which provides trainees with an introduction to *method study*. In the current UK version of TWI, this programme is known as 'job methods'.

job relations. One of the programmes in *training within industry*. It is designed to provide an understanding of human relationships with particular emphasis on the prevention of problems and effective handling of problems that do arise.

job rotation. Transferring an employee from one job to another at a similar level in an organization in order to give him experience before promotion.

job safety. One of the programmes in *training within industry*. It is designed to create the right attitude of mind towards accident prevention.

job satisfaction. The gratification (in the sense of mental pleasure following from the satisfaction of needs, desires or hopes) that a person derives from the job that he is employed to perform.

job security. Any form of promise to, or belief by, a person that there is a low probability that his employment in a particular job will be ended.

job sheet. Form used by a worker to record the jobs he has been engaged on, the quantities produced and the time spent on each. (Also known as a 'time sheet'.)

job shopper. A person who is continually looking for a new job and changes jobs frequently so as to gain small increases in pay.

job specification. A description of the personal characteristics required for performing a *job* [1]. A job specification normally states the type of employee required for a job, in terms of skill, experience and special aptitudes, and summarizes the working conditions found in the job.

job ticket. A document used to instruct a worker to perform a particular operation on specified pieces of work. It is usually returned by the worker to signify that the operation is complete, often with a statement of time spent from which wages or costs may be calculated. (Also called a 'work ticket'.)

job title. The name given to a particular *job* [1].

joint consultation. Discussion between the representatives of *management* and the employees of an enterprise of matters of common interest, especially the way that plans for the future of the enterprise will affect its employees. Matters that are normally the subject of negotiation between trade unions and employers (such as pay and conditions) are normally excluded from joint consultation.

joint consultative comittee. A committee established for the purposes of *joint consultation*.

joint consultative machinery. Institutions and procedures that enable regular *joint consultation* to take place.

joint cost. A *cost* [2] incurred in manufacturing *joint products* before they are individually recognizable.

joint industrial council (JIC). A voluntarily established permanent body for the consideration of terms and conditions of employment in a particular industry or sector of an industry. A JIC is made up of equal numbers of representatives of employers and employees.

joint probability. The *probability* that two outcomes will both occur together.

joint product. Products that a manufacturer produces from the same initial materials and where some operations are performed before the products are individually recognizable.

joint product offer. A form of *sales promotion* in which consumers are offered a *banded pack* of two or more different products from the same or from different manufacturers, at a reduced price.

joint-stock bank. A British *deposit bank*. (Such banks were usually *joint-stock companies*, in the early nineteenth century, unlike *merchant banks* which were usually *partnerships*. Both types of bank are now always *limited companies* but the distinguishing name has survived.)

joint-stock company. A trading organization whose *capital* (or 'stock') was supplied by a number of investors who appointed 'directors' or 'governors' to manage the business. This form of organizing business originated in the sixteenth century (with the Muscovy Company) and is the forerunner of the modern *limited company*. The name persists in the phrase *joint-stock bank*.

joint venture. A business activity undertaken jointly by two or more firms that are otherwise independent.

joint works committee. A committee of representatives of workers and management in a factory who meet to discuss matters of common interest.

journal. A list of financial transactions recorded in the order in which they occur and without the detailed analysis and classification found in a *ledger*, which is compiled from the entries in journals. (Also known as a 'daybook'.)

journeyman. A *craftsman* who, having finished his period of *apprenticeship*, works for wages (originally computed daily—*i.e.* per 'journey'.)

judgment creditor. A person who is entitled to be paid a *judgment debt*.

judgment debt. A sum of money which a court has ordered to be paid. The person who must pay it is a 'judgment debtor' and the person to whom the money is due is a 'judgment creditor'.

judgment debtor. A person who has been ordered to pay a *judgment debt*.

junior board. A committee of people in a company below the status of *top management* (often trainee managers) which meets like a *board of directors*, reviews the progress and plans of the company and makes recommendations to top management.

junior subordinated debenture. See *subordinated debenture*.

k

kangaroo court. A mock court in which the principles of law and justice are ignored.

Kennedy round. A series of negotiations, from 4 May 1964 to 30 June 1967, on extensive reductions of *import duties,* involving all major trading nations of the world within the framework of the *General Agreement on Tariffs and Trade.* The impetus for the negotiation came from President John F. Kennedy who asked Congress to pass the Trade Expansion Act in 1962 which authorized the necessary cuts in US import duties.

key. 1. A symbol on a *coupon* [3] in an *advertisement* that identifies the place where the advertisement appeared. 2. One or more characters that are used to identify a unit of data or a single *record.* (Also called a 'label'.)

key area (or key result area). See *key results analysis* [1]

key event. Synonym for *milestone.*

key results analysis. 1. Activity of identifying the areas (usually 5–8 of them) of a manager's job that are crucial to the success of the job in the organization ('key areas' or 'key result areas') and of quantifying the results that the manager must achieve in each area. *Also* a record of such an analysis. 2. Activity of identifying the objectives that it is crucial for an organization to achieve. *Also* a record of such an analysis.

keyword. The word in the title of a book or article or other piece of information which is selected as best characterizing the contents of the item and is therefore used to index it in certain kinds of information retrieval system. Thus a book called *Making the Most of Metrication* would be indexed under 'metrication' in a keyword index.

kickback. Part of a person's payment for doing a job that he gives to someone else for getting him the job.

kinaesthesia (or kinaesthesis). (Spelt kinesthesia or kinesthesis in USA.) Synonym for *kinaesthetic sense*.

kinaesthetic sense (kinesthetic sense in USA). The nervous mechanism that provides information about the position of parts of an animal's own body and about the pressures being exerted by those parts. (Also known as 'kinaesthesia' or 'kinaesthesis'.)

kind. Goods or commodities as opposed to money. (As in 'payment in kind'.)

kit. 1. The parts needed to make an *assembly* [1]. 2. A collection of duplicated or printed documents, brochures and so on given to delegates to a conference or to journalists (a 'press kit').

kite. 1. An *accommodation bill*. 2. A *cheque* drawn by someone who knows there is no money in the bank *account* [3] he is drawing on.

Knights of Labor. An American trade union formed in 1869, originally as a secret society with oaths and religious trappings called the Noble and Holy Order of the Knights of Labor. 'Noble and Holy' was dropped from the name in 1881 when the union began to dominate the American labour movement. It had 702 924 members in 1886. Its aim was to be a single union for all workers, regardless of type of employment, nationality or sex (equal pay for women was one of its earliest demands). However, it declined rapidly in the face of opposition from employers and the growth of *craft unions*. It was formally dissolved in 1917.

knock-for-knock agreement. An agreement between *insurers* that whenever a vehicle insured by one of them is involved in an accident with a vehicle insured by the other then each insurer will pay for the damage to the vehicle he has insured. This procedure is adopted—instead of the normal one in which an insurer (exercising his right of *subrogation*) pursues a claim for *damages* against the person alleged to have caused the accident—in order to simplify settlement of claims.

knocking copy. *Copy* in an *advertisement* which directly, or by implication, discredits a competitive product.

know-how. Knowledge of the techniques or practical details that enable a process or operation to be carried out efficiently.

know-how agreement. An agreement by which the possessor of *know-how* promises to disclose it to someone else. When the disclosure is made to enable the other person to perform his own research or to evaluate the usefulness of the know-how, the agreement is called a 'secrecy agreement'. When the disclosure is made so that the other can use it in commercial production, the agreement is called a 'know-how licence'.

know-how licence. See *know-how agreement*.

kurtosis. The degree to which a *frequency curve*, *frequency diagram* or *frequency polygon* has a high central peak. Also a *statistic* [1] that measures kurtosis.

LicBAA. Abbreviation of 'licentiate of the British Association of Accountants and Auditors' (see *British Association of Accountants and Auditors*.

LME. Abbreviation of *London Metal Exchange*.

LOB. 1. Abbreviation of *line of balance*. 2. Abbreviation of *Location of Offices Bureau*.

LOB diagram. Abbreviation of *line-of-balance diagram*.

LOB network. Abbreviation of *line-of-balance network*.

LP. Abbreviation of *linear programming*.

LPA. Abbreviation of 'Local Productivity Association' (see *British Productivity Council*.

L.S. Abbreviation of *locus sigilli*—i.e. the place of the seal—used on a copy or printed reproduction of a document to indicate that a *seal* was attached to the original in order to authenticate it.

Ltd. Abbreviation of *Limited*.

label. 1. A slip (e.g. of paper or cloth) attached to something and carrying indentifying information—especially, one that identifies a producer of goods. Extended to be a synonym for *brand*. 2. Synonym for *key* [2].

laboratory training. Synonym for *group dynamics training*.

labor cost. US spelling of *labour cost*.

labor exchange. US spelling of *labour exchange*.

labor force. US spelling of *labour force*.

labor law. US spelling of *labour law*.

labor market. US spelling of *labour market*.

labor mobility. US spelling of *labour mobility*.

labor-only subcontracting. US spelling of *labour-only subcontracting*.

labor organization. (Chiefly US.) Synonym for *trade union* [1].

Labor Reform Law. Popular name for the US Labor-Management Reporting and Disclosure Act 1959. Among other things this lays down minimum standards for the conduct of union affairs and requires unions to file annual financial reports. (Also known as the Landrum-Griffin Act.)

labor relations. (Chiefly US.) Relations between *trade unions* [1] and employers, or between an employer and the unions representing his employees. (Usually called 'industrial relations' in the UK.)

labor stability index. US spelling of *labour stability index*.

labor turnover. US spelling of *labour turnover*.

labour cost (spelt labor cost in USA). A *cost* [2] that relates to an *expenditure* on *remuneration* for employees. *Also* the total of such costs associated with a particular activity, product or *cost centre*, or over a particular period.

labour exchange (spelt labor exchange in USA). (Now obsolete.) Synonym for *employment office*.

labour force (spelt labor force in USA). 1. The people in an economy who are available to perform work. 2. The collection of people who perform the work of an organization.

labour law (spelt labor law in USA). The law concerning relationships between employers and employees—covering, among other things, standards for working conditions, conduct of industrial relations, payment of wages and the respective rights and duties of employers and employees.

labour market (spelt labor market in USA). The *market* [1] for labour in a particular area: the available workers, the firms that wish to employ them and the kinds of contracts they enter into (including rates of pay).

labour mobility (spelt labor mobility in the USA). Movement of workers from job to job.

230

labour-only subcontracting (spelt labor-only subcontracting in the USA). Practice of employing people under a *contract for services* in circumstances where a *contract of employment* would be more appropriate. The workers do not provide any of their own tools or equipment (thus the contract is for 'labour only') and claim to be self-employed. The worker does not have income tax or social security payments deducted from his wages because these deductions are only made for people who work under a contract of employment. Wages are, therefore, paid as a lump sum—hence the popular name of 'the lump' for the arrangement.

labour stability index (spelt labor stability index in the USA). Ratio of the number of employees of a firm who have been employed by that firm for one year or more at a specified date to the total number of employees one year before the specified date.

labour turnover (spelt labor turnover in the USA). The rate at which employees leave an organization. Usually measured by the ratio:

$$\frac{\text{number of employees leaving during a year}}{\text{average number of employees during that year}}$$

(Also known as 'manpower turnover'.)

laches. Negligent or unreasonable delay by a person in claiming what is due to him—e.g. unreasonable delay in presenting a *cheque* for payment.

ladder activities. In a *network*, two overlapping *activities*, one of which is continually supplying information, parts or goods etc. to the other.

laisser-faire (in USA, usually *laissez-faire*). The doctrine that governments should not interfere in economic affairs.

lame duck. Someone who, or an enterprise which, fails to pay debts; a defaulter.

Landrum-Griffin act. Popular name for the *Labor Reform Law*.

Lang factor. Ratio of the cost of the equipment in a plant used in a *process industry* to the total cost of erecting the plant. The ratio is observed to be a constant for a large number of plants in broadly defined categories (e.g. all plants processing fluids). (Named after Hans L. Lang.)

231

Laspeyres index. An *index number* that relates a *weighted arithmetic mean* of observations in one period to a weighted arithmetic mean of observations in the base year, using weights that are determined in the base year. For example, if the observations are the prices $p_{10}, p_{20}, \ldots, p_{n0}$ of goods $1, \ldots, n$ in the base period; quantities $q_{10}, \ldots, q_{n0}$ of these goods were bought in the base period; and the prices in year t are $p_{1t}, p_{2t}, \ldots, p_{nt}$ then the Laspeyres price index for year t is:

$$100 \sum_{i=1}^{n} p_{it}q_{i0} \bigg/ \sum_{i=1}^{n} p_{i0}q_{i0}$$

A Laspeyres price index measures the change in the price of a standard 'basket' of items (cf. *Paasche index*). Named after its inventor, the German statesman and economist, Étienne Laspeyres (1834–1913).

last-bag system. Synonym for *two-bin system*.

last in first out. See *LIFO*.

lateral communication. Passage of information about what one department of an organization is doing from that department to other departments.

late shift. 1. The *afternoon shift* in a *double day-shift system* 2. The *afternoon shift* or *evening shift* in a *three-shift system*.

latest allowable date. Synonym for *latest event time*.

latest event time. The latest possible time at which an *event* in an *activity-on-arrow network* can occur without increasing the total duration of the project. (Also known as 'latest allowable date'.)

latest finish time of an activity (or latest finish date of an activity, or latest finish). The latest possible time by which an *activity* in an *activity-on-node network* can finish without increasing the total duration of the project.

latest start time of an activity (or latest start date of an activity, or latest start). The latest possible time by which an *activity* in an *activity-on-node network* can be started without increasing the total duration of the project.

law merchant. Synonym for *lex mercatoria*.

law of diminishing return. A frequently observed phenomenon that when output depends on several inputs (such as labour, machines and materials) and some of the inputs are constant then, beyond a certain limit, increases in the other inputs result in smaller and smaller increases in output.

law of the situation. A phrase used by Mary Parker Follett (1868–1933), the American political and business philosopher, to describe the action that must be taken because of the circumstances that exist and not because a superior has given an order to a subordinate. Miss Follett suggested that reliance on common acceptance of the law of the situation would depersonalize orders and thus make them more acceptable.

layoff (noun). Instance of laying off.

lay off (verb). 1. To cease to employ someone, usually temporarily, especially because of: (a) a contraction of business; or (b) a strike in part of the firm or in a firm that is a major supplier or customer. 2. To reduce risk by carrying out *reinsurance*.

lay-off agreement. An agreement by an employer to give *lay-off pay* to its workers.

lay-off pay. A payment given to workers who have to be sent home because there is no work for them to do.

lead time. The length of time between ordering the supply of something and receiving it. *Also* an estimate of such a length of time.

learning curve. A graph that shows improvement in the performance of a task, by an individual or a group, as it is repeated and more is learned about it.

lease (noun). A contract by which one person grants possession of some of his property (especially land, buildings or machinery) to another for a certain period of time. (Also known as a 'demise'.)

lease (verb). 1. To grant to someone a *lease* over one's property. 2. To be the *lessee* of something.

leaseback. See *sale and leaseback*.

least squares line. The *graph* [1] of the *regression equation* found by the *method of least squares* in *simple regression analysis*.

ledger. A classified record of a firm's financial transactions which are listed in separate 'ledger accounts' each of which records transactions only with a particular person (a 'personal account') or only relating to a particular class of the firm's *assets* [2] or *liabilities* [2] (an 'impersonal account'). It is usual to divide the ledger up, for the practical work of bookkeeping, into separate records of particular types of account—e.g. a 'sales ledger' containing accounts of the firm's customers, a 'bought ledger' containing accounts of the firm's suppliers and an 'impersonal ledger' containing impersonal accounts.

legacy. A gift made by someone in his will (apart from a gift of *real property*, which is called a 'devise'). (Also known as a 'bequest'.)

legacy duty. A UK tax on the value of *personal property* bequeathed to someone that was payable by the beneficiary and was abolished in 1949.

legalized invoice. A copy of an invoice on which a *chamber of commerce* has certified that the details are accurate.

legal tender. *Money* that a creditor has no legal justification for refusing when it is offered (tendered) as payment.

legislation. The action or process of preparing laws or rules, according to regulated procedures, performed by an authoritative body or individual. *Also* the laws or rules so prepared.

lessee. One who is given possession of someone else's property by means of a *lease*.

lessor. One who gives possession of his property to someone else by means of a *lease*.

letter-box company. A *company* which has been incorporated in a particular country merely because that country charges low taxes or exercises little control over the operations of companies and which does not transact any of its business in that country. The office that the company has in its country of incorporation is nothing more than a letter-box.

letter of allotment. A document, sent by an *issuer* of new *securities* [1] to an *allottee* informing him of acceptance of his offer to buy securities and of the number he has bought. Most letters of allotment are 'renounceable' or 'provisional'—i.e. the allottee can, within a certain period (usually 6 weeks), sell his new securities to someone else and substitute him as the allottee. (Also known as an 'allotment letter'.)

letter of attorney. Synonym for *power of attorney*.

letter of credit. See *credit* [4].

letter of hypothecation (or letter of lien or letter of pledge). A document setting out the terms on which a *pledge* [1] is made and specifying the goods that are pledged.

letter of regret. A letter sent, after a *public offer* of new *securities* [1], to people whose applications to purchase securities have had to be refused because there have been applications to buy more securities than are being issued.

letters of administration. A document in which the *High Court* gives authority to a named person (the 'administrator') to act as *personal representative* of a person who died *intestate* or who died without appointing an *executor* [1].

letters patent. A document by which the Crown grants *authority* [1] to someone. To stress the fact that the authority should be available for everyone to read, the document is not folded—i.e. it is 'patent' or 'open'.

leverage. See *financial gearing*.

lex mercatoria (or law merchant). Customary commercial practices that are accepted by courts of law throughout the world.

liability. 1. An obligation, especially an obligation to pay money. 2. (Plural.) The amounts of money that a firm owes to others, usually classified as *current liabilities* and *long-term liabilities*.

licence (in USA, usually spelt license). 1. Permission granted to someone (called the 'licensee') by a competent authority for the licensee to do something that would otherwise be unlawful. *Also* a document containing evidence of such permission. 2. Permission given by one person (called the 'licensor') to another (called the 'licensee') for the licensee to use the licensor's property. In particular, permission to exercise the licensor's *patent rights*.

license (noun). US spelling of *licence*.

license (verb). To grant a *licence*.

licensee. 1. A person who is entitled to do something (that is otherwise unlawful) under the terms of a *licence* [1]. 2. A person who is entitled to use someone else's property under the terms of a *licence* [2].

licensor. A person who grants a right to use his property to someone else by means of a *licence* [2].

lieu bonus. A payment made to a worker who, for special reasons, is not able to participate in an *incentive payment system* or who is unable, because of abnormal circumstances, to do the work required to entitle him to an *incentive payment*.

lien. A right to take (or retain) possession of goods in order to persuade their owner to pay a debt. For example, a carrier has a right to retain possession of goods until his charges for carrying them have been paid.

life assurance. An arrangement under which an *insurer* promises to pay a fixed sum if a named person (called the 'life assured') dies within a specified period ('term life assurance') or to pay a fixed sum when a named person dies ('whole life assurance') or to pay an *annuity* to a named person if he does not die. Payments after death go to the *estate* [2] of the deceased person for payment to his heirs.

LIFO. (Acronym from 'last in first out'.) A method of estimating the change in value, over a period, of a stock of some good. It is used in the same circumstances as *FIFO* but it is assumed that the stock remaining at the end of the period is the oldest stock (i.e. that a withdrawal is always of the most recently purchased stock).

limitation period. Period fixed by statute after which legal action may not be taken.

Limited (Ltd). Being a *limited company* (put as the last word of a company's name).

Limited and Reduced. Being a *limited company* of which the *nominal share capital* has been reduced (written as the last three words of the company's name, usually by order of the court that sanctioned the reduction).

limited company. A *company* [1] that has *members* who are liable to contribute only a known limited amount of money to help pay off the company's debts if the company is dissolved without having sufficient funds to pay its debts.

Usually the limit of a member's liability is the *nominal value* (or par value) of the *shares* he holds. In practice this money is usually paid to the company when it issues the shares so that any holder of them has no further liability. However, if shares are issued partly paid then a holder may be liable to pay the remainder of their nominal value.

In some countries (e.g. Belgium and almost all states of the USA) a company may issue *no-par shares*. A shareholder's liability is then limited to the *issue price* of the share—when he has paid that to the company his liability in ended.

See also *guarantee company*.

limited liability. A *liability* [1] or possible liability that is limited in extent to a definite amount—especially the liability that a *member* of a *limited company* could have for paying the company's debts.

limited-line strategy. Strategy of offering very few variants within a single *product line*.

linear function. A *function* [2] that has the properties:

$$f(ax) = af(x)$$
$$f(x+y) = f(x) + f(y)$$

The *graph* [1] of a linear function of one variable is a straight line.

linear programmed instruction. *Programmed instruction* in which the frames are presented in the same sequence for all learners. In each frame there is a question for the learner to answer in order to test his learning but the questions are usually phrased so that they suggest the right answer—hence the alternative name of 'constructed-response programmed instruction'.

linear programming (LP). The techniques of *mathematical programming* that can be applied when the objective function is a *linear function* and all the constraints are linear functions. Any linear programming problem can be expressed in the form:

237

maximize $\quad \sum_{j=1}^{n} c_j x_j$

subject to $\quad \sum_{j=1}^{n} a_{ij} x_j \leqslant b_i \quad$ for $\quad i = 1, 2, \ldots, m$

and $\quad\quad\quad\quad x_j \geqslant 0 \quad$ for $\quad j = 1, 2, \ldots, n$

where $x_1, \ldots, x_n$ are the decision variables,

$$\sum_{j=1}^{n} c_j x_j$$

is the objective function and the two sets of inequalities are the constraints.

linear regression analysis. *Regression analysis* of which the object is to find a regression equation that expresses the dependent variable as a *linear function* of the independent variables.

line authority. *Authority* [1] that is, or is like, the authority exercised by a *line manager*.

line balancing. Arranging a *production line* so that equal amounts of work are allocated to each *work station*.

line management. 1. The function performed by *line managers*. 2. The *line managers* of a firm.

line manager. A member of an organization who is responsible for the success or failure of a section of the organization in performing part of the principal work of the organization. (Cf. *staff specialist*.)

line of balance (LOB). A line drawn on a *line-of-balance diagram* showing the *balance quantity* at each *event*.

line-of-balance diagram (LOB diagram). A diagram that shows, for every *event* in a *line-of-balance network*, the number of *parts*, *subassemblies* or other items that have reached the manufacturing stage represented by that event.

line-of-balance network (LOB network). A *network* that shows the sequence of activities required to manufacture and assemble a batch of identical units of a finished product, and which is used to calculate the *line of balance* for the manufacturing process.

line of command. The sequence of people in an organization through whom instructions from the *chief executive* pass before reaching a particular employee. (Also known as a 'chain of command'.)

line of credit. Synonym for *credit line*.

line relationship. Relationship between two members of an organization, one of whom may issue instructions and delegate authority to the other.

line responsibility. Responsibility of, or like that of, a *line manager*.

link. 1. Synonym for *edge*. 2. Synonym for *sequence arrow*.

link financing. An arrangement whereby a firm borrows the amount of a *compensating balance* from someone else.

liquid asset. An *asset* [1] that either is *cash* or can be turned into a known amount of cash very quickly (such as a *Treasury bill*).

liquidate. 1. To ascertain, by agreement or by litigation, the extent of a debt—see *liquidated damages*. 2. To sell an *asset* [1] for cash (i.e. convert it into a *liquid asset*). 3. To sell all the *assets* of a firm and arrange its affairs so that it can be brought to an end. (Synonymous with 'wind up'.)

liquidated damages. *Damages* of an amount that is fixed as one of the terms of a contract. For example, suppose two companies sign a contract under which one promises to install some machinery by a certain date. The contract may state that if the date is not kept, damages of £50 a day must be paid—these are liquidated damages. If no sum was specified in the contract, the aggrieved party would have to ask a court to decide the proper amount of damages which would then be 'unliquidated damages'.

liquidating value. Synonym for *break-up value*.

liquidation. 1. The action or process of *liquidating*. 2. The state of being *liquidated* [3] (in the phrase, 'go into liquidation').

liquidator. A person appointed by a court to carry out the *winding up* of a *registered company*. A 'provisional liquidator' (nearly always an *official receiver*) is appointed in the *winding-up order* (or, in exceptional cases, before that order is made). The provisional liquidator calls meetings of all *contributories* and *creditors* [1] of the company at which they state whom they would like to be appointed as liquidator.

liquidity. 1. Ability to produce *cash*; especially a firm's ability to produce cash to pay its debts. 2. Ease with which a *security* [1] or an investment may be turned into cash. (Thus a *Treasury bill* has high liquidity but a specialized machine has low liquidity.)

liquidity ratio. 1. The ratio of a bank's total holdings of *cash* and *near cash* (i.e. its *liquid assets*) to its total *deposits* [1]. 2. A ratio that indicates a firm's ability to pay its debts—e.g. the *acid-test ratio* or the *current ratio*.

list. To include in a list of *securities* [1] that are permitted to be bought and sold on an *organized market* for securities. ('Listed' is synonymous with 'quoted'; 'listing' is synonymous with 'quotation'.)

listed company. A *company* that has issued *securities* [1] that are *listed* on a *stock exchange* [1]. (Also known as a 'public company' or a 'quoted company'.)

litigation. Activity or process of asking a court to settle a dispute.

little Neddy. An *economic development committee*.

livery. Style of design adopted by an organization for the uniform decoration of the commercial vehicles that it owns.

Lloyd's. An *organized market* for insurance in London which originated in a seventeenth-century coffee house run by Edward Lloyd. Members of Lloyd's are individual insurers (called Lloyd's *underwriters*) who are grouped in partnerships called syndicates. They will only deal with *brokers*.

load (noun). The use that is to be made of a production facility (e.g. a machine, a *work centre*, a worker) over a period (usually expressed in units of time—e.g. *machine-hours*).

load (verb). To assign *loads* to particular production facilities (e.g. a factory, a *shop* [1], a machine, a *work centre*).

load chart. A chart that shows the future work *load* of machines, *work centres* or other production systems.

load factor. In *work measurement*, when the time a worker takes to perform a job depends on the speed at which a machine works, the load factor for the job is the proportion of the time of one *work cycle* [1] during which the worker is occupied on necessary work when he is working at *standard performance*.

loan. Something lent for the borrower's temporary use; especially money lent with conditions about repayment and the payment of interest.

loan capital. Synonym for *debt capital*.

loan capital duty. A UK tax which was paid by a corporation or body of persons on the amount of any loan that it proposed to raise by selling *marketable securities*. The tax was abolished as from 1 January 1973.

loan shark. Someone who lends money at exorbitant rates of interest; a usurer.

lobster shift. Synonym for *midnight shift*.

local. A local branch of an American *trade union* [1].

local authority. A *corporation* consisting of members elected by the inhabitants of a particular area, but independent of the central government of the country, with powers to provide certain services in that area and the power to raise money by taxation. (Often called an 'authority'.)

local bargaining. *Collective bargaining* over terms and conditions of employment at a particular workplace.

local productivity association (LPA). See *British Productivity Council*.

location. A part of a *store* [4] in a computer that can retain a small quantity of data treated as a unit by the computer. Each location in a store has an *address*.

Location of Offices Bureau (LOB). A *commission* [4] established by an *Order in Council* in 1963. The members (at present 3 plus a chairman) are appointed by the Secretary of State for the Environment. The Bureau was established to encourage movement of office employment from congested central London to suitable centres elsewhere. The Commission's staff give a free advisory service to London businessmen on the availability of offices.

Address: 27 Chancery Lane, London WC2A 1NS (01-405 2921).

lockout (noun). Action by an employer to prevent his employees from performing their work (and earning wages) in order to influence the course of an industrial dispute.

lock out (verb). To enforce a *lockout*.

locus sigilli. See *L.S.*

logic network. Synonym for *flow-chart form of network*.

log normal distribution. The *probability distribution* of a *random variable* X where $\ln X$ (i.e. the natural logarithm of X) has a *normal distribution*.

logo. A distinctive symbol used repeatedly by an organization for identifying itself. Often consists of the organization's name in distinctive lettering. (Originally, a shortening of 'logotype'—i.e. one piece of printers' type with a whole word on it—from the practice of supplying a printer with a logotype when a name in distinctive lettering is to be included in, e.g., an advertisement.)

London allowance. Synonym for *London weighting*.

London metal exchange (LME). An *organized market* for the sale of copper, tin, lead, zinc and silver founded in 1877 and moved to its present premises (Whittington Avenue, London EC3) in 1882. Only a small number of dealers are entitled to trade on the market; their representatives sit in a circle and the dealers are, therefore, known as 'The Ring'. Transactions are concluded during two five-minute trading sessions each day for each metal. Most transactions are for *futures contracts*.

London weighting. A payment made to employees who work in London, which is in addition to the pay they would receive if they did the same job out of London and is intended to compensate for the additional cost of accommodation and travel in London. (Sometimes called a 'London allowance'.)

long position. State, of a dealer in some *commodity* [3] or in *securities* [1], of possessing, or being committed to buying, more of a specific item than he currently has contracts to sell. The dealer is said to be 'long of' the item. (Also known as a 'bull position'.)

long-range planning. The activity, process or study of preparing plans that cover long periods (usually, five years or more).

longs. *Government stocks* that are to be redeemed more than 15 years hence.

long-term liability. A debt that is not to be repaid for some time (for most purposes, 12 months).

loop. 1. In a *graph* [2], an *edge* that has the same *vertex* at each end. 2. A sequence of instructions in a *program* [1] that are to be obeyed repetitively by the computer.

loose insert. An *advertisement* in the form of a printed single sheet of paper or pamphlet that is inserted in (but not attached to) copies of a publication.

loose rate. 1. A *piece rate* that is high enough to enable a worker to earn a lot without too much effort (cf. *tight rate*). 2. Synonym for *loose time value*.

loose time value. In *work measurement*, an inaccurately measured time for a job which actually requires less time. (Also known as a 'loose rate'.)

loss. 1. An amount by which the *revenues* [1] of a firm are less than all *expenses* [3] and *lost costs* over a period. (Also known as 'net loss'.) 2. An amount by which the *proceeds* of selling something are less than the *expenses* [3] associated with the sale.

loss adjuster. An independent consultant who, for a fee, will advise an *insurer* on the extent of his liability to pay a claim from an *assured*.

loss assessor. An independent consultant who will, for a fee, advise an *assured* on the presentation of a claim to an *insurer*.

loss leader. Something which a retailer sells at a loss in order to attract customers to his shop where they will buy other goods (on which he hopes to make a large profit).

lost cost. An amount of *expenditure* by a firm for which it has not received any benefit.

lost-time accident. An accident that injures an employee and prevents him from continuing his normal work on the day or shift after that on which the accident occurred.

lot. Synonym for *batch*.

lot production. Synonym for *batch production*.

low-level language. A *programming language* which has few or no *macro-instructions* but has a code for instructions that is more easy to remember and use than *computer instruction code*. (Also known as a 'symbolic language'.)

lump, the. See *labour-only subcontracting*.

Lutine bell. A bell (salvaged in 1859 from the sunken frigate

Lutine) which hangs in the dealing room at Lloyd's and is rung to announce important news (once for bad news, twice for good news). (*Lutine*— the name is French for 'sprite'— was surrendered to the British by the French in 1793 and sank in 1799 carrying a vast quantity of gold and silver that was insured by members of Lloyd's.)

m

M₁, *M₂*, *M₃*. See *money stock*.

MAD. 1. Abbreviation of *mean absolute deviation*. 2. (Acronym from 'Michigan algorithmic decoder'.) A *procedure-oriented language* based on an early version of *ALGOL* and used for teaching programming in the USA.

MBIM. Abbreviation of 'member of the British Institute of Management' (see *British Institute of Management*).

MBO. Abbreviation of *management by objectives*.

MCD. Abbreviation of *Master Clerical Data*.

MDW. Abbreviation of *measured daywork*.

MIEx. Abbreviation of 'member of the Institute of Export' (see *Institute of Export*).

MIEx (Grad). Abbreviation of 'graduate member of the Institute of Export' (see *Institute of Export*).

MIMC. Abbreviation of 'member of the Institute of Management Consultants' (see *Institute of Management Consultants*).

MInstM. Abbreviation of 'member of the Institute of Marketing' (see *Institute of Marketing*).

MIWM. Abbreviation of 'member of the Institution of Works Managers' (see *Institution of Works Managers*).

MLH. Abbreviation of *minimum list heading*.

MLR. Abbreviation of *minimum lending rate*.

MRA. Abbreviation of *multiple regression analysis*.

MRG. Abbreviation of *Management Research Groups*.

MSD. Abbreviation of *Master Standard Data*.

MTM. Abbreviation of *methods-time measurement*. Different parts of the system are called MTM–1, MTM–2 and MTM–3.

machine code. Synonym for *computer instruction code*.

machine-hour. A unit for measuring the usage of machines which is equivalent to the use of one machine for one hour. Thus a use of 3 machines for 1 hour each, or 6 machines for $\frac{1}{2}$ hour each, etc., are measured as 3 machine-hours.

machine idle time (or idle time). Time during which a machine is available to perform work but is not used (e.g. because nobody is available to operate it).

machine instruction. An instruction, for a *computer* to perform a single operation, which is in *computer instruction code* so that it can be obeyed directly by the computer.

machine instruction code. Synonym for *computer instruction code*.

machine tool. A device for shaping metal (e.g. by drilling, planing, milling, boring, turning or grinding) in which either the piece of work to be shaped or the cutting tool is mechanically driven.

macroeconomics. The study of an economy as a whole.

macro-instruction. A single expression, in a *programming language*, which represents a number of elementary instructions to a *computer*. A *program* [1] containing macro-instructions is given to the computer in conjunction with a second program that translates macro-instructions into their component instructions.

magnet board (or magnetic board). A *display board* of which the surface is magnetized so that items carrying small magnets can be attached to it.

magnetic core. Synonym for *core*.

mail order. System of retailing in which customers send orders to the seller by post (mail) and goods are delivered to the customer's home.

mail-order advertising. *Advertising* intended to persuade people to buy goods by *mail order*. Note that mail-order advertising may or may not be *direct-mail advertising* though the terms are often confused.

maintenance. Work undertaken on plant, equipment or machinery in order to keep it at, or restore it to, an acceptable standard.

maintenance engineering. Activity, process, or study of maintaining *plant* (including buildings and machinery involved in production processes) and of inspecting and lubricating machinery.

maintenance factor. Synonym for *hygiene factor*.

main frame. Synonym for *central processing unit*.

make-ready time. Synonym for *set-up time*.

make-up pay. In *payment by results* each worker is usually guaranteed a minimum weekly wage. Make-up pay is given if the worker fails to do the work that could earn him the minimum wage and is the difference between the payment for the work he has done and the guaranteed minimum.

manage. To carry out the task of ensuring that a number of diverse activities are performed in such a way that a defined objective is achieved—*especially* the task of creating and maintaining conditions in which desired objectives are achieved by the combined efforts of a group of people (which includes the person doing the managing).

management. The process, activity or study of carrying out the task of ensuring that a number of diverse activities are performed in such a way that a defined objective is achieved—*especially* the task of creating and maintaining conditions in which desired objectives are achieved by the combined efforts of a group of people (which includes the person carrying out the management). *Also* a group of people within an organization who are primarily concerned with the management of the activities of that organization.

‘Management’ is used to indicate the diversity and multiplicity of the activities to be managed (e.g. in such phrases as ‘management of the economy’) as well as the fact that the activities are largely performed by people other than the manager. The activities are not necessarily performed by people in a work group containing the manager. For example, *financial*

247

management, *risk management* and *personnel management* are often carried out by managers with little more than a secretary. However, it is often suggested that these 'staff functions' are really only particular components of the task of management which, for convenience, have been assigned to specialists and that those specialists are carrying out the *administration* [3] of policies determined by managers. (The term 'personnel administration' is more common in the USA than 'personnel management'.) Certainly the study of management has concentrated on the performance of a particular role within a more or less stable group of people. Wilfred Brown (see *Glacier Project*) in *Organization* (London: Heinemann Educational Books, 1971), suggests the following characterization of a manager: (1) he has *subordinates*; (2) he can, at least, veto the appointment of particular individuals to be his subordinates; (3) he assigns work to subordinates; (4) he assesses the performance of subordinates and can remove them from their jobs if they fail to produce an adequate standard of work.

Henri Fayol (see *administrative management theory*) analysed the work of a *chief executive* and suggested there are five essential elements of the management process: planning, organization, command, coordination and control. Subsequent writers have made similar analyses, though giving different emphasis to the elements. For example, in E. F. L. Brech (editor), *The Principles and Practice of Management*, 2nd edition (London: Longmans, 1963), it is suggested that management has 'four essential elements—planning, motivation, coordination, control' (p. 17). H. Koontz and C. O'Donnell, in *Principles of Management: An Analysis of Managerial Functions*, 5th edition (New York: McGraw-Hill, 1972), identify five managerial functions—planning, organizing, staffing, directing, controlling—and say that 'all managerial knowledge can be organized under these five categories' (p. 2). Later in their book, Koontz and O'Donnell say that coordination is 'the essence of managership, for the achievement of harmony of individual effort toward the accomplishment of group goals is the purpose of management. Each of the managerial functions is an exercise in coordination.'

248

(p. 50.) A similar view is taken by F. E. Kast and J. E. Rosenzweig, in *Organization and Management: A Systems Approach*, 2nd edition (New York: McGraw-Hill, 1974): 'Management involves coordination of human and material resources toward objective accomplishment' (p. 6). However, Ernest Dale, in *Management: Theory and Practice*, 2nd edition (New York: McGraw-Hill, 1969), says that 'the directing phase of the management job is what many people think of as management itself: telling people what to do and seeing that they do it' (p. 424). In International Labour Office, *Introduction to Work Study*, revised edition (Geneva: ILO, 1969), 'organization' is taken to be the key: 'Management is the organization and control of human activity towards specific ends. The word "organization", here used in a broad sense, includes the activities of planning on the basis of facts obtained, direction and co-ordination' (pp. 25–6).

A somewhat different view of management is given by Robert L. Katz in *Management of the Total Enterprise* (Englewood Cliffs NJ: Prentice-Hall, 1970): 'The most crucial requirements for a manager are that he be an analyst of conditions affecting his unit; a procurer and allocater of the resources to be used by his unit; and a diagnostician of the interpersonal relationships, values, and norms within his unit. These requirements are common to all managerial positions.' (p. 51.) Katz distinguishes three types of management skill: (1) technical skill —concerned with what is done; (2) human skills—concerned with how it is done; and (3) conceptual skills—concerned with why it is done. He points out that conceptual skills become more important at higher levels in an organization.

In the past, particularly when administrative management theory was the dominant viewpoint for thinking about management, the word 'administration' was more popular than management. In his preface to the second translation of Fayol's 'Administration, industrielle et générale', Urwick expressed great disquiet that the title had been translated as 'General and Industrial Management'. He thought that 'management' had too many bad connotations; for example, the *Shorter Oxford English*

Dictionary notes one meaning as: 'The use of contrivance for affecting some purpose; often in bad sense, implying deceit or trickery.' Curiously, this bad connotation is preserved in one popular (anonymous) definition, 'Management is getting things done through other people'. Dale discusses the inadequacy of this definition in chapter 1 of his book; Koontz and O'Donnell say: 'Most people would agree that [management] means getting things done through and with people' (p. 42).

From the above definitions it is clear that management as an activity is not restricted to profit-seeking business firms nor even to a capitalist economy but is required in any situation involving complex activity. This is the view taken by the editors—Paul Pigors, Charles A. Myers & F. T. Malm—of *Management of Human Resources*, 2nd edition (New York: McGraw-Hill, 1969), when they write: 'In any organization, management's task is to develop and coordinate the willing efforts of employees in accomplishing organizational goals. This is just as true in government agencies and nonprofit organizations as it is in private enterprises.' (p. 2.) However, the influential writer, Peter Drucker, sees management purely as the process of efficiently providing *economic goods* (whether in a free-enterprise or a centrally planned economy). 'Management must always, in every decision and action, put economic performance first. It can only justify its existence and its authority by the economic results it produces'—P. F. Drucker, *The Practice of Management* (London: Heinemann, 1955), p. 7.

See also, *POSDCORB, scientific management.*

management accounting. Preparation and analysis of financial information about a firm's operations for use within the firm to assist in the formulation of policy and in day-to-day control of operations.

management audit. A systematic, detailed examination of the quality of *management* in an *organization* in order to suggest improvement.

management board. See *two-tier board.*

management by exception. Technique of carrying out the *control* [1] function of management by paying attention only to deviations from a *plan*. The process of *monitoring* the system (and, by implication, judging what constitutes a deviation from the plan) is *delegated* [1]. The phrase was first used by F. W. Taylor (see *scientific management*). See also Lester R. Bittel, *Management by Exception: Systematizing and Simplifying the Managerial Job* (New York: McGraw-Hill, 1964).

management by objectives (MBO). A systematic procedure for planning the work of managers in an organization which is characterized by collaboration between each manager and his superior in analysing the manager's tasks and establishing quantified objectives to be achieved by the manager within specified time-limits. Emphasis is usually placed on integrating the objectives set for individual managers with those of the whole organization and on having a well-established procedure for ascertaining whether a manager achieves his objectives and for regularly reviewing objectives. The phrase, 'management by objectives' is usually attributed to the American management consultant, Peter Ferdinand Drucker (born in Austria, 1909)—see P. F. Drucker, *The Practice of Management* (London: Heinemann, 1955). For detailed descriptions of MBO systems, see G. S. Odiorne, *Management by Objectives: A System of Managerial Leadership* (New York: Pitman Publishing Corporation, 1965/London: Pitman Publishing, 1970), W. J. Reddin, *Effective MBO* (London: Management Publications, 1971) and J. Humble, *Management by Objectives* (London: Management Publications, 1972).

management company. A company which decides what *securities* [1] should be bought and sold by a *unit trust* and arranges the sale of *units* in return for a fee that is deducted from the fund's income.

management consultant. Someone whose principal business activity is *management consulting*.

Management Consultants Association (MCA). An association, founded in 1956, of management consulting firms. Its principal objectives are to safeguard and improve the standards of the profession. Member firms are bound by a technical and ethical code of professional conduct and a code of practice for executive selection consultants which ensure an ethical and objective approach to their work. The association provides a free advisory and information service.

   Address: 23 Cromwell Place, London SW7 2LG (01–584 7285).

management consulting. The activity of identifying and investigating, as an independent expert, problems concerned with the policy, organization, procedures and methods of any kind of organization, of recommending action that is appropriate to the problems investigated, and of helping to implement recommendations.

management development. An activity, taking place in an organization, with the objective of making managers into better managers. It includes training, in the sense of acquisition of *skills,* and improvements in attitudes and personality.

management game. A training or educational activity in which a trainee must take a sequence of decisions relating to a simulation of a real-life management problem and is presented with the results of each decision after he has taken it. A game may be played by trainees working individually or as teams or by a number of trainees competing against each other. In the competitive type of game, the result of an individual decision is the response, or the next move, of the other competitors. In the individual type of game, the response is provided by a trainer, or by a computer, according to predetermined rules. (Also called a 'business game', or 'game'.)

management guide. A document used in some systems of *management by objectives.* There is one for each manager in the organization, showing: (1) outline of the manager's job; (2) the results of the last *key results analysis* [1] of his job; (3) his *job improvement plan.* (Also known as a 'management job description' or 'manager's guide' or 'results guide'.)

management job description. Synonym for *management guide.*

management ratio. Synonym for *business ratio.*

Management Research Groups (MRG). A voluntary non-profit-making association of business enterprises, government regional offices, professional firms and institutions concerned with education and training for industry and commerce. MRG was founded in 1926 to promote the efficiency of management in commerce and industry by encouraging the study of management problems, the exchange of experiences and ideas between member organizations and by providing information. Member organizations (150 in December 1974) belong to groups (13 in December 1974) on a geographical basis which hold regular meetings at which chief executives and other directors can discuss subjects of mutual concern. New members can be admitted to a group only if existing members agree. In addition MRG organizes a general conference every 3 years, visits to member firms, surveys, and inter-group meetings.

Address: Beacon House, 113 Kingsway, Strand, London WC2B 6QR (01–242 1114).

management science. Application of scientific techniques, research and results to problems of management. Virtually synonymous with *operations research* although it is sometimes suggested that management science is concerned with general theories while operations research is concerned with solving particular problems.

management share. See *deferred share.*

management style. Synonym for *managerial style.*

manager. A person who has been appointed to carry out a job of *management. Also* a person who undertakes such jobs as a profession.

managerial economics. The part of the theory of *economics* that is concerned with, or applicable to, the management of business enterprises.

managerial effectiveness. Defined by W. J. Reddin as 'the extent to which a manager achieves the output requirements of his position'. See, e.g. W. J. Reddin, *Effective MBO* (London: Management Publications, 1971).

managerial grid (often capital M and G). 1. A representation of *managerial styles* on a two-dimensional grid. The dimensions are: concern for production (horizontal axis) and concern for people (vertical axis). Each dimension has 9 possible ratings from

1 (low) to 9 (high). 2. A systematic method of *organization development* which was devised by Robert R. Blake and Jane Srygley Mouton. The objective of the method is to induce an overall change in *managerial style*, throughout an organization, in the direction of a '9, 9 managerial style' (i.e. combination of high concern for production and high concern for people).

Further information is given in R. R. Blake and Jane S. Mouton, *The Managerial Grid* (Houston: Gulf Publishing Company, 1964).

managerial structure. The established relationships between *managerial positions* in an organization—usually described in terms of *responsibility* and *authority* [1].

managerial style. The way in which a manager characteristically conducts his dealings with his subordinates. (Sometimes called 'management style'.)

manager's guide. Synonym for *management guide*.

managing director. Title often given to the *chief executive* of a company in the UK.

managing system. A *system* (of individual people) that is concerned with regulating the transactions between the *operating systems* [2] in a firm and the environment of the firm.

man-hour. A unit for measuring employment equivalent to the employment of one person for one hour. Thus employment of 3 men for 1 hour each, or 6 men for ½ hour each, etc., are measured as 3 man-hours.

man-machine chart. A *multiple-activity chart* that shows the activities of a machine and the worker who operates it.

manpower. The persons available to do work.

Manpower and Productivity Service. Title, until 1 March, 1972 of the *Conciliation and Advisory Service*.

manpower inventory. Summary of information about the quality of *manpower* that an organization employs.

manpower planning. Estimating how many employees and what types of employees an organization or a nation will require at some time in the future and making plans to meet those requirements.

Manpower Services Commission. A *corporation* established on 1 January 1974 under the Employment and Training Act 1973 with 10 members (one of whom is chairman) appointed by the Secretary of State. The main function of the Commission is 'to make such arrangements as it considers appropriate for the purposes of assisting persons to select, train for, obtain and retain employment suitable for their ages and capacities and to obtain suitable employees'. The Commission has only a small staff and most of its work is delegated to two agencies, the *Employment Service Agency* and the *Training Services Agency*. The Commission controls the activities of the *industrial training boards*.

manpower turnover. Synonym for *labour turnover*.

man-type flow process chart. See *flow process chart*.

manual dexterity. Ability of a person to make controlled skilful movements with his hands and arms.

manual dexterity test. A test of which the purpose is to measure a person's ability to perform tasks with his hands.

manufacture. 1. To change the form of materials—e.g. by shaping or by assembling components—in order to create something new—especially when done repetitively and employing machinery. 2. To create a specified thing by changing the form of materials.

manufacturer. A firm that *manufactures*.

manufacturer's agent. A firm that acts as an *agent* in selling to retailers the goods of several (usually not competing) manufacturers.

manufacturing management. See *production management*.

MAPI formula (or MAPI system). A method (published by the Machinery and Allied Products Institute—MAPI) for assessing whether it is worth while to replace existing equipment with new equipment. See G. Terborgh, *Business Investment Policy* (Washington, DC: MAPI, 1958).

margin. 1. Synonym for *profit margin*. 2. A cash *deposit* [2] paid by someone to a *broker* who lends him money to purchase *securities* [1] or *futures contracts*. The borrower hopes that he will soon be able to sell his securities or futures contracts for more than the purchase price so that he can repay the broker's loan, have his margin returned and take his profit. This procedure is known as 'speculating on margin'. (Margin is also sometimes known as 'cover'.)

marginal cost. An additional cost which is caused by producing just one more unit of production.

marginal costing. Synonym for *variable costing*.

marginal-income ratio. Ratio of the *net profit* [1] (or 'income') derived from selling just one more unit of production to the *marginal revenue* of that unit. It is often assumed that net profit is a linear function of the number of units sold; if that is so then the marginal-income ratio is also the ratio of the *contribution* from the sales of a specified quantity to the sales revenue from that quantity.

marginal relief. If a *personal relief* is given only when income is below a particular amount then a proportion of the relief is usually given to people with incomes that are slightly above the limit. This proportion is called marginal relief.

marginal revenue. The increase in revenue that is caused by selling just one more unit of production.

markdown. A reduction in a price charged by a retailer.

marked cheque. A *cheque* that has a note on it, from the bank that is the *drawee*, which signifies that the *drawer* does have adequate funds in his account for the cheque to be paid. Marked cheques are no longer issued in the UK where *bank drafts* are used instead. (Also known as a 'certified cheque'.)

market. 1. The conditions determining the number and nature of transactions for leasing or sale of particular goods or services, for performance of work by people, or for lending money, during a specified period in a specified geographical location or among specified people and firms. Such conditions include the quantity of goods (or capacity for performing services, or number of employable people, or quantity of money) available, the demands for the available goods, and the actions of governments or other institutions. 2. The habitual or potential buyers of a particular product. 3. A group of people or firms with specified characteristics, considered as potential buyers either of specified products

or of anything (e.g. 'the teenage market', 'the Brazilian Market').
4. A place people regularly go to in order to buy and sell, especially an *organized market*. *Also* an identifiable group of people, usually acting as *brokers*, who regularly deal in specified goods and have established rules for trading.

marketable security. A *security* [1] that is capable of being sold on a *stock exchange* [1].

market capitalization rate. The reciprocal of a *P/E ratio*— i.e. the ratio of the *EPS* of a company over a specified period to the price of one share at a specified time.

marketer. A manager who is responsible for *marketing* a firm's products.

marketing. The activities, of a firm, that are concerned with acquiring and maintaining *markets* [2] for the firm's *products* [2] and for ensuring that the firm's output reaches those markets.

marketing game. A *management game* in which the management problem that is simulated is primarily concerned with *marketing*.

marketing mix. The combination of methods used by a firm for *marketing* its *products* [2].

marketing research (US). Synonym for *market research*.

market price. The price at which specified goods can be sold in the *market* [2] for those goods.

market research. Systematic and objective search for, and analysis of, information concerning the actual or potential *markets* [2] for *products* [2]. (Usually called 'marketing research' in the USA.)

market segment. A group of buyers within a *market* [2] for a product who can be identified as being especially interested in a particular variant of the product.

market segmentation. Introduction, by an enterprise, of separate products specifically designed for *market segments* to which the enterprise once sold a single product.

market share. The ratio of a firm's sales of a product (either the number of units sold or the value of sales) during a period in a specified *market* [3] to the total sales of that type of product during the same period in that market.

market value. The market value of something at a particular time is the price that any buyer might reasonably be expected to pay for it at that time if he was able to make a considered judgment of its value and was not influenced by any special relationship with the seller.

markup. The difference between the selling price of a product and its cost to the seller; especially when the seller calculates it as a standard percentage of the cost.

markup pricing. Setting prices at which goods are to be sold by applying a standard *markup* to the cost of the goods.

mass production. Production (usually by machinery) of large quantities of something—either a repeated, undifferentiated product or a repeated basic structure with minor individual variations (e.g. in colour or accessories).

Master Clerical Data (MCD). A *predetermined motion-time system* developed by a firm of management consultants, Serge A. Birn Company Inc. It is based on *methods-time measurement* and is intended for use in measuring office work. See S. A. Birn, R. M. Crossan and R. W. Eastwood, *Measurement and Control of Office Costs: Master Clerical Data* (New York: McGraw-Hill, 1961).

Master Standard Data (MSD). A *predetermined motion-time system* described in: R. M. Crossan and H. W. Nance, *Master Standard Data: The Economic Approach to Work Measurement*, revised edition (New York: McGraw-Hill, 1972).

matched orders. A method of creating a *false market* in which two orders are given by one person to two different *brokers* who deal in the same *organized market*. One order is to sell a quantity at not less than a stated price (above the prevailing *market price*); the other order is to buy at up to that price. The brokers carry out the deal which is then reported to the public and gives the impression that market prices are rising.

materials. The goods that a *manufacturer* buys for conversion into manufactured products. *Also* the value of a manufacturer's stock of unconverted materials.

materials cost. A *cost* [2] associated with an *expenditure* on *materials* or *supplies*. *Also* the total of such costs associated with a particular activity, product or *cost centre,* or over a particular period.

materials handling. The activity, or study, of moving *materials* to a factory, moving *work-in-progress* through the factory and moving *finished goods* to customers.

materials management. Activity, or study, of planning, organizing and controlling the flow of a firm's *materials* at all stages between the firm's suppliers and its store of finished goods.

materials requisition. A document which authorizes and records the issue (from a stock) of *materials* for use.

material-type flow process chart. See *flow process chart.*

mathematical programming. Mathematical techniques for finding *optimum* programmes of action within given constraints. The typical programming problem involves a number of 'decision variables' which are measures of the extent to which each of a number of related activities is carried out. The overall effect of these activities is expressed as a *function* [2] of the decision variables (called the 'objective function'). There are limits (called 'constraints') on the values that the decision variables can take. The problem is to find the values of the decision variables (within the constraints) that will give an optimum value to the objective function.

The simplest form of the problem is when the objective function is a *linear function* and all the constraints are linear functions of the decision variables; it is then a problem of *linear programming*—a subject which has been studied extensively. If any of the functions involved is not linear the problem is one of *nonlinear programming.* See also, *dynamic programming.*

For a survey of mathematical programming, see P. G. Moore and S. D. Hodges (editors), *Programming for Optimal Decisions: Selected Readings in Mathematical Programming Techniques for Management Problems* (Harmondsworth: Penguin, 1970).

matrix. A rectangular array of data in which individual items are arranged in 'rows' (i.e. written or printed so that they are read from left to right); each row has the same number of items and the rows are written or printed following each other so that the items fall into 'columns'. E.g. in the matrix:

$$\begin{pmatrix} a\ b\ c \\ d\ e\ f \end{pmatrix}$$

(*abc*) is the first row and (^a_d) is the first column. If the numbers of rows and columns are the same the matrix is called a 'square matrix'. (The plural is 'matrices'.)

maturity. 1. The time when a debt becomes repayable. (Also known as 'maturity date'.) 2. The period for which money is loaned.

maturity curve. A graph which is sometimes used when determining salaries. In the method a survey is made of all people working in a particular kind of professional or technical career. The survey establishes the salary of each individual and the number of years he has been working in his profession (or sometimes number of years since first degree, or sometimes just chronological age). The distribution of salaries is plotted for each year. The 90th *percentile* (for example) maturity curve can then be derived by plotting all the 90th percentiles of these distributions on a graph of salary against years in profession. Similar maturity curves are derived for other percentiles. The salary of an individual working in that profession can then be determined by assessing which percentile the individual corresponds to (assessing him as corresponding to the 90th percentile, for example, is equivalent to saying he is better than 90 per cent of the other people in his profession with the same experience) and then reading off his salary according to his years of experience from the maturity curve for that percentile. (A maturity curve is also known as a 'career curve'.)

maturity date. The date on which a debt is repayable—especially when a *security* [1] is to be *redeemed*.

maximin criterion. A criterion used when making decisions that the decision taken should maximize the minimum *payoff* [1] that can be achieved.

maximize. To make as large as possible.

maximum working area. The space within which a seated or standing worker can reach and use tools, materials and equipment by moving his arms but not the rest of his body (cf. *normal working area*).

mean. 1. The *weighted arithmetic mean* of all values capable of being taken by a *random variable* where each value is weighted by its *probability*. More precisely, the mean of a *probability distribution* of a *discrete random variable* is:

$$\sum_i p_i x_i$$

where p_i is the probability of occurrence of the value x_i. The mean of a probability distribution $f(x)$ of a *continuous random variable* is:

$$\int_{-\infty}^{\infty} xf(x)\mathrm{d}x$$

(Also known as the 'population mean' or the 'expectation' of the random variable.) 2. The *arithmetic mean* of observed values (in a *frequency distribution*) of a *random variable*. Usually denoted by m. (Also called a 'sample mean'.)

mean absolute deviation (MAD). The MAD of n numbers $x_1, \ldots, x_n$, whose *arithmetic mean* is m, is:

$$\left(\sum_{i=1}^{n} |x_i - m| \right) \Big/ n$$

where the vertical rules represent *absolute value*. (Sometimes called 'average deviation' or 'mean deviation'.)

measured daywork (MDW). *Payment by results* in which a fixed *bonus* is paid to a worker whenever his performance is at or above a predetermined level.

measured work. Work for which *standard times* [1] have been set using techniques of *work measurement*. (Cf. *estimated work*.)

media planning. Activity or process of choosing the media that are to carry specified *advertising*.

median. 1. The value of a *random variable* for which its *distribution function* is equal to $\frac{1}{2}$ (i.e. there is a *probability* of $\frac{1}{2}$ that the random variable will occur with a value less than or equal to the median). 2. The median of a *frequency distribution* is the value of the *random variable* that is exceeded by half the items in the sample.

mediums. *Government stocks* that are to be *redeemed* between 5 and 15 years hence.

member. A person who has acquired rights and duties *vis-à-vis* a *corporation* by agreeing to the conditions of membership contained in the corporation's constitution. The precise rights and duties are detailed in the constitution or by the laws governing the corporation.

The usual condition for membership of a business corporation (e.g. a *company limited by shares* in the UK) is that a person must be a *shareholder*. Thus shareholder and member are virtually synonymous. However, a person can be a member of an English *unlimited company* or of a *company limited by guarantee* without being a shareholder since such companies often do not issue shares. A person who owns a *share warrant* is technically not a member unless he exercises his right to exchange his warrant for a *share certificate*.

memomotion photography. Time-lapse photography of the performance of a task for purposes of *work study*.

memorandum of association. A document setting out the basic aims and structure of a British *registered company*. A company's memorandum must be sent to the *Registrar of Companies* when the company is first registered and any alterations to the memorandum must also be sent to the Registrar, who makes these documents available for public inspection.

The memorandum must state: (1) the name of the company; (2) the objects of the company; (3) whether the *registered office* is to be in England or Scotland (but not the actual address); (4) whether the company is a *limited company*; (5) the *nominal share capital* of the company.

mental ability test. A test of which the purpose is to measure or assess a person's intellectual functions. (Also known as an intelligence test.)

mercantilist. A member, or follower, of a group of economists (chiefly English) in the seventeenth century who concentrated attention on the relationship between a country's foreign trade and the state of the country's economy and proposed that governments should impose *trade controls*.

merchandise (noun). Goods that a firm has bought with the intention of reselling them without altering their physical form.

merchandise (verb). 1. To buy and sell goods, either as a *wholesaler* or a *retailer*, without altering the physical form of the goods. 2. To take action intended to help *retailers* to sell products one has manufactured. For example, by supplying *point-of-sale advertising* or designing packaging. *Also* to inform retailers of one's plans to *advertise* a product and persuade them to stock up their shops to meet the demand created by the advertising.

merchandiser. 1. Someone who *merchandises*. 2. A firm that buys and sells goods, either as a *wholesaler* or a *retailer*, without altering the physical form of the goods.

merchant (noun). Someone who buys and sells goods without altering their physical form. In the UK the term usually excludes *retailers* and is not frequently used; in the USA it usually includes retailers and is often used to mean a retailer only.

merchant (verb). To buy and sell goods without in any way altering them physically.

merchant bank. A firm of which the main activity is the provision of finance for trade and industry. The older merchant banks originated as 'merchants' (i.e. buyers and sellers of goods —mainly in international trade) who turned to financing other people's trading activities. Merchant banks now provide a wide variety of financial services, including advice on *public offers* and *mergers*, and acting as *issuing houses* and *accepting houses*.

merchant middleman. An *intermediary* that takes possession and ownership of goods. (Also known as a 'reseller'.)

merge. 1. To come under common ownership or control. 2. To form a single *sequenced* collection of units of data by combining two or more collections that have each been sequenced (according to the same rules) already. (Synonymous with 'collate'.)

merger. Action by which two firms come under common ownership or control. Similar terms include 'acquisition', 'amalgamation', 'consolidation' and 'takeover'. Merger tends to be the term with the most general meaning in both the UK and the USA, though US (but not UK) lawyers often restrict it to mean a situation in which one of the merged firms continues in existence while the other loses its separate identity and is incorporated in the first. 'Acquisition' implies that one of the firms loses its identity and that it has been purchased by the firm that continues in existence; 'takeover' adds to 'acquisition' the implication that there was opposition to the merger from some of the owners, senior managers or directors of the firm that has lost its identity. 'Amalgamation' and 'consolidation' tend to indicate agreement between the original owners of the merged firms: 'consolidation' implies that a completely new firm is created from the merged firms.

See also, *conglomerate merger, horizontal merger, vertical merger*.

merit increase. An increase in pay given to an employee if his performance satisfies some criterion.

merit payment. An addition to a standard *time rate,* for a particular type of work in an enterprise, that is paid to individual workers because of their special skills or responsibilities.

merit rating. Assessing an employee's performance and personal qualities—usually so that his pay can be determined (see *merit increase*). *Also* such an assessment of an employee.

Merrick differential piece-rate system. A *payment system* for repetitive production work in which three *piece rates* and a standard rate of output are set. The lowest piece rate is paid to workers who produce less than $83\frac{1}{3}\%$ (five-sixths) of the standard output, the middle rate for between $83\frac{1}{3}\%$ and 100% of the standard and the highest rate for production in excess of the standard.

metamarketing. The principles and practices of *marketing* applied to the tasks of increasing public acceptance of ideas, giving to charities, support for political leaders and other matters not directly concerned with the purchase of goods and services.

method of least squares. A method of *regression analysis* in which the form of the regression equation is assumed leaving only its *parameters* to be calculated. The parameters chosen are the ones that make:

$$\sum_j (Y_j - \hat{Y}_j)^2$$

as small as possible, where Y_j is an observed value of the independent variable and $\hat{Y}_j$ is the corresponding predicted value given by the regression equation.

methods engineering. Synonym for *work study*.

methods-time measurement (MTM). A *predetermined motion-time system* in which a job to be measured is analysed into the elementary types of human movement for which times have been established, first by members of the Methods Engineering Council in the USA and later under the auspices of the International MTM associations in many countries which provide training in, and prescribe codes of practice for, the application of MTM. For a description of the origins of the system, see: H. B. Maynard, G. J. Stegemerten and J. L. Schwab, *Methods-Time Measurement* (New York: McGraw-Hill, 1948).

method study. Systematic recording and critical examination of existing and proposed ways of performing tasks involving human activity in order to develop and apply easier and more effective methods and reduce costs. (Also known as 'motion study'.)

metropolitan shift system. A *rapidly rotating shift system* in which the change from working one type of shift to working another type occurs every two days.

microchronometer. A timing device, graduated in *winks*, which is photographed by a movie camera at the same time as the performance of a task for purposes of *method study*. A microchronometer has a dial (cf. *wink counter*).

microcopy. A copy of a document that is too small to be read by the unaided eye—e.g. a copy on a *microfiche*.

microeconomics. The study of the economic activity of individuals, individual firms and *markets* [1] for particular goods.

microfiche. A sheet of photographic film (the British Standard Size is 105mm × 148mm, which is the A6 international paper size) on which a number (up to 72 on the BS microfiche) of *microcopy* images have been recorded in a standard format. (Also known as a 'fiche'.)

micromotion analysis. Analysis of the performance of repetitive work into constituent basic elements of bodily movement (*therbligs*). It is usual to analyse a film or videotape record of the work.

middleman. Synonym for *intermediary*.

middle management. The *middle managers* in an organization.

middle manager. A manager in an organization who is not a *first-line supervisor* and is not in a *general-management* position. *Also* a person in an organization with the same status as middle managers in that organization.

middle rate. The *arithmetic mean* of the buying and selling rates in a *quotation* [2] of *exchange rates*.

midnight shift. A *shift* that begins about midnight.

migrant (or migrant worker). Person who moves (especially from one country to another) in order to find work.

migrant worker. Synonym for *migrant*.

milestone (or milestone event). An *event* picked out as particularly important when applying a *project network technique*. (Also known as a 'key event'.)

milline rate. Unit used for measuring the cost of advertising in a US newspaper. It is the notional cost of having one 'agate line' (a space of which the width is one of the newspaper's columns and the depth is one-fourteenth of an inch) of advertising in 1 000 000 copies of the newspaper.

minicomputer. A *computer* of small size and low cost.

minimax criterion. A criterion used when making decisions that the decision taken should minimize the maximum loss that can occur.

minimax theorem. The fundamental theorem of *game theory* which states that in a *two-person zero-sum game* there is a number v (called the 'value of the game') such that each player can adopt a *mixed strategy* which will guarantee that player 1 always has a payoff of at least v (his 'minimum' payoff) and player 2 can ensure that 1 never gets more than v (thus making it his 'maximum' payoff).

minimum lending rate (MLR). The lowest rate of interest at which the *Bank of England* will make short-term funds available to London *discount houses* [1]. It is usually set each Friday to be $\frac{1}{2}\%$ above the average discount rate of the tenders accepted that day for *Treasury bills* [1] (rounded to the nearest $\frac{1}{4}\%$ higher). However, the Bank may set a different rate when required by its economic policy.

minimum list heading (MLH). A heading in a list of government statistics which have been subject to a minimum degree of analysis according to the *Standard Industrial Classification*.

minimum stock. Synonym for *safety stock*.

minority interest. An amount recorded in *consolidated accounts* to represent the *book value* of shares in subsidiaries of the holding company that are not owned by the holding company.

mint par (or mint par of exchange). The ratio of the gold content of two currencies which are regulated by the *gold standard*.

minute. 1. An official memorandum recommending a course of action. 2. (Plural.) An official record of the proceedings of a meeting.

minute book. A book containing the *minutes* [2] of meetings; specifically one containing the minutes of meetings of *directors* of a company or of *general meetings* of a company.

misrepresentation. A false statement of fact, made by one party to a *contract*, which induces the other party to enter into the contract.

Mitbestimmung. German for *codetermination*.

mixed economy. An economy in which a significant proportion (but not all) of industrial and commercial activity is carried out by the state or (usually) by state-owned corporations, there is some government control of and intervention in economic activity, but where much economic activity is carried out in conditions approaching *free enterprise*.

mixed strategy. In *game theory*, a rule adopted by a player specifying the *probabilities* of his selecting each of a number of choices. (Cf. *pure strategy*.)

mode. 1. The value of a *randon variable* that occurs most often in a sample of its occurences (i.e. in a *frequency distribution*). 2. The value of a *random variable* for which its *frequency function* is a maximum.

module. One of a series of items designed for use together in any combination that the user chooses.

monetarism. The theory that the activity of an economy and problems such as *inflation* and depression can be controlled simply by controlling the *money stock* in the economy.

monetary policy. The policy of a government regarding the *money stock* in its country.

money. Something generally accepted as a means of discharging debts, making payments and measuring value. (See also *money stock*.)

money broker. A person who arranges deals, on behalf of his clients, on a *money market*.

money market. A *market* [4] for the purchase and sale of *liquid assets*—especially *bills of exchange, Treasury bills* and other *securities* [1] that are due to be *redeemed* within a very short time and where there is very little risk of default.

money-off pack. Synonymous with *flash pack*.

money shop. An office of a bank that provides a wide range of financial services to individual customers rather than businesses and which is designed to look more like a shop than a traditional banking office.

money stock (or money supply). The total amount of *money* in a country, measured in various ways. The two measures of money used in UK official statistics are M_1 and M_3.

M_1—the 'narrowly defined money stock'—is the total value of *cash* (*bank notes* and coins) and *demand deposits* at banks that are held by members of the public and firms (not by banks or the government) that are resident in the UK. (Only deposits in sterling are counted.)

M_3—the 'widely defined money stock'—is the total value of cash in private circulation plus all resident deposits with banks (i.e. both sterling and non-sterling, demand deposits and *time deposits* held by firms, individuals, government and local authorities).

At one time an intermediate definition, M_2, was also used in which a distinction was drawn among private-sector deposit accounts between time deposits with *deposit banks* and with *discount houses* [1] and other banks.

monitor (noun). 1. A device for observing continuously the activity or output of a system so as to indicate deviations from a planned or normal state. 2. Synonym for *supervisory program*.

monitor (verb). To observe or measure continuously the activity or output of a system in order to discover variations from a planned or normal state.

monitored control system. Synonym for *closed-loop control system*.

monitoring feedback. In a *control system*, transmission of information about the controlled condition along a separate path provided for that purpose, comparison of the information with information about the desired state of the controlled condition and production of information about difference between actual and desired states.

monitor program. Synonym for *supervisory program*.

Monopolies and Mergers Commission. Permanent commission set up in 1948 to investigate and make public reports on various kinds of monopolistic practices in the UK. It was originally called the Monopolies and Restrictive Practices Commission; it was renamed the Monopolies Commission in 1956 (when the *Restrictive Practices Court* was established) and given its present title on 1 November 1973.

The Commission has not less than 10 and not more than 25 regular members appointed by the Secretary of State. One of the regular members is appointed chairman by the Secretary of State.

The Commission's main function is to investigate and report on questions referred to it by the *Director General of Fair Trading* or by the Secretary of State. The Commission may be asked to say whether a 'monopoly situation' or a proposed *merger* is likely to be detrimental to the public interest and, if so, what action should be taken.

A 'monopoly situation' exists if one person, or one company or group of companies supplies more than one-quarter of the

UK market for particular goods or services, or if more than one-quarter of the UK supplies of particular goods or services are bought by one buyer.

The Commission can also be asked to investigate a situation in which suppliers refuse to supply in the UK goods or services of a particular description.

A proposed merger may be referred to the Commission if either the company to be taken over has assets worth more than £5 million or if the merger will create a monopoly situation.

The Commission has wide powers to require people to give evidence to it and to produce documents.

Monopolies Commission. See *Monopolies and Mergers Commission.*

monopoly. Domination of a *market* [1] by a single seller.

monopsony. Domination of a *market* [1] by a single buyer.

moonlighter. One who engages in *moonlighting.*

moonlighting. Being employed by two employers simultaneously; especially doing one job during the day and another at night. (Also called 'double jobbing'.)

morale survey. An *attitude survey* [1] carried out among employees of a firm to determine what they think of their current employment.

moratorium. An agreement between the *creditors* [1] of someone who is in financial difficulty that they will not press for payment of their debts for a period (say, six months) to give the debtor an opportunity to improve his fortunes.

morning shift. A *shift* that is worked mainly in the late morning—e.g.: (1) the earlier shift during a day in a *double day-shift system;* (2) a shift that is worked mainly in the late morning in a *three-shift system,* typically worked from 0600 to 1400; (3) a *part-time shift* worked, for example, from 0800 to 1200.

morphological analysis. A technique for encouraging creative thinking. Solving a problem is seen as finding the right combination of alternative factors; to facilitate this, all possible factors are listed in classes and all possible combinations of factors with one factor from each class are tested for suitability as a solution.

mortgage (noun). A transfer of some rights over a person's property, which is made by him as *security* [2] for a loan to him and on condition that the rights must be returned to him when he repays the loan. (Sometimes called a 'fixed charge'.)

The person who gives the rights (i.e. the borrower) is called the 'mortgagor' and the person who receives the rights (the lender) is the 'mortgagee'. A mortgage gives the mortgagee the right to 'foreclose'—i.e. to ask a court to transfer *all* rights of ownership to him—if the mortgagor does not pay his debt on time. In practice, the drastic step of foreclosure is rarely taken, and mortgage agreements give other rights—such as the right to appoint a *receiver*, or the right to sell property and pay the debt from the proceeds—if the debt is not paid on time. The mortgagor is usually not allowed to do anything with the property that might affect the mortgagee (e.g. sell it or lease it).

mortgage (verb). To give someone rights over one's property by means of a *mortgage*.

mortgage bond. Equivalent in the USA to a *mortgage debenture*.

mortgage debenture. A *debenture* [2] issued by a company that has *mortgaged* specific assets to a trustee for the debenture holders.

mortgagee. The person who acquires rights over property by means of a *mortgage*.

mortgagor. The person who gives rights over his property by a *mortgage*.

most likely time. An estimate of the time taken to complete an *activity* in *PERT* that the estimator feels the activity would most often take if it were repeated again and again.

most optimistic time. An estimate of the time to complete an *activity* in *PERT* that has a probability of 0.01 of being correct and which is based on the assumption that there will be no problems at all.

most pessimistic time. An estimate of the time to complete an *activity* in *PERT* that has a probability of 0.01 of being correct and is based on the assumption that everything will go wrong.

motion and time study. Synonym for *work study*.

motion study. Synonym for *method study*.

motivate. To create circumstances in which a particular individual will acquire *motivation* [1] to behave in a particular way.

motivation. 1. The causes of particular behaviour by an individual—especially causes (e.g. emotions) related to the internal state of the individual. 2. Process or study of *motivating* people to behave in a particular way.

motivation-hygiene theory. The view, advanced by the American psychologist Frederick Herzberg (born 1923), that an employee derives *job satisfaction* from two separate sources: 'hygiene factors' and 'motivators'.

The 'hygiene factors' are matters not directly connected with the task to be performed in the job; they are, for example, working conditions, remuneration, interpersonal relationships and the managerial styles of superiors. Herzberg suggests that if these factors do not reach a certain standard then they will cause dissatisfaction but that when they are at an acceptable standard they will not contribute to satisfaction.

The 'motivators' are concerned with the tasks to be performed; they are, for example, the nature of the tasks, the possibility that the job offers for career advancement, and the opportunities for assuring oneself that one has done a good job. If these factors are good then they will cause satisfaction but if they are poor it is unlikely they will cause dissatisfaction.

Evidence for the theory is given in F. Herzberg, B. Mausner and Barbara Snyderman, *The Motivation to Work* (New York: Wiley, 1959). See also, F. Herzberg, *Work and the Nature of Man* (New York: World Publishing Co., 1966/London: Staples Press, 1968).

motivator. An aspect of a job that can contribute to the satisfaction but not the dissatisfaction of the job holder according to the *motivation-hygiene theory*.

moving average. If $x_1, x_2, x_3, \ldots, x_m$ is a sequence of numbers then a 'moving average of order n' (where n is a positive whole number) is the sequence of *arithmetic means*:

$$(x_1 + \ldots + x_n)/n, \ (x_2 + \ldots + x_{n+1})/n, \ (x_3 + \ldots + x_{n+2})/n, \text{ etc.}$$

Moving averages are often used to describe *time series*. When a time series consists of annual observations then a moving average of order *n* is called an '*n*-year moving average'. For example, if annual observations are 2000, 6000, 1000, 5000, 3000, 7000 then the three-year moving average is:

$$(2000 + 6000 + 1000)/3, (6000 + 1000 + 5000)/3,$$
$$(1000 + 5000 + 3000)/3 \text{ etc.}$$

i.e. 3000, 4000, 3000 etc.

multi-factor incentive scheme. An *incentive payment system* in which the incentive payment depends on several factors—e.g. performance, quality of output and wastage of materials.

multinational (adjective). Operating in many countries.

multinational (noun). A firm that operates in many countries.

multinational company (or multinational corporation). A *company* (or *corporation*) that operates in many countries. (Also known as an 'international company'.)

multi-pack. A package containing several separate items which is sold as one unit.

multi-packaging. Packing several small items together for sale instead of selling them individually.

multiple. An enterprise that owns and operates a number of retail establishments. (Also known as a 'chain'.)

multiple-activity chart. A chart showing the interrelated activities of two or more subjects (e.g. of several workers in a team) in the order in which the activities occur. If a timescale is added, such a chart is known as a 'multiple-activity time chart'.

multiple branding. The practice, by a manufacturer, of selling similar products, or the same product, under different *brands* in competition with each other.

multiple exchange rates. *Exchange rates* which a country enforces for its currency through *exchange controls* and which differ according to the type of transaction for which a payment is made.

multiple management. A system of *employee participation* devised by Charles P. McCormick of McCormick & Co. Inc.

(producers of spices and foods in Baltimore, Maryland) during the 1930s. Committees are formed to represent the employees in particular areas of a firm and there is also a *junior board*. Committees are able to discuss freely any subject and may present unanimous motions to the board of directors for consideration. See, e.g. C. P. McCormick, *The Power of People: Multiple Management up to Date* (New York: Harper and Brothers, 1949).

multiple regression analysis (MRA). *Regression analysis* involving two or more independent variables.

multiple time plan. 1. Synonym for *measured daywork*. 2. Synonym for *double daywork*.

multiplexing. Simultaneous or almost simultaneous transmission of a number of different messages through a single communications channel.

multiplexor. A device for combining several messages for simultaneous transmission using one communications channel.

multiplier effect. The phenomenon that creation of additional *capital goods* (investment) by the business enterprises in an economy increases *national income* by more than the value of the investment. The ratio between the increase in income and the increase in net investment is called the 'multiplier'.

multiprocessing. Use of two or more linked *computers* (or two or more linked *central processing units*) with a single *control unit* so that several different jobs can be performed simultaneously. The main control unit determines which processing unit is to perform a particular operation.

multiprogramming. Using a single *central processing unit* (CPU) in a *computer* to perform several jobs simultaneously. This is possible because *peripheral equipment* operates more slowly than the central processing unit; thus while the CPU is waiting for a peripheral unit to carry out an operation the CPU can be used to work on a different job.

multi-project scheduling. Planning how to allocate resources and time to a number of activities.

multi-unionism. Existence of a number of trade unions in one place of employment.

mutual fund (US). A *collective investment institution* organized as a *corporation* in which the investment fund is the corporation's *contributed capital*. The corporation usually promises to re-purchase its stock from holders whenever they ask it to (i.e. to acquire it as *treasury stock*); a mutual fund also sells its stock continuously. (Thus, like a *unit trust*, a mutual fund is 'open-ended'.)

mutual life assurance company. A company whose business is providing *life assurance* but in which all *policyholders* are *members* of the company (and all members are policyholders). The profits of the company are distributed to policyholders as *bonuses*.

n

NBPI. Abbreviation of *National Board for Prices and Incomes.*

NCC. Abbreviation of *National Computing Centre.*

NCQR. Abbreviation of *National Council for Quality and Reliability.*

NDP. Abbreviation of *net domestic product.*

NEC. 1. Abbreviation of 'not elsewhere classified'—i.e. a category for miscellaneous items in a classification. 2. Abbreviation of 'national executive committee' (of a trade union or political party).

NEDC. Abbreviation of *National Economic Development Council.*

NEDO. Abbreviation of *National Economic Development Office.*

NIESR. Abbreviation of *National Institute of Economic and Social Research.*

NIRC. Abbreviation of *National Industrial Relations Court.*

NNP. Abbreviation of *net national product.*

NPV. Abbreviation of *net present value.*

NV. Abbreviation of *naamloze vennootschap.*

naamloze vennootschap (NV). 1. A *limited company* organized according to the laws of the Netherlands. 2. Flemish name for a *société anonyme* [2].

naked debenture. A *debenture* [2] issued by a company that has not given any *security* [2] for the loan. (Also known as a 'simple debenture'.)

name day. Synonym for *ticket day.*

276

narration. An explanation, written in the account, of an entry in an *account* [1].

National Association of British Manufacturers. An association formed in 1915 to represent the interests of individual firms in manufacturing industry (especially small firms) and which became part of the *Confederation of British Industry* in 1965. It was called the National Union of Manufacturers until 1961.

National Board for Prices and Incomes (NBPI). Body set up by a Labour government in the UK in 1965 to examine wage claims and price increases referred to it by the government. The Board did a great deal of research into payment systems and pricing structures which was published in its reports. The Board was disbanded in 1971 by a new, Conservative government. In 1973 the *Pay Board* and *Price Commission* were set up.

National Computing Centre (NCC). Non-profit-making UK organization, financed by industry and government, the purpose of which is to promote knowledge of and use of computers in the UK.

National Confederation of Employers' Organizations. See *British Employers' Confederation.*

National Council for Quality and Reliability (NCQR). An organization which assists industry, commerce, the professions and the government in promoting the quality of all types of British products and services. It had 300 subscribing members in 1974. NCQR was originally set up under the *British Productivity Council* but now operates as an independent body. It publishes a quarterly bulletin.

Address: 1 Birdcage Walk, London SW1H 9JJ (01–839 1211).

National Debt. The total amount that has been borrowed by the government.

national defence contribution. An additional tax on the earnings of companies in the UK (which at that time paid *income tax*) which was introduced in 1937 and renamed *profits tax* in 1947.

National Economic Development Council (NEDC or Neddy). National forum for economic consultation between government, management and unions in the UK. Monthly meetings are held of the council, which consists of 6 representatives of the *Confederation of British Industry*, 6 of the *Trades Union Congress*, 2 chairmen of nationalized industries, 2 independent members, the Secretaries of State for Employment and for Trade and Industry, the Director-General of the *National Economic Development Office* and the Chancellor of the Exchequer (who is chairman). Meetings are held in private to discuss national economic policies. The council first met in 1962.

National Economic Development Office (NEDO). Independent organization, financed from public funds, that provides information, research, and services for the *National Economic Development Council* and the *economic development committees*.

National Giro. A *giro* transfer and deposit-banking service run by the British Post Office.

national income. The *gross national product* of a country at factor cost during a period minus an estimate of the *depreciation* [2] of the country's *capital goods* during that period. It represents the total remuneration of the elements used in production (land, labour, capital and entrepreneurship).

National Incomes Commission. Body set up in 1962 by a Conservative government in the UK to examine pay claims referred to it by the government, unions or employers. It was ignored by trade unions and replaced in 1965 by the *National Board for Prices and Incomes*.

National Industrial Relations Court (NIRC). British court established on 1 October 1971 with jurisdiction over a wide range of disputes between employers and employees. Trade unions generally refused to take any part in proceedings in the NIRC and it was abolished by the *Trade Union and Labour Relations Act 1974* as from 31 July 1974. (Also known as the Industrial Court.)

National Institute of Economic and Social Research (NIESR). An independent *guarantee company* formed in 1938 to conduct research in order to increase knowledge of the social and economic conditions of contemporary society. NIESR publishes a quarterly journal, *National Institute Economic Review*, which presents a quarterly analysis of the economic situation and prospects.

Address: 2 Dean Trench Street, Smith Square, London SW1P 3HE (01–222 7665).

nationalization. 1. Action or process of *nationalizing*. 2. State of being *nationalized*.

nationalize. To transfer ownership of something (usually compulsorily) from private individuals to the government of a country.

National Labor Relations Act 1935. US statute which governs relations between unions and employers. The Act (1) declares that public policy is to encourage and facilitate *collective bargaining* through *trade unions* [1]; (2) defines the rights of employees to join trade unions of their own choice; (3) prohibits action by employers that is defined as 'unfair labor practices' (such as interference with employees' rights to join unions); (4) created the National Labor Relations Board to administer the Act.

National Loans Fund. An *account* [3] of the *Treasury* at the *Bank of England* established on 1 April 1968. Any surplus at the end of a day in the *Consolidated Fund* is paid into the National Loans Fund. Withdrawals from the National Loans Fund are made for government loans to nationalized industries, local authorities and similar bodies.

National Union of Manufacturers. Until 1961, the title of the *National Association of British Manufacturers.*

near cash. Something that can be converted into a known amount of *cash* at very short notice—for example, a *demand deposit.*

near money. Something which may be easily converted into *money* at short notice—for example, *Treasury bills,* a *time deposit.*

Neddy. The *National Economic Development Council.*

need. 1. Something that is required by an individual for his health and wellbeing. If a need is not satisfied then an internal disturbance (either physiological or psychological) called a 'drive' is set up which tends to make the individual aware of his unsatisfied need and acts as a *motivation* [1] for him to take action to satisfy the need. 2. Something that an individual wants with sufficient regularity or consistency for it to be treated as a feature of his personality.

negligence. Failure to exercise the care that a prudent person usually exercises. *Also* an act or instance of negligence.

negotiable. 1. Capable of being negotiated. 2. May be modified during negotiations (as in 'negotiable demand').

negotiable instrument. A document that entitles its owner to payment of money by someone else (e.g. a *currency note, cheque* or *bill of exchange*) and which, if delivered, or delivered with an *endorsement* [1], by one person to a second person is indisputably the property of the second person.

negotiable warehouse receipt. A *warrant* [4].

negotiate. 1. To discuss with someone with whom one has a difference or dispute possible terms for the settlement of the difference or dispute. 2. To transfer something to someone in such a way that he is the undisputed owner of it. 3. To deal with an event, a problem, or a difference with someone. 4. To proceed successfully.

negotiating machinery. The institutions for conducting negotiations between employers and trade unions and the rules governing such negotiations.

negotiation. Action or process of *negotiating*.

net (adjective). 1. After specified deductions have been made. 2. Not subject to any further deductions. 3. From which no deductions may be made; as in 'net price' (a minimum price). 4. Sold at net prices.

net (verb). 1. To gain as a *net* [1] amount. 2. To compute a *net* [1, 2] amount.

net annual value. The result of subtracting a statutory repairs allowance from the *annual value* of land under the system of taxing income from land in the UK (Schedule A) that was abolished in 1963.

net assets. 1. Total *assets* [2] of a firm less *current liabilities*. This is equal to the capital employed. 2. Total *assets* [2] of a firm less *current liabilities, debt capital,* any other long-term loans and *provisions*. This is equal to the *owners' equity*.

net cash. A phrase used to announce that no *cash discount* or *credit* [3] will be given.

280

net cash flow. 1. *Net profit* [1] (after payment of *corporate income tax*) of a firm over a period. 2. See *cash flow* [3].

net current assets. Difference between the values of a firm's total *current assets* and its total *current liabilities* at a particular time. (Also known as 'net working capital'.)

net domestic product (NDP). The *gross domestic product* of an economy over a particular period minus an estimate of the *depreciation* [2] of the economy's *capital goods* during the period.

net income. The *net profit* [1] of a firm over a period measured after deducting payments of *corporate income tax*, interest on *debt capital* and (usually) *preference dividends*. Note that net income (unlike *net operating income*) includes receipts from transactions that are not related to the firm's main activities and also includes the cost of paying interest on loans and debt capital.

net loss. See *loss* [1].

net national product (NNP). The *gross national product* of an economy over a particular period minus an estimate of the *depreciation* [2] of the economy's *capital goods* during the period. If the NNP is measured at factor cost it is called 'national income'.

net operating income. The *profit* made on a firm's main operations over a period. It is made up of the *net sales* minus *cost of sales* and other *operating expenses*. No account is taken of receipts from transactions not related to the firm's main activities (e.g. *dividends* [2] from *portfolio investments*) or of the cost of finance (i.e. interest on loans and *debt capital*). (Also known as 'net operating profit'.)

net present value (NPV). The net present value of an *investment project* is the *present value* of the sequence of *cash inflows* associated with the project minus the present value of the sequence of *cash outflows* associated with the project.

net profit. 1. A financial gain which is achieved by a firm over a period or from a particular activity and which is measured after allowing for all *expenses* [3] and *lost costs* incurred during the period. It may be measured with or without deducting payments of *corporate income tax*, interest on *debt capital* and *preference dividends*. (See also, *net income* and *net revenue*.) 2. The amount by which the *proceeds* of a sale exceed the total *expenses* [3] associated with the sale.

net profit margin. The ratio of *net profit* [1] acquired by a firm over a specified period from the sale of a specified product (or from all its activities) to the *revenues* [1] it received during that period from the sale of the product (or from all its activities). (Usually expressed as a percentage.)

net revenue. Synonym for *net profit* [1].

net sales (or net sales revenue). Total invoiced charges for the sale of goods or services over a period less *cash discounts* taken by customers, the value of *returns* [3] by customers and any other allowances. (See *sales revenue*.)

net statutory income. The amount of an individual's income for a *year of assessment* that is liable to UK *income tax* after deduction of *personal reliefs*. In legislation, this amount is referred to as 'total income'.

Net statutory income is computed by: (1) Adding together the amounts of taxable income received from each of the sources of income that are described in the *Income Tax Acts* by six Schedules (called Schedule A, B, C, D, E and F). For each Schedule there are rules for calculating the taxable income by taking the actual income for a particular period (not necessarily the year of assessment) and making deductions to allow for the expense of getting that income. (2) Adding to (1) the amount of income from which tax was deducted by the payer. (3) Sub-tracting amounts paid to others from which tax has been deducted and certain other allowable deductions.

net terminal value. The *terminal value* of the *cash inflows* associated with an investment project minus the terminal value of the *cash outflows* at a specified time (usually the time when the investment is likely to be abandoned).

network. A diagram, used in *project network techniques*, that represents the component *activities* and/or *events* in a *project* [4] and shows their interrelationships. A network consists of lines, called 'arrows', that join points (or circles or rectangles) called 'nodes'. A network is a *graph* [2] but users of project network techniques have developed a terminology that is almost entirely different from that used by mathematicians who have built up the theory of graphs. (Also known as an 'activity network' or a 'project network'.)

network analysis. Analysis of a project using a *project network technique*. (Also known as 'project network analysis'.)

network-beginning event. Synonym for *start event*.

network-ending event. Synonym for *end event*.

net working capital. The difference between the values of a firm's total *current assets* and its total *current liabilities* at a particular time. (Also known as 'net current assets'.)

network planning. Using a *project network technique* for planning.

net worth. Synonym for *owners' equity*.

night shift. A *shift* that is worked mainly at night (see *nightwork*). (Colloquially known as a 'graveyard shift'.)

nightwork. Work performed at night. The conventions adopted by the *International Labour Organisation* for the control of nightwork define 'night' as 'a period of at least 11 consecutive hours including the interval between 22 00 and 05 00'.

node. An end of an *arrow* in a *network*.

node diagram. Synonym for *activity-on-node network*.

nominal capital. Synonym for *nominal share capital*.

nominal share capital. The total *nominal value* of all the *shares* that a company is authorized by its constitution to issue. (Also known as 'authorized capital' or 'nominal capital'.)

nominal value. A value assigned to something purely for purposes of description or identification or as a basis for some calculation. (Also known as 'par value'.)

nominee. A person who acts in name only; *specifically* a person who is entered in a company's *register of members* as the owner of shares which are in fact controlled by someone else who wishes to be anonymous or is technically not allowed to own shares.

nomogram (or nomograph). Three or more scales (straight or curved) drawn and arranged so that when a straightedge is laid across them it intersects them at the related values of a number of variables.

non-contributory pension scheme. A scheme for providing

pensions to employees that does not involve payments by the employees.

noncurrent asset. An *asset* [1] that is not a *current asset*.

nondurable goods. *Goods* [2] that can usually be used only once or a few times or have a useful life that is very much less than one year.

nonexecutive director. A *director* of a *company* [1] who is not also a full-time employee of the company. (Also known as an 'outside director'.)

nonlinear programming. The techniques of *mathematical programming* that are used to solve problems in which either the objective function or the constraints, or both, are not *linear functions*. Particular types of nonlinear programming are: *quadratic programming* and *separable programming*.

nonparametric test. A test used in *statistical inference* in which no assumption is made about the form of the *probability distribution*.

nonvoting share. An *ordinary share* in a company that carries no entitlement to vote at shareholders' meetings.

no-par share. A *share* that is not given a *nominal value* (or 'par value') in its *share certificate* (or *stock certificate* [1]) or in dealings on *stock exchanges* [1]. No-par shares are usually assigned a nominal value (called the 'stated value') for purposes of accounting and taxation. In most EEC countries (except Belgium) companies may not issue no-par shares. (*Unlimited companies* in the UK are allowed to issue no-par shares, but this is a minor exception.) In the USA they are legal but their popularity is declining. (Also called a 'share of no par value'.)

normal curve. *Graph* [1] of the *normal distribution*.

normal density function. The *frequency function* of the *normal distribution*.

normal distribution. A *probability distribution* of which the *frequency function* is:

$$f(x) = \frac{1}{\sigma\sqrt{(2\pi)}} e^{-(x-\mu)^2/2\sigma^2}$$

where σ (the *standard deviation* [1]) and μ (the *mean* [1]) are constants.

284

The normal distribution is very important in *statistics* [3] because it corresponds to the frequency distribution of many natural phenomena.

normal population. A *population* associated with a *random variable* that has a *normal distribution*.

normal working area. The space within which a seated or standing worker can reach and use tools, materials and equipment when his elbows fall naturally by the side of the body (cf. *maximum working area*).

normative. Establishing, or seeking to establish, norms; attempting to set out the proper course of action; stating what should be rather than what is, was or will be.

Norris-La Guardia Act. US statute of 1932 which restricts the use of injunctions in industrial disputes and outlaws *yellow-dog contracts*.

notary public. An individual who is appointed to draw up and certify documents in order to guarantee their authenticity. In England a 'general notary' is appointed by the Court of Faculties following a five-year apprenticeship; a general notary may practise anywhere. A 'district notary' in England is allowed to practise only in a defined area.

note (noun). Synonym for *promissory note*.

note (verb). To attach a certificate to a *bill of exchange* stating that it has been presented for payment (usually by a *notary public*) and has been *dishonoured*.

notice. 1. A formal declaration to a person of an intention to take action that will affect him. 2. An indication by one party to a *contract* that he will treat the contract as being ended as from a specified time in the future. *Also* the period of time between giving such an indication and ending the contract.

numerical control. Control of an operation (especially of a *machine tool*) by a computer.

nursed account. A supplier whose invoices are always paid immediately by a firm which does not bother to pay other firms' invoices. The nursed account will provide a good *trade reference* to a new supplier.

O

O & M. Abbreviation of *organization and methods*.

OECD. Abbreviation of *Organisation for Economic Co-operation and Development*.

OR. 1. (US.) Abbreviation of *operations research*. 2. (UK.) Abbreviation of *operational research*.

obiter dictum. A remark made by a judge when explaining in court his decision in a case but which is not a reason for making that decision.

objective (adjective). Expressing or involving the use of facts without distortion by personal feelings or prejudices.

objective (noun). The desired result of some effect or activity.

objective test. A *test* consisting of questions to be answered by the testee in which each question has only one correct answer. Thus the opinion of the person marking the test does not influence the rating he gives the testee.

object program. The result of translation, by a *computer* using a *translating routine*, of a *source program*. The object program is in a form more readily usable by the computer than the source program.

objects clause. A clause in the *memorandum of association* of a British *registered company* which states the objects of the company (i.e. the activities it was set up to perform).

obligee. The person for whose benefit a promise is made in a *bond* [1].

obligor. The person who makes a promise in a *bond* [1].

obsolescent. Becoming *obsolete;* nearly obsolete.

obsolete. No longer in use; disused; outmoded.

occupation. 1. A class of *jobs* [1], which people are employed to perform, that are sufficiently similar in their main tasks to be grouped together for purposes of description, analysis or classification. 2. The *office* [1], *employment* [5], *trade* [2], *profession* or *vocation* that a person is engaged in.

occupational psychology. The study of psychological problems associated with work and which arise in connection with, for example, vocational guidance, design of *aptitude tests,* personnel selection, training, *work study* or *ergonomics.* (Also known as 'industrial psychology'.)

occupational role. A *role* adopted by someone in order to pursue his *occupation* [1]. E.g. a specific *job* [1] or an arrangement for practising a *profession.*

occupational title. The name given to an *occupation* [1].

odd pricing. Practice of *pricing* goods in odd amounts (e.g. £1.99 rather than £2.00) in order to suggest a bargain.

offer. A proposal made by one person (called the 'offeror') to another person (called the 'offeree') of the terms of a *contract* and an indication that if the offeree *accepts* [2] the proposal then the offeror will consider himself bound by the contract. Sometimes the offeror specifies the way in which acceptance must be communicated to him or puts a time-limit on acceptance.

offer by tender. A method of making a *public offer* of *securities* [1] in which the public is invited to submit *tenders* [3] for purchasing the securities.

offeree. A person to whom an *offer* is made.

offer for sale. A *public offer* of *shares* in a company which is made by an *issuing house* and in which the shares being sold are not new shares but have been sold to the issuing house by existing shareholders.

offeror. Someone who makes an *offer.*

offer price. 1. The price at which the *management company* of a *unit trust* will sell units. 2. The price at which a *jobber* [2] will sell a *security* [1].

office. 1. A collection of duties and responsibilities carried out by an appointed person (called the 'holder' of the office)—especially where several people may be appointed holder in succession with no change in the nature of the duties and responsibilities, and where the holder is not under a *contract of employment* or the duties are of a public nature. 2. A place where business (especially clerical and administrative rather than retailing and manufacturing) is carried out. 3. The room that a particular person or group of people use to perform non-manual work. 4. A firm of *insurers*.

Office of Fair Trading. UK government agency headed by the *Director General of Fair Trading* and carrying out his work concerning consumer protection and control of monopolies and mergers.

Address : Chancery House, 53 Chancery Lane, London WC2A 1SP (01–242 2858).

official receiver. A government official in the UK who assists in the process of *liquidating* [3] companies.

official reserves. The assets that a country's *central bank* has available for making payments to nonresidents: they consist of stocks of gold, holdings of *special drawing rights* and holdings of foreign currencies. (Also known as 'exchange reserves' or 'reserve assets'.)

official strike. Strike which has the support of a trade union—which usually provides money for the strikers, provides officials to negotiate on their behalf with their employer and deals with public relations.

off-line. Not *on-line*.

offshore. Not subject to regulation (especially in relation to protection of investors and taxation) by the country in which operations are carried out. Used, in particular, of *companies* which are registered in *tax havens* or in countries where there is little regulation of financial activity.

off-the-job training. Any *training* that takes place while the *trainee* is not performing his normal job.

ogive. The *graph* [1] of a *distribution function*.

oligopoly. A *market* [1] that is dominated by a small number of sellers.

oligopsony. A *market* [1] that is dominated by a small number of buyers.

on call. Available to perform work immediately a request is made.

oncost. Synonym for *indirect cost*.

on demand. At such time as a request is made. For example, if a *bill of exchange* or *promissory note* is stated to be 'payable on demand' it must be paid immediately a request for payment is made.

one-point arbitrage. Synonym for *simple arbitrage*.

on-line. Directly connected to the *central processing unit* of a *computer*.

on-the-job training. Any *training* that takes place while the *trainee* is in his normal place of work and (to a large extent) doing his normal job.

open account. A system of trading in which a seller sends goods and an invoice to a buyer who is expected to make payment within a reasonable time.

open-door policy. Attitude taken by a manager or supervisor that any of his subordinates who have a problem can feel free to come to discuss it at any time.

open-ended. Not of a fixed size. Used, e.g., (1) to describe a *collective investment institution* that uses an investment fund which is unlimited in size (see *mutual fund* and *unit trust*); (2) to describe a question (especially on a *questionnaire*) which invites an unlimited statement of opinions or feelings rather than a limited statement of facts; (3) to describe a commitment to spend or lend money of unlimited amount; (4) to describe a meeting with no fixed finishing time.

open-loop control system. A *control system* without *monitoring feedback*. An open-loop control system is not affected by the actual state of the controlled condition. (Also known as an 'unmonitored control system'.)

open position. A *short position*.

open shop. A place of employment in which no trade union is recognized by the employer as representing his employees.

open system. A *system* of regularly interacting components whose activity is largely concerned with converting material or energy (called 'inputs' or 'imports') taken in from outside the system (i.e. from the 'environment') into some 'output' or 'export' that is returned to the environment.

There is a considerable amount of theory about how simple open systems, such as biological organisms or mechanical or chemical systems operate. This *systems theory* is of interest in management because a firm can be considered to be an open system, taking in materials and exporting products. Furthermore, it is possible to identify several *subsystems* within a firm—e.g. a production system and a marketing system. Systems theory provides insights into, for example, what constitutes a system and how a system can be controlled and directed.

open union. A *trade union* [1] that will accept as a member anyone who wishes to join.

operating assets. The *assets* [1] of a firm that are used in, or derived from, its normal operations.

operating cycle. The average time taken by a firm to convert materials or bought-out components into a finished product, sell it and collect payment for the sale.

operating expenses. The *expenses* [3] incurred by a firm, over a period, in carrying out its normal operations apart from financing expenses such as payment of interest on *debt capital*. The term is often taken to exclude *cost of sales* but there is no standard usage.

operating profit. *Profit* derived by a firm over a period from its normal operations.

operating system. 1. A set of *programs* [1] (including a *supervisory program* and several *utility programs*) that perform routine tasks within a *computer* but do not contain instructions for processing data. 2. A system that includes people performing work and which has been identified for purposes of discussion and analysis that concentrate attention on the performance of work. The term is often used by A. K. Rice and his associates— see, e.g. A. K. Rice, *Productivity and Social Organization: The Ahmedabad Experiment* (London: Tavistock Publications 1958) or E. J. Miller and A. K. Rice, *Systems of Organization* (London:

Tavistock Publications, 1967).

operation. 1. Intentional action to change the physical or chemical characteristics of something. 2. Intentional action to change the location of data or to derive further data according to an established rule (e.g. by addition).

operational research (OR.) (Chiefly UK.) Synonym for *operations research.*

operation chart. Synonym for *two-handed process chart.*

operation process chart. Synonym for *outline process chart.*

operations management. Application of the principles and techniques of *production management* to the management of nonmanufacturing organizations.

operations research (OR). Activity, process, or study of applying scientific (especially mathematical) methods to the solution of problems involving the operations of a *system.* The usual aim of OR is to provide those in control of the system with an *optimum* plan for the operation of the system.

operator performance. The ratio of the total *standard times* for all *measured work* and *estimated work* performed by a particular individual during a period to the time he actually spent performing the work during that period. (Usually expressed as a percentage.)

opportunity cost. The value of some course of action which one could take but does not. For example, the opportunity cost of holding *cash* in a *current account*]1] instead of investing it in *securities* [1] (because it is thought necessary to have the money instantly available) is the value of the interest that is forgone. (Sometimes called 'cost'.)

optimality. State, or quality, of being *optimum.*

optimization. The process of determining an *optimum.*

optimize. 1. To make *optimum.* 2. To achieve an *optimum* state. 3. To calculate an *optimum* value.

optimum (adjective). As favourable or as satisfactory as is possible under specified conditions.

optimum (noun). State in which matters are as favourable or as satisfactory as possible under specified conditions.

optimum order quantity. Synonym for *economic lot size.*

option. An arrangement by which one person (called an 'option holder') may buy specified goods from (or sell them to) another person at a fixed price at any time he chooses within defined limits. With some options it may be possible to do nothing at all. A fee (see *option money*) is paid by the option holder. See *call option, double option, option forward, put option, share option, stock option*.

option forward (or option forward contract). A contract by which one person undertakes to sell—at an agreed *exchange rate*—a stated amount of foreign currency at a time in the future to be chosen by the buyer (within specified limits). *Also* a similar contract in which the seller chooses the time of delivery. Note that in an option forward, delivery must take place whereas with an *option*, the holder of the option can choose to do nothing if he wishes. Option forwards are used in foreign-exchange markets (but options are not) whereas options are used in commodity and security markets.

option money. The fee paid by the holder of an *option* for the option. The holder is sometimes called the 'giver' of option money and the other party is called the 'taker' of option money (though sometimes the taker of option money is called the 'giver' of the option and the giver of option money is called the 'taker' of the option).

Order in Council. *Delegated legislation* made by the Crown, by and with the advice of the *Privy Council*.

ordinary resolution. A *resolution* taken or to be discussed by a company's *general meeting* and which is binding if more than half of the votes cast at the meeting are in favour of it.

ordinary share. A *share* in a *company* [1] which carries a right to a *dividend* [2] if the *directors* recommend that one should be paid, the right to vote at *general meetings* of the company, and the right to a proportion of whatever is left of the company's *assets* [1] after it has been liquidated [3]. (The equivalent in the USA is a share of *common stock*.)

ordinary shareholder. Someone who owns one or more *ordinary shares* of a particular company [1].

Organisation for Economic Co-operation and Develop-

ment (OECD). An international organization founded in September 1961 to promote high economic growth and employment among member countries, to coordinate and improve development aid and to help expand world trade. The members are: Australia, Austria, Belgium, Canada, Denmark, Finland, France, Federal Republic of Germany, Greece, Iceland, Irish Republic, Italy, Japan, Luxembourg, Netherlands, Norway, Portugal, Spain, Sweden, Switzerland, Turkey, UK and USA. (Also known by its French title, Organisation de coopération et de développement économiques.)

organization. 1. The act or process of *organizing*. 2. A result of *organizing* [1]; a set of definitions of positions which are intended to enable the position holders to work together to carry out certain tasks. *Also* the group of people holding positions in an organization.

organizational behaviour (spelt 'organizational behavior' in USA). The behaviour of people when they are acting as members of *organizations* [2].

organizational change. Change in the *organization structure* or in the usual forms of *organizational behaviour* in a particular organization.

organizational climate. The points of view, particularly on how employees should be treated, that are common to most senior people in an organization.

organization and methods (O & M). The body of knowledge concerning *data-processing systems,* including ways of arranging flows of work, methods of performing tasks and the design and use of data-processing equipment.

organization chart. A chart which shows one or more aspects of relationships between positions in an *organization* [2]; usually showing the way responsibility is allocated.

organization costs. (US.) Synonym for *preliminary expenses.*

organization development. The activity of improving an organization's ability to achieve its goals by using people more effectively.

Organization for Trade Cooperation. An international organization, on the lines of the abandoned *International Trade*

293

Organization, which was to have been set up under a treaty signed in 1955. The treaty has not been ratified by enough countries for it to come into force and so the organization has never come into existence.

organization meeting (US). A meeting of the owners of a newly incorporated *corporation* at which formalities concerning the setting-up of the corporation are dealt with (e.g. the adoption of *bylaws* [2] or election of a *chief executive*).

organization planning. Deciding on the form of organization appropriate to an enterprise. The process includes grouping activities, delineating authority and responsibility, and establishing working relationships.

organization structure. The established pattern of relationships between members of an organization.

organization theory. The body of knowledge about *organizational behaviour* and *organization structure.*

organize. 1. To specify some of the characteristics of a number of *roles* (usually called 'positions') so that they form an interdependent system (an 'organization'). The usual reason for organizing is so that when suitably chosen people take up the specified roles then the specifications will enable them to work together to achieve a definite purpose. Therefore, an important aspect of organizing is to specify the tasks and duties that are expected to be undertaken in each role. It is also usual to specify the *authority* [1] that the holders of some positions will possess to take actions that affect others (such as issuing directives to the holders of other positions in the organization, or representing the organization in dealings with outsiders). Finally, it is usual to make each holder of a position of authority *responsible* [2] to another position holder for the exercise of that authority (apart from some position holders who are responsible only to people outside the organization or to no one at all—as in an *autocracy*).

2. To form, or persuade workers to join, a *trade union* [1].

organized market. An institution that provides facilities for approved people to buy and sell particular goods (often intangible property such as *securities* [1], or *futures contracts*). Transactions are usually agreed verbally and at great speed; there are usually facilities for informing the public of the terms of every transaction; the people who are allowed to trade in the market usually act as *brokers* for members of the public; transactions must usually be agreed in a specific room of a building (known as a 'trading floor'). (Often known as an 'exchange'.)

orientation program. (US.) Synonym for *induction procedure.*

outdoor publicity. Advertising by means of posters on hoardings, on or inside buses, bus shelters, telephone kiosks or by similar methods.

outlay tax. Synonym for *expenditure tax.*

outline process chart. A *process chart* for the manufacture of an item that shows only operations and inspections. No timescale is given. (Also known as an 'operation process chart'.)

output. 1. The product of an activity. 2. The quantity produced by a person, a machine, a factory or some other unit in a period of time. (Sometimes called 'production'.) 3. Power or energy that is delivered by a generator or engine.

output tax. See *value added tax.*

outright forward (or outright forward contract). A contract for the delivery of goods at a fixed future date. (Cf. *option forward.*)

outside director. Synonym for *nonexecutive director.*

outstanding stock. The number of *shares* in a US *corporation* that are held by shareholders (i.e. excluding *treasury stock*). *Also* the total *nominal value* or *stated value* of such shares.

outwork. Work done outside of a factory, especially work done, for a factory owner, in the home of the worker.

outworker. One who performs *outwork.*

overcapitalized. Having more *contributed capital* than is justified by the scale of operations so that it will not be possible to pay adequate *dividends* [2].

overdraft. The extent to which a *current account* [1] at a bank is *overdrawn.*

overdraw. To draw out money from one's *current account* [1] at a bank to such an extent that the *balance* [1] of the account is negative—i.e. one has borrowed money from the bank.

overhead. Synonym for *indirect cost.*

overhead absorption. Process, or methods, of assigning portions of *indirect cost* to specific activities, products or *cost centres* according to arbitrary (but justifiable) rules as part of *cost accounting*. (Also called 'absorption'.)

overhead rate. The ratio of a firm's *indirect costs* over a period to some specific characteristic of a *cost centre* (e.g. number of man-hours worked, number of machine-hours worked, cost of *direct materials*), which is used as a basis for *overhead absorption*.

overmake. Production in excess of the required or ordered quantity. *Also* an item that is part of such excess production.

overseas sterling area. The countries which were *scheduled territories* but ceased to be as from 23 June 1972.

over-the-counter. Relating to dealings in *securities* [1] that are not made on a *stock exchange* [1].

overtime. Time worked in excess of normal hours.

overtime multiplier. The ratio of the *time rate* for *overtime* to a *basic rate* [1]. Often expressed as, e.g., 'time and a half' (i.e. overtime hours are paid for at $1\frac{1}{2}$ times the rate for normal hours).

overtrading. Expansion of a firm's production and sales without adequate financial support.

own brand. The *brand* of a retailer. (Also known as 'own label' or 'private brand'.)

owners' equity. The value of a firm to its owners as presented in a *balance sheet;* it consists of the value of the firm's total *assets* [1] minus its total *current liabilities, debt capital,* any other long-term loans and *provisions.* Owners' equity in a *company* [1] is equal to *contributed capital* plus *retained earnings.* (Also called 'shareholders' equity', 'stockholders' equity', 'net assets' or 'net worth'.)

own label. Synonym for *own brand.*

p

p.a. Abbreviation of per annum—i.e. yearly.

PAYE. Abbreviation of *pay as you earn*.

PBR. Abbreviation of *payment by results*.

PDM. Abbreviation of 'physical distribution management'—i.e. management of a *physical distribution* system.

PER. Abbreviation of *Professional and Executive Recruitment*.

P/E ratio. Abbreviation of 'price-earnings ratio'—i.e. the ratio of the price at a specified time of one share in a *company* [1] to the *EPS* of that company over a specified period. (Also called a 'price-earnings multiple'.)

PI. Abbreviation of *programmed instruction*.

PL. Abbreviation of *programmed learning*.

plc. Abbreviation of *public limited company*.

PL/1. (Abbreviation of 'programming language 1'). A *procedure-oriented language* for programming computers which has been designed as a general-purpose, high-level language to combine the features of *COBOL* and *FORTRAN*.

PMTS. Abbreviation of *predetermined motion-time system*.

p.p. According to authority delegated by. Used when someone is signing a document on behalf of someone else (e.g. as an employee, *agent, proxy* or in exercise of a *power of attorney*) and written before the name of the person that the signer is acting for. (Although p.p. is used in the sense just defined, it seems to be an abbreviation of the Latin *per procurationem*, i.e. 'by the agency of' and is sometimes put before the signature.)

PPBS. Abbreviation of *planning-programming-budgeting system.*

PR. Abbreviation of *public relations.*

prem. Abbreviation for *premium* (especially for forward foreign exchange—see *premium* [1]).

PSD. Abbreviation of *Primary Standard Data.*

PV. Abbreviation of *present value.*

Paasche index. An *index number* which is like a *Laspeyres index* except that weighting factors are related to the year for which the index is calculated. Thus if the observations in the time series are that prices of goods $1, \ldots, n$ are $p_{10}, \ldots, p_{n0}$ in the base period and $p_{1t}, \ldots, p_{nt}$ in year t and that, in year t the quantities bought were $q_{1t}, \ldots, q_{nt}$ then the Paasche price index is:

$$100 \sum_{i=1}^{n} p_{it} q_{it} \Big/ \sum_{i=1}^{n} p_{i0} q_{it}$$

A Paasche index measures the change in the price of the quantities of items actually bought (cf. Laspeyres index). Named after the German economist, Hermann Paasche (1851–1925).

packaging. A process or operation by which a finished product is made ready for transportation, storage or delivery. *Also* the body of knowledge concerning such operations.

packing note. A document enclosed with a parcel of goods sent to a customer, which informs him of what the parcel contains. Often a copy of an *advice note.*

Page report. The report of a committee appointed in 1971 by the Chancellor of the Exchequer to consider the future role and development of the National Savings movement. The chairman of the committee was a local-government administrator, Sir Harry Robertson Page (born 1911). The report recommended the abolition of National Savings stamps and the voluntary National Savings movement (but these recommendations were rejected by the government) and major restructuring of *trustee savings banks.* See: Committee to Review National Savings, *Report,* Cmnd 5273 (London: HMSO, 1973).

paid-in capital. Synonym for *contributed capital.*

paid-in surplus. (Chiefly US.) Money (or a measurement in monetary terms of the value of property or services) received by a *company* [1] in exchange for issuing its *shares* and which is in excess of the *nominal value* or *stated value* of those shares. The term is regarded by the accounting profession as being misleading because it suggests the money is surplus to requirements and can be quickly distributed to shareholders. Also known as 'capital surplus'. Equivalent in the UK is *share premium*. See also, *contributed capital.*

paid-up capital (or paid-up share capital). The total *contributed capital* of a *company* [1]. Note that this is a measure of the actual value received by the company rather than the *nominal value* of the shares issued.

panel interview. A *selection interview* with two or more interviewers.

Panel on Takeovers and Mergers. A body of representatives of the London financial community that considers *takeover bids* made for companies listed on the *Stock Exchange* [2]. The Panel has a permanent secretariat, headed by a director-general, to carry out routine business. Alleged breaches of the *City Code on Takeovers and Mergers* can be referred to the Panel for decision; the Panel can make a private reprimand, a public statement of censure, or recommend more serious action as necessary. It is possible to appeal against any of the Panel's decisions to an Appeal Committee.

paper. Colloquial term for *securities* [1]—especially *promissory notes* sold by firms (which are sometimes called 'commercial paper').

paper gold. Colloquial name for *special drawing rights* or similar suggested schemes.

paper money. Printed or written paper that is used as money, including *bank notes* and *cheques.*

par. The *nominal value* of a *security* [1].

parallel import. Importation of a *branded* product into a country by some firm other than a firm that has been granted exclusive rights to distribute the brand in that country.

parallel pricing. Practice of increasing the price of a product that is sold by several manufacturers by the same amount at approximately the same time by all the manufacturers.

parameter. A measurement or other attribute which determines the size, scale or location of something but not its form or type. For example in the equation of a straight line, $y = ax + b$, the parameters a and b determine the inclination and position of the line but, whatever the values of a and b, the equation always represents a straight line.

parent company. A *company* [1] that owns a majority of the *shares* (or a majority of shares that carry a right to vote at *general meetings*) of another company. (Also known as a 'holding company'.)

pari passu. Equally; without preference.

parity. 1. Equality of status. 2. Synonym for *peg*. 3. State of being in the same class; for example, (of two numbers) being both even or both odd. 4. Equality of payment (of workers).

Parkinson's law. The aphorism, 'Work expands so as to fill the time available for its completion,' written by the English author, historian and journalist, Cyril Northcote Parkinson (born 1909). See C. N. Parkinson, *Parkinson's Law or the Pursuit of Progress* (London: John Murray, 1958). Parkinson also produced a second law, 'Expenditure rises to meet income', in *The Law and the Profits* (London: John Murray, 1960).

part. A manufactured item which is used by a firm in making *assemblies* [1] but is not itself an assembly (or *subassembly*).

part-exchange. See *exchange* [1].

participating preference share. A *preference share* that carries the right to an additional *dividend* [2], without limit, whenever the directors recommend that one should be paid. (Sometimes called a 'preferred ordinary share'.)

participative management. A *managerial style* characterized by extensive use of the *group-decision method* and in which each person is given wide opportunity to exercise *discretion* [1] in his work. The style represents a complete contrast to *authoritarian management*. People practising participative management usually believe that people can be emotionally committed to doing jobs well. They would accept McGregor's *Theory Y*, would have

300

'9, 9 managerial style' according to Blake and Mouton's *managerial grid* [1], and would be practising *System 4* management according to Likert's analysis. A leading proponent of participative management is the American psychologist, Norman Raymond Frederick Maier (born 1900). See, e.g. Norman R. F. Maier & John J. Hayes, *Creative Management* (New York: Wiley, 1962). (Sometimes known as 'democratic management'.)

participator. For the purposes of the *Income Tax Acts*, a person who has a share or interest in the capital or income of a company is a participator in that company.

particular average. Liability of an owner of property to bear a share of a *particular average loss*.

particular average loss. A partial loss of property during a sea voyage or while loading or unloading which is to be borne partly by the owner of the property and partly by an *insurer*.

partly paid share. A *share*, only a part of the *nominal value* of which has been received by the company that issued it.

part method. A method of training in which the operation to be learned is divided into small parts and the trainee practises each part separately and combinations of parts (e.g., according to the *cumulative-part method* or the *progressive-part method*) until the whole operation is learned.

partner. One of the members of a *partnership*.

partnership. An arrangement whereby two or more people ('partners') agree to carry on a business (often a profession) together and to share the profits. *Also* an organization formed to carry out the business of a partnership. A partnership is not a *corporation* : all contracts made by a partnership are made by the partners acting jointly and all partners are liable for all the debts of their business.

part-time shift. A *shift* that is shorter than 8 hours, especially when it is always worked by a group of *part-time workers*.

part-time worker. A person who is employed to work for significantly fewer hours each week than most employed persons. E.g. in UK statistics a person who works 30 hours or less a week.

party. 1. One of the two sides in a legal action. 2. One of the people who have promised to do something by making a *contract*.

par value. 1. A value for a country's currency that the country notifies to the *International Monetary Fund* (IMF) and is recognized as the fixed value of the currency in dealings with the IMF. The value is measured in gold or (usually) in US dollars.

A member of the IMF is obliged to ensure that dealings on the *foreign-exchange market* involving its currency are conducted so that the *cross-rate* [2] between the currencies of any two other members of the IMF is within a specified margin of the cross-rate calculated from the par values of their currencies. On occasion, members of the IMF have been allowed to abandon their par values so that their currencies *float* [1].

2. Synonym for *peg*.

3. The *nominal value* of a *security* [1].

passing-off. Falsely representing that goods being offered for sale are those of a particular producer or dealer—e.g. by unauthorized use of a *brand*.

patent (noun). A document by which an individual or a corporation (called a 'patentee') is granted certain rights (called 'patent rights') to prevent, for a defined period of time, anyone else from making, using, or selling goods made in a defined way or using a defined manufacturing process without permission of the patentee. The document is, in the UK, in the form of *letters patent* (hence the name patent).

Under UK law, a patent can be granted only for a 'manner of new manufacture' and can be granted only to the 'true and first inventor' of the manner of manufacture (or to a person or corporation nominated by the inventor). The period covered by a UK patent is 16 years so long as the patentee pays prescribed fees after the 4th year. The rules in other countries are very similar.

patent (verb). To obtain a *patent* for a particular invention.

patentee. A person to whom *patent rights* have been granted for a specified invention.

patent exchange. An arrangement under which two firms in different countries grant each other *licences* [2] to operate *patents* each owns.

patent pool. An agreement between a number of firms with similar activities that if one firm is granted a *patent* for a particular process it will automatically grant a *licence* [2] to any other firm in the group that wishes to use the process. Usually standard rates of royalty are set for licences.

patent rights. The rights that a person acquires when he is granted a *patent*.

paternalism. *Managerial style* characterized by a belief that subordinates are necessarily less mature and less capable of looking after themselves than their bosses—i.e. treating one's subordinates as children. The attitude often leads to an emphasis on behaving in a kindly and fair-minded way and preoccupation with providing welfare facilities. Paternalistic managers normally listen to the views of their subordinates but insist on retaining decision-making power for themselves.

paternalistic management. A *managerial style* (especially when practised throughout an organization) characterized by provision of a wide range of valuable rewards for employees and a belief that employees will work well out of gratitude, and out of fear that they could lose the important benefits if they did not work well. Wages are high, promotion prospects are good and there are numerous fringe benefits under paternalistic management. It is usual for people practising paternalistic management to use *consultative management*.

In extreme forms of paternalistic management, managers believe they are responsible for all aspects of their employees' welfare and living conditions.

(See also *hygienic management*.)

path. 1. A sequence of connected *directed edges* which can be traced (following the indicated directions) without going through the same vertex twice. 2. An unbroken sequence of *arrows* [2] in a *network*. 3. A sequence of connected *edges* in which each edge occurs only once. If the edges are *directed edges* this is also called a *chain*.

Pay as You Earn (PAYE). System for collection of UK *income tax* under which an employer deducts tax from all remuneration he pays to employees and sends the tax to the tax collector.

payback method. Technique of appraising *investment projects* for capital expenditure by calculating their *payback periods*.

payback period. The length of time necessary for the *returns* [1] (usually measured after tax has been paid) from an *investment project* to equal the initial sum invested in the project. (Also known as 'payoff period'.)

Pay Board. Statutory body established, by the Counter-Inflation Act 1973, on 1 April 1973 and abolished on 26 July 1974. The members of the Board were appointed by the Secretary of State for Employment. The Board's principal duty was to ensure that all increases in remuneration in the UK were in accordance with the *Price and Pay Code*. Proposed pay increases affecting 1000 or more employees had to be notified to the Board before they could be implemented; pay increases affecting between 100 and 1000 employees had to be notified within seven days of implementation. The Board had the power to restrict any kind of remuneration by issuing an order or a notice and anyone contravening such a restriction was liable to a fine.

The Board also carried out studies on general problems related to pay that were referred to it by the Secretary of State for Employment.

pay curve. Graph of a person's actual or projected earnings from employment, measured periodically, over his working life— either with one employer or with several employers in succession.

payee. The person who is to receive payment according to a *bill of exchange, cheque, draft* or *promissory note*.

payment by results (PBR) (or payment-by-results system). A *payment system* in which a worker's earnings are related to the work he has done and to other factors within the control of the worker (or of the team or group to which he belongs).

payment system. The principles, rules and procedures by which the rates of pay of employees in an organization are determined. (Also known as a 'pay plan'.)

payoff. 1. The actual result of some past action, or the estimated result of some possible future action; *especially* when expressed quantitatively. 2. In *game theory*, a measure of the value to a player of an outcome of a game.

payoff matrix. A *matrix* formed from the *payoffs* [2] of a two-

person game. If the game is a *zero-sum game* it is necessary to show only the payoffs to one player (since the payoffs to the other player are exactly opposite); conventionally, one player is designated player 1 and the matrix shows the payoffs to him; a row represents all the payoffs resulting from a particular choice by player 1 according to the choices of player 2.

payoff period. Synonym for *payback period*.

payola. Bribery. A bribe. Especially in the entertainment industry.

payout ratio. Synonym for *dividend payout ratio*.

pay pause. A period during which a government attempts to prevent any increases in wages as part of an *incomes policy;* especially the period from July 1961 to March 1962 when the UK government announced that no increase in wages would be given to its employees and that other employers should not give increases either.

pay plan. (Chiefly US.) Synonym for *payment system*.

pay relativity. Synonym for *relativity*.

payroll. 1. A list of amounts to be paid by an employer to his employees. 2. The total cost of wages and salaries to a firm over a period. 3. Cash to be used to pay wages.

payroll tax. A tax that is paid by an employer and is related to the number of his employees.

pay structure. The fixed arrangements or formulae by which an employer determines the pay of individual employees within a defined group; especially when such arrangements are known to all the employees concerned.

peer goal-setting. Activity of setting personal objectives (as in *management by objectives*) by groups of people of similar status in an organization.

peg. An *exchange rate* for a currency which is regarded as normal —usually because *central banks* will take action to prevent the rates at which the currency is actually bought and sold in the *foreign-exchange market* from deviating from the peg by more than a known amount. (Also known as a 'parity' or 'par value'.)

pegboard. A device for measuring a person's psychomotor skills (i.e. skills involving mental control of bodily movement): a testee is required to insert pins, pegs or more complex items into holes in a board and his performance is timed. (Also known as a 'formboard'.)

penetration price. A price for a product set according to a policy of *penetration pricing.*

penetration pricing. Setting a low price for one of an enterprise's products (particularly a new product which the enterprise is the first to supply in large quantities). The object is to maximize the number of units sold and to discourage competitors who would find it difficult to achieve a similarly low price.

pension. A regular payment to someone who has retired from work.

pension fund. A fund of money from which *pensions* are, or are to be, paid. *Also* the *trustees* or managers of such a fund, considered as an organizational or legal entity.

per annum. Yearly.

per capita. For each person.

percentile. 1. The nth percentile of a *probability distribution* (where n is a number between 1 and 100) is the value of the *random variable* for which the *distribution function* equals $n/100$. Thus the 100 percentiles divide the distribution into 100 equal parts. The number n is called the 'percentile rank'. 2. The nth percentile of a *frequency distribution* is the value of the *random variable* that is exceeded by $(100 - n)\%$ of the items in the sample.

percentile rank. See *percentile.*

perceptual set. State of concentration of an individual on a particular range of sensory stimuli.

per diem. Daily.

perfect market. An abstract model of a real *market* [1] in which it is assumed that: (1) no buyer or seller can affect prices by, for example, offering very large quantities for sale; (2) all buyers and sellers have equal access to all information about the goods being traded in the market that could influence decisions to buy or sell; (3) information costs nothing and there are no *transaction costs.* This model is frequently used in economic analyses.

performance appraisal. Assessment of how well an employee does his job; especially an assessment carried out as part of an organization's formal procedure in which regular assessments are made, records kept of the results, and action taken to improve performance. (Also known as 'appraisal'.)

performance review. In a system of *management by objectives,* the regular meeting between a manager and his boss to agree a new *job improvement plan.*

performance standard. The result that is to be achieved in each key area in a *key results analysis.*

peril. An event that may occur (but is not certain to occur) and which, if it does, will cause a loss to someone.

period bill. Synonym for *time bill.*

peripheral equipment (or peripheral). Parts of a *computer* other than its *central processing unit.* In large computers most of the peripheral equipment is physically separate from the central processing unit.

permanent night shift. A group of employees who always work a *night shift.*

perpetual debenture. A *debenture* [2] for which there is no final date for *redemption.*

perpetual inventory. Records of *stocks* [1] (recording either their quantity or value) in which every inflow or outflow is noted so that *stock levels* are known at all times.

per pro. Synonym for *p.p.*

personal account. An *account* [1] that records all the transactions of a firm with a particular person or other firm.

personal allowance. Synonym for *personal relief.*

personal income tax. A tax on the *income* [1] of individual people (rather than *corporations*).

personality promotion. A form of *sales promotion* in which a person or team in distinctive dress (or, occasionally, a well known 'personality') tours an area handing out gifts to people who have bought a particular product.

personality test. A procedure (or *instrument* [2]) for measuring some aspect of an individual's personality.

personal property (or personalty). 1. *Property* [1] that is not *real property.* 2. An item or collection of *tangible property* that is not *real property.*

personal relief. An amount which a UK taxpayer may deduct from his *net statutory income* before tax is levied. The amount is related to the number of people the taxpayer has to support. For example, a single person may deduct £625 and a married man £865 (rates fixed in Finance Act 1974). (Also known as a 'personal allowance'.)

personal representative. A person appointed to take over all the assets of a deceased person, use them to pay off his debts and distribute the remainder according to the deaceased's will or according to law. If a personal representative was appointed by the deceased in his will, he is called an 'executor'; if he was appointed by a court he is called an 'administrator'.

personal selling. *Selling* carried out by a *salesman* who has some direct communication with the individual he is selling to—e.g. through conversation (in person or by telephone) or by letter.

personal tax. A tax payable by individuals (principally *income tax* and *capital gains tax*) on their personal wealth as opposed to tax payable by corporations (*corporation tax*).

personalty. Synonym for *personal property*.

personnel. All or a group of the employees of an organization.

personnel agency. (US.) An *employment agency*.

personnel management. Activity, function or study of helping managers in an organization to make the best use of the human resources of the organization.

PERT. (Acronym from Programme Evaluation and Review Technique.) A *project network technique* developed by the US Navy Special Projects Office and the management consulting firm Booz, Allen & Hamilton.

An *activity-on-arrow network* is used in PERT and three estimates (most optimistic, most likely and most pessimistic) are made of the duration of each activity. An 'expected elapsed time' for an activity is calculated from the formula:

$$\text{expected elapsed time} = \tfrac{1}{6}(\text{most optimistic time} + 4 \times \text{most likely time} + \text{most pessimistic time})$$

It is usual to write the expected elapsed time to be taken by each activity alongside its arrow and sometimes the name of the activity also.

Critical path analysis of the network is based on these expected elapsed times. Various modified versions of PERT are in use. For more details, see Jerome D. Wiest and Ferdinand K. Levy, *A Management Guide to PERT/CPM* (Englewood Cliffs, NJ: Prentice-Hall, 1969).

Peter principle. The aphorism that 'in a hierarchy every employee tends to rise to his level of incompetence'. Named after the Canadian educationalist, Laurence Johnston Peter (born 1919) and explained in L. J. Peter and R. Hull, *The Peter Principle* (New York: William Morrow/London: Souvenir Press, 1969).

petty cash. A fund of cash held by an organization and used to make small payments.

phantom stock plan. An arrangement by which an employee of a company is given a number (usually related to salary) of 'units' each of which will entitle him to be paid the amount by which the price on a *stock exchange* [1] of one *share* of the company increases over a fixed period in the future.

photocopy. A copy—of an image (e.g. a document)—made on paper that has been coated with an emulsion of a light-sensitive substance—as in photography.

physical distribution. Movement of *finished goods* from manufacturer to customer—usually, as organized by the manufacturer.

physical inventory. Synonym for *stocktaking*.

physical working conditions. Synonym for *working conditions*.

physiocrat. (Literally, 'rule of Nature'.) A member, or follower, of a group of French economists, led by François Quesnay (1694–1774), who believed that wealth is derived from the land and that governments should not interfere in the operation of 'natural' economic laws.

picket (noun). Person posted outside a workplace, as a representative of strikers, whose task is to inform people of the objectives of a strike and persuade them to join or support it.

picket (verb). To act as a *picket*.

piece rate. The amount to be paid for each unit of output in a *piecework* payment system.

piecework. Payment system used especially for *direct* workers in which an employee's earnings are proportional to the number of units of output produced by him. The simplest form is that in which an employee is paid a piece rate of so much for each item of work he does. Normally a minimum wage is guaranteed and there are sometimes arrangements for penalizing inadequate work and rewarding above-average work.

pie chart. A diagram showing the relative sizes of the components of some quantity by means of a circle divided into sectors the areas of which are proportional to the sizes of the components.

piggybacking. Practice, by a firm, of marketing another firm's (usually complementary) products in addition to (but on a smaller scale than) its own.

piracy. Unauthorized use of someone else's production, invention or conception; especially infringement of *copyright* or *patent rights*.

pirate (noun). One who commits or practises *piracy*.

pirate (verb). 1. To take by *piracy;* for example to infringe *copyright.* 2. To lure an employee away from his employer by offering better conditions when he has not thought of changing his job. (See also, 'raiding'.)

placement. 1. Assignment of a person to a job. 2. Synonym for *placing*.

placing (in USA, usually 'placement'). An *issue* of a block of *securities* [1] by a company to a small number of buyers (often only one) following private negotiation about price and other terms as opposed to a *public offer*. Often the initial buyer is an *issuing house* which intends to resell the securities quickly at a profit either to its clients or to authorized dealers on a *stock exchange* [1] so that the securities can eventually be held by the general public. Placings that are made with no intention of the securities being traded on a stock exchange are called 'private placings'.

plan (noun). A projected course of action that is designed to lead to desired results.

plan (verb). To prepare a *plan*. Planning is usually seen as one of the essential elements of *management*. See also *control*.

planning-programming-budgeting system (PPBS). A systematic application of *programme budgeting*.

plant. 1. The physical objects used by a firm to carry out its business but which are not incorporated in its products. The term covers buildings, machinery and office equipment but is often used rather vaguely or in combinations such as 'plant and machinery'. Hand tools are usually not thought of as plant. 2. A factory or workshop.

plant engineering. Part of *industrial engineering* concerned with the design of *plant*. Often considered to include *maintenance engineering*.

plantwide incentive payment. *Incentive payment* that is related to the value or quantity of work done by a whole factory or other production unit.

pledge (noun). 1. An act of *pledging*. 2. Property that is *pledged*.

pledge (verb). To give someone possession of one's property as *security* [2] for a loan from him. If the debt is not repaid on time the lender can sell the property; if the debt is repaid on time he must return the property to the borrower. A person who pledges property is called a 'pledger' and the person to whom it is pledged is called a 'pledgee'.

plenary session. A part of a conference which all delegates attend.

plural executive. A group of people (e.g. a committee or board) who are given *responsibility* to jointly exercise *authority* [1] over specified activities of others. A plural executive is often said to carry out 'management by committee'.

point of purchase. Synonym for *point of sale*.

point of sale (or point of purchase). A place where a *product* [2] is shown to a customer and where the customer can purchase the product if he wishes. Usually applied by a manufacturer to the position in a retail establishment where his products are offered for sale.

point-of-sale advertising. *Advertisements* at a *point of sale*.

point system (or point rating method or points rating method).

311

A method of *job evaluation* in which: (1) a number of *job factors* are defined; (2) for each factor, a *rating scale* is defined (with numerical values called 'points'); (3) a rating (according to the rating scale) is given to each factor of each job and the total number of points for a particular job then represents its evaluation.

Poisson distribution. A *probability distribution* of which the *frequency function* is:

$$f(x) = \lambda^x e^{-\lambda}/x!$$

where λ is a constant. (λ is equal to both the *mean* [1] and the *variance* [2] of the distribution.) The Poisson distribution represents the probability that a rarely occurring outcome will actually occur a particular number of times (x) when there is a large number of opportunities for it to occur (for example, the number of typographical errors in a well-set book). Named after the French mathematician, Siméon Denis Poisson (1781–1840), who discovered it.

policy. 1. Principles and objectives which guide decision-making on particular matters and which express broad intentions or attitudes. **2.** A general, outline plan of action. **3.** A document setting out the terms of a *contract of insurance*.

policy allowance. An addition (other than a *bonus increment*) to *standard time* which is made so that a worker can achieve a satisfactory wage for a particular level of performance.

policyholder. A person who is insured under a *contract of insurance*—especially a contract of *life assurance*.

policy-making. The activity or process of deciding on a *policy* [1, 2] to be followed in future.

Political and Economic Planning (PEP). A non-profit-making organization established in 1931 to contribute to better planning and policymaking, particularly in government, industry, the social sciences and the relations between them. The staff of PEP, with outside advisers, carry out studies of selected problems and publish their results. Over 560 'broadsheets' and 90 books have been published by PEP.

Address: 12 Upper Belgrave Street, London SW1X 8BB

(01–235 5271).

polyarchic. Lacking *superiors* and *subordinates.*

polyarchy. An *organization structure* characterized by absence of *superiors* and *subordinates.*

population. 1. The complete collection of objects, events or people about which data are obtained in a *survey.* If the data are numerical they can be regarded as values of a *random variable.* 2. The complete collection of possible outcomes of an 'experiment' being analysed by the use of *probability theory.* (Also known as a 'sample space'.)

population mean. Synonym for *mean* [1].

population parameter. A *parameter* that describes the *probability distribution* relating to a complete *population.*

population standard deviation. Synonym for *standard deviation* [1].

population variance. Synonym for *variance* [2].

portfolio. 1. A collection of *securities* [1]. 2. A set of *investment projects.*

portfolio investment. An investment in *securities* [1] made by a company purely for financial reasons and not as a *trade investment.*

POSDCORB. Acronym from 'planning, organizing, staffing, directing, coordinating, reporting and budgeting' devised by the American expert on public administration, Luther Halsey Gulick (born 1892), to describe the functions of a *chief executive.* See L. Gulick, 'Notes on the theory of organization', in *Papers on the Science of Administration,* edited by L. Gulick and L. Urwick (New York: Institute of Public Administration, Columbia University, 1937 reissued 1969 by Augustus M. Kelly, New York).

position. A collection of tasks and duties within an organization, the performance of which requires the service of one person.

position description. *Job description,* especially one relating to a managerial or senior job.

position of authority. A *position* in an *organization* of which the occupant (whoever he is) automatically has *authority* [1].

position statement. Synonym for *balance sheet.*

313

post (noun). A *position;* the *job* [1] someone is employed to perform.

post (verb). To make an entry in one accounting record based on an entry in another record. Especially to make an entry in a *ledger* summarizing and classifying an entry in a *journal*.

postaudit. A critical review of the way in which a project was carried out, undertaken when the project is complete.

post-date. To give a document (especially a *cheque*) a date that is later than the actual date of writing the document.

post-entry closed shop. A place of employment where all employees performing certain types of work must belong to a particular trade union but the employer may take on new employees who are not union members so long as they join the union after they have entered employment. (Also known as a 'union shop'.)

post-test. A *test* that is administered to a trainee after a training activity to ascertain the level of ability reached by him.

potential assessment (or potential review). 1. Assessment of an employee's future career in an organization. 2. Procedure for regularly assessing the future careers of all employees in an organization.

potential review. Synonym for *potential assessment*.

power. Capability of a person to influence other people to act in accordance with his intentions (usually within specified limits). A person may acquire power from many different sources: the commonest kind derives from *authority* [1] and the acceptance of that authority by the people who are to be influenced. A person may have power over someone because he is skilful in making effective threats (e.g. a blackmailer) or because he is able to exert general influence over people to make them follow him (e.g. a religious leader).

power of attorney. Document by which one person (called the 'donor') appoints another person or a *corporation* (called the 'attorney') to act on his behalf in specified matters. (Also known as a 'letter of attorney'.)

power position. A *position* in an *organization* of which the occupant (whoever he is) automatically has *power*.

power structure. The distribution of *power* within an *organization*.

predetermined cost. An estimate of the amount of a *cost* [2] to be incurred in the future.

predetermined motion-time system (PMTS). A technique for *work measurement* in which times established, by previous research, for elementary types of human movement are used to build up the time for performing a particular task which has been analysed into elementary types of movement. *Methods-time measurement* is one such technique.

pre-entry closed shop. A place of employment where no person may be employed unless he is a member of a particular trade union.

preference dividend. A *dividend* [2] due or paid to the holders of *preference shares*.

preference share. A *share* in a company which carries rights that are in some respects superior to the rights carried by the *ordinary shares* of the company. Usually, preference shareholders are entitled to a fixed *dividend* [2] (a 'preference dividend') whenever the company makes sufficient profit to pay it (the ordinary shareholders receive a dividend only if there is any profit left after paying the preference dividend). Preference shareholders usually have no right to vote at *general meetings*. Often preference shareholders are entitled to be paid the *nominal value* of their shares, if the company is *liquidated* [3], before any payment is made to holders of ordinary shares. The owners of preference shares often do not have a right to share in the surplus assets (the 'equity') of the company after liquidation and to that extent preference shares are more like *debentures* [2] than shares. However, the money received by the company in exchange for issuing preference shares counts as *contributed capital* and cannot be diminished, e.g. by being used to pay dividends or returned to shareholders. (Equivalent to shares of *preferred stock* in the USA.)

preference share capital. The part of actual or potential *share capital* of a company received in exchange for *preference shares*. (Equivalent to *preferred stock* in the USA.)

315

preference shareholder. Someone who owns one or more *preference shares* of a particular *company* [1]. (Equivalent to *preferred stockholder* in the USA.)

preferential creditor. A *creditor* [1] whose debt ranks as a *preferential debt*.

preferential debt. 1. A debt that must be paid, when a person is declared *bankrupt*, before any other debts apart from *pre-preferential debts*. Preferential debts include taxes incurred in the 12 months preceding the date of the *receiving order* and wages of the bankrupt's employees for a period of 4 months preceding the date of the receiving order. 2. A debt that must be paid, when a *winding-up order* is made for a company, before any other debts apart from the costs of the winding-up.

preferential shop. A place of employment where the employer agrees that for certain types of work he will give preference to members of certain trade unions when recruiting new employees.

preferred ordinary share. Another name for a *participating preference share.*

preferred stock. A part of the *authorized capital* of a US *corporation* received in exchange for *securities* [1] (called 'shares of preferred stock' or, simply, 'preferred stock') that give rights in some way superior to those carried by shares of *common stock.* Usually, preferred stockholders are entitled to a fixed *dividend* [2] whenever the corporation makes sufficient profit to pay it (the ordinary stockholders receive a dividend only if there is any profit left after paying the preferred stock dividend). Preferred stock usually carries no right to vote at meetings of the corporation. Preferred stock is usually 'callable' (i.e. the corporation may demand surrender of shares, in return for a fixed sum of money, at any time) and is sometimes 'convertible' (i.e. a stockholder may exchange shares of preferred stock for shares of common stock at his option). (Equivalent to *preference share capital* in the UK.)

preferred stockholder. Someone who owns one or more shares of the *preferred stock* of a US corporation. (Equivalent to a *preference shareholder* in the UK.)

preliminary expenses. Legal costs and fees paid in connection with the incorporation of a new *company* [1]. (Also known as 'formation expenses' and, in the USA, as 'organization costs'.)

premium. 1. An addition to the normal, or previous, price of something which buyers are willing to pay because they have a high or recently increased estimation of the value of the thing. *Specifically :* (*a*) an increase in the market price of a *security* [1] over its *issue price ;* (*b*) the difference between the issue price of a security and its (lower) *nominal value ;* (*c*) the difference between the price for delivery of a quantity of a foreign currency at a fixed date in the future and the (lower) price for immediate delivery of the same quantity.

Note. The conventional method of quoting a premium for a foreign currency is to state two figures : the higher figure is the number of units of the foreign currency that a seller of the currency will subtract from his *indirect rate* for a sale involving immediate delivery (the *spot rate*) when computing the *forward rate* ; the lower figure is the number of units a buyer of the foreign currency will subtract from his spot rate for purchase. For example, suppose the closing rates for US dollars in London on a particular day were : spot $2.3910–20 ; 1 month forward 1.25–1.15¢ premium. Then a dealer selling US dollars for delivery in 1 month would give $2.3910 - 0.0125 = 2.3785$ US $ per pound ; a buyer would want $2.3920 - 0.0115 = 2.3805$ US $ per pound.

2. A prize (see, e.g., *premium savings bond*).

3. Something extra that is offered as a special inducement to others to take some action. *Specifically* an object of value or interest that is given away or offered at a low price to buyers of a particular product as a form of *sales promotion.* (See also, *premium bonus scheme.*)

4. The money paid by an *assured* to an *insurer* as the *consideration* for acting as an insurer.

5. A lump sum paid to an employer for taking on an *apprentice.*

6. A lump sum paid to a landlord for the grant of a lease.

premium bonus scheme (or premium bonus system). A system of *payment by results* in which an *incentive payment* is based on

317

the 'time saved', which is the difference between the *allowed time* or *standard time* for a job and the time taken performing it. (Also called 'time-saved bonus scheme'.) Payment may or may not be directly proportional to results. If the incentive payment per unit of time saved increases as the time saved increases, then the scheme is called an 'accelerating' or 'progressive' scheme. If the incentive payment per unit of time saved decreases as the time saved increases, then the scheme is called a 'decelerating' or 'regressive' or 'gain-sharing' scheme.

premium package. A package of a *consumer product* in which the product is in a container that is itself usable (e.g. a storage jar containing instant coffee) and which is offered as a form of *sales promotion*.

premium pricing. Synonym for *prestige pricing*.

premium savings bond. A document sold by the UK government for an amount (the 'denomination') stated on the bond (always a whole number of pounds). Interest (at present $4\frac{3}{4}\%$ a year) is paid on the amount received from the sale of the bonds into a 'prize fund'. Each bond has a set of numbers (one for each pound of the denomination). Draws are made weekly of numbers that qualify the holder for prizes ('premiums'). Bonds will be *redeemed* at the holder's request for their face value but may not be transferred.

prepaid expense. A measurement, for the purposes of accounting, of the cash value of an *expenditure* that has been recorded in a firm's accounts but which was made for a benefit that has not yet been used by the firm. The term is normally used to refer only to expenditure on benefits that will be used in a short period (one year or one *operating cycle*); expenditure on benefits to be used after a longer period is called a 'deferred charge'. Prepaid expenses are classified as *current assets* because they represent items which, if not prepaid, would have to be paid for out of current assets.

pre-preferential debt. A debt which must be paid, when a person is declared *bankrupt*, before any other debts. For example, if the bankrupt holds any funds of a *friendly society* because he is an officer of the society then these must be repaid to the society before any other debts are paid.

pre-process stocks. The *stocks* [1] that a manufacturer has of *materials* (including *bought-out* components) and *supplies* (including *consignment stocks*) which have not yet been subjected to any operation or process by the manufacturer.

preproduction. Associated with, or performed in, the time immediately before a new product is first produced.

present value (PV). The present value of a *cash flow* of x that is to occur n periods of time after the present is:

$$P = \frac{x}{(1+i)^n}$$

i is called the 'discount rate' (per period of time) and is usually stated as a percentage.

It is usual to take the present value of a *cash inflow* as positive and the present value of a *cash outflow* as negative.

The present value of a sequence of cash flows is the sum of their individual present values.

The present value of a future cash flow may be thought of as the amount someone is willing to give up now in order to receive that future amount. Note that:

$$x = P(1+i)^n$$

which is the *terminal value* of an investment of P at an interest rate i.

president. 1. (US.) Title often given to the *chief executive* of a corporation. 2. (UK.) Title sometimes given to the *chief executive* of a company on retirement.

press kit. A collection of duplicated information, leaflets, etc., given out to journalists at a press conference.

prestige pricing. Practice of setting high selling prices for goods regardless of manufacturing cost because customers would not believe that quality was satisfactory if they were asked to pay a lower price. (Also called 'premium pricing'.)

pre-test. A *test* that is administered to a trainee (or potential trainee) before he takes part in a training activity and which is intended to ascertain his existing level of ability and/or his capacity to benefit from the proposed training.

319

preventive maintenance. Work undertaken on plant, machinery or equipment that has not developed any faults in order to prevent the occurrence of faults (e.g. lubrication, painting, replacement of parts).

Price and Pay Code. A document prepared by the Treasury in accordance with section 2 of the Counter-Inflation Act 1973 and specifying principles to be followed when determining prices and wages. Two codes were prepared. The first (SI 1973/658) came into force on 1 April 1973; it was replaced by the second (SI 1973/1785) which came into force on 1 November 1973 (with respect to prices) and 7 November 1973 (with respect to pay). When the government changed in early 1974, two amendments (SI 1974/661 and SI 1974/785) were made to the second code. When the *Pay Board* was abolished (on 26 July 1974) the name of the code was changed to the Price Code and responsibility for its preparation was transferred to the Secretary of State.

Price Code. A document prepared by the Secretary of State in accordance with section 2 of the Counter-Inflation Act 1973 which was amended by the Counter-Inflation (Abolition of Pay Board) Order 1974 (SI 1974/1218). The code sets out principles to be followed when determining prices and charges. The *Price Commission* is required to ensure that the code is implemented.

Price Commission. Statutory body established, by the Counter-Inflation Act 1973, on 1 April 1973. The members of the Commission are appointed by the Secretary of State and the Minister of Agriculture, Fisheries and Food for periods of up to three years; one of the members is chairman; members may be full- or part-time. (There may be between five and twelve members.) The Commission may issue an order or notice to restrict any prices or charges for the sale of goods or the performance of services in the course of business in the UK. It has this power until 31 July 1977. Orders and notices are enforced by local weights and measures authorities (or the Ministry of Commerce in Northern Ireland). Anyone contravening an order or notice of the Commission is liable to a fine. The Commission must follow the principles laid down in the *Price Code* when restricting prices. The Commission can hold

320

inquiries as it thinks necessary and may summon people to appear to give evidence on oath. The Commission receives regular information about proposed price increases from large firms.

price-earnings multiple. Synonym for *P/E ratio*.

price-earnings ratio. See *P/E ratio*.

price-fixing. Setting, by agreement between them, the prices at which different firms will sell apparently competing products.

price leader. A firm that is one of the suppliers in an *oligopoly* and usually is the first of the suppliers to change its price—the other suppliers making similar changes soon after the price leader.

price-lining. Practice, by a seller, of having a small number of standard prices for the type of goods he sells though there are a large number of different items for sale with varying costs to the seller. Price-lining is practised, for example, by record publishers.

price maker. A firm that produces goods and sells them at prices which it can determine itself.

price relative. An *index number* which gives the price of a standard quantity of a good at one date as a percentage of its price on an earlier base date.

Prices and Incomes Board. Popular, but erroneous, name for the *National Board for Prices and Incomes*.

price taker. A firm that produces goods and sells them for their *market price*, which the firm cannot influence. For example, most farmers are price takers.

price war. A situation in which competing suppliers of a good reduce their prices drastically in the hope that one competitor will find it impossible to continue supplying that good and will then leave the market.

pricing. The activity, process or study of setting selling prices for a firm's products.

primary market. 1. A market for a good in which the sellers are the producers of the good. 2. A market for *securities* [1] in which the sellers are the *issuers* of the securities.

primary producing country. A country whose foreign trade is dominated by the export of *primary products*.

321

primary product. An *economic good* that is a result of agriculture, forestry, fishing, mining or quarrying and has been subjected to little or no processing or transformation by humans apart from the activity involved in extracting it from its natural environment.

primary production. The activities of agriculture, forestry, fishing, mining or quarrying concerned with yielding *primary products*.

Primary Standard Data (PSD). A *predetermined motion-time system* of *work measurement* which is a simplified version of *methods-time measurement*.

prime cost. The sum of the *direct materials cost*, *direct labour cost*, and *variable direct expenses* associated with a particular product.

principal. 1. The original sum of money that a person has lent or invested (as opposed to the *interest* that has been added to that sum). 2. The person on whose behalf someone acts as an *agent*. 3. A person who is not acting as an *agent* for, or on behalf of, someone else.

principles of motion economy. See *characteristics of easy movement*.

prior claim. A debt incurred by a firm on conditions that entitle the creditor to repayment before other, specified, creditors of the firm are repaid. The creditors who have to wait until the prior claim is paid off are said to be 'subordinated' to the prior claim.

priority task. A single item on a *job improvement plan*.

private Act of Parliament. An Act of Parliament that applies to only one person or *corporation* or only in a local area and which is enacted after a special 'private Bill' procedure starting with the presentation of a petition by representatives of the people who want the Act to be passed.

private brand. Synonym for *own brand*.

private company. A *company* [1] that is not allowed by the laws under which it is incorporated to make general invitations to members of the public to buy its *securities* [1]. Private companies are often small, family businesses and, in most countries, they can be formed more simply and are subject to less extensive controls than *public companies* [1].

In particular, a British private company is a *registered company*, the *articles of association* of which: (1) prohibit any invitation to the public to *subscribe* [3] for *shares* or *debentures* [2] of the company; (2) limit the number of *members* of the company to 50 (excluding employees); and (3) restrict the right of the company's *shareholders* to *transfer* their shares.

A British private company may, at present, be a *limited company* or an *unlimited company*.

In the USA, the law does not distinguish between public companies and private companies and, in principle, all companies may make *public offers* of their securities.

private label. Synonym for *own brand*.

private limited company. A *limited company* which is a *private company*.

private placing (in USA, usually private placement). A *placing* of *securities* [1] made with no intention that the securities will be traded on a *stock exchange* [1].

privilege. Synonym for *option*.

privileged subscription. Synonym for *rights issue*.

Privy Council. A body, consisting of an unlimited number of people (at present, about 300) appointed by the Crown, which has the power to legislate by issuing Orders in Council on a wide variety of matters (notably in relation to foreign and Commonwealth affairs). In practice this legislation is prepared by government departments and formally approved by the Council. It also appoints certain office holders and grants *charters*. Its committees include the *Board of Trade* and the Judicial Committee which acts as a final court of appeal from the Channel Islands, the Isle of Man, and British colonies. The Lord President of the Council is a politician nominated by the current Prime Minister.

probability. The likelihood or relative frequency of occurrence of something; usually expressed as a number between 0 and 1 (or a percentage)—see *probability theory*.

probability density (or probability density function or density

323

or density function). A *frequency function,* especially of a *continuous random variable.*

probability distribution. The pattern of probabilities associated with a *population* [2] when using *probability theory.* A probability distribution is usually described by a *function* [2], either of the items in the population or of a *random variable* based on these items, called a *frequency function.* Some probability distributions are found to occur very often and have been extensively studied in probability theory: they include the *binomial distribution,* the *chi-square distribution,* the *F distribution,* the *normal distribution,* the *Poisson distribution* and the *t distribution.* One of the main uses of *statistical inference* is to determine the complete probability distribution associated with a natural phenomenon from observations of a *sample* [1] of actual occurrences of the phenomenon.

probability function. The *frequency function* of a *discrete random variable.*

probability theory. Part of mathematics that deals with abstract models of phenomena that occur unpredictably (such as the number of sales made by a firm in one day or the number of defective articles produced by an imperfect machine in one hour). It is possible to apply probability theory if the phenomenon being analysed can be considered as an 'experiment'—i.e. a single activity which results in an outcome that is unpredictable ('random') but must be one of a number of known possible outcomes. (For example, an imperfect machine must produce a countable number of defectives in an hour but it is not possible to predict in advance, with certainty, the exact number of defectives it will produce in a particular hour.)

The complete collection of possible outcomes is known as a 'population' or 'sample space'. Each outcome can be assigned a number between 0 and 1 (called the 'probability' of the outcome) which represents the likelihood of occurrence of the outcome or its frequency of occurrence in several repetitions of the experiment. Probabilities can also be assigned to combinations of outcomes (e.g. 'either 15 or 16 defective products in an hour'). However, the probabilities must conform with two rules:

(1) the sum of the probabilities of all possible distinct outcomes is 1 ; (2) if two outcomes are 'mutually exclusive' (i.e. both cannot occur simultaneously) then the sum of their individual probabilities is the probability that either of them will occur.

Because mathematics deals with numbers it is often necessary to have an intermediate stage in which each outcome is assigned a numerical value by a *random variable*. The probabilities are then assigned to the individual values of the random variable.

Probabilities may be assigned: (1) on the basis of past experience by calculating the relative frequency of occurrence of outcomes; or (2) by subjective estimate.

probationary period. A short period at the start of a person's employment with a firm during which the suitability of the person for his job (and of the job for the person) is tested.

problem-oriented language. A *high-level language* for writing computer programs that is designed to facilitate the solution of a particular class of problems. Problem-oriented languages often do not include any way of specifying the method to be used to solve the problem. The programmer usually specifies only the details of the particular problem he has. Several languages of this type have been devised; one that is intended for general business use is *RPG*.

procedure agreement. An agreement between trade unions and employers that defines the procedure to be followed for attempting to settle a dispute between an employer and his employees without resorting to a strike or *lockout*.

procedure chart. Synonym for *data flow chart*.

procedure flow chart. Synonym for *data flow chart*.

procedure manual. A document that sets out one or more procedures that are to be followed in specified circumstances by members of an organization.

procedure-oriented language. A *high-level language* for programming computers that is designed to facilitate, by providing easily memorable *macro-instructions*, the accurate description of procedures to be used by computers in data-processing tasks. Examples are *ALGOL, FORTRAN* and *PL/1*.

325

proceeds. The total amount of money or other valuable benefits received from selling something.

process (noun). 1. Action, operation or treatment carried out to transform something (e.g. by altering its shape, effecting a chemical change or changing its location). 2. Action taken as part of the procedure available to a court to compel a defendant in a case to appear in the court or to enforce a judgment of the court. Specifically, an order requiring the attendance of someone at a court.

process (verb). 1. To subject something to treatment intended to transform it, physically or chemically, or change its location. 2. To carry out *data processing*.

process average. The average percentage of *defectives* (or number of *defects* per 100 units) in the output from a production process.

process block flow diagram. A simplified or outline version of a *process flow sheet*.

process chart. A diagram showing a sequence of events, usually using standard process-chart symbols, in order to aid visualization and analysis of a process. The American Society of Mechanical Engineers proposed a standard set of symbols in 1947 to represent 'operation', 'transport', 'permanent storage', 'temporary storage or delay' and 'inspection'. There is usually no indication of timescale on a process chart.

process charting. The activity of preparing *process charts*.

process chart—man analysis. Synonym for 'man-type flow process chart' (see *flow process chart*).

process chart—product analysis. Synonym for 'material-type flow process chart' (see *flow process chart*).

process consultancy. Activity by a consultant that is intended to help a group of people to work together more effectively by analysing and improving *group processes*.

process-control system. A *control system* that affects a *parameter* of a *process* [1].

process costing. Practice or activity of determining the *cost* [2] per unit of output of a product by a manufacturing firm through dividing total costs by total output. (Also known as 'unit costing'.)

process engineering. Synonym for *production planning*.

process flow sheet. A detailed diagram of the path along which bulk material flows through *plant* [1] used by a *process industry*.

process industry. An industry which is concerned with converting bulk materials (liquid, powder, granulated, or irregularly sized pieces) into workable form.

process layout. Arrangement of machines in a factory according to functional type so that an item of work may be taken along various routes through the factory according to the operations to be performed on it. The layout is associated with *batch production*.

processor. Synonym for *central processing unit*.

process planning. Synonym for *production planning*.

produce (noun). The result of production—now used only to refer to fruit and vegetables.

produce (verb). 1. To yield, or cause to come into being, as a result of natural or human or mechanical activity. 2. To *manufacture*.

producer goods. Synonym for *industrial goods*.

producer market. Synonym for *industrial market*.

product. 1. A result of *production* [1]; an output. 2. An item, or a class of identical items, that an enterprise offers for sale—extended to mean a type of service that an enterprise offers to its customers.

product development. Synonym for *engineering development*.

production. 1. The act or process of *producing*. 2. Synonym for *output* [2].

production control. Activity or process of ensuring that a firm produces planned quantities of its products according to a specified design, to a specified quality, at planned costs. In many firms there are production control departments that are not responsible for all of these matters but they are usually responsible for producing products on time. Production control may include *production planning*.

production line. A sequence of *work stations* at which successive operations are performed on a piece of work which is moved from station to station—especially one organized to manufacture one specific product and where individual items

327

move almost continuously. A line may be a 'fabrication line' (where, at each station, an alteration is made to the shape or form of an item) or an 'assembly line' (where at each station *assembly* [1] is carried out).

production management. Management of all aspects of an enterprise concerned with transforming materials into finished products. Although the techniques and principles of production management were developed within a context of *manufacturing*, they are applicable to organizations with other kinds of 'products' (e.g. enterprises providing services). The name 'operations management' is sometimes used to emphasize the general applicability of the discipline; 'manufacturing management' is used to emphasize application to manufacturing enterprises.

production planning. Activity of deciding the processes and operations, and their sequence, to be used to manufacture a firm's product in required quantities to a specified design and of specified quality. The activity may include deciding the layout of production facilities, designing tools, and specifying work methods. (Also known as 'process engineering' or 'process planning'.)

production transfer. Movement of an employee from work that is declining in importance to work that is expanding.

productive work. Work which alters the physical or chemical nature of something or is a necessary contribution to the completion of a process that changes the physical or chemical nature of something.

productivity. Output per unit of input. For example, output per man-hour or output per £1 of investment.

productivity agreement. An agreement between employers and employees that higher wages will be paid in return for changes in the way work is performed that will achieve an increase in *productivity*.

productivity bargaining. *Collective bargaining* over a *productivity agreement*.

product layout. Arrangement of machines in a factory that is determined by the order in which operations must be performed on one product. The layout is associated with *continuous production*.

product life cycle. A commonly observed pattern of changes over time in the volume of sales of a *product* [2] consisting of four stages: (1) 'introduction' (commencing when the product is first sold) during which sales increase very slowly; (2) 'growth' when, if the product is successful, sales increase rapidly; (3) 'maturity' during which sales are fairly constant; (4) 'decline' during which sales decrease.

product line. A group of *products* [2], offered by a single firm, that have similar uses.

product manager. An employee of a firm who is responsible for developing and promoting one or more of the firm's *products* [2] (but not all of them). (Also known as a 'brand manager'.)

product market. The *market* [2] for a *product* [2] of a firm.

product mix. The selection of *products* [2] offered for sale by an enterprise.

product planning. Activity or process of specifying future new products within a known *product line* for a firm. The emphasis in product planning is on identifying what would be profitable for the firm to sell (rather than the technological aspects of what it could produce).

profession. An *occupation* [1] requiring predominantly intellectual skills acquired after lengthy training.

Professional and Executive Recruitment (PER). A service operated by the *Employment Service Agency* for recruiting managerial, professional, scientific and technical employees. Fees are charged to the employer but not to employees.

professional institute. An association, of people who practise a particular profession, of which the principal purposes are: (1) to specify the skills and knowledge that should be possessed by a person who wishes to practise the profession; (2) to conduct *achievement tests* to determine whether individuals do have the specified skills and knowledge, and to certify their competence; (3) to specify ethical standards or codes of conduct for people who practise the profession.

proficiency test. Test of how well a person can perform a particular task (cf. *aptitude test*).

profit. An excess of *revenues* [1] over associated *expenses* [3] for

329

an activity or over a period or for a particular transaction.

Terms with similar meanings include 'earnings', 'income', 'margin' and 'profit'; all these (and profit) may be qualified by the adjectives *gross* and *net*.

'Revenue', 'gross revenue' and 'gross income' invariably refer to the amount of a receipt of money with no deductions, whereas the other terms usually mean revenue minus an amount that represents some or all of the expenses of getting the revenue. 'Income' sometimes means 'revenue'—especially when referring to non-profit-making organizations—but is often used to mean only receipts that are not *capital receipts*.

All the terms can be used to describe the results of selling goods and services over a period but only 'earnings' and 'income' are used to describe the remuneration an individual receives from employment.

Only 'profit' is used to describe the results of a single transaction (the revenue from a single transaction is usually called the *proceeds* of the transaction).

'Earnings', 'income', 'margin' and 'profit' all mean the difference between revenue and expenses. Depending on the purpose of the calculation different items are included as expenses; however, none of the 4 words (each of which may be preceded by 'gross' and 'net' making 8 terms in all) has ever been firmly established as referring to financial gain measured in a particular way. The following is a guide to the most common usages: 'margin' usually means *gross profit* and is usually expressed as a percentage of revenue; 'profit' is usually measured without deducting payments to the suppliers of the firm's *capital* (i.e. interest on *debt capital, preference dividends* and *dividends*) or payments of *corporate income tax*; 'profit' is often expressed as a percentage of revenue. 'Income' and 'earnings' are never expressed as a percentage and are usually calculated after deducting payment of corporate income tax, preference dividends and interest on debt capital. ('Net income' and 'net revenue' mean a sum calculated in this way when 'gross income' and 'gross revenue' are used to mean revenue.) See also, *EBIAT, EBIT* and *retained earnings*.

330

profitability. Quality or state of being *profitable*.

profitability index. Synonym for *discounted gross benefit-cost ratio*.

profitable. 1. Producing benefits; especially in the sense of creating additional wealth. 2. Yielding a *profit*.

profit and loss account. An *income statement*.

profit centre (spelt profit center in USA). A part of a firm that is regarded as having its own financial targets to achieve and has the manpower and material resources necessary to achieve those targets.

profit margin (or margin). 1. Synonym for *profit*. 2. Ratio of *profit* to *revenues* [1].

profit plan. A forecast, made at the beginning of an accounting period, of a firm's *income statement* for that period. It is based on a forecast of sales for the period and on budgets which show the planned costs of the operations necessary to achieve those sales.

profit planning. The process or activity of drawing up a *profit plan*.

profit sharing. An arrangement by which employees of a firm receive a share of the profits of the firm, in addition to their fixed wages, and the method of calculating the share is fixed in advance.

profits tax. A UK *corporate income tax* which has been abolished and is not payable on earnings received after April 1966 (when *corporation tax* was introduced). Profits tax was called 'national defence contribution' until 1947 and was charged in addition to *income tax* (which companies paid before the introduction of corporation tax).

profit-volume chart. A graph of the *net profit* [1] from selling a product against the number of units sold (or the *sales revenue*).

program (noun). 1. A sequence of individual instructions to a *computer* which determines how it will carry out a particular data-processing job. 2. US spelling of *programme*.

program (verb). To devise a *program* [1] for a computer.

program budget. US spelling of *programme budget*.

program budgeting. US spelling of *programme budgeting*.

program evaluation and review technique. See *PERT.*

program flow chart. A diagram giving a visualization of how a computer *program* [1] will deal with a particular item of data. (Also known as a 'flow chart'.)

programme (spelt program in USA). 1. A *plan*—especially when expressed in very general terms. 2. A *schedule* [2]. 3. An important category of the activites of an organization with a common purpose—especially one identified for purposes of *programme budgeting*. 4. A group of activities with a common purpose carried out within an organization especially when incidental to the main activities of the organization or existing only for a defined period. 5. A complete set of material for providing *programmed instruction* in a particular topic.

programme budget (spelt program budget in USA). A *budget* [1] produced in *programme budgeting*.

programme budgeting (spelt program budgeting in USA). An approach to the formulation of plans (especially *budgets* [1]) for an organization in which attention is concentrated on the organization's objectives and the organization's activities are grouped into 'programmes' where each programme is concerned with achieving a single objective. Budgets and other plans are set out for each programme (rather than for departments of the organization) and the accounting information required to control activities is analysed according to programmes.

programmed instruction (PI). Method of self-instruction in which the material to be taught is split up into small items (called 'frames') and recorded in permanent form (e.g. printed or tape-recorded). The material is presented in such a way that the learner can see or hear only one frame at a time. The learner works through a sequence of frames. Usually the learner has to make some response to each frame (such as answering a question) and his response determines which frame he should look at or listen to next. The complete set of material presented to a learner is called a 'programme'. (Also known as 'programmed learning'.)

programmed learning (PL). Synonym for *programmed instruction.*

programme evaluation and review technique. See *PERT.*

programmer. A person who prepares *programs* [1] for computers.

programming language. A set of standard symbols (and, often, groups of symbols) and rules for combining the symbols so that they represent instructions for a *computer* to carry out specific operations. (Also known as a 'code'.) A computer is designed to interpret instructions that are written in its *computer instruction code*, which is a very elementary language using a very restricted range of symbols. Computer instruction codes are virtually impossible for programmers to use and much effort has been devoted to devising languages that are more convenient. The first stage is the use of *low-level languages* in which many instructions are represented by mnemonics. The next stage is the use of *high-level languages* (such as *ALGOL, COBOL, FORTRAN* and *PL/1*) which use *macro-instructions,* often represented by approximations to English words.

progressive-part method. A method of training in which the operation to be learned is divided into small parts and the trainee practises the first two parts separately, then the first two combined, then the third part on its own, then all three combined, and so on.

progressive scheme. Synonym for *accelerating premium bonus plan.*

project. 1. A proposal or scheme. 2. An *investment project.* 3. A piece of research. 4. An activity (or, usually, a number of related activities) carried out according to a plan in order to achieve a definite objective within a certain time and which will cease when the objective is achieved. 5. A task undertaken by a group of students to apply or supplement teaching.

project management. The study, or the body of knowledge concerning, the management of *projects* [4].

project manager. A manager who is responsible for the successful completion of a single *project* [4].

project network. Synonym for *network.*

project network analysis. Synonym for *network analysis.*

project network technique. Any of a group of methods of describing, analysing, planning and controlling *projects* [4] and which involve the use of *networks*.

promissory note (or note). A document which entitles its holder to payment, by the 'maker' of the note, of a sum of money at some fixed date (or 'at sight'—that is, when it is presented to the maker).

A promissory note is a *negotiable instrument* and is like a *bill of exchange* of which the drawer and drawee are the same person.

promotion. 1. Activity that is intended to increase the numbers of buyers of a product or to improve public acceptance of an idea—e.g. *advertising* [2], *personal selling* or *sales promotion*. *Also* an instance of promotional activity. 2. Movement of an employee to a job that has greater responsibilities and/or involves more skill and/or has higher status and/or, especially, has a higher rate of pay.

promotional game. Synonym for *consumer contest*.

promotional mix. 1. The methods employed by a firm for the *promotion* [1] of its *products* [2]. (Also known as the 'communications mix'.) 2. The methods employed by a firm for *below-the-line* [2] promotion of its products.

property. 1. A right of ownership of a specified benefit. *Also* the benefit owned. 2. An item of *tangible property*. 3. Land and buildings (i.e. *real property*).

prospectus. An advertisement for something that is to be sold in the future which is intended to persuade people to place advance orders. Specifically: (1) an advertisement for a *public offer* of *securities* [1]; (2) a detailed description of a new publication; (3) a description of a forthcoming educational course.

prospectus issue. Synonym for *public offer*. So called because the laws of most countries require the publication of a detailed prospectus of the financial condition of any firm that makes a public offer of securities.

protectionism. The view that a government should take action to ensure that domestic producers of goods do not have to compete with imported foreign goods—e.g. by limiting quantities of imports or by imposing *protective duties* or by imposing *exchange controls* on payments for foreign goods.

protective duty. A *customs duty* that is imposed by a government in order to make particular imported goods expensive and thus protect domestic producers of those goods. In the UK, protective duties are always imposed by the Treasury making an order under the Import Duties Act 1958 or the Customs Duties (Dumping and Subsidies) Act 1969 and they are invariably *ad valorem* taxes. (Cf. *revenue duty*.)

protective practice. Synonym for *restrictive practice*.

protest (noun). A certificate that a *bill of exchange* has been *dishonoured*.

protest (verb). To make a certificate that a *bill of exchange* has been *dishonoured*. Usually done by a *notary public* who simultaneously *notes* the bill.

protocol. 1. The minutes or records of a diplomatic conference; especially a note of agreement on subsidiary matters which supplements a *treaty*. 2. A code of diplomatic etiquette and precedence.

proving. Demonstrating that something is free from faults or that a piece of equipment can be used to perform particular tasks.

provision. A sum of money set aside (especially from the profits of a firm) in anticipation of a future *liability* [1].

provisional liquidator. See *liquidator*.

Provisional Register. A register, maintained by the *Chief Registrar of Trade Unions and Employers' Associations* from 1 October 1971 until 16 September 1974 to enable organizations that had been registered under previous legislation to continue receiving the benefits of such registration until their registration under the *Industrial Relations Act 1971* was completed.

proxy. A document authorizing a person to vote on someone else's behalf at a meeting. *Also* the person so authorized.

psychological price. Price which is commonly used for goods —see *psychological pricing*. (Also known as a 'charm price'.)

psychological pricing. Setting selling prices at commonly used amounts (called 'psychological prices' or 'charm prices'). For example, in the USA in 1969, 29¢ was a common price in grocery stores but 26¢ was very rarely used.

public authority. A person or administrative body entrusted with functions to perform for the benefit of the public and not for private profit.

public company. 1. A *company* [1] that is allowed by the laws under which it is incorporated to make general invitations to members of the public to buy its *securities* [1]. In particular, a British *registered company* that is not a *private company*. 2. Synonym for *listed company*.

public corporation. 1. (UK.) Synonym for *statutory corporation* [1]. 2. (US.) A *corporation* established for a governmental purpose or for the management of affairs of public concern— e.g. Michigan State University.

public general Act of Parliament (or public Act of Parliament). An Act of Parliament that affects everyone or a large number of people and which is enacted after a procedure that commences with presentation of a Bill to one of the Houses of Parliament by a member of that House.

publicity. Information about a firm, or its products, that is carried by media of communication without payment by the firm.

public limited company (plc). A *limited company* which is a *public company* [1].

public offer (or 'public offering'). A general invitation to the public to buy *securities* [1]. (Often called a 'prospectus issue'.)

public relations (PR). Activity, practice or study of efforts to bring about a favourable estimation of an organization by the public in general or by particular people who are important to the organization.

public utility. A service (e.g. of passenger transport) or supply (e.g. of water or gas or electricity) available to and used by a whole community. Such services are usually subject to municipal or government control or ownership. *Also* a firm or organization that provides such a service or supply.

punched card. A card in which holes are punched to represent data. The most widely used type of card is the 80-column card, which is rectangular ($3\frac{1}{4}$ in × $7\frac{3}{8}$ in), 0.007 in thick and has the upper left corner cut off; the holes are also rectangular and can be punched in any of 960 positions arranged in a grid of 80 columns (numbered from left to right) and 12 rows (numbered

12, 11, 0, 1, 2, . . . , 9 from top to bottom).

Particular types of data-processing equipment use 90-column cards (same dimensions as 80-column cards but with circular holes) or 96-column cards (also using circular holes but smaller than 90-column cards).

purchase order. A written order from a firm for goods (and sometimes services) that it wants to buy. Often on a preprinted form incorporating information about acknowledgement, delivery and payment.

purchase tax. A tax which was payable in the UK when certain goods were sold by 'registered traders' (roughly the equivalent of *wholesalers*) to people who were not registered traders. The tax was a percentage of the wholesale price of the goods. Purchase tax was introduced in 1940 but ceased to be payable after 1 April 1973 when *value added tax* was introduced.

purchasing agent. An *agent* who purchases materials for his principals (usually manufacturers).

pure rent. Synonym for *rent* [2].

pure strategy. In *game theory*, a rule adopted by a player that he will definitely make a particular choice. (Cf. *mixed strategy*.)

put option. An *option* under which the option holder may, at any time within a set period, decide to sell, to the other party to the arrangement, a specified quantity of something (e.g. *securities* [1]) at a specified price. The holder may decide to do nothing but, whether he sells or not, he has to pay a fee ('option money') to the other party.

pyramid of ratios. A set of *financial ratios* for analysing the activity of a firm which can be represented by a pyramid-shaped diagram because each ratio analyses one component of another ratio (apart from the ratio at the apex of the pyramid). For example, if one ratio is A/B and $A = A_1 + A_2 + A_3$ then that ratio will be analysed into three ratios: A_1/B, A_2/B and A_3/B. The ratio at the apex of the pyramid is usually the ratio of *operating profits* for a period to the average value of *operating assets* during that period.

q

quadratic programming. A particular case of *nonlinear programming* in which the function to be optimized or the constraints are quadratic functions—i.e. any variable, x, appears as x or x^2.

qualified-circulation journal/magazine. Synonym for *controlled-circulation journal/magazine*.

qualified worker. See *standard performance*.

quality control. Activity, process or study of ensuring that the output of production processes conforms with a prescribed standard.

quality control chart (or control chart). A chart used in *statistical quality control* to show the performance of a production process. Periodically a sample is taken from the output of the process and measured; a statistic calculated from the measurements (e.g. the *mean* [2] or the *range*) is plotted on the control chart. Lines (called 'control limits') are drawn on the chart which represent the limits of variation of the statistic that would be expected if the process was 'in control'—i.e. if the only variation in the output was unpredictable and due to random, uncontrollable factors.

quantile. Synonym for *fractile*.

quantity discount. A reduction in the price of a *product* [2] that a seller offers to anyone who buys more than a minimum quantity.

quantum meruit. As much as he (or she) deserved. Used to describe a claim in a court for payment for work done when there was no agreement about the amount to be paid and the court must decide what is reasonable.

quartile. 1. The first, second and third quartiles of a *probability distribution* are the values of the *random variable* for which the *distribution function* is equal to $\frac{1}{4}$, $\frac{1}{2}$ and $\frac{3}{4}$ respectively. 2. The first, second and third quartiles of a *frequency distribution* are the values of the *random variable* that are exceeded by $\frac{3}{4}$, $\frac{1}{2}$ and $\frac{1}{4}$ respectively of the items in the sample.

The second quartile is also called the *median*.

questionnaire. A document (especially one reproduced in large numbers) containing a set of questions intended to elicit useful information.

queue. A number of persons, items of *work-in-progress*, or units of anything, that are, at a particular time, awaiting attention or processing. (Also known as a 'waiting line'.)

queuing theory. Part of mathematics that deals with analysing *queues* and predicting their sizes. (Also known as 'theory of queues' or 'waiting-line theory'.)

queuing time. The time spent waiting in a *queue*.

quick ratio. Synonym for *acid-test ratio*.

quid pro quo. One thing in return for another; *consideration*.

quorum. A fixed number of members of a committee, a meeting, etc., whose presence is necessary for the valid transaction of business.

quotation. 1. A statement, in response to a request by a prospective buyer, of what a firm would probably charge for supplying specified goods or services. 2. A statement by someone trading in a *market* [4], especially an *organized market*, of his prices for buying and for selling specified goods (a 'two-way quotation') in response to an enquiry from another trader in the market. (The person giving the quotation is usually supposed not to know whether the enquirer wants to sell or buy.) 3. Synonym for *listing*. (See *quoted*.)

quoted. *Listed* on a *stock exchange* [1]. (Traders on a stock exchange are permitted to give *quotations* [2] only for listed securities.)

quoted company. Synonym for *listed company*.

r

RA. Abbreviation of *relaxation allowance*.

R & D. Abbreviation of *research and development*.

ROI. Abbreviation of *return on investment*.

ROP advertisement. Abbreviation of *run-of-paper advertisement*.

RPG. (Abbreviation of 'report program generator'.) A *problem-oriented language* for programming computers. A programmer using RPG has to specify the available files of information and the output desired but is not concerned with the method to be used by the computer to generate the output. Unlike other *high-level languages*, there are different versions of RPG for different computers. Two books that cover the general principles of RPG languages are: Joyce Currie Little, *RPG : Report Program Generator* (Englewood Cliffs NJ : Prentice-Hall, 1971) and S. M. Bernard, *System/3 Programming : RPG II* (Englewood Cliffs NJ : Prentice-Hall, 1972).

rack jobber. A *wholesaler* (or occasionally a manufacturer) who supplies retailers with a restricted range of goods on the basis that on one visit the rack jobber leaves a selection, chosen by himself, in a separate display area (the 'rack') in a retail establishment and on his next visit collects payment for whatever has been sold and replenishes the stock.

rack rent. A rent equal to or not much less than the *annual value*.

Radcliffe gap. Lack of facilities for supplying capital to independent inventors, which was pointed out in the *Radcliffe report*.

Radcliffe report. The report of a committee appointed by the Chancellor of the Exchequer in 1957 to inquire into the working of the monetary and credit system. See: Committee on the Working of the Monetary System, *Report,* Cmnd 827 (London: HMSO, 1959). The chairman of the committee was Sir Cyril John Radcliffe, Viscount Radcliffe (born 1899).

raiding. Practice of luring employees away from their jobs to take up a job with another employer. (Also known as 'pirating'.)

random. Unpredictable.

random numbers. A sequence of numbers such that one number cannot be predicted from knowing the previous numbers in the sequence.

random sample. A *sample* [1] of a given size from a *population* which has been chosen in such a way that any possible sample of that size could have been chosen with a known *probability*. The term usually refers to a 'simple random sample'—i.e. one in which any possible sample has an equal probability of being chosen.

random sampling. *Sampling* [1] in such a way that a *random sample* is chosen.

random variable. A *function* [2] that assigns a number to every element of a *population*. See *probability theory*. (Also known as a 'stochastic variable' or 'variate'.)

range. The difference between the greatest and least observation in a sample.

rank (noun). A position in a series of things that have been *ranked*.

rank (verb). To list or arrange things in order of importance (according to some concept of what makes them important) or in order of the degree to which they possess some specified attribute.

ranking method. Method of *job evaluation* in which all the jobs to be evaluated are *ranked* according to some consistent system (e.g. by asking someone to put the jobs in order of importance after considering *job descriptions*).

341

rapidly rotating shift system. A *rotating shift system* in which the change from working one type of *shift* to another occurs at intervals of less than a week.

rate. 1. A charge or payment (e.g. of discount, interest or wages) expressed as an amount per unit of what is paid for. 2. (Usually plural.) A tax levied by a *local authority* in the UK on the occupation (or sometimes ownership) of property within its area. The tax is related to the amount of rent for which it is believed the property could be let for a year.

rate-buster. A worker who is paid a *piece rate* and who, according to his colleagues, produces too much work. Colleagues of a rate-buster dislike this behaviour because they believe it will encourage management to reduce the piece rate on the grounds that the work is obviously easier than was first thought.

rate card. A list prepared by the proprietor of a communication medium to show his standard charges for carrying *advertisements*. (It is often printed on a standard-sized record card.)

rate-fixer. An employee who carries out *rate-fixing*.

rate-fixing. Activity or process of setting *piece-rates* by experience and judgment rather than by using *work measurement*. (Also called 'rate-setting'.)

rate-for-age scale. A *payment system* in which all employees of the same age and doing similar work are paid the same wages. Usually it covers only employees under an 'adult' age (between 18 and 21) and all older employees are paid an 'adult rate'.

rate of return. The ratio of the *return* from the investment of a sum of money over a period (usually a year) to the amount of money invested. (Also known as 'yield' or 'accounting rate of return' or 'return on investment'.)

The calculation can be made before or after tax is taken into account. The amount of money invested may be measured by the amount of the initial investment or by the average investment over the life of the asset—i.e. $\frac{1}{2}$ (initial investment minus scrap value).

rate-setting. Synonym for *rate-fixing*.

rating. An estimation or assessment of something expressed in relative terms (e.g. 'A is better than B')—especially when it is compared with a commonly used standard. *Also* a numerical value assigned to such an estimation in accordance with a *rating scale*.

rating scale. A method of assigning numerical values to *ratings*. The ratings may be: (1) classified (e.g. ratings of 0, 1 and 2 mean bad, average and good respectively); (2) by interval measurement (e.g. if A is rated at 45, B at 50 and C at 60 then the difference between B and C is twice the difference between A and B); or (3) on a ratio scale in which there is interval measurement and one rating (usually 0) corresponds to complete absence of the quality being rated.

ratio. The result of dividing one quantity by another.

ratio analysis. Use of *financial ratios* to assess an enterprise's efficiency and to help to find reasons for inefficiency.

ratio-delay study. *Activity sampling* in order to determine the allowance that should be included in *standard times* [1] for unavoidable delays. The ratio of the number of observations of a worker when he is not performing any work to the total number of observations gives a measure of the fraction of time during which delays occur.

raw score. A score of a testee that has not been converted into a *standard score*.

real estate. Synonym for *real property*.

real property. A right of ownership, for an indefinite period, of land or something that is annexed to or affixed to land (such as buildings, minerals or trees) or of a benefit deriving from land (such as a right of way). (Also known as 'real estate' or 'realty'.) *Also* a piece of land or other property (or a collection of such property) over which such rights may be exercised.

real-time. Of, or relating to, the operation of a *computer* so that it processes data immediately in response to some activity outside the data-processing system. For example, a computer controlling a production process reacts immediately to changes in the aspects of the process that it monitors; when operating in a *conversational mode* (as in airline booking systems) a computer immediately processes the data presented to it by the user. Real-time operation

343

may be contrasted with *batch processing* in which individual jobs are dealt with according to a predetermined schedule and may, therefore, spend some time waiting their turn.

realty. Synonym for *real property*.

rebate. A deduction from a sum of money to be paid; a *discount*. Specifically a deduction from the sum to be paid according to a *bill of exchange* when the bill is presented for payment before the date specified on it.

receipt. 1. A sum of money, or quantity of goods, received. 2. A written acknowledgement that one has received money or goods.

receivable. A debt; an amount owed to one.

receiver. An independent person, appointed by a court or by the creditors of an *insolvent* person or firm to receive all money paid to the person or firm, or all the money paid in connection with particular property, and use it to repay creditors.

receiving order. An order made by a court for the appointment of a *receiver* of the property of a person (as a first stage in *bankruptcy* proceedings) or of a company (which has defaulted on payments of interest on a *debenture* [2]).

recitals. Statement of the events leading up to, or reasons or justification for the signature of, a formal legal document, such as a deed or treaty. Each clause usually begins with the word, 'whereas'.

recommended retail price. A price for a *consumer product* that is notified to retailers by the manufacturer of the product as being a suitable price at which to sell it.

record. A collection of related items of data.

recruitment. Obtaining employees for an organization.

recruitment advertising. Advertising of which the objective is to inform people of the existence of a job and to persuade suitable candidates to apply for it.

red book. Colloquial name for the third (1972) edition of the *City Code on Takeovers and Mergers* (cf. *blue book*).

redeem. To end an obligation to someone else by making a suitable payment. Specifically: (1) to buy back a *security* [1]; (2) to end a *mortgage* by paying off the relevant loan.

redeemable. Capable of being *redeemed*. Used to describe a *security* [1] when the *issuer* may demand its surrender in return for a cash payment. (Synonymous with 'callable'.)

redeemable bond. A *bond* [2] that is *redeemable*. (Also known as a 'callable bond'.)

redeemable preference share. A *preference share* that the issuing company can exchange (or 'redeem') either for cash or for new shares at some time in the future.

redeemable stock. *Stock* [4] that is *redeemable*.

redemption. Repayment of a loan *especially* by buying back a document (a *debenture* [2], *stock certificate* or *bond* [2]) that acknowledges indebtedness.

redemption premium. The difference between the price received for a *debenture* [2] or similar instrument when it was issued and the (higher) price paid for it on *redemption*.

redemption yield. *Internal rate of return* of an investment project that consists of buying a *redeemable stock* or a *redeemable bond*, keeping it until it is *redeemed* and receiving the proceeds of redemption.

rediscount. To sell (at a *discount*) a *bill of exchange* or *promissory note* that one bought at a discount.

redundancy. 1. Quality or state of being *redundant*. 2. A person who is *redundant*.

Redundancy Fund. Fund set up by the *Redundancy Payments Act 1965*. Employers pay a weekly sum for all employees into the Fund. When an employer makes a redundancy payment he is entitled to receive half the payment back from the Fund.

redundancy payment. A payment to a dismissed employee made by his employer under the *Redundancy Payments Act 1965*.

Redundancy Payments Act 1965. UK statute that: (1) set up the *Redundancy Fund*; (2) requires an employer to make a 're-dundancy payment' to any employee, who is aged between 18 and 65 (60 for women) and whom he has continuously employed for more than two years, whom he dismisses because of redundancy.

redundant. Surplus to requirements. Used to describe an employee who is no longer required because the work he does is no longer necessary to his employer.

reference. A statement about one or more aspects of a specified person's character or behaviour or of the way that a specified firm usually conducts its business which has been given by someone named by the person or firm at the request of a person who intends to employ, do business with or extend *credit* [3] to the person or firm.

reference group. A *group* [1] that an individual compares himself with in order to help develop his beliefs, attitudes and values and to guide his behaviour.

refresher training. Training that is intended to improve trainees' performance of their current job. (Also known as 'booster training'.)

refund. 1. To return the money someone has paid for goods because he is dissatisfied with his purchase. 2. To repay a loan by means of a further borrowing.

regional development grant. A cash grant given by the Secretary of State, under the Industry Act 1972, to firms in *development areas* and *intermediate areas*. The grant is a fixed percentage of the cost of new buildings or machinery purchased by firms.

regional employment premium. A payment made by the UK government to every employer in manufacturing industry in the *development areas*. The payment is of a fixed amount each week for each employee (currently £3 for men over 18, £1.50 for women over 18 and boys under 18, and 95p for girls under 18). The premium was first payable in September 1967.

register. 1. A written record consisting of entries added from time to time containing standardized items of data relating to people, corporations or other objects that satisfy specific requirements. 2. A small *store* [4] in a *computer* which is used for some special purpose.

registered accountant. An associate or a fellow of the *British Association of Accountants and Auditors.*

registered bond. A *bond* [2] issued as a *registered security.*

registered company. A *corporation* established in Great Britain by registering documents (including *articles of association* and a *memorandum of association*) with the *Registrar of Companies* in accordance with whichever *Companies Act* was in force at the time of registration. A registered company comes into existence on the date of incorporation that is stated on its *certificate of incorporation* [1], and its first *members* are the *subscribers* to its memorandum. A registered company may be either a *limited company* or an *unlimited company*. The great majority of registered companies have *shares*.

registered debenture. A *debenture* [2] issued as a *registered security*.

registered office. The address which a *registered company* states, to the *Registrar of Companies*, to be the address to which all official correspondence (including writs and summonses) may be sent. Correspondence sent to the registered office of a company is presumed in law to have been brought to the company's attention.

registered security. A *security* [1] the name of the owner of which must be entered in a register kept, usually, by the *issuer*. If the holder of a registered security wishes to transfer it to someone else then an alteration must be made in the register. (Cf. *bearer security*.)

registered share. A *share*, the name of the owner of which is recorded by the company that issued it.

registered stock. *Stock* [4] of which ownership is evidenced by a *registered security*.

registered trademark. A *trademark* that has been entered in a publicly available register in accordance with the laws of a country so that only the person registered as the owner of the trademark is entitled to use it. (See also *registered user*.) In the UK registered trademarks were introduced in 1875; the current law is the Trade Marks Act 1938 and the UK Register of Trade Marks is maintained by the Comptroller-General of Patents, Designs and Trade Marks.

registered user. Under UK trademark law, only the owner of a *registered trademark* is normally entitled to use that trademark. If another firm is to use the trademark it must be entered in the Register of Trade Marks as a 'registered user'; the Registrar must be satisfied that the owner of the trademark will exercise control over the quality of goods made or sold by the registered user and that the public will not be deceived by the arrangement.

register of members. A list kept by a British *registered company* of the names and addresses of all its *members* and (if the company has *shares*) a statement of the number of shares held by the member. A company's register of members must be available for inspection by anyone, for a maximum fee of 5p, during business hours.

registrar. 1. An official who is responsible for maintaining a register. 2. An official of a law court who is in charge of administrative work and who judges straightforward cases. 3. (Plural.) An organization (often a subsidiary of a bank) that carries out the work of maintaining a company's *register of members* and issues *share certificates*.

Registrar of Companies. An official appointed by the Secretary of State (at present the Secretary of State for Trade) who is responsible for receiving and approving applications for the incorporation of new *registered companies* and for receiving, and making available to the public, annual reports and other information relating to companies.

Registrar of Restrictive Trading Agreements. An official who was appointed to supervise the registration of *restrictive trading agreements* and to bring proceedings in the *Restrictive Practices Court*, in accordance with the Restrictive Trade Practices Act 1956. The office was abolished on 1 November 1973 and all its functions are now exercised by the *Director General of Fair Trading*.

regression analysis. Techniques of *statistical inference* that are used to determine the pattern of *correlation* between one quantity (called the 'dependent variable') and one or more other quantities (called 'independent variables'). If only one independent variable is involved the technique is called 'simple regression analysis'; if two or more independent variables are involved, the technique is called 'multiple regression analysis'. The object of the analysis is to find a 'regression equation' which can be used to predict the dependent variable from the independent variable(s).

regression equation. An equation, found by using *regression*

348

analysis, from which values of a dependent variable can be predicted from values of one or more independent variables.

regression line. The graph of a *regression equation* found by using *simple regression analysis*.

regressive scheme. Synonym for *decelerating premium bonus plan.*

regulating system (or regulator). A *control system* the purpose of which is to hold constant the controlled condition or to vary it in accordance with a predetermined programme.

reimbursement credit. An arrangement similar to an *acceptance credit* but where the importer's bank in country A guarantees reimbursement of *bills of exchange* drawn on the *accepting house* in country B. The importer's bank makes all arrangements with the accepting house which, therefore, does not have to assess the importer's creditworthiness.

reinstatement. Employing a person in a job again after dismissing or suspending him from it.

reinsurance. Arrangement by which an *insurer* finds a second insurer (the 'reinsurer') who will *indemnify* him against all or part of any claims he has to pay, either under a specific contract ('facultative reinsurance') or under any contract of a particular type ('treaty reinsurance').

relative. An *index number* which is the observation for a particular year expressed as a percentage of the observation for the base.

relativity (or pay relativity). A difference between the wage rates or total remuneration of different individuals or groups of workers which has not been planned as part of the *pay structure* for a particular workplace. There may be relativities (called 'internal relativities') between workers in the same workplace if there has been no coordinated policy for determining a pay structure for the workplace. In general, a relativity is a difference in pay that has arisen haphazardly while a *differential* is a difference that is a result of a conscious comparison of two jobs.

relaxation allowance (RA). An addition to the *basic time* for a job or element of a job which is intended to cover the time needed by the worker to recover from the physiological and psychological effects of carrying out the work ('fatigue allowance')

349

and to allow for attention to personal needs ('personal needs allowance'). The amount of the allowance depends on the nature of the job.

reliability. Property of a manufactured implement, tool or machine, of acting in a specified fashion when required without maintenance work being performed on it.

relief. An amount of income on which tax need not be paid.

remit. To send money from one place to another—especially in payment of a bill.

remittance. A sum of money that has been sent from one place to another.

remittance man. A person living abroad on *remittances* sent from home.

remunerate. To give *remuneration* to someone.

remuneration. Payment for service or work done. Usually restricted to payments of money as opposed to *employee benefits* and payments in *kind*.

Terms with similar meaning include: 'compensation', 'emoluments', 'salary' and 'wage'. 'Remuneration', 'compensation' and 'emoluments' are all used as general terms to denote payment of any nature to employees for their work: 'compensation' is frequent in the USA but rare in the UK; 'emoluments' is used only with reference to UK *income tax*. 'Salary' and 'wage' imply regular payments of money calculated in some systematic way: 'wage' is traditionally used for weekly payments to manual workers, 'salary' for monthly payments to white-collar or managerial employees.

rent (noun). 1. A payment made by one person (usually at fixed intervals) for the use of someone else's property. 2. The difference between the amount actually paid for using a *factor of production* and the minimum payment which would bring it into use. (Sometimes called 'pure' or 'economic' rent.)

rent (verb). 1. To let someone use one's property in return for a payment of *rent*. 2. To pay *rent* for the use of something.

rental (adjective). Of, or relating to, *renting* or *rent*.

rental (noun). An amount paid or collected as *rent*.

reorder point (or reorder level or reordering level). A *stock level* at which more of the *stock-keeping unit* must be ordered to replenish the stock.

replacement analysis. Analysis of the problem of when to replace a firm's machinery or other equipment, given that the machinery gradually wears out or that new, more efficient versions of the machinery become available. The problem has been extensively studied in *operations research*.

replacement chart. An *organization chart* that shows, for each key manager in an organization, who in that organization could replace him. (Cf. *succession plan*.)

replacement cost. The *cost* of replacing an *asset* [1] at a specified time.

reporting pay. A guaranteed minimum payment to any employee who reports for work (unless he has been told not to) whether there is work for him to do or not.

reprography. Copying of documents or other graphic or printed matter.

resale price maintenance. System by which a manufacturer sets a uniform price at which all retailers must sell his product (i.e. the price at which a resale is made). Although once widespread the practice is now used for only a small part of retail trade (e.g. for books and magazines in the UK).

research and development (R & D). Activities that are directed towards finding improvements or innovations in a firm's products and solving the technical problems of producing such improved or new products. The 'research' aspect may involve any efforts to increase knowledge about natural phenomena that may be relevant to the activities of the firm. 'Developing' is usually thought of as being concerned with solving specific problems and is sometimes divided into *exploratory development*, *advanced development* and *engineering development*.

Emphasis in these activites is usually on the technological aspect of what a firm might produce rather than what it might sell. (Cf. *product planning* and *market research*.)

reseller. Synonym for *merchant middleman*.

reserve. 1. (Often plural.) *Retained earnings* which have not been set aside for particular purposes (such as an estimated tax liability). 2. Synonym for *safety stock*.

reserve assets. Synonym for *official reserves*.

reserve currency. A currency that commonly forms a major part of countries' *official reserves*. The US dollar, pound sterling (to a declining extent) and the French franc (in a limited number of countries) are examples.

reserve liability. If a British *limited company* issues *partly paid shares* it may pass a *special resolution* that some of the amount unpaid on the shares cannot be *called up* until the company is *wound up*. The total amount covered by such a resolution is called the reserve liability of the company.

resolution. A formal statement of a decision taken (usually by voting) by a meeting. *Also* a proposed statement of this kind put up for discussion at a meeting. (Sometimes a proposed resolution is called a 'motion' or 'proposal'.)

resource. 1. A material or an abstract quality that a person or organization uses to perform work (e.g. tools, stocks, time, employees). 2. Something one can turn to in case of need. Especially financial backing.

resource aggregation. Summation, period by period, of the *resources* [1] available or required for a *project* [4].

resource allocation. Process, or study, of *scheduling* activities and the *resources* [1] required by those activities given limits on the availability of resources (including time).

resource planning. Synonym for *scheduling*.

resource smoothing. *Scheduling* activities in a way that reduces fluctuations in the demands on individual *resources* [1].

responsible. 1. Having *responsibility* for the performance of a specified task. 2. Having an obligation to a specified person (or group of people) to perform a specified task or *job* [1]. 3. Synonym for *accountable*. 4. Involving *responsibility*. (As in 'responsible job'.) 5. Trustworthy; able to answer for one's conduct and obligations.

responsibility. Obligation, of a person, to perform some task (or see that others perform it) in a way that satisfies criteria laid down by another person or group of people. *Also* a task that a person must perform under an obligation of that type.

restrictive endorsement. An *endorsement* [1] which forbids the *endorsee* from making a further endorsement.

restrictive practice. 1. A practice adopted by workers which serves (as they see it) to protect their employment but which employers think prevents improvement of methods of working. (Also known as a 'protective practice'.) 2. Synonym for *restrictive trade practice*.

Restrictive Practices Court. Court created in 1956 to hear cases concerning *restrictive trade agreements*. It has 5 judges (3 from the *High Court*, 1 from the Court of Session in Scotland and 1 from the Supreme Court of Northern Ireland) and not more than 10 other members appointed by the Crown on the basis of knowledge of industry, commerce or public affairs. The quorum for hearing a case is 2 of the lay members and 1 judge. The *Director General of Fair Trading* may bring proceedings in the Court against: (1) anyone who has refused to give assurance that he will cease to indulge in a business practice that the Director General considers detrimental to the interests of consumers; (2) any parties to a restrictive trading agreement who are required to show that the agreement is in the public interest.

restrictive trade practice (or restrictive practice). An arrangement between producers or suppliers of goods to limit competition among themselves—e.g. by agreeing minimum prices for their products or agreeing to restrict their outputs.

restrictive trading agreement. An agreement between producers or suppliers of goods to adopt a *restrictive trade practice*.

results guide. Synonym for *management guide*.

retail (adjective). Of, relating to, or engaged in *retailing* [1].

retail (adverb). From a *retailer*.

retail (verb). 1. To act as a *retailer*. 2. To be sold by *retailers*.

retail banking. Aspect of a banking business that is concerned with providing *current accounts* [1] for individuals (cf. *wholesale banking*).

retailer. A firm that buys *consumer goods* in order to resell them at a profit (without altering them in any way) to consumers.

retained earnings. The profits of a firm that are not distributed to the firm's owners or paid out as interest on *debt capital*, or paid out as tax, or set aside as a *provision* for specific future liabilities. (Also known as 'earned surplus', 'retained income', 'retained profits' or 'retentions'.)

retained income. Synonym for *retained earnings*.

retained profits. Synonym for *retained earnings*.

retention. 1. A part of the charge for work done by a contractor that is not paid until some time after the work is completed so that deductions can be made if the work turns out to be faulty. 2. The amount which an *insurer* might still be liable to pay himself after transferring some of his potential liability by *reinsurance*. 3. (Plural.) Synonym for *retained earnings*.

retire. 1. To cease one's job or occupation because of age. 2. To *redeem* a *security* [1].

retraining. Training that is intended to enable a person to take up an occupation that is different from the one for which he was previously trained.

return. 1. The value that results from the use of something; especially the money that is produced by using or investing a sum of money, often expressed as a percentage of the sum invested. 2. A formal or official report, especially one compiled regularly and giving statistics, that has been ordered by an authority. 3. Merchandise that has been returned as unsatisfactory or surplus.

return on investment (ROI) (or return on assets). 1. Ratio of *net income* (after taxes have been paid) of a firm (or a division of a firm) over a period to the average value during that period of the *operating assets* of the firm. 2. Synonym for *rate of return*.

revaluation. 1. Action by the government of country A to change a *peg* for its currency in terms of the currency of country B so that in future a unit of currency A will be exchanged for more units of currency B. 2. A fresh *valuation* of *assets* [1].

revenue. 1. An amount of money, or other valuable benefits, received or receivable by a firm—apart from *contributed capital* and loans made to the firm. 2. Synonym for *sales revenue*. 3. The receipts of a government or state. 4. (Usually capital R.) The department of a government responsible for collecting taxes.

revenue account. An *income statement*, especially of an *investment trust* or a company specializing in buying and selling *real property*.

revenue duty. A *customs duty* or an *excise duty* that is imposed by a government mainly in order to raise *revenue* [3] for itself. Revenue duties in the UK are always imposed by a *Finance Act* and are invariably charged according to the quantity of goods involved rather than their value. (Cf. *protective duty*.)

revenue reserve. *Retained earnings* that have not been set aside as *capital reserves*.

reverse bid (or reverse takeover bid). A *takeover bid* made to effect a *reverse takeover*.

reverse split. Synonym for *consolidation* [2].

reverse takeover. A *merger* between two *companies* [1] of unequal size brought about in the following way: the smaller company makes an offer to purchase a large number of the *shares* of the larger company and to pay for them with newly issued shares of its own. The number of newly issued shares exceeds the previous number of existing shares so that the majority of shares in the smaller company are held by the previous shareholders of the larger company who can then proceed to vote for a merger. Although the smaller company has, formally, made the *takeover bid*, in fact it is the bidder that is taken over.

reversion. Return of ownership of property to someone after a specified event (such as the expiration of a *lease*).

Review Body on Top Salaries. A committee appointed in May 1971 to advise the Prime Minister on the remuneration of the chairmen of the boards of nationalized industries, the highest judiciary, senior civil servants, and senior officers in the armed forces.

revocation. An act or instance of *revoking*.

revoke. To reverse or withdraw a previous statement or promise (e.g. by cancelling a contract or a will). In particular, to state that a *Statutory Instrument* is to have no effect after a specified date.

revolving credit. A facility granted to a specific person whereby he may borrow money, or buy goods on credit, up to a known initial limit; when money is borrowed or goods are bought, the credit limit is reduced by the value of the borrowing, etc.; it can be increased again by the amount of any money paid to the granter of the facility, but never to more than the initial limit.

rig. To create a *false market*, especially by *cornering*.

right. An entitlement to *subscribe* [3] for a defined number of *securities* [1] at an advantageous price that is granted in connection with a *rights issue*.

rights issue. An *issue* of new *securities* [1] by a company in which each of the existing holders of its securities is given a number (proportional to the number of securities he already holds) of 'rights', each of which entitles him to *subscribe* [3] for a specified number of the new securities at an advantageous price. A holder can either take up his allotment by paying the required cash, or sell the rights but not his existing securities, or sell his securities 'cum rights' (i.e. so that the buyer has the benefit of the privileged price for the new issue), or do nothing. A rights issue may be made by sending out *subscription warrants* or 'provisional' *letters of allotment* (which the allottees may reject, or sell, or accept).

right-to-work law. Legislation passed by about 19 states in the USA that prohibits employers from discriminating against employees or candidates for employment on the grounds that they are not union members. Right-to-work laws prohibit *pre-entry closed shops* and *post-entry shops* and some prohibit *agency shops*.

ring. 1. Group of individuals or firms who agree not to compete against each other in bidding at a public *auction* of goods or in *tendering* [2] for a contract. Instead, one member of the ring is nominated to bid against people outside the ring (thus giving the impression that there is little interest so that the nominee can secure the goods or contract at an advantageous price). Later the nominee conducts a separate auction (or asks for tenders for the contract) but only among members of the ring. 2. (Usually capital R.) The members of the *London Metal Exchange*.

risk. 1. The *probability* of failure or loss associated with a particular course of action. 2. A hazard covered by a *contract of insurance*.

risk analysis. Estimating the *probability distribution* of each factor affecting an *investment project* and then simulating the possible combinations of the value of each factor to determine the range of possible outcomes and the probability associated with each possible outcome. See D. B. Hertz, 'Risk analysis in capital investment', *Harvard Business Review*, vol. 42, no. 1 (January–February 1964), pp. 95–110.

risk-free rate of interest. The rate of interest that is paid for a loan of money when the risk that the interest will not be paid may be considered to be zero. Usually, the rate paid by a government. It may be considered as the lowest rate of interest that lenders are willing to accept.

risk management. The process, activity or study of reducing the risk of loss to a firm, particularly loss caused by accidents. Risks, once they have been identified may be reduced by: (1) taking preventive action (e.g. improving fire precautions or security); (2) setting aside a fund to pay for losses; (3) transferring the risk to someone else (e.g. by *insurance*).

risk manager. An employee of a firm who carries out *risk management* for the firm.

risky. Having several possible outcomes, *probabilities* of which are known.

Robens report. The report, *Safety and Health at Work*, Cmnd 5034 (London: HMSO, 1972), of a committee appointed in 1970 by the Secretary of State for Employment and Productivity to review the provision made for the safety and health of persons in the course of their employment. The chairman of the committee was Alfred Robens, Baron Robens of Woldingham (born 1910, created a life peer 1961).

role. A set of expectations of how the occupant of a particular position in an organization ought to behave. Specifically, the function performed by a person in an organization.

role-play. To assume a specified *role* and act out a situation involving that role as a form of training.

role playing. A technique, used in training, in which a trainee is asked to assume a specified *role* and act out a situation involving that role.

role reversal. Version of *role playing*, during training, in which two trainees role-play a situation and then exchange their roles.

role rotation. Variation of the *role-playing* technique of training, in which each member of a group of trainees successively plays a particular role.

Rorschach (or Rorschach technique or Rorschach test). A method of assessing personality in which a *testee* is shown a series of ink-blots in several colours and is asked to describe what he sees in each blot. (Named after Hermann Rorschach, a Swiss psychiatrist.) An experienced examiner can obtain insights into a testee's personality by analysing his responses to ink-blots.

rotating shift system. A *three-shift system* in which one group of workers works one type of *shift* for a period (commonly a week) then a second type of shift for the same period and then a third type of shift for the same period.

route card (or route sheet). A document which accompanies a batch of work during a manufacturing process and shows the operations that have to be performed and the *work centres* involved.

route diagram. Synonym for *flow diagram*.

routine. 1. A course of action that is regularly repeated or is intended to be the standard method of carrying out some task. 2. The whole or part of a *program* [1].

Rowan incentive payment system. A *premium bonus scheme* in which a *standard time* is set for a job and wages are calculated as

$$\left(\text{time taken} + \frac{\text{time taken} \times \text{time saved}}{\text{standard time}} \right) \times \text{rate per hour}$$

Named after its inventor, the Scottish marine engineer, James Rowan.

Royal Commission on Trade Unions and Employers' Associations. See *Donovan report*.

royalty. Money paid to someone in return for being allowed to exercise, but not take over entirely, specified rights of his—

especially the right to work a mine, or the right to publish a *copyright* work. The amount of a royalty. is almost invariably related to the benefit from exercising the specified right.

Rucker plan (or Rucker share-of-production plan). An arrangement, similar to a *Scanlon plan,* in which a *plantwide incentive payment* is related to improvements in the ratio of labour cost to *value added.* Committees of representatives of management and workers ('share-of-production committees') are usually set up to assess suggestions for improvements in working methods. Named after Allen W. Rucker, president of the Eddy-Rucker-Nickels Company of Cambridge, Massachusetts, who devised the plan.

ruled-bin system. A variation of the *two-bin system* of *stock control* in which the stock is kept in a container which has a line drawn inside it at a particular level. When the stock falls below the line it is time to reorder the unit.

run. The processing of a single *batch* of work.

running maintenance. *Maintenance* carried out on an item of plant, machinery or equipment while it is being used.

running yield. The ratio of the income derived during one year from a *security* [1] to the cost of that security (cf. *redemption yield*). For an *ordinary share,* it is the same as the *dividend yield*. (Also known as 'current yield', 'flat yield' or 'straight yield'.)

run-of-paper advertisement (ROP advertisement). A *display advertisement* that is to be inserted wherever the publisher thinks is convenient.

S

SA. 1. Abbreviation of *société anonyme*. 2. Abbreviation of *sociedad anónima*.

sàrl (or Sàrl or sarl or SARL). Abbreviation of *société à responsabilité limitée*.

SDR. Abbreviation of *special drawing right*.

SE. Abbreviation of *societas europaea*.

SEC. Abbreviation of *Securities and Exchange Commission*.

SET. Abbreviation of *selective employment tax*.

SI. Abbreviation of *Statutory Instrument*.

SIC. Abbreviation of *Standard Industrial Classification*.

SIS. Abbreviation of *short-interval scheduling*.

SpA (or spa or SPA). Abbreviation of *società per azioni*.

SPRL. Abbreviation of *société de personnes à responsabilité limitée*.

srl (or SRL). Abbreviation of *società à responsabilità limitata*.

SQC. Abbreviation of *statistical quality control*.

safety officer. Employee in an organization who is responsible for recommending safe methods of working, educating employees in safe working methods and investigating accidents.

safety stock. A quantity of an item that is held in *stock* [1] to allow for unpredictable variations in usage or delays in supply. (Also known as 'buffer stock', 'reserve' or 'minimum stock'.)

salary. A fixed regular payment to an employee for work done.

360

Usually restricted to payments to non-manual workers and payments made at intervals of a month or longer. (See *remuneration*.) *Also* the amount a person receives as salary in a particular period.

salary administration. Activities concerned with fixing and, sometimes, paying *salaries* in an organization.

salary structure. The principles, rules and procedures by which the *salaries* of an organization's employees are determined.

sale. 1. A change of ownership over goods in return for money. 2. An agreement to sell specified goods to someone. 3. An *auction*. 4. An offer by a retail establishment of reductions in the prices of many goods for a restricted period. 5. (Plural.) The total quantity of goods (or goods of a particular type) sold by an enterprise over a period. 6. (Plural.) Synonym for *sales revenue*.

sale and leaseback. An arrangement whereby A sells something (usually a building) to B and B immediately *leases* [1] it to A.

sale or return. An arrangement by which goods are supplied, by a manufacturer or *wholesaler*, to a *retailer* on condition that he may return any that he does not sell within a specified period and no charge will be made for the returned goods.

sales force. The people employed to sell a firm's *products* [2].

sales forecast. A forecast of the sales of one of a firm's *products* [2] (in terms of number of units or value of sales) that will be made in a specified future period.

salesman. Someone who is employed to sell his employer's *products* [2].

sales promotion. Any device or arrangement, except *advertising* using media of mass communication, used by a firm at some cost to itself and intended to draw the attention of potential buyers to one or more of the firm's *products* [2]. Probably the most common form of sales promotion is a reduction in selling price for a limited period. Other forms include *consumer contests, premiums* [3] and, for retailers, *trading stamps*. (See also, *below-the-line* [2] and *promotion* [1].)

sales revenue (or revenue or sales). The total amount of money (or a measurement, in monetary terms, of the total value of property or services) receivable by a firm in exchange for goods or services of specified kinds supplied by the firm during a specified period. For some firms, e.g. a firm operating a super-market, sales revenue is simply the total cash taken during the period. For other firms a decision must be made about when to recognize the fact that revenue is receivable; the usual convention is that revenue is recorded for a transaction when the goods have been despatched (or the services completed) and an *invoice* has been sent. The amount of revenue recorded is the charge stated on the invoice. It may be necessary to deduct something from the sales revenue recorded by this method in order to reflect returns of surplus or faulty goods and *cash discounts*; the remaining amount is then sometimes called 'net sales'.

sample (noun). 1. A set of items from a *population* chosen for measurement during *sampling* [1]. 2. A very small but repre-sentative portion which is extracted from a quantity of something that is offered for sale and which can be used by potential buyers to judge the quality, style or colour of the whole quantity. 3. A small amount of some *product* [2] (usually a *consumer product*) that is given free in order to introduce people to the product and persuade them to buy more.

sample (verb). 1. To choose some items from a *population* for measurement in order to discover, by using *statistical inference*, information about the whole population. Sampling can be done either 'with replacement'—i.e. once an item has been chosen and measured it is 'returned' and it is possible for it to be chosen again—or 'without replacement'—i.e. any one item can be chosen only once. 2. To distribute free *samples* [3].

sample mean. Synonym for *mean* [2].

sample space. Synonym for *population* [2].

sample standard deviation. Synonym for *standard deviation* [2, 3].

sample survey. The activity of collecting standard items of data concerning each item in a *sample* [1] taken from a defined collection of objects, events or people.

sample variance. Synonym for *variance* [3, 4].

362

sampling distribution. The *probability distribution* of a *random variable* that is defined as some characteristic (a *statistic* [1]) of a *sample* [1] of a particular size drawn from a given *population.* Thus the sampling distribution of a statistic shows the pattern of occurrence of that statistic in all possible samples of a given size.

sampling frame (or frame). A means of identifying all the items of a population to be *surveyed*—e.g. a list of households or a map of an area—so that a *sample* [1] can be chosen.

sampling procedure. Practical rules for obtaining a *sample* [1] from a *population* [1].

sandwich course. An educational course consisting of alternate periods of study at an institution of higher education (such as a university or polytechnic) and practical industrial, professional or commercial experience working as an employee.

satellite. An enterprise that sells its *products* [2] to only one or two large firms and is, therefore, dependent on their success for its existence.

satisficing. Achieving or attempting to achieve an outcome or state of affairs that satisfies known conditions without necessarily being an *optimum.*

scab. (Chiefly US.) A *blackleg.*

scalar principle. A principle, often followed when *organizing* [1], that each member of the organization should have one and only one *superior* (apart from one *chief executive* who has no superior within the organization but may be *responsible* [2] to people outside it). The idea is that if a *subordinate* (A) has a superior (B) who, in turn, is the subordinate of superior C then C should have no direct *authority* [1] to issue directives or control the activities of A.

Scanlon plan. A method of *motivating* production workers based on the practice of *participative management* plus a *plant-wide incentive payment.* The incentive payment system works as follows: a major proportion (50–100%) of any improvement in the value of work done by a production unit is paid to the workers in that unit. Improvement in value of work may be measured in any appropriate or feasible way: one method is to establish a standard ratio of labour cost to value of production; each month the actual ratio is calculated and if it is less than the standard then the saving is paid to the workers. The other important feature of the plan is a system of joint employer-employee committees to examine and evaluate suggestions for cost saving. Named after its inventor, an American trade-union official, Joseph N. Scanlon (died 1956).

scattergram. A *graph* [1] in which observations are recorded only as points to show whether they fall into groups and whether some are scattered outside the groups.

schedule (noun). 1. A statement of supplementary details appended to a legal document, Act of Parliament or other legislative document. 2. A *plan* expressed in terms of the timing of events. 3. (Usually capital S.) One of the six categories of receipts of money by individuals on which UK *income tax* is charged. The Schedules are called A, B, C, D, E and F. Schedules D and E are subdivided into 'cases'.

schedule (verb). 1. To include in a *schedule* [1, 2]. 2 To prepare a *schedule* [2].

scheduled territories. A geographical area in which payments are free from UK *exchange control*. A payment by a resident of the UK may be made to someone resident outside the scheduled territories only if the Treasury gives permission. The scheduled territories used to include the whole of the Commonwealth plus several other countries but from 23 June 1972 the area was reduced to the UK, the Channel Islands, the Isle of Man and the Republic of Ireland. Gibraltar was added on 1 January 1973. The term 'scheduled territories' is used because the first list of them was in the first *schedule* [1] to the Exchange Control Act 1947.

scheduling. Activity or process of planning when particular actions are to be carried out. In particular, planning when particular items are to be manufactured. (Sometimes called 'resource planning'.)

scientific management. The principles of management, relating mainly to the management of production work, that were formulated by the American engineer, Frederick Winslow Taylor (1856–1915). Taylor's view was that a manager should:

(1) develop, through scientific analysis and experiment, the best method for performing each task; (2) select and train workers to use the best methods; (3) cooperate with workers and view management and productive work as two equal components in an enterprise. In Taylor's own words: 'The principal object of management should be to secure the maximum prosperity for the employer, coupled with the maximum prosperity for each employee.'

Taylor's views were extended and developed by his colleague, Henry Laurence Gantt (1861–1919) and by the industrial engineers, Frank Bunker Gilbreth (1868–1924) and Lillian Evelyn Moller Gilbreth (1878–1972) who laid the foundations of the modern science of *work study*.

Taylor's views were first presented in a paper, 'Shop management', *Transactions of the American Society of Mechanical Engineers*, vol. 24 (1903), pp. 1337–1480. The name, 'scientific management', seems to have been coined in 1910 during discussions between the lawyer Louis Dembitz Brandeis (1856–1941), Frank Gilbreth and the management consultant, Harrington Emerson (1853–1931), when Brandeis was preparing to argue before a tribunal that American railroad operators should not be allowed to raise their rates because they were so inefficient. Emerson appeared as a witness and suggested that if the railroads followed Taylor's (and Emerson's) methods of 'scientific management' they could save one million dollars a day. The case aroused enormous public interest and, in 1911, Taylor published a book called *The Principles of Scientific Management* and *Shop Management* was simultaneously reissued as a book. (Scientific management is also sometimes called 'Taylorism'.)

Taylor's principal writings were collected in: F. W. Taylor, *Scientific Management* (New York: Harper & Brothers, 1947). Other writing from this school of management thought is in: Alex W. Rathe (editor) *Gantt on Management: Guidelines for Today's Executive* (New York: American Management Association/American Society of Mechanical Engineers, 1961), and William R. Spriegel and Clark E. Myers (editors), *The Writings of the Gilbreths* (Homewood, Ill: Irwin, 1953). See also: L.

Urwick and E. F. L. Brech, *The Making of Scientific Management,* vol. 1, 'Thirteen pioneers' (London: Management Publications Trust, 1945/reissued 1951 by Pitman, London).

scrambled merchandising. Offering for sale, in a retail establishment, an assortment of goods not traditionally or usually offered by that type of retailer (as when a pharmacist sells books and records).

scrap. Material that is no longer of any use to a firm and is to be disposed of.

scrip. A *letter of allotment.* (From shortening of 'subscription receipt', an obsolete name for a letter of allotment.) Extended to mean any kind of *security* [1].

scrip dividend. A *dividend* [2] that is paid by issuing additional *shares* or other *securities* [1] to *shareholders,* instead of paying cash.

seal. A design impressed on a piece of wax, or similar substance, which is attached to a document as evidence of the authenticity of the document. *Also* the piece of wax so impressed. *Also* the device used for making such impressions.

seasonal index. An *index number* that shows the relative sizes of the figures in a monthly *time series* and which is used to produce *seasonally adjusted* data.

seasonality. A variation, in a sequence of measurements taken at regular time intervals, that occurs to the same extent at the same time every year. In many industries, monthly sales figures exhibit seasonality. (Also called 'seasonal movement' or 'seasonal variation'.)

seasonally adjusted. Presented so that *seasonality* is ignored (as in 'seasonally adjusted sales figures').

seasonal movement (or seasonal variation). Synonym for *seasonality.*

secondary market. 1. A *market* [1] for a good in which the producers of the good do not participate as sellers. 2. A *market* [1] for *securities* [1] in which the *issuers* of the securities do not participate as sellers.

secondary worker. A person who can work but works only occasionally or part time—for example, a housewife or a retired person.

second-injury fund. A fund subscribed by all employers in most states of the USA which provides an extension of the *workmen's compensation* system, in conjunction with 'second-injury laws'. If a person has been disabled by an accident at work and is taken on by a new employer a further injury in his new job could increase the effects of the first injury. In such an event, the second employer pays workmen's compensation only for the effects of the second injury; compensation for the aggravated effects of the first injury is paid from the second-injury fund.

second-injury law. See *second-injury fund*.

secrecy agreement. See *know-how agreement*.

Secretary of State. One of the holders of the office of Secretary of State (there are 14 at present) who exercise an enormous range of powers conferred on them by statute and administer the common law prerogatives of the Crown. The office of Secretary of State originated as a secretary to the Sovereign—i.e. the person who acted as a channel of communication between Sovereign and subjects. The Secretaries are now the senior members of the government. Each is responsible for a government department: foreign and Commonwealth affairs, Northern Ireland, defence, the home department, social services, the environment, education and science, Scotland, trade, industry, Wales, employment, prices and consumer protection, and energy.

secured creditor. A *creditor* [1] who has arranged, as *security* [2] for his debt, a *mortgage, charge* [1] or *lien* on some or all of the property of the person who owes him the debt.

Securities and Exchange Commission (SEC). US government agency established principally to regulate *public offers* of *securities* [1]. Any company that makes an offer of more than $300 000 worth of securities must register a detailed prospectus in the prescribed form with the SEC. The SEC can refuse to accept registration until it is satisfied that a full and fair disclosure of all material facts has been made. *Organized markets* for securities (securities exchanges) and *stockbrokers* trading in the *over-the-counter* market must also register with the SEC which prescribes rules for trading in securities. The SEC also

367

has extensive powers to investigate the creation of *false markets, insider deals* and other forms of fraud.

security. 1. A document given by a person or *corporation* or government called the 'issuer' and acknowledging that the issuer has received money, or some other valuable consideration, for issuing the security and that some specified person is, in return, entitled to certain rights against the issuer. The rights may be, e.g., an entitlement to an annual payment of *interest*. The specified person may be the *bearer* of the security or the person who is registered by the issuer as being entitled to the specified benefits (in which case it is called a 'registered security'). The term includes a *share certificate* and is therefore extended to mean a *share* in a *company* [1].

Often corporations and governments issue large numbers of identical securities, e.g. *bonds* [2], *debentures* [2] or *stocks* [4]. 'Securities' is usually used to refer to such documents plus shares in companies as bought and sold on organized *stock markets*.

2. Something that is deposited or given by someone who has promised to do something and will be forfeited if he does not fulfil his promise.

3. Measures taken to guard against criminal or malicious interference with property and protect secrecy of operation. Often taken to include measures to ensure safety of employees.

security dollars. *Investment currency* in the form of US dollars.

segregated trust. Synonym for *split-level investment trust*.

selection board. A committee that is given the task of selecting new employees from among applicants.

selection interview. An *interview* that is intended to help the interviewer decide whether to select the interviewee for employment.

selective employment tax (SET). A tax, which had to be paid in the UK by every employer, of a fixed sum for each employee. The tax was payable between September 1966 and April 1973 (when it was abolished). The tax was 'selective' because it was refunded to every employer classified in orders 1 (agriculture, forestry, fishing), 2 (mining, quarrying) and 22 (transport and communication) of the *Standard Industrial Classification*. In addition, SET was refunded with an additional 'premium' payment to all employers classified in orders 3 to 16 (i.e. all manufacturing industries). Thus the burden of the tax fell on the service and distributive industries.

self-actualization. Making the most of one's potentialities; becoming all that one is capable of becoming. (Also called 'self realization'.)

self-liquidating premium. A *premium* [3], which is offered to customers, as a form of *sales promotion,* at a price that covers the cost of the premium goods to the manufacturer who makes the offer.

self-optimizing control system. Synonym for *adaptive control system.*

self-realization. Synonym for *self-actualization.*

sell. 1. To transfer ownership over some piece of property to someone else in exchange for money. 2. To assist and/or persuade a specific person to buy something. 3. Regularly to offer specified goods for sale. 4. To be employed as a salesman.

sellers' market. A situation in which demand for a good is high so that a seller finds it easy to sell it at a price that yields him a good profit.

selling. The process or activity of persuading and/or assisting individuals to make purchases.

selling cost. The *cost* [2] of all goods, services and labour used by a firm for the purpose of *marketing* its products. Often the cost of transporting products from the firm to its customers is excluded from selling cost and is called 'distribution cost'.

selling expenses. The *expenses* [3] incurred by a firm that are directly related to the *marketing* of its products. (See also, *selling cost, distribution cost*.)

sell short. To make a contract to sell goods at some time in the future although one does not own the goods at the time of signing the contract.

semifixed cost. Synonym for *semivariable cost.*

semimanufactures. Goods that consist of raw materials converted into a form suitable for use by manufacturers to produce goods for consumption.

semiskilled work. Work that is rated less highly than *skilled work* [2] but more highly than *unskilled work*. Semiskilled work usually requires a high level of *manual dexterity* but limited to a well-defined work routine which does not call for the exercise of independent judgment.

semiskilled worker. One who performs *semiskilled work*.

semivariable cost. A cost that is incurred by a firm in manufacturing something and which will increase only if the quantity manufactured is significantly increased (for example, the cost of supervisors' wages). (Also known as a 'semifixed cost'.)

sensitivity analysis. Analysis of how errors in one or more estimates would affect the conclusions drawn from the estimates.

sensitivity training. Training in interpersonal behaviour skills using *T-groups*.

separable programming. Technique of *mathematical programming* that is used when a constraint is not a *linear function* but can be separated into pieces that are each nearly linear.

separation rate. Ratio of number of employees who leave an employer for any reason during a period to average number of persons employed by that employer during that period.

sequence. To arrange units of data so that the *keys* [2] used to identify them are in a specified order. For example, if the keys are numbers, the order would probably be numerical.

sequence arrow. An arrow used in an *activity-on-node network* to represent the sequence of activities in a project. (Also known as a 'dependency arrow' or 'link'.)

serial bond. A *bond* [2] that is issued as one of a large number of bonds with differing *maturity dates*.

service. 1. To pay interest on (a loan). 2. To carry out maintenance work.

service level. The ratio of the number of occasions on which an order for a *stock-keeping unit* is met (i.e. there is not a *stockout*) to the number of orders during a period.

service routine. Synonym for *supervisory program*.

set. 1. A collection of objects of thought that is defined by a rule which unambiguously determines whether or not something is included in the collection. 2. A state of psychological preparedness, of limited duration, which is characteristically taken up in anticipation of a particular type of stimulus or situation.

set-off (noun). An act or instance of setting off a debt owed by A to B against a debt owed by B to A.

set off (verb). To use money that one owes to someone for the purpose of reducing his debt to oneself.

settlement day. Synonym for *account day*.

settlement discount. Synonym for *cash discount*.

settling day. Synonym for *account day*.

set up. To make a production facility ready for performing a particular task.

set-up cost. The *cost* of *setting up* a production facility.

set-up time. The time necessary to *set up* a production facility for a particular task. (Also known as 'make-ready time'.)

seven-point plan. A list of questions arranged under seven headings that serve as a checklist for assessing people for employment (either for vocational guidance or for selection for a particular job). The list was devised by the British occupational psychologist Alec Rodger (born 1907)—see Alec Rodger, *The Seven Point Plan* (NIIP Paper No. 1), third edition (London: National Institute of Industrial Psychology, 1970).

severance pay. Compensatory payment to an employee who has been dismissed because of circumstances beyond his control. See also *redundancy payment*.

share. A set of rights that a person called a 'shareholder' has *vis-à-vis* a *company* [1] which are defined in the company's constitution and which may be regarded as a share of the ownership and control of the company.

Usually there are in existence a large number of shares in a company, all with equal rights and one shareholder may possess one or more such shares. With some companies there are a large number of shares divided into a small number of 'classes' and all the shares of a particular class have the same rights.

A shareholder may have acquired his share (or shares) either:

371

(1) direct from the company by paying money or giving property or services to the company (see *contributed capital*); or (2) from another shareholder—e.g. by purchase or inheritance. (In addition, in the USA, a company may buy its shares back from shareholders and later sell them again to new shareholders.)

The rights carried by particular shares vary enormously but usually cover the following points: (1) right to transfer the share (for holders of shares in *public companies*, the possibility of making a gain on selling their shares is an important reason for having them; the right to transfer shares in *private companies* is restricted); (2) right to an annual *dividend* [2] (the extent of this right varies considerably: holders of *ordinary shares* are entitled to a dividend if the *directors* recommend that one should be paid; holders of *preference shares* are entitled to a fixed dividend whenever the company makes sufficient profits to pay one); (3) right to vote at meetings of shareholders (some companies have *nonvoting shares* which do not carry this right); (4) right to a proportion of whatever is left of the company's assets after it has been *liquidated* [3].

share capital. Actual or potential *contributed capital* of a *company* [1] measured in various ways but usually excluding *share premium*—e.g.: (1) *issued share capital*; (2) *paid-up capital*; (3) *nominal share capital*.

share certificate. A document issued by a *company* [1] to one of its *shareholders* certifying that he is the owner of a specified number of shares.

shareholder. Someone who owns one or more of a company's *shares*.

shareholders' equity. The *owners' equity* of a company, which is owned by its *shareholders*.

shareholding. The *shares* that a specified person owns.

share-of-production plan. A scheme for motivating employees based on the ideas of the *Scanlon plan*. Emphasis is placed on accurately calculating a *plantwide incentive payment*: this is done by computing the average ratio of labour costs to *value added* over a number of years before the scheme starts; each month after the scheme starts the value added during the month is calculated; if there is any increase in value added then workers are paid a proportion of it corresponding to the established ratio of labour costs to value added. Share-of-production committees are set up with representatives of management and workers to receive suggestions about improved working methods but there tends to be less emphasis on this aspect than in Scanlon plans. See, e.g., F. R. Bentley, *People, Productivity and Progress: Obtaining Results through Share of Production Plans* (London: Business Publications, 1964).

share option. A right, given by a *company* [1] to someone (especially an employee), to require the company to issue a new *share* to him at a fixed price at some time in the future. Normally the person who has the option can choose when to exercise it but for current UK tax purposes there is a time-limit of 7 years.

share premium. (UK.) Money (or a measurement in monetary terms of the value of property or services) received by a company in exchange for issuing its *shares* and which is in excess of the *nominal value* of those shares. (See also, *capital surplus, paid-in surplus*.)

share warrant. A document issued by a *company* [1] which states that the bearer is the owner of a specified number of *shares* in the company. Share warrants may be sold without registering the change of ownership with the company and the company has no record of who owns share warrants. An owner of a share warrant usually has the right to surrender it to the company in exchange for a *share certificate* and his name is then entered on the *register of members*; this would be necessary if he wanted to vote at a shareholders' meeting.

shell company. A *limited company* which has virtually no assets and transacts no business—especially one that is *listed*.

Sherman Act 1890. US statute under which any agreement among firms which has the effect of unreasonably restraining trade or commerce among the states is illegal. Any person who is an owner or director of a firm restraining interstate trade is guilty of a misdemeanour. Named after its promoter in the Senate, John Sherman (1823–1900).

shift (noun). A period during which a particular group of employees of a firm work continuously at their jobs, apart possibly from a meal break and short rest breaks. *Also* the group of employees who work during such a period.

shift (verb). To arrange that the burden of paying a tax falls on someone other than the person on whom the tax is assessed. For example, when a manufacturer puts up his prices in order to cover his tax payments.

shift premium. A payment in addition to a *basic rate* that is made to employees who work on *shifts* other than a *day shift* [1]. The premium may be a fixed amount or a percentage of the basic rate. (Also known as 'shift allowance', 'shift bonus', or 'shift differential'.)

shiftwork. 1. An arrangement under which a particular type of work in a firm is performed during more than one *shift* in a period of 24 hours for most or all of each week. 2. An arrangement of an employee's working hours under which, over a period of time, he works on different *shifts*.

shipbroker. A person who acts as an *agent* in anything concerned with the use, *chartering* [2] or selling of ships.

shipments policy. A credit-insurance policy issued by the *Export Credits Guarantee Department* by which the risks are covered from the time goods are shipped (rather than the time a contract is signed for producing the goods).

shop. 1. A department of an enterprise where manufacturing or a specific manufacturing process is carried out. 2. An establishment where retail business is carried on. 3. An *advertising agency*.

shop order. An instruction to a manufacturing department to make or assemble specified items.

shopping goods. High-priced *consumer goods* (especially *consumer durables*) which consumers will usually buy only after careful consideration of available alternatives and, if possible, after visiting a number of shops. (Cf. *convenience goods*.)

shop steward. An unpaid, part-time trade-union official who represents a small number of workers in a part of a factory, office, etc, and who is elected by them.

short bill. A *bill of exchange* that is due to be paid in a short time (usually less than 10 days).

shortfall. The difference between the amount that a *close company* distributes to its *participators* during an *accounting period* and the company's 'relevant income' during that period. Relevant income is, roughly, the amount that could have been distributed to participators without prejudicing the company's operations.

If a close company has a shortfall then a tax inspector can charge the participators income tax as if the shortfall had been distributed to them. The object of this is to prevent the shareholders of a limited company avoiding tax by not transferring the company's profits to themselves.

short-interval scheduling (SIS). Planning and controlling the execution of routine work by dividing it into small amounts each of which can be dealt with by one worker in a short interval (typically, one hour), assigning each amount to a particular worker and regularly checking each worker's performance. See, e.g. M. R. Smith, *Short-interval Scheduling: A Systematic Approach to Cost Reduction* (New York: McGraw-Hill, 1968).

short position. State, of a dealer in some *commodity* [3] or in *securities* [1], of being committed to sell more of a particular item than he currently possesses or has contracts to buy. The dealer is said to be 'short of' the particular item. (Also known as a 'bear position' or an 'open position'.)

shorts. *Government stocks* which are due to be *redeemed* in less than five years.

short-term. Occurring over, or relating to, a relatively short period of time—usually not more than 12 months.

short-time working. Arrangement made by an employer for his employees to work less than the usual number of hours a week because of adverse conditions.

shutdown maintenance. *Maintenance* carried out on large-scale or immovable items while they are not in use.

sick pay. Payment by an employer to an employee who is unable to work because of illness.

sight bill. A *bill of exchange* which is to be paid immediately it is presented to the *drawee*.

simo chart. A chart showing the results of *micromotion analysis* of a worker's performance of a task. It shows the sequence of *therbligs* performed by different parts of the body on a common timescale. (From shortening of 'simultaneous motion cycle chart'.)

simple arbitrage. Taking advantage of the existence of two different market prices for something by *arbitrage*. For example, a dealer in foreign exchange in London wishes to exchange £100 000 for French francs. A dealer in Paris says that he will sell francs at 10.57 francs per pound or at 6.90 francs per 1000 lire while a dealer in Milan will sell lire at 1535 lire per pound. The London dealer can then sell his sterling for 153.5 million lire and then sell the Italian currency for $153\,500 \times 6.9 = 1\,059\,150$ francs which is 2150 francs more than he would have got if he had exchanged the sterling directly for francs. (Also known as 'one-point arbitrage' because one extra transaction is involved.)

simple contract. A contract not contained in a *deed*.

simple debenture. Synonym for *naked debenture*.

simple discount. A *discount* calculated by *simple discounting*. (Also known as 'banker's discount' because when a bank buys *bills of exchange* it calculates the discount by simple discounting.)

simple discounting. Computing a *discount* according to the formula:

$$d = niP$$

where P is the amount from which the discount, d, is to be subtracted, i is the 'discount rate' per unit of time and n is the number of units of time.

simple regression analysis. *Regression analysis* in which there is only one independent variable.

simplex method. An *algorithm* for solving a *linear programming* problem by determining successive possible solutions and testing them for *optimality*.

simplified PMTS. A *predetermined motion-time system* which was developed by the English industrial engineer Russell M. Currie and colleagues at ICI as a simplified version of *methods-*

time measurement. The *synthetic data* and instructions for use have been published in R. M. Currie, *Simplified PMTS: A Manual for Practitioners and Trainers* (London: British Institute of Management, 1963).

simulation. Representation of a system (a physical device such as an aeroplane or an abstraction such as the economy of a country) by a device that imitates the behaviour of a system. For example, the behaviour of a real aeroplane can be simulated by a scale model, the behaviour of the economy of a country can be simulated by a computer program.

simultaneous motion cycle chart. Synonym for *simo chart*.

single bond. Synonym for *bond* [1]—see *double bond*.

single-concept film. Synonym for *film loop*.

sinking fund. A fund of money that is set aside and invested to earn interest so that it can be used to 'sink' (i.e. pay off) a debt.

sitdown strike. A strike during which employees remain at their place of work but do no work.

six-tenths rule. A rough guide to the cost of constructing a plant of a specified size *a* (measured by capacity, area or other indicator) when a similar plant of size *b* has already been constructed at a known cost *C*. The rule is that the cost of the new plant will be:

$$Ce(a/b)^{6/10}$$

where *e* represents the amount of inflation between the dates of construction of the two plants.

skill. The ability, innate or acquired, which enables someone to perform a task proficiently.

skilled work. 1. Work that is, or can only be, performed by *craftsmen*. 2. Work that is rated more highly than *semiskilled work* (usually because it requires ability to make independent judgments about the application of a wide range of manipulative *skills*). 3. Work that has been performed very skilfully; the product of a *craftsman*.

skilled worker. 1. Synonym for *craftsman*. 2. Someone who performs *skilled work*. 3. A worker who possesses a wide range of *skills*.

skills analysis. A technique of *method study*, used in analysing jobs in order to train people to perform them, in which particular attention is paid to the way the worker interprets sensory information (touch, sight, *kinaesthetic sense*, etc.) and uses it to guide his actions.

skills inventory. Summary of the skills possessed by employees of an organization.

skimming price. A high price for a product that is set in order to gain the maximum *sales revenue* from buyers who are not concerned about cost (thus, figuratively, skimming the cream off the market).

skimming pricing. Setting a *skimming price* for a product.

slack. The slack of an *event* in an *activity-on-arrow network* is the difference between its *latest event time* and its *earliest event time*.

slip. A document given by an *insurance broker* to a *Lloyd's underwriter* with brief details of the risk he wants insured. If the underwriter accepts it he initials the slip and states the amount he will insure. An initialled slip is a *cover note* and also a binding promise by the underwriter to prepare a *policy* [3] setting out complete details of the *contract of insurance*.

slogan. A brief, memorable statement used in *advertisements*.

smoothing constant. See *expontential smoothing*.

snapback timing. Synonym for *flyback timing*.

social responsibility. Duty of a privately owned enterprise to ensure that it does not adversely affect the life of the community in which it operates. The extent of the duty is not clearly defined but it is usually thought of as a duty not to cause pollution, not to discriminate in employment, not to make money from unsavoury or immoral activities and not to withhold information from consumers about one's products. It has also been thought of as a duty to make positive contributions to the life of the community.

social security. Arrangements made by a government to provide money for people who are unable to provide for themselves.

sociedad anónima (SA). A *public limited company* organized according to the laws of Spain.

sociedad de responsabilidad limitada. A *private limited company* organized according to the laws of Spain.

sociedade anonima. A *limited company* organized according to the laws of Portugal.

società à responsabilità limitata (srl or SRL). A *private limited company* organized according to the laws of Italy.

società per azioni (SpA or spa or SPA). A *public limited company* organized according to the laws of Italy. An SpA must have *contributed capital* of at least 1 million lire.

societas europaea (SE). A form of *public company* [1] which would be incorporated according to draft rules proposed by the *Commission of the European Communities.* An SE would be a 'European company' registered with the *Court of Justice of the European Communities* and recognized as having the same status in each EEC country as a public company registered in that country. The Commission published its proposals in 1970 but they have not yet been acted on.

société anonyme (SA). 1. A *limited company* organized according to the laws of France. It must have a minimum *contributed capital* of 100 000 French francs if it is not going to make *public offers* of its *securities* [1] (i.e. if it is a *private company*). If it is to make public offers (i.e. if it is a *public company* [1]) then it must have a minimum contributed capital of 500 000 French francs. There must be either a *board of directors* (*conseil d'administration*) elected by the *shareholders* or a directorate (*directoire*) appointed by a committee of supervision (*conseil de surveillance*) that is elected by the shareholders (see *two-tier board*). 2. A *public limited company* organized according to the laws of Belgium. There must be a *board of directors* (*conseil d'administration*) appointed by the *shareholders* and a number of supervisors (*commissaires*) also appointed by the shareholders (see *two-tier board*). (Also called a *naamloze vennootschap.*) 3. A *public limited company* organized according to the laws of Luxembourg and similar to a Belgian SA. 4. A *public limited company* organized according to the laws of any member of the *European Communities.*

société à responsabilité limitée (sàrl or Sàrl or sarl or SARL).
1. A *private limited company* organized according to the laws of
France. An sàrl can have no more than 50 *shareholders* and a
shareholder can transfer his shares to someone who is not already
a shareholder only with the consent of the holders of 75% of the
sàrl's shares. Shareholders appoint managers (*gérants*) who are
roughly equivalent to *directors* of a British company. The minimum *contributed capital* of an sàrl is 20 000 French francs. 2. A
private limited company organized according to the laws of
Luxembourg with a similar structure to a French sàrl except
that the maximum number of shareholders is 40.

société de personnes à responsabilité limitée (SPRL). A *private
limited company* organized according to the laws of Belgium, with
a similar structure to a French *société à responsabilité limitée*. An
SPRL must have a minimum *contributed capital* of 250 000
Belgian francs.

Society for Long Range Planning. An association formed in
1967 to: (1) awaken the need for, and understanding of, long-
range planning; (2) enhance the skills of long-range planners;
(3) exchange and extend the information available to long-range
planners.

Activities of the Society include conferences and seminars,
meetings of study groups and the promotion of research. It
sponsors a quarterly journal, *Long Range Planning*.

Membership is open to individuals and to corporations (which
are each represented by 5 individuals) that support the society's
objectives. In April 1974 there were nearly 900 individual
members and 48 corporate members.

Address: 8th Floor, Terminal House, Grosvenor Gardens,
London SW1W 0AR (01–730 0466).

Society of Company and Commercial Accountants. A
professional institute formed in 1974 by the amalgamation of the
Institute of Company Accountants (founded 1928), the Society
of Commercial Accountants (1942) and the Incorporated Association of Cost and Industrial Accountants (1937). The institute is
for accountants in industry and commerce who are concerned
more with *management accounting* than with *financial accounting*.

Membership is by examination only. There are two grades: associates (designated ASCA) and fellows (designated FSCA). A fellow must have been an associate for some years and must hold a position of responsibility. There were approximately 10 000 members at the time the institute was formed.

Address : 11 Portland Road, Birmingham B16 9HW (021–454 8791).

sociotechnical system. A *system* that includes people performing work and which has been identified for purposes of discussion and analysis concentrating attention on the interaction between the people and their methods of working (including the physical production facilities, materials, machinery, tools, quality standards, pace of work, etc.).

softening price. A price that is decreasing.

software. The maintenance manuals, training manuals, instructions for particular jobs and other material that accompanies *hardware*. In particular, *programs* [2] for a computer.

soldiering. Pretending to work while actually shirking.

sole licence (in USA, spelt sole license). A *licence* [2] of *patent rights* with a promise by the licensor that he will grant no other licences. (Unlike an *exclusive licence,* the licensor may exercise the rights.)

sole trader. A person who carries on a business for his own profit, not in *partnership* with others and not by forming a *company* [1] to carry on the business.

solvency. Quality or state of being able to pay debts as they fall due.

source program. A *program* [1] for a computer that is not written in *computer instruction code*. It must be translated before the computer can work with it. A special program, often called a 'translating routine' or 'compiler', is used for this purpose. The version of the program it produces, in computer instruction code, is called an 'object program'.

space advertising. Printed *advertisements* appearing in newspapers, magazines, books, timetables or other publications not published by the advertiser.

space arbitrage. *Arbitrage* that consists of taking advantage of different market prices in two different geographical locations.

span of authority. Synonym for *span of control*.

span of control. Number of subordinates to whom a manager delegates his authority, or who are responsible to a manager. (Also known as 'span of authority' or 'span of management'.)

span of management. Synonym for *span of control*.

Special Commissioner. A person appointed by the Treasury to judge appeals made by taxpayers against assessments for income tax. Special Commissioners hear appeals that are complex or involve points of law.

special crossing. See *crossing*.

special deposit. An amount of cash a commercial bank must deposit with the *Bank of England*.

special development area. Part of a *development area* which has been designated by the Secretary of State and in which enterprises may be eligible for a *regional development grant* of 22% instead of 20%. The areas were first designated in August 1972 and consist of parts of the Scottish, Northern and Welsh development areas.

special drawing right (SDR). The *unit of account* for the *official reserves* that were created by the *International Monetary Fund* in accordance with an agreement between its members that came into force on 28 July 1969. The unit was originally expressed in terms of gold (0.888671 grammes of fine gold—the value of US$ at the time) but as from 1 July 1974 its value is calculated daily as the US dollar equivalent of the following 'basket' of currencies: US $ 0.40 + DM 0.38 + £0.045 + FF 0.44 + ¥ 26 + $ Can 0.071 + Lit 47 + Fl 0.14 + FB 1.60 + Sw Kr 0.13 + $ Aus 0.012 + D Kr 0.11 + N Kr 0.099 + Pta 1.10 + Sch 0.22 + Rand 0.0082. Each member of the Fund that participates in the SDR scheme is allocated a number of SDRs every January. The IMF's board of governors decides the basis of allocation following a proposal by the IMF's managing director. (The first allocation was based on members' quotas.) Each country participating in the scheme has promised that, when required by the IMF, it will provide another participant with *convertible currency* in exchange for SDRs. This means that SDRs can be regarded as

382

a means of settling international debts between *central banks*.

special endorsement. An endorsement [1] that specifies who is to be the *endorsee*.

special resolution. An *extraordinary resolution* that must be notified to members 21 days before the meeting at which it is to be considered. A special resolution is necessary, for example, to change the *articles of association* of a company.

specialty advertising. *Advertising* using *advertising specialties*.

specialty contract. A *contract* embodied in a *deed*.

specialty goods. *Consumer products* which have a limited but intense appeal so that consumers will expend considerable time, effort, and, often, money to obtain them.

specialty shop. A retail establishment selling mainly or exclusively *specialty goods;* usually offering a large and diverse selection of a very narrow range of goods.

specie. Coins.

speculate. To purchase goods or *securities* [1] or *futures contracts* in the hope of reselling them at a profit because their market price will increase as opposed to, e.g., buying goods for use in manufacturing or for resale as an *intermediary* or buying securities because they give an entitlement to interest payments.

speculation. An act or instance of *speculating*.

spirit duplicating. Synonym for *hectographic process*.

split commission. A *commission* [1] that is shared between a salesman who obtains an order for equipment and an engineer who supervises installation and after-sales service for that order.

split-level investment trust. An *investment trust* that has two classes of *shares*: one which entitles holders to a share of the profits made each year from the trust's revenue and one which entitles holders to a share in the surplus assets of the trust when it is *liquidated* [3] at a fixed time in the future. Basically all the dividends go to holders of the income shares and all the gains or losses in asset value to the capital shares. (Also called 'split trust', 'segregated trust' or 'dual-purpose trust'.)

split shift. Two periods of time, within a period of 24 hours, during which a particular group of employees of a firm work continuously at their jobs, apart possibly from short rest breaks, e.g. 06 00 to 10 00 and 16 00 to 20 00. A split shift is really a *shift* that has been divided into two parts and is common in passenger transport to cater for periods of peak activity.

split trust. Synonym for *split-level investment trust*.

spin-off. An unplanned, usually minor, application of the results of *research and development*.

spot (adjective). 1. Of, or relating to, *delivery* immediately. For example, 'spot price' (the price at which someone will sell a commodity and deliver it to the buyer immediately). 2. (US.) Of, or relating to, broadcast *advertising* that is carried by individual stations and not by networks—i.e. the advertiser has chosen a particular 'spot' for his advertisement.

spot (noun) (or spot time). Time for which a single advertisement is broadcast on radio or television.

spot price. The price at which someone is willing to buy or sell something for immediate delivery.

spot rate. An *exchange rate* at which someone will buy or sell foreign currency for immediate delivery.

spread. The difference between the buying and selling prices for something in a two-way *quotation* [2].

staff relationship. Relationship between two members of an organization, one of whom looks to the other for advice and information but neither of whom issues instructions to, or delegates authority to, the other.

staff specialist. Member of an organization who provides specialized services or advice to *line managers* in the organization.

stag. A person who *subscribes* [3] for a large quantity of *securities* [1] in a *public offer* because he expects that, when trading opens in the *secondary market* for those securities, other people will be willing to buy them from him at a higher price than he has had to pay.

stagflation. A state of an economy in which prices are rising (*inflation*) but there is no increase in industrial output (stagnation). The higher prices do not act as an incentive for producers to make more goods.

stamina building. Training activity that is intended to improve the performance of a trainee who can achieve the equivalent of *experienced worker standard* for only a short period of time (e.g. for one *work cycle* [1]).

stamp duty. A tax, payable on specified documents, for which evidence of payment is given by a stamp on the document. (In the UK, often an *impressed stamp* put on the document by the government department that receives payment of the tax.)

standard cost. A *predetermined cost* of using some resource (such as labour or materials) in the production of something by a manufacturer which, according to the person who estimated it, is the cost that would be incurred if production were carried out under specified conditions. Such an estimate is used as a standard with which to compare actual costs in order to discover inefficiencies.

standard costing. The process of determining *standard costs* of producing something under specified conditions. The process is invariably associated with the process of recording actual costs and analysing *variances* [1] between actual costs and standard costs.

standard data. Synonym for *synthetic data*.

standard deviation. 1. A measure of the extent to which a *probability distribution* is dispersed about its *mean* [1]. Normally denoted by the Greek letter σ and equal to the positive square root of the *variance* [2]. (Also called the 'population standard deviation'.)

2. A measure of the extent to which a *frequency distribution* is dispersed about its *mean* [1]. Usually denoted by the letter s. If there are n observations $x_1, \ldots, x_n$ with mean m then:

$$s = \sqrt{\{\sum(x_i - m)/n\}}$$

(Also called 'sample standard deviation'.)

3. An unbiased estimate, denoted by $\sqrt{k_2}$, of the *standard deviation* [1] σ of the *probability distribution* of a *random variable*. If n observations of the random variable are $x_1, \ldots, x_n$ and their *mean* is m then:

$$\sqrt{k_2} = \sqrt{\{\sum(x_i - m)/(n-1)\}}$$

(Also called 'sample standard deviation'.)

Note: when n is large there is little difference between $\sqrt{k_2}$ and s. In practice s rather than k_2 is more convenient as an estimate of the value of σ for a random variable.

standard error. The *standard deviation* [1] of a *sampling distribution* or a *statistic* [1] that provides an estimate of such a standard deviation.

standard hour. Unit used when measuring work. It is the work performed in one hour by a worker with *standard performance* when no delays occur that are beyond the worker's control (e.g. shortage of materials or delays caused by the way a machine operates).

standard-hour payment system (or standard-hour plan). Synonym for *standard-time payment system*.

Standard Industrial Classification (SIC). A classification of UK industries prepared by the Central Statistical Office and used in preparing and analysing official statistics. The most recent (third) version was published by HMSO in 1968. Industries are classified under 181 'minimum list headings' (i.e. the headings used for lists of statistics when the minimum degree of analysis has been performed), which are identified by three-digit codes. The codes go from 001 for 'agriculture and horticulture' to 906 for 'local government service' with gaps in the numbering so that new headings can be introduced. The minimum list headings are grouped into 27 'orders' identified by roman numerals (from I for 'agriculture, forestry, fishing' to XXVII for 'public administration and defence'). For some of the minimum list headings there are subdivisions identified by arabic numerals.

standardized time. Synonym for *basic time*.

standard minute. One-sixtieth of a *standard hour*.

standard operator performance. Synonym for *standard performance*.

standard performance. Used in *work measurement* to mean the rate of output which 'qualified workers' will naturally achieve when performing a specified task without overexertion as an average over a working day or shift, provided they adhere to a specified method and are motivated to apply themselves to their work.

A 'qualified worker' is one who is accepted as having the necessary physical attributes, who possesses the required intelligence and education and has acquired the necessary *skill* and knowledge to carry out the work to satisfactory standards of safety, quantity and quality.

Standard performance corresponds to taking the *basic time* plus *relaxation allowance* to perform the work. (Also known as 'standard operator performance'.)

standard rate. The rate of *income tax* that was paid in the UK on all income left after deducting *personal reliefs* from *net statutory income*. The term 'standard rate' has not been used since the 1972/73 year of assessment when the *unified tax system* (which has a *basic rate*) was introduced.

standard rating. The *rating* (in numerical terms) of the pace of working at a particular job which is the average at which 'qualified workers' (see *standard performance*) would naturally perform the job, provided they adhere to a specified method and are motivated to apply themselves to their work. On the British Standard *rating scale*, standard rating is 100 (and 0 is the rating for no activity at all).

standard score. If a test is administered to a number of testees and the result is a number of scores $x_1, \ldots, x_n$ then it is easier to compare the scores if they are 'standardized' as follows: if m is the *mean* [2] of the scores and s is the *standard deviation* [2] then the standard score corresponding to the score x_i is:

$$z_i = (x_i - m)/s.$$

standard time. 1. The time, as determined by *work measurement*, that should be taken to perform a job under specified conditions. (Also known as a 'time standard'.) It consists of: (*a*) *basic time* plus (*b*) *relaxation allowance* plus (*c*) an allowance for additional work (i.e. infrequent or irregular tasks that the worker has to perform or time spent consulting a supervisor) plus (*d*) an allowance for 'unoccupied time' caused because a worker has to wait for other members of a team to finish their job or to wait for machinery to be ready. The sum of items

387

(*a*), (*b*) and (*c*) is sometimes called the 'work content' of a job.

2. A time set, usually without using *work measurement*, as a normal time for the performance of a particular job in order to establish *standard costs* or as the basis of an *incentive payment system*. (See also *allowed time*.)

standard-time payment system (or standard-time plan). A system of *payment by results* in which a *standard time* is set for producing one unit of output. A worker is paid:

$$\text{number of units produced} \times \text{standard time per unit}$$
$$\times \text{wage rate per unit of time}$$

There is usually a guaranteed minimum pay, which is:

$$\text{time actually worked} \times \text{wage rate per unit of time}$$

(Also known as 'hour-for-hour plan', 'standard-hour payment system', or 'time piecework'.)

standby pay. Pay given to employees who have been asked to report for work in case they are needed but do not actually perform any work.

start event. An *event* in a *network* with no preceding activities. (Also known as a 'network-beginning event'.)

stated value. The minimum amount that a company will accept as payment for issuing a *no-par share*. Stated values may be set by law, by the constitution of the company or by a resolution of the company's *directors*.

statement (or statement of account). A list, sent periodically to a firm's customer, of his financial transactions with the firm and the balance owed by or to him.

statement of affairs. A statement of *assets* [2] and *liabilities* [2] that shows the financial position of a person who is being declared *bankrupt* or a firm that is being *liquidated* [3].

statistic. 1. A number calculated from data acquired by observation, measurement or experiment and used to characterize the data or to estimate characteristics of the *frequency distribution* from which the data came. 2. (Plural.) Numerical data acquired by observation, measurement or experiment. 3. (Plural.) The part of mathematics that deals with methods of

388

collecting, organizing and analysing data.

statistical inference. Act, process, or study of deriving information about a *probability distribution* by using *samples* [1] taken from it and estimating the accuracy of that information using *probability theory*.

statistical quality control (SQC). Application of the theory of *statistics* [3] to *quality control*.

statistical test. Any procedure (especially, a frequently used, standardized procedure) used in *statistical inference* for determining whether a hypothesis can be said to have a specified probability of being true.

status. The status of an individual is the evaluation of him, relative to others, that is made by a specified group of people (or by society generally). The status of some attribute of people (such as job title, size of personal wealth, type of physique, or nature of political views) is the evaluation that a group would normally give to a person with that attribute if they knew little else about him.

statutory audit. An *audit* [1] carried out to satisfy legal requirements.

statutory company (UK). A *corporation* created by a specific *private Act of Parliament* usually to provide some *public utility*, and having a form similar to a *registered company*. The Act of Parliament is usually necessary to provide the company with powers to purchase land compulsorily or to make *bylaws* [1]. The majority of existing statutory companies supply water.

statutory corporation. 1. A *corporation* created by a specific *public general Act of Parliament*, usually to manage a nationalized industry—e.g. the National Coal Board established by the Coal Industry Nationalisation Act 1946. (Sometimes called a 'public corporation'.) 2. Any *corporation* established under an Act of Parliament as opposed to corporations established by royal *charter*.

Statutory Instrument (SI). A document containing orders, rules, regulations or other kinds of delegated legislation made by a Minister, government department or by the Crown in Council (i.e. by the *Privy Council*).

statutory meeting (UK). A *general meeting* of the *members* of a *public company* [1] held within three months of its incorporation to ensure that members are given basic information about their company.

statutory undertaker. A person (or *corporation*) authorized by a statute to provide *public utilities*—such as electricity, railways and canals.

sterling area. A group of countries whose monetary systems were linked to sterling (although they each issued their own national currencies). They: (1) used sterling as the normal means for making international payments; (2) held the major part of their *official reserves* in sterling; (3) cooperated in international monetary affairs. The importance of the sterling area declined rapidly in the early 1970s: sterling ceased to form a major part of foreign countries' official reserves when the UK joined the EEC.

stochastic decision tree. A *decision tree* in which outcomes associated with each decision are treated as *continuous random variables* for which *probability distributions* are given. The optimum decision is found by *risk analysis*.

stochastic game. 1. In *game theory*, a game in which some or all of the outcomes are determined randomly. However, each player knows the possible outcomes from each combination of the players' choices and also knows the *probability distribution* of the possible outcomes for each combination. E.g. the rules of a *two-person game* may be that if player 1 makes choice α and player 2 makes choice β then 1 receives 100 points with probability 0.1 or loses 1 point with probability 0.9.

2. A *management game* in which some of the events that the trainees have to deal with are determined randomly. E.g. if the game is concerned with managing production facilities they may be confronted with a machine breakdown at an unpredictable point in the game.

stochastic variable. Synonym for *random variable*.

stock. 1. A quantity of something that is kept or stored for use as the need arises. Especially a quantity of *materials, work-in-progress* [2], *finished goods* or *supplies*. (Also known as *inventory* [1].) 2. (Plural.) The total amount or total value of a firm's stocks

390

of materials etc. 3. (US.) Synonym for *capital stock*. Also the shares in the capital stock of a particular *corporation*. 4. (UK.) An entitlement—initially sold by the government or by a *public company*—to a regular payment (usually known as a *dividend* [3]). The extent of the entitlement to dividend possessed by a particular owner of stock is called the *nominal value* (expressed in pounds) of his stock (the dividend is expressed as a percentage of the nominal value). The price at which stock is bought and sold is customarily expressed as so much per £100 of nominal value. Stock may be *convertible*, *irredeemable* or *redeemable*. 5. (UK.) Synonym for *capital stock*. Also a *security* [1] issued by a company which represents a share in its capital stock and has most of the characteristics of an *ordinary share* except that a holder may resell any part of his holding and names of holders are not usually registered with the issuing company.

stockbroker. A person who arranges the purchase and sale of *securities* [1] on behalf of others. A stockbroker acts as an *agent* in transactions and never has ownership of the securities he deals in. (Often called a 'broker'.)

stock certificate. 1. (US.) A document issued by a *corporation* to one of its *stockholders* [1] certifying that he is the owner of a specified number of shares of the corporation's *capital stock*. 2. (UK.) A document stating that a person is the owner of *stock* [4,5] of a specified *nominal value*.

stock control. Activity, process or study of ensuring that quantities of *stocks* [1] (e.g. of materials, supplies or finished goods) are such that a satisfactory *service level* is maintained for all *stock-keeping units* while *stockholding costs* are minimized. (Also known as 'inventory control'.)

stock exchange. 1. An *organized market* for *securities* [1]. (Also called a 'stock market'.) 2. (Capital S and E.) The *organized market* for *securities* [1] in the UK and the Republic of Ireland formed in March 1973 by the amalgamation of the London Stock Exchange and several exchanges in other cities. The Stock Exchange is divided into 7 'administrative units' (AUs) as follows: London AU, Belfast AU, Irish AU, Midlands and Western AU, Northern AU, Provincial AU, and Scottish AU.

Each AU has a 'unit committee' and the whole exchange is administered by a 'council'.

Members are elected annually by the council and are in two categories: *jobbers* [2] and brokers (i.e. *stockbrokers*). Members are of three types: individual persons, *unlimited companies* (members of which must be members of the Stock Exchange) and *limited companies* (*directors* of which must be Stock Exchange members). Only individual persons are entitled to elect the council and unit committees but individuals are not allowed to transact business on their own behalf: all business must be transacted in the name of an unlimited company or limited company member or in the name of a *partnership* of individual members. All partnerships and company members must submit annual audited accounts to the council.

Transactions can only take place in securities *listed* by the council (or by other stock exchanges) and *government stocks*. Each firm trading as a jobber must provide a list of the securities it will deal in. Brokers must normally deal only with jobbers and may not deal directly with each other unless no jobber deals in the particular security required.

Stock Exchange Daily Official List. A list of prices and dealings in securities which is published after each day's business by the *Stock Exchange* [2].

stockholder. 1. A person who owns a specified type of *stock* [3, 4, 5]. 2. A firm that has a *stock* [1] of specified goods (e.g. a *wholesaler* that has a stock of a particular manufacturer's goods).

stockholders' equity. The *owners' equity* of a US *corporation*, which is owned by its *stockholders* [1].

stockholding cost. The *cost* [1] incurred because a *stock* [1] of something is kept for a time. E.g. the rent of storage space, the wages of a storekeeper, the cost of stock records.

stock-in-trade. The goods which an enterprise possesses with the intention of selling them as part of its normal activity.

stockjobber. Synonym for *jobber* [2].

stock-keeping unit. A category of *stocks* [1] (e.g. of materials, supplies or finished goods) that an enterprise identifies as distinct for the purpose of *stock control*.

stock level (or inventory level). The magnitude of a *stock* [1] of something.

stock market. An *organized market* for *securities* [1]. (Also called a 'stock exchange'.)

stock option. Equivalent in a US *corporation* to a *share option* in a UK *company* [1].

stock order. An instruction to produce a quantity of a finished product which is to be stored by the enterprise—i.e. is not to fulfil an order from a customer.

stockout. A state of having no stock of some *stock-keeping unit*.

stock split. Replacement of a number of *shares* in a US *corporation* by a larger number with a correspondingly lower market value.

stocktaking. Measuring the quantities of items of *stock* [1] that an enterprise has in order to obtain an accurate list of it. (Also known as 'physical inventory' or 'inventory'.)

stock tender offer. See *tender offer*.

stock turnover. 1. The ratio of the *sales revenue* of a firm for a period to the average value of its *stock-in-trade* (or stocks of *finished goods*) during that period. 2. The ratio of the total quantity of a *stock-keeping unit* issued during a period to the average quantity of the item held in stock during that period. (Sometimes called the 'stock-turn rate'.)

stock-turn rate. Synonym for *stock turnover* [2].

store. 1. Something that is kept for future use; a *stock* [1]. 2. (Often plural.) A place where *stocks* [1] are kept. 3. An establishment where retail business is carried on; especially where a diverse selection of goods is offered for sale. 4. A part of a computer or of *peripheral equipment* that records data or *programs* [1] for use when required by the *control unit*.

storyboard. A form of script used for television *commercials* in which drawings of key scenes are linked to the written text.

straightline depreciation. *Depreciation* [2] of a *fixed asset* by the same amount each year.

straight yield. Synonym for *running yield*.

stranger group. In *group training* a group that consists of people who do not know each other.

strategic plan. A *plan* which sets out general methods or policies for achieving specified objectives; especially a plan of future *corporate strategy*.

strategic planning. The activity, process or study of preparing *strategic plans*. (Also known as 'corporate planning'.)

strategy. 1. A general method or policy for achieving specified objectives. 2. In *game theory* a rule by which one player selects his choice. The rule may be a 'pure strategy'—i.e. a rule that he will definitely select a specified choice—or a 'mixed strategy' —i.e. a rule that gives the *probabilities* of his making each of a number of choices.

stratified sampling. A *sampling procedure* in which the *population* [1] is classified into groups or 'strata' according to some characteristic and a *random sample* is taken from each stratum. The sizes of the samples will depend on the relative extents or importance of the strata.

stress interview. A *selection interview* in which the interviewer deliberately behaves in an aggressive way to the interviewee.

strike. Refusal by a group of employees to carry out their assigned work in order to bring pressure on their employers to change some aspect of their working conditions.

strike manual. A book giving details of procedures to be carried out during a strike. When issued by a union it covers matters such as strike pay, strategy, meeting and authority. When issued by a company it details how essential services, maintenance and so on are to be kept going during a strike.

striker. Person participating in a *strike*.

string diagram. A scale plan or model, used in *method study*, in which a thread traces and measures the path of workers, materials or equipment during a specified sequence of events.

Student's *t* distribution. Synonym for *t distribution*.

study group. 1. A group of people who meet in order to examine some matter, usually benifiting from each other's point of view. 2. Synonym for *T-group*.

subassembly. An *assembly* [1] that is only a part of a complete machine, structure or other assembly.

subcontract (noun). A *contract* by which one firm *subcontracts* work to another. *Also* the work to be done according to such a contract.

subcontract (verb). To make a *contract* with another firm, called the 'subcontractor', for the subcontractor to do work that one has contracted to do.

subcontractor. A person or firm that carries out part of the work that a *contractor* has undertaken to perform.

subliminal advertising. *Advertisements* that are displayed very briefly in a cinema or on television. It is suggested that viewers will not consciously notice a brief display but that it will have a subconscious influence. Subliminal advertising has generally been banned.

suboptimization. Act or process of *suboptimizing*.

suboptimize. To make less than *optimum;* to fail to achieve an optimum. Especially by achieving or calculating a result that is optimum for a *subsystem* but not for the *system* as a whole.

subordinate. A member of an organization is a subordinate of a second member (called a 'superior') if the superior has *power* over the subordinate by virtue of the *authority* [1] attached to the position the superior holds.

subordinated debenture. A *debenture bond* that is issued by a company when there already exists a debt that constitutes a *prior claim* on the assets of the company. If then a further debenture is issued it is called a 'junior subordinated debenture'.

subrogation. If a person suffers a loss because of the action of a second person but is entitled to be recompensed for his loss by an *insurer* then, after the insurer has paid the claim of the assured, the insurer is entitled to take over all rights the assured had to pursue a claim for *damages* against the person who caused the loss. Pursuit of a claim by an insurer in these circumstances is called 'subrogation'.

subroutine. A part of a *program* [1] which is used at more than one stage in the program or is self-contained to the extent that it can be used in constructing other programs.

subscribe. 1. To signify one's assent or approval. 2. To state that one is a party to some course of action. Specifically, to sign the *memorandum of association* of a proposed new *registered* *company* and thereby become one of the first *members* of that company. 3. To promise (usually in writing) to purchase and pay for something not yet in existence—especially *securities* [1] that are about to be issued, or books or periodicals about to be published. 4. To make a regular, advance payment in return for a service.

subscriber. Someone who *subscribes*.

subscription warrant (or warrant). A *security* [1] which entitles its holder to buy another security from the same issuer (usually an *ordinary share* or share of *common stock*) for a fixed price. Sometimes, there are time-limits for exercising the entitlement.

subsidiary. A *company* [1] most *shares* of which are owned by one other company called its 'holding company' or 'parent company'. In particular, a 51%/75%/90%/etc. subsidiary is a company of which 51% etc. of the shares are owned by one other company.

subsidize. 1. To reduce the price of something by paying a *subsidy*. 2. To assist a firm or an industry by paying *subsidies*.

subsidy. A payment to a producer of goods or a provider of services which is made either in order to reduce the cost of those goods or services to a defined group of consumers or in order to enable the recipient to continue in a business that might otherwise be unprofitable. *Also* any other arrangement (such as a payment to defined consumers) having the same effect.

substitution effect. Phenomenon of a consumer ceasing to buy something that goes up in price and buying a cheaper substitute instead.

subsystem. A *system* that is part of a larger system.

succession plan. A document that shows, for each management position in an organization (or each position above a certain level): (1) the name of the present job holder; (2) estimated date he will leave; (3) name and experience of person (from within the organization) who will succeed him, or note that no one in the organization can replace him.

succession planning. Activity of drawing up *succession plans*.

suggestion scheme. An arrangement by which an organization provides a reward to employees who suggest improvements in methods of work.

sum insured. The maximum amount that an *insurer* might have to pay to an *assured* under a particular *contract of insurance*.

summons. An order for a named person to appear before a judge or magistrate.

sum of the years' digits (or sum of the digits method). A method of arriving at the *depreciation* [2] of a *fixed asset*. The useful life, *l*, of the asset is estimated and the sum:
$$s = 1 + 2 + 3 + \ldots + l = \tfrac{1}{2}l(l+1)$$
(i.e. the 'sum of the years' digits') is computed. Then, in the *n*th year of the asset's life the depreciation is
$$\text{(cost of the asset)} \times (l-n)/s.$$

sunk cost. The *cost* [1, 2] of acquiring a *fixed asset* for a firm.

sunlighting. Holding a full-time job after retirement.

superior. A member of an organization is a superior of a second member (called a 'subordinate') if he has *power* over the subordinate by virtue of the *authority* [1] attached to the position the superior holds. (Also known as a 'superordinate'.)

supermarket. A large, mostly self-service, retail establishment specializing in food.

superordinate. Synonym for *superior*.

super-profits. Excess of the actual profit of a firm over the amount necessary to pay interest at a reasonable rate (considering the type of business and the risks involved) on the firm's *contributed capital*.

supervisor. 1. A *manager* whose main role is to ensure that tasks specified by others are performed correctly and efficiently by a defined group of people—especially when none of those people are themselves managers (see *first-line supervisor*). 2. Synonym for *supervisory program*.

supervisory board. See *Aufsichtsrat* and *two-tier board*.

supervisory control program. Synonym for *supervisory program*.

supervisory program (or supervisory routine). A *program* [1] which is permanently stored in a computer and which performs certain routine functions (such as locating a program that is stored in *peripheral equipment* and transferring it to a store in the *central processing unit* when it is needed). (Also known by a large number of other names, including 'executive routine', 'executor', 'monitor', 'monitor program', 'service routine', 'supervisor' and 'supervisory control program'.)

supplement. 1. Synonym for *insert*. 2. A separate section of a newspaper—especially one containing short articles on a single theme and intended by the newspaper publisher to attract advertisers to insert *advertisements* relating to that theme.

supplies. Goods (such as paper clips) that are used by a firm but are not incorporated in its final products.

supply curve. A *supply schedule* presented as a *graph* [1].

supply schedule. A list of the quantities of a good that its suppliers are willing to sell at various prices.

supportive. Providing support; especially by contributing to a person's belief in his own worth and importance.

support point. An *exchange rate* for a country's currency which is considered to be too far from the *peg* for that currency so that if rates at which the currency is actually bought and sold in the *foreign-exchange market* reach the support point then *central banks* will take action to force the rates nearer the peg.

surface bargaining. Bargaining conducted without full determination to achieve the best result, especially bargaining in a way that inevitably leads to breakdown of negotiations.

surrendering company. See *group relief*.

surtax. A tax which used to be charged (in addition to *income tax*) on UK personal incomes in excess of £2000 a year. Surtax has been abolished and is not payable on income received after 5 April 1973.

survey (noun). The activity of collecting standard items of data concerning each one of a number of defined objects, events or people (a 'population'). Often the data are collected only from a *sample* [1] of the complete population and an exercise of this kind is called a 'sample survey'. Information about the complete population is derived from a sample survey by using *statistical inference*.

survey (verb). To made a *survey* of a specified *population* [1].

398

surveyor of taxes. Obsolete title for one of *Her Majesty's inspectors of taxes*.

suspense account. A *ledger* account which records transactions that are not yet complete—e.g. payments in advance—or unidentified receipts.

swap. A pair of transactions arranged almost simultaneously by which one person agrees either: (1) to purchase a stated sum of foreign currency for immediate delivery (a *spot* [1] purchase) and to sell the same sum at a fixed date in the future (a *forward* sale); or (2) to make a spot sale and a forward purchase.

swap arrangement. An arrangement between two *central banks*, A and B, which is designed to prevent B's currency becoming more expensive in terms of A's currency on the *foreign-exchange market*. A lends a quantity of its currency to B and B lends an equivalent amount of its currency to A; A then sells its holding of B's currency on the foreign exchange market in order to reduce the demand for B's currency and thus prevent its price rising. After a specified time A must buy back its currency from B at the prevailing rate. Thus B cannot lose if the operation fails and its currency does become more expensive.

switch selling. A technique of personal selling in which: (1) a prospective customer responds to an advertisement that has emphasized the low cost of the advertiser's product; (2) a salesman calls and demonstrates that product which is clearly of poor quality; (3) when the prospect expresses disappointment the salesman produces a far more expensive (usually overpriced) version of significantly higher quality and, if he is successful, sells that to the prospect. A common variation is for the salesman to announce, when he calls on the prospect, that there has been an overwhelming response to the advertisement and so there is now a very long waiting list for the cheap product but that immediate delivery can be given of a more expensive model.

symbolic language. Synonym for *low-level language*.

sympathetic strike. A strike held by employees to demonstrate support for another strike rather than to protest about their own conditions of employment.

syndicate. 1. A small group of students, from a larger class, formed to discuss and report on a set problem or jointly carry out a training exercise. (Also known as a 'buzz group'.) 2. An association of independent firms formed to carry out business of common interest—e.g. to buy materials used by all the firms.

synergy. Cooperative or combined activity, by two people or organizations, which is more effective or more valuable than their independent activities.

synectics. An approach to encouraging creative thinking by a group of people who are meeting together. Synectics is based on the thesis that creativity stems from recognizing relationships between apparently unconnected ideas. The synectics approach requires the group to be uninhibited in articulating ideas (as in *brainstorming*) and requires deliberate use of analogy and metaphor to stimulate the production of novel ideas. Unlike brainstorming there is often evaluation and discussion of ideas and the approach is intended to produce a single good idea rather than a large number of ideas of unknown quality. Detailed techniques have been devised for applying synectics. See, for example, W. J. J. Gordon, *Synectics : The Development of Creative Capacity* (New York: Harper & Row, 1961) and G. Price, *The Practice of Creativity* (New York: Harper & Row, 1970).

synthetic data. Data relating to the timing of elementary types of human movement which are used when applying *predetermined motion-time systems*. (Also known as 'standard data'.)

system. A group of component items that are interdependent and may be identified and treated as an entity.

systematic sampling. A *sampling procedure* in which the items in the sample are chosen according to some simple rule such as 'take every 20th item beginning with item 12'.

system chart. Synonym for *data flow chart*.

System 1, System 2, System 3, System 4. The names given —by the American social scientist, Rensis Likert (born 1903), and his colleagues at the Institute of Social Research of the University of Michigan—to four *managerial styles* and the results of practising those styles.

At first the Systems were called 'exploitive-authoritative', 'benevolent-authoritative', 'consultative' and 'participating group', respectively. The neutral 'System 1' etc., names were adopted to avoid influencing people during research.

Each of the Systems is given a lengthy description in Likert's book, *The Human Organization: Its Management and Value* (New York: McGraw-Hill, 1967). System 1 corresponds to *authoritarian management*, System 4 to *participative management* and Systems 2 and 3 are between those extremes.

systems analysis. Activity, process or study of critically examining the ways of performing frequently occurring tasks that depend on the movement, recording or processing of information (i.e. data processing) by a number of people within an organization.

systems flow chart. Synonym for *data flow chart*.

systems theory. Theory of the working of *systems*.

t

TDS. Abbreviation of *training development services.*

TIMS. Abbreviation of *The Institute of Management Sciences.*

TMU. Abbreviation of *time measurement unit.*

TOPS. Abbreviation of *Training Opportunities Scheme.*

TSA. Abbreviation of *Training Services Agency.*

TSB. Abbreviation of *trustee savings bank.*

TT (or T/T). Abbreviation of *telegraphic transfer.*

TUC. Abbreviation of *Trades Union Congress.*

TUI. Abbreviation of *trade union international.*

Table A. A model set of *articles of association* for a *company limited by shares.* It is part of the first schedule to the Companies Act 1948 although there were earlier versions in the 1862, 1908 and 1929 Companies Acts.

tactic. A method adopted for achieving a minor objective within the context of a *strategic plan.*

Taff Vale case. Famous legal case (Taff Vale Railway Company *v* Amalgamated Society of Railway Servants, [1901] AC 426) in which the House of Lords decided that a British trade union, even though it was not a *corporation,* could be sued for *tort.* The decision was overruled by the *Trade Disputes Act 1906.*

Taft-Hartley Act. Popular name for the Labor-Management Relations Act 1947, a US statute which: (1) defined 'unfair labor practices' of trade unions paralleling those for employers defined in the *National Labor Relations Act*; (2) provided for a 'cooling-off period' in national strikes; (3) limited political activities of unions and required   ion officials to swear they were not Communists (a requirement t at has been modified by subsequent legislation).

take-home pay. Amount of payment an employee receives from his employer over a period after the employer has made any normal deductions for tax, social security, union subscriptions etc.

takeover. Gaining control of a company by making a successful *takeover bid*. Use of the word often implies that there was initial objection by the owners or directors of the company taken over (cf. *merger*).

takeover bid. An offer made by one person or company (the 'offeror') to buy the issued *shares* of another company (the 'offeree') from the existing shareholders so as to gain control of the offeree.

talon. Part of a *share warrant* or similar *bearer security* which is torn off by the owner when he has used all the *coupons* [1] from the security and is exchanged, by the issuer of the security, for new coupons.

tangible assets. Physical objects over which someone has rights that confer valuable benefits to him.

tangible property. An object, of which humans may enjoy physical possession, that is owned by someone. (Also known as a 'chose in possession' or a 'thing in possession'.) *Also* a collection of such objects.

tap. A large quantity of *securities* [1] held by someone who is therefore able to sell to anyone who wants to buy (so that buying is like turning on a tap). *Treasury bills* [1] issued 'through the tap' are those sold direct to government departments instead of by tender.

tare. A deduction made from the weight of a consignment to represent the weight of the packaging involved.

tariff. 1. A list of the *import duties* imposed by a government on the goods that are imported into its country. *Also* one of the rates of duties in such a list. 2. A list of charges, especially for a *public utility*.

task. A requirement for the exertion of human effort leading to a recognizable achievement.

task analysis. Systematic analysis of the behaviour required to carry out a repetitive job in order to identify areas of difficulty and to devise appropriate methods of training people to perform the job.

task force. A small *ad hoc* group of managers (say 4–6) in an organization whose objective is to make a concerted determination of the course of action to be taken in a critical area of the organization's activities. Task forces are a feature of organizations that have a system of *management by objectives,* where they are formed to examine how corporate performance can be improved.

task-work. Manual work for which payment depends on achieving a standard rate of output so that any worker who does not reach the standard can be dismissed or his wages reduced.

tax. A charge (almost always monetary) imposed by national or local government on individuals or corporations.

tax credit. An amount that a UK taxpayer can offset against any *income tax* or *corporation tax* that he has to pay or can have paid to him in cash by the Board of Inland Revenue.

In particular, a credit equal to the amount of *advance corporation tax* paid on a dividend or other distribution of a company's profits. This credit is allowed to the recipient of the dividend.

Also, a credit that, it has been proposed, should be allowed to individuals. The size of this credit would be related to the number of dependants an individual has. The credit would be offset against income tax to be paid or would be repaid in cash if the individual's tax liability was smaller than his tax credit. See: *Proposals for a Tax-credit System,* Cmnd 5116 (London: HMSO, 1972).

tax deposit certificate. A certificate issued by the *Commissioners of Inland Revenue* to a company that has deposited at least £5000 with the Commissioners. If the deposit is used for paying the company's *corporation tax* then interest is paid on it by the Commissioners. (See also *tax reserve certificate.*)

Taxes Management Act 1970. UK statute that consolidates the law relating to the administration and collection of *income tax, corporation tax* and *capital gains tax.*

tax haven. A place where very low taxes (especially *income taxes*) are charged but which has a stable government favouring free enterprise and a simple system for incorporating companies.

tax-loss company. A *company* [1] that makes a loss which can be offset against the profits of an *associated company* or *holding company* [2] under the rules for *group relief*, when computing liability for *corporation tax*.

tax point. The time at which the UK *value added tax*, on a particular supply of goods or services, becomes due for payment to the supplier.

tax reserve certificate. Document formerly issued by the *Bank of England* certifying that the holder had deposited a specified sum of money. A tax reserve certificate could be presented to a collector of taxes as payment for tax and, if that was done, interest was given. If the certificate was surrendered then only the deposit was returned. The system was abandoned in 1973—see *tax deposit certificate*.

tax return. A document containing details of an individual's income and expenses and his claims for *personal reliefs* that is used to assess his *income tax*.

Taylor differential piece-rate payment scheme. An *incentive payment system* in which a standard level of output per worker and two *piece rates* are set: one piece rate is paid to any employee producing less than the standard number of units of output a week and the other is paid to any employee producing more than the standard number. Named after the American industrial engineer, Frederick Winslow Taylor (1856–1915) who used the system at the Midvale Steel Company and published a description of it in 1895.

Taylorism. Synonym for *scientific management*.

***t* distribution.** If m is the *mean* [2] of the *frequency distribution* of a *sample* [1] of size N from a *normal population* then a *random variable* may be defined by:

$$t = N^{\frac{1}{2}}(m - \mu)/k_2^{\frac{1}{2}}$$

where $k_2^{\frac{1}{2}}$ is the sample *standard deviation* [3] and μ is the population mean [1]. The distribution of this random variable is

405

called the '*t* distribution' or 'Student's *t* distribution' (it was first described by the English statistician, William Sealy Gosset (1876–1937), who used the pen name 'Student').

teaching machine. A device for displaying a programme in *programmed instruction*. In its simplest form, the programme is on a roll of paper. The trainee winds the roll so that he can read a frame through a window in the machine, reads it, writes his response on a second roll of paper through another window, then winds on so that the correct response is displayed and he can compare it with his own. If he is correct, he winds on again to the next frame; if he is not correct, he can wind back to re-read the frame and try to resolve his difficulty.

teamwork. Work done by a number of associated people who are all agreed on and committed to doing it. Each person does a part of the work and his part is coordinated with the efforts of the others.

tear sheet. A printed *advertisement* torn out of the publication in which it appeared and sent to the advertiser or *advertising agency* as proof of publication.

telegraphic transfer (TT or T/T). Instruction—contained in a telegram sent by a bank in one country to an agent, branch or correspondent in another country—to pay a specified sum of money to someone (by crediting it to his account or in cash when he applies for it).

telephone selling. *Personal selling* in which the salesman telephones prospective customers and, usually, does all the selling during a telephone conversation.

tel quel rate. The effective *exchange rate* at which someone offers to pay in one currency to purchase a particular *financial instrument* that represents an entitlement to payment in a foreign currency. (*Tel quel* is French for 'such as it is'.) For example, the price a bank will pay for a *bill of exchange* due for payment some time in the future will depend on exactly how long a period there is until the bill is due for payment.

tender (noun). 1. A formal, unconditional offer—specifically of something that will discharge a debt (see *legal tender*) or obligation. 2. A formal offer to perform work (which has been specified by the person or organization to which the offer is put) at a fixed

406

price. *Also* the price so stated. (Also known as a 'bid'. 3. An unconditional offer to buy something (previously described by the person to whom the offer is made) at a particular price.

tender (verb). 1. To proffer something unconditionally—especially something intended to discharge a debt or obligation. 2. To make a *tender* [2]. (Synonymous with 'bid'.)

tender offer (US). A *takeover bid* in which the offeror company makes a public announcement that it is willing to buy all shares in the offeree company at a specific price—either in cash (a 'cash tender offer') or in its shares (a 'stock tender offer'). (So called because the shareholders are invited to *tender* [1] their shares to the offeror.)

term bill. Synonym for *time bill.*

terminal market. A *futures market.* (Because a *futures contract* specifies delivery after a fixed 'term'—i.e. period of time.)

terminal value. The terminal value, at an interest rate $r\%$, of a *cash flow* [1] of x, at a time n years after the cash flow occurred, is:

$$x\left(1+\frac{r}{100}\right)^n$$

It is the result of investing the £x at *compound interest* for n years. The terminal value of a *cash inflow* is usually taken to be positive and the terminal value of a *cash outflow* as negative. The terminal value, at a specified time, of a stream of cash flows is the sum of their individual terminal values at that time. The factor $1 + (r/100)$ is called an 'accumulation factor'.

term loan (US). Abbreviation of 'intermediate-term loan'. A loan by a bank to a firm for a period of between 1 and 15 years which is to be repaid according to an agreed schedule of instalments.

Terms and Conditions of Employment Act 1959. UK statute which gives a procedure under which employees can claim that an employer is not observing the terms and conditions of employment generally recognized in their industry. The Secretary of State must take steps to settle the claim, if necessary referring it to the *Industrial Arbitration Board.*

test. A series of questions or exercises or other means of measuring some characteristic of individual personality or behaviour (e.g. an *aptitude test*).

testee. A person whose reactions or responses are studied by means of a test (such as an *aptitude test*).

testimonial. A statement in which someone commends a person or a *product* [2] on the basis of his own experience of knowing or employing the person or using the product.

test marketing. Marketing a new product in a small geographical area in order to assess whether it will be successful.

T-group. A small group of people that meets, with a trainer, for the purpose of improving members' skills in interpersonal behaviour by talking and thinking about their effects on each other during group meetings. (T stands for 'training'.) (Sometimes called a 'study group'.)

T-group training. *Group training* using *T-groups*.

The Institute of Management Sciences (TIMS). An international society founded in 1953 to identify, extend and unify scientific knowledge that contributes to the understanding and practice of management. Membership is open to individuals who are interested in promoting the growth of management science and its practice. In May 1974 there were 5400 regular members and 700 student members from 77 countries. TIMS publishes *Management Science* (monthly) and *Interfaces* (quarterly) and conducts local, regional, national and international meetings.

Address: 146 Westminster Street, Providence, Rhode Island 02903, USA (401-274-2525).

thematic apperception test. A method of assessing personality in which a *testee* is shown a set of black-and-white pictures depicting various scenes and is asked to say what is happening in the picture, what led up to the events in the picture and what the outcome will be. An experienced examiner can obtain insights into a testee's personality by analysing his responses to the pictures.

theory of games. Synonym for *game theory*.

theory of queues. Synonym for *queuing theory*.

Theory X. A set of assumptions about human behaviour that D. McGregor considered to be implicit in much managerial policy and practice. The assumptions are:

1. The average human being has an inherent dislike of work and will avoid it if he can.

2. Because of this human characteristic of dislike of work, most people must be coerced, controlled, directed, threatened with punishment to get them to put forth adequate effort toward the achievement of organizational objectives.

3. The average human being prefers to be directed, wishes to avoid responsibility, has relatively little ambition, wants security above all.

(Quoted from D. McGregor, *The Human Side of Enterprise,* McGraw-Hill, 1960.) Cf. *Theory Y.*

Theory Y. A set of assumptions about human nature and human behaviour that D. McGregor considered to be more consistent with current research knowledge of those subjects than *Theory X.* McGregor also considered that if a manager assumed Theory Y then his subordinates would be more highly motivated than if he assumed Theory X. The assumptions are:

1. The expenditure of physical and mental effort in work is as natural as play or rest.

2. External control and the threat of punishment are not the only means for bringing about effort toward organizational objectives. Man will exercise self-direction and self-control in the service of objectives to which he is committed.

3. Commitment to objectives is a function of the rewards associated with their achievement.

4. The average human being learns, under proper conditions, not only to accept but to seek responsibility.

5. The capacity to exercise a relatively high degree of imagination, ingenuity, and creativity in the solution of organizational problems is widely, not narrowly, distributed in the population.

6. Under the conditions of modern industrial life, the intellectual potentialities of the average human being are only partially utilized.

(Quoted from D. McGregor, *The Human Side of Enterprise,* McGraw-Hill, 1960.)

therblig. One of 17 basic elements of bodily movement that humans use when working. The elements were orginally described by the American industrial engineer, Frank Bunker Gilbreth (1868–1924) (hence the name) and are used in describing and analysing manual work in *work study*, particularly in *micromotion analysis*. For example the therblig, 'grasp' has the following definition. It 'begins when hand or body member touches an object. Consists of gaining control of an object. Ends when control is gained.' Each therblig has a graphic symbol, a letter symbol and a colour code. For lists of therbligs and symbols see, e.g., British Standards Institution, *Glossary of Terms used in Work Study* (BS3138: 1969), p. 9; International Labour Office, *Introduction to Work Study*, revised edition (Geneva: ILO, 1969), p. 190; or M. E. Mundel, *Motion and Time Study: Principles and Practices*, 4th edition (Englewood Cliffs, NJ: Prentice-Hall, 1970), pp. 245–8.

therblig chart. A man-type flow process chart (see *flow process chart*) in which the operation is analysed into individual *therbligs*. Unlike a *simo chart*, no timescale is shown.

thermal copier. A device for copying documents by means of *thermography*.

thermography. A process for making copies of documents onto special copy paper that is coated with a chemical that changes colour when subjected to heat. The original document, with the copy paper laid on top of it, is passed under an infrared light. The infrared rays generate heat where they strike ink on the document (though only with certain kinds of ink). This pattern of heat is reproduced as a change of colour on the copy paper.

thing in action. An item of *intangible property*.

thing in possession. An item of *tangible property*.

three-bin system. A variation of the *two-bin system* of *stock control*, in which a third part of the stock is kept aside as a *safety stock*.

3-D theory. (From 'three-dimensional'.) A theory of *managerial styles* developed by William J. Reddin. Managerial styles are analysed along three dimensions: task orientation, relationships orientation and effectiveness. The first two correspond to the dimension of the *managerial grid* [1]: concern for production and concern for people. Reddin defines effectiveness as the extent to which a manager achieves the output requirements of his position. More details are given in W. J. Reddin, *Managerial Effectiveness* (New York: McGraw-Hill, 1970).

three-shift system. A system of *shiftwork* [1] in which three *shifts* are worked in each period of 24 hours in most or all of each week.

The commonest arrangement is for the three shifts to be of 8 hours each. According to timing and industry, they are called: (1) morning, afternoon and night shifts; (2) morning, evening and night shifts; (3) foreshift, backshift and nightshift; or (4) early, late and night shifts.

3-2-2 shift system. Synonym for *continental shift system.*

Three Wise Men. Popular name for the *Council on Prices, Productivity and Incomes.*

threshold arrangement (or threshold agreement). An arrangement between an employer and one or more of his employees that if the *cost of living* (in the UK, usually measured by the *General Index of Retail Prices*) increases by more than a certain amount then the employer will add a predetermined sum to the remuneration of the employees.

threshold worker. A new employee who has not previously been employed.

ticket. A document given by a *stockbroker* to a *jobber* [2] on the *Stock Exchange* [2] after the broker has bought shares from the jobber. The ticket states the name of the broker's client.

tight rate. 1. A *piece rate* that is so low that a worker has difficulty in earning a reasonable wage. (Cf. *loose rate* [1].) 2. Synonym for *tight time value.*

tight time value. In *work measurement,* an inaccurately measured time for a job which actually requires more time. (Also called a 'tight rate'.)

time-and-duty study. Observation of a salesman at work by someone who accompanies him for one or two working days and records and classifies the time spent on various activities.

time-and-motion engineering. Synonym for *work study.*

time-and-motion study. Synonym for *work study.*

time arbitrage. *Arbitrage* that consists of taking advantage of discrepancies between either: (1) *spot price* and *forward price* for a *commodity* [3] or for *foreign exchange* [1]; or (2) forward prices for different delivery dates.

time bill. A *bill of exchange* that is due to be paid after a fixed interval of time—typically a few months after it is drawn or a few months after it is presented to the *drawee* for *acceptance*. (Also known as a 'period bill' or 'term bill'. Cf. *sight bill*.)

time card. Synonym for *clock card*.

time clock. A clock with a device attached that stamps an employee's *clock card* with the times at which he starts and finishes work.

time deposit. A sum of money deposited with someone at a bank or similar institution (such as a savings bank or building society) on condition that it can be withdrawn at any time if a set period of *notice* [2] is given. Interest is paid for time deposits.

time measurement unit (TMU). Unit, used in *methods-time measurement*, equal to 0.00001 hour.

time piecework. Synonym for *standard-time payment system*.

time rate. A rate of payment for an individual's work based on the amount of time spent at work. (Also known as a 'day rate' or 'timework rate'.)

time saved. The difference between the time taken to produce a unit of output and the *standard time* or *allowed time* for that job.

time-saved bonus scheme. Synonym for *premium bonus scheme*.

timescale. 1. A graduated line drawn on a chart or graph to indicate how time intervals are represented. 2. The length of time involved in a *project* [4].

time series. A sequence of observations of some phenomenon taken at regular intervals of time (e.g. annual sales of a product).

time-sharing. Use of a *computer* for two or more concurrent operations.

time sheet. Synonym for *job sheet*.

time-span of discretion. The maximum time for which the holder of a specified job would normally work on a task without being reviewed or checked by his superiors. The time-span of discretion is a measurement of the job not of the particular person

412

who holds the job at a given time—it may be safe to allow a particular job holder to exercise his own discretion for much longer than would be considered normal for that job.

time standard. Synonym for *standard time* [1].

time study. 1. (UK.) Recording the time it takes people to perform tasks (often analysed into small 'elements' for convenience of measurement). Time study is one of the techniques used in *work measurement*. 2. (US.) Synonym for *work measurement*.

time ticket. A document recording the time taken by a worker in performing a particular task.

timework. Work that is paid for by a *time rate*. (Also known as 'daywork'.)

timeworker. Someone who is paid a *time rate*. (Also known as a 'dayworker'.)

timework rate. Synonym for *time rate*.

tolerance. The amount by which some measurement of a piece of work may vary from a predetermined specification without the piece being unacceptable to whoever made the specification.

tool. Any device or instrument, either manual or mechanical, that is used to perform work.

tooling. Devices that are attached to a *machine tool* for use on particular jobs (e.g. patterns, cutting tools).

top management. Loosely, the chief executive of an organization and managers close to him in the organization's structure.

tort. An injurious act done by someone, causing someone else harm or loss (apart from a criminal act or a breach of a *contract* between the two), for which the harmed person can claim *damages* in a court.

total float. The time by which an *activity* in a *network* may be delayed or extended without affecting the total duration of the project.

total income. Synonym for *net statutory income*.

track system. A *payment system* used especially for professional employees in which: (1) a salary is set, by comparison with rates paid in other organizations, for a senior job; (2) the performance of a junior employee is assessed to determine how long he is expected to take to be promoted to the senior job; (3) at regular intervals his salary is increased by a constant percentage determined so that at the end of the expected period for promotion he is paid the rate of the senior job.

Salary increases are usually determined by referring to a graph on which salary lines (called 'tracks') are drawn to show salary levels for fast, normal and slow advancement to the senior position.

trade. 1. An *occupation* [1] requiring the exercise of manual or mechanical *skills*. 2. The activities of buying and selling goods for profits without altering them. 3. An *industry* [2]. *Also* the firms in a particular industry. 4. An instance of *bartering*.

trade acceptance. A *bill of exchange,* which has been accepted by the *drawee*, and which represents the price of goods purchased by the drawee from the *drawer*.

trade association. An organization set up by firms in a particular *industry* [2] to provide common services, e.g. by collecting information or by representing the industry to government.

trade bill. A *bill of exchange* which represents the price of goods purchased by the *drawee* from the *drawer*.

trade board. *Wages councils* were called trade boards from the time they were first introduced in 1909 until 1945.

trade control. A limitation imposed by a government on the import or export of specified goods.

trade credit. Facilities by which firms who purchase *industrial goods,* or the *intermediaries* in any channel of distribution, are permitted to delay payment for goods they have bought.

trade cycle. A period (of about 8–10 years) during which economic activity changes from a peak (when production, wages and profits are high and unemployment is low) to a trough (when unemployment is high and production and profits are low) and back to a peak again. This kind of cycle occurred with distressing regularity throughout the western world until the 1950s. Determined control of economic activity by governments has cured the cycle by eliminating large troughs like the 1930s depression but fluctuations in economic activity still occur.

414

trade deal. A temporary reduction in the price retailers pay for a product, made by the manufacturer of the product as an inducement to retailers to buy more of it.

trade debtor. A *debtor* whose debt represents a purchase of *industrial goods* or of goods which the debtor intends to resell as an *intermediary*.

Trade Descriptions Act 1968. UK statute which makes it an offence, punishable by a fine or by imprisonment for up to 2 years, to apply a false trade description to goods or to supply goods to which a false trade description is applied. It also makes it an offence to make a statement known to be false about a service provided in the course of trade or business. A 'trade description' is defined in section 2 of the Act in very wide terms to include any indication of size or quantity, method of manufacture or country of origin which might be of interest to a potential buyer.

trade discount. A deduction made from a standard price of a firm's product when it sells to firms in the same *trade* [3].

trade dispute. A term defined in the *Trade Union and Labour Relations Act 1974* to mean: 'a dispute between employers and workers, or between workers and workers, which is connected with one or more of the following, that is to say—
(*a*) terms and conditions of employment, or the physical conditions in which any workers are required to work;
(*b*) engagement or non-engagement, or termination or suspension of employment or the duties of employment, of one or more workers;
(*c*) allocation of work or the duties of employment as between workers or groups of workers;
(*d*) matters of discipline;
(*e*) the membership or non-membership of a trade union on the part of a worker;
(*f*) facilities for officials of trade unions; and
(*g*) machinery for negotiation or consultation, and other procedures, relating to any of the foregoing matters, including the recognition by employers or employers' associations of the

415

right of a trade union to represent workers in any such negotiation or consultation or in the carrying out of such procedures.'

Trade Disputes Act 1906. An English statute which considerably increased the freedom to strike by making it almost impossible for an employer to claim *damages* (e.g. for loss of profits during a strike) from trade unions. The Act stated that no court could hear a claim for damages for a *tort* committed by any trade union (see *Taff Vale case*). It also gave strikers a right to *picket* peacefully. The Act was repealed as from 28 February 1972 by the *Industrial Relations Act 1971*, which: (1) made it possible to claim compensation for action by trade unions (or by individuals) that constituted an *unfair industrial practice*; (2) made it possible to sue for damages if a union that was not registered under the Act (or an individual) persuaded workers to break their *contracts of employment*; (3) made it illegal to picket a person's home. Under the *Trade Union and Labour Relations Act 1974*, complete immunity from being sued for tort in connection with *trade disputes* has been restored to trade unions.

trade in. To give a retailer an article in part-exchange (see *exchange* [1]) for a newer or more expensive article of the same kind.

trade-in offer. A form of *sales promotion* for *consumer durables* in which people who already own a product of a particular type are offered the opportunity to trade it in for a new model at a reduced price.

trade investment. A purchase by one company of *shares* in a second company for the purpose of acquiring some control over the management of the second company (rather than acquiring income or capital gains).

trademark (often spelt trade mark). A *brand*; especially one that is protected by law as a *registered trademark*.

trade off. To set an advantage against a disadvantage and consider only the excess of benefit or loss.

trade press. Periodicals that specialize in providing information about business in a particular *industry* [2].

trade price. The price at which a good is sold by one firm in a *channel of distribution* to another in the channel.

trade reference. A statement of the creditworthiness of a firm given by another firm that has supplied goods to it.

Trades Union Congress (TUC). An association of UK *trade unions* [1] founded in 1868 to promote the development of trade unionism and the improvement of the social and economic conditions of working people. The congress of delegates from affiliated unions meets once a year. Between these meetings the TUC's affairs are managed by an elected general council and its committees, assisted by a permanent staff headed by a general secretary.

The TUC maintains relations with the government and with the *Confederation of British Industry* both directly and through tripartite bodies such as the *National Economic Development Council*. Publications include an annual economic review, an annual report, a monthly information broadsheet and booklets.

The TUC is affiliated to the *International Confederation of Free Trade Unions* and the *European Trade Union Confederation*, and nominates the British workers' delegates to the *International Labour Organisation*.

Address: Congress House, Great Russell Street, London WC1B 3LS (01-636 4030).

trade union. 1. An association of people of which the main objectives are to regulate wages and conditions of work for its members. (Usually called a 'union' in the USA and often in the UK. The plural is now always 'trade unions'; the older form—trades unions—survives only in the name of the *Trades Union Congress*. Sometimes called a 'labor organization' in the USA.) 2. An association of employers of which the main objectives are to regulate the wages and conditions of work of people employed by its members. (Now obsolete except in the titles of a few organizations, e.g. the National Farmers' Union. Such an organization is now known as an 'employers' association'.)

Trade Union and Labour Relations Act 1974. A British statute which repealed the *Industrial Relations Act 1971* and largely restated the law on industrial relations as it existed before the 1971 Act.

trade union international (TUI). An international association

417

of national trade unions within a specific industry or occupation formed under the auspices of the *World Federation of Trade Unions* (cf. *international trade federation, international trade secretariat*).

trading account. A statement of the *gross profit* of an enterprise for a period. It usually includes a summary of major categories of *revenues* [1] and *expenses* [3].

trading company. A *merchant*; especially one that buys goods in one country and sells them in another.

trading down. Introduction, by an enterprise, of new *products* [2] that are distinctly cheaper than the products it has sold in the past.

trading floor. The place, usually a specific room in a building, where transactions on an *organized market* are agreed.

trading stamp. An adhesive stamp given by a retailer to a customer as a form of *sales promotion*. The number of stamps given is in proportion to the value of purchases. The stamps are sold to the retailer by a firm (called a 'promoter of a trading stamp scheme') which promises that customers who collect them can exchange them for goods or cash.

trading up. Introduction, by an enterprise, of new *products* [2] that are distinctly more expensive than the products it has sold in the past.

trained-worker standard. The standard of ability to perform a job that should be reached at the end of a *training programme*.

trainee. A person who is receiving *training*.

training. Systematic development and improvement of an individual's ability to perform a specific task or job.

training development services (TDS). One of the training programmes that forms part of *training within industry*. It provides instruction in the use of systematic, analytical training methods.

training levy. A levy imposed by an *industrial training board* on firms in the industry it covers. The funds raised by the levy are paid out as grants to firms in the industry to reimburse them for expenditure on training employees. A firm may apply to its training board for exemption from paying the levy on the grounds that its training schemes are adequate.

training manual. A document setting out prescribed or recommended methods of instruction and other details of a *training scheme* or of a particular training activity.

Training Opportunities Scheme (TOPS). A scheme run by the *Training Services Agency* to provide vocational training for unemployed people over 19 who have spent three years away from full-time education.

training programme (spelt training program in USA). A detailed list of the training activities to be undertaken by specified trainees.

training scheme. A series of activities planned to provide a specific type of *training*.

Training Services Agency (TSA). A UK government agency, established on 1 April 1974 as a *corporation* under the Employment and Training Act 1973, to carry out aspects of the work of the *Manpower Services Commission* that are concerned with training. The three members of the agency are appointed by the Manpower Services Commission and one of them acts as director of the TSA. The TSA has stated that its aims are: (1) to increase the efficiency and effective performance of manpower; (2) to help people to fulfil their needs and aspirations in their jobs; (3) to increase the effectiveness and efficiency of training. The TSA is responsible for the operation of *industrial training boards*.

training specification. A detailed statement of what a trainee needs to learn based on a comparison between his *job specification* and his present level of ability, training or experience.

training within industry (TWI). A series of training programmes designed to develop skills needed by supervisors. Six training programmes covering different aspects of supervisory work are conducted by training officers employed or approved by the *Training Services Agency* in the UK. The scheme started in the USA during the Second World War when the *job instructor training* programme was developed.

transaction cost. Legal fees, *brokerage* [1], *stamp duty* or incidental expenses that are paid when a particular transaction occurs.

transfer (noun). 1. An act of *transferring*. 2. A document by which one person (called the 'transferor') gives ownership of his property (especially of *securities* [1]) to another person (called the 'transferee').

transfer (verb). To change the ownership of a piece of property—especially of *securities* [1] when the action is voluntary and not by order of a court or by inheritance (cf. *transmission*).

transferee. The person who acquires ownership of something by a *transfer*.

transfer line (or transfer machine). A *machine tool* in which an item of work is automatically transported from one *work station* to another within the machine.

transferor. The person who gives up ownership over something by a *transfer*.

transfer price. A price charged by one division of a firm for supplying goods or services to another division.

transfer risk. The risk, when selling goods to another country, that *exchange-control* regulations will change so as to prevent or delay payment.

translating routine. A *program* [1] which provides instructions to a *computer* to translate a *source program* written in one *programming language* into an *object program* in another language (usually *computer instruction code*). (Also known as a 'compiler' or a 'compiling routine'.)

transmission. A change of ownership over property (especially *securities* [1]) that comes about by operation of law (e.g. by inheritance or by order of a court) rather than the voluntary action of the first owner.

transnational. Not identified with a particular nation. As in 'transnational enterprise' (a firm whose owners and top management do not come predominantly from one nation); 'transnational merger' (a *merger* of firms from different nations to create a transnational enterprise).

transportation problem. A *linear programming* problem in which a commodity (e.g. oil) has to be transported from depots to consumers in such a way that the total cost of transportation is a minimum but each customer's demand is satisfied.

There are special techniques for solving problems of this kind.

travellers cheque. A *bank draft* which is payable when it has been countersigned by a named person.

Treasury. Central government department in the UK concerned with the supervision and control of national finance. It is responsible for: (1) allocating money and resources to other government departments; (2) assisting other government departments on economic and financial matters and helping them to maintain proper practice in the expenditure of public money; (3) the overall efficiency of the civil service; (4) the development of management services throughout the public service, taking the initiative in the introduction of new management techniques and keeping an oversight over the management practice of all departments.

The politicians controlling the Treasury are, theoretically: (1) the members of the Treasury Board, namely: the First Lord of the Treasury (invariably the Prime Minister), the Chancellor of the Exchequer and five Lords Commissioners (or 'Junior Lords') who, despite their title, are usually members of the House of Commons and act as government whips; (2) the Secretaries to the Treasury, namely: the Chief Secretary, the Financial Secretary and the Parliamentary Secretary (who acts as a government whip). In practice, the Junior Lords and the Parliamentary Secretary have little to do with running the Treasury, the Treasury Board never meets, and overall control is exercised by the Chancellor of the Exchequer.

Treasury bill. 1. A *promissory note* sold by the UK Treasury and entitling its holder to payment from the *National Loans Fund* 91 days after the date it was issued. Treasury bills are sold by *tender* each Friday. 2. A similar note issued by the US Treasury.

treasury stock. *Shares* in the *capital stock* of a US *corporation* that have been purchased by the corporation itself.

treaty. A *contract,* originally one concluded after negotiation or 'treating', now used only: (1) to refer to an important agreement between governments; (2) in the phrase 'private treaty' (a contract for the sale of goods arrived at after private negotiations rather than public *auction*); and (3) in the phrase 'treaty rein-surance' (see *reinsurance*).

Treaty of Rome. Popular name for the treaty establishing the *European Economic Community* signed at Rome on 25 March 1957. A second treaty establishing the *European Atomic Energy Community* was also signed at Rome on the same day.

tree. A *graph* [2] in which there are no *loops* [1] or *circuits* but there is a *path* [3] from each *vertex* to every other vertex.

trial balance. A list of all *balances* [1] of the *ledger* accounts of an enterprise. The totals of *credit* [1] balances and *debit* [1] balances should always be the same in a *double-entry book-keeping* system.

Truck Acts. Series of UK statutes (Truck Act 1831, Truck Amendment Act 1887, Truck Act 1896 and Truck Act 1940) that require employers to pay employees for 'manual labour' in legal tender. The Acts outlaw the nineteenth-century 'truck system' whereby wages were paid in the form of vouchers which could only be exchanged at a 'truck shop' (or 'tommy shop') that was run by the employer and gave poor value. (From the now-obsolete use of 'truck' to mean 'barter'.)

true discount. Synonym for *compound discount*.

trust. 1. An arrangement by which one person (called a 'trustee') has ownership and possession of specified property but any income he derives from the property must go to a second person (called the 'beneficiary') or must be used for specified purposes (called the 'objects' of the trust). In dealings between trustee and beneficiary, the trust property is considered to belong to the beneficiary but in dealings with third persons it is considered to belong to the trustee. The person who appointed the trustee and gave him the trust property is called the 'donor' of the trust. Beneficiary and donor may be the same person but often are not.

2. A *monopoly*; especially one that arises because previously independent firms come under common control. This use derives from a popular form of monopoly arrangement made in the USA in the nineteenth century: the *stockholders* [1] of previously competing *corporations* were persuaded to give all their stock to a

single board of trustees in exchange for 'trust certificates'; the trustees were required to exercise the voting rights carried by their stock so as to manage the corporations in the best interests of the holders of trust certificates and to distribute *dividends* [2] to them. The first trust of this kind was the Standard Oil Trust formed in 1879 but by 1888 they had been declared illegal.

trust deed. A *deed* which sets out the terms of a *trust* [1].

trustee. One to whom property is entrusted to be administered for the benefit of another.

trustee company. See *unit trust*.

trustee savings bank (TSB). A non-profit-making institution that accepts *deposits* [1] of money from people and pays interest (usually *compound interest*) on them. The deposits may be withdrawn at short notice. The property of a TSB is *vested* in four 'custodian trustees' of the TSB, which is not a *corporation*. A TSB may also operate a *current account* [1] for a depositor.

turnkey contract. An arrangement by which a client commissions a specialist firm to arrange the design and construction of a complex project and leaves all decisions to the specialist firm until the project is complete and he can 'turn a key' to set it working.

turnover. 1. *Sales revenue* for a period. 2. The ratio of *sales revenue* for a period to the average value of a class of the firm's *assets* [1] during that period (e.g. turnover of *operating assets* or of stocks of *finished goods*).

twilight shift. A *part-time shift* that is an *evening shift*.

two-bin system. A system of *stock control* in which the stock of a particular *stock-keeping unit* is divided into two parts. The first part is for normal use, the other part can be used only when the first is exhausted. Exhaustion of the first part is the signal to reorder the unit. (Also known as the 'last-bag system'.)

two-handed process chart. A *process chart* that analyses the actions of one worker when performing a single task. It is usual to present the motions of each hand separately on the same chart. (Also known as an 'operation chart'.)

two-person game. In *game theory*, a game with only two players.

two-person zero-sum game. In *game theory*, a *two-person game* that is a *zero-sum game*.

two-shift system. A system of *shiftwork* [1] in which two *shifts* are worked in each period of 24 hours.

two-tier board. A group of people who are responsible for the conduct of a *company* and are divided into two committees: (1) a 'management board' consisting of full-time employees of the company who are responsible for the company's day-to-day operations; (2) a 'supervisory board' responsible for protecting the interests of the company's *shareholders* and, possibly, of its employees. Usually, the management board is appointed by, and may be dismissed by, the supervisory board. The supervisory board is elected by shareholders and, possibly, employees.

two-tier gold system. An arrangement between some members of the *International Monetary Fund* (IMF) that, from March 1968, they would use their holdings of gold only for transactions between *central banks* and that such transactions would be at IMF *par values* [1] (based on US $35.00 an ounce, raised to US $38.00 an ounce from 18 December 1971 and raised to US $42.00 an ounce from 13 February 1973). Specifically, they would cease buying and selling gold to private individuals in order to maintain a uniform price for gold. Private individuals conducted their own market for gold where the price reached $127.00 an ounce in June 1972. From 18 December 1971 the USA suspended the convertibility of dollars into gold and central banks virtually ceased to use gold in their transactions. The agreement for the two-tier system was formally ended in November 1973 although central banks continued not to sell gold to the private market (where the price rose to $195.50 an ounce in December 1974) until 6 January 1975 when the US Treasury held an auction to sell 2 million ounces. In fact only 750,000 ounces were sold at the auction.

u

UNICE. Abbreviation of *Union des industries de la Communauté européenne.*

ultra vires. Latin for beyond power—that is, outside the *competence* [1] or legal authority of someone or some body of people.

***ultra vires* rule.** Rule of English law until 1973 that a company could not be liable for debts connected with activities that it was not authorized to engage in by its *memorandum of association.*

unaided-recall method. Technique for assessing the effectiveness of *advertisements* in which an interviewer asks someone which advertisements he remembers having seen or heard.

unattended time. A period during which a machine is not being used and is not being attended by a maintenance engineer.

uncalled capital. The difference between *issued share capital* and *paid-up capital* (when paid-up capital is less than issued share capital).

uncontrollable cost. A cost that is not a *controllable cost.*

underinsure. To insure something for less than its actual value.

undertrading. Underutilization by a firm of its assets.

underwrite. 1. To act as an *insurer.* 2. To guarantee to purchase any of a *public offer* of *securities* [1] that are not bought by anyone else.

underwriter. One who *underwrites.*

underwriting commission. *Commission* [1] paid to someone who *underwrites* [2] a *public offer* of *securities* [1].

undiscounted gross benefit-cost ratio. Ratio of the total forecast *cash inflows* for an investment project to the total forecast *cash outflows* for the project.

undiscounted net benefit-cost ratio. If I_1 , . . . , I_n are the forecast *cash inflows* from an investment project in years $1, . . . , n$; D_1 , . . . , D_n are *depreciation expenses* of the project in years $1, . . . , n$ and O_1 , . . . , O_n are the forecast *cash outflows* then:

$$\sum_i (I_i - D_i)/\sum_i O_i$$

is the undiscounted net benefit-cost ratio of the project.

undistributed profits. Synonym for *retained earnings*.

unemployed. 1. (Of a person.) Not *employed* [2] by anyone. 2. (Of a machine or plant.) Not in use. 3. (Of money.) Not invested.

unemployment. The state of being *unemployed*.

unexpired cost. The *cost* [1] of an *asset* [1] that belongs to a firm and which it can use to produce future *revenue* [1].

unfair dismissal. Dismissal from employment that is deemed to be unfair by an *industrial tribunal* in accordance with the *Trade Union and Labour Relations Act 1974*. A tribunal may award damages to an employee who has been unfairly dismissed. The employer has to show that the dismissal was not unfair.

unfair industrial practice. Any of various activities, by unions, employers' associations, employers and others, which were defined as unfair industrial practices by the *Industrial Relations Act 1971* (e.g. it was an unfair industrial practice for anyone to organize a strike in order to induce an employer to interfere with his employees' right to refrain from joining a trade union). If anyone suffered loss as a result of an unfair industrial practice he could ask the *National Industrial Relations Court* for an injunction to stop the practice and for damages. The 1971 Act has been repealed under the *Trade Union and Labour Relations Act 1974* and unfair industrial practices no longer exist in English law.

426

unfair labor practice. US equivalent of an *unfair industrial practice*. Unfair labor practices are defined in the *National Labor Relations Act 1935*, the *Taft-Hartley Act* and similar legislation.

unfunded debt. A debt that has to be repaid at some time in the future (cf. *funded debt*).

unified tax system. The system of *personal income tax* introduced into the UK on 6 April 1973 in which the previously separate 'income tax' and *surtax* have been replaced by a single *income tax*.

unincorporated association. A group of people who have voluntarily associated themselves to promote common interests (e.g. the *Trades Union Congress*) or to carry out a business (e.g. a firm of solicitors) but have not formed a *corporation* for that purpose.

union. A *trade union* [1].

Union des industries de la Communauté européenne (UNICE). An association of the central industrial federations of the members of the European Communities. UNICE was founded in 1958 and now has 13 members plus 12 associate members (organizations from European countries outside the EEC). UNICE's principal objectives are: (1) to promote the formulation of an industrial policy based on the European idea; (2) to act as the official spokesman for industry in the EEC when dealing with the institutions of the European Communities; (3) to represent European industry in dealings with other countries.

Address : 6 rue de Loxum, 1000 Bruxelles, Belgium (512 67 80 or 513 45 62).

unionized. *Organized* [2] into *trade unions* [1].

union shop. Synonym for *post-entry closed shop*.

unissued capital. The difference between *authorized capital* and *issued share capital*.

unit. A *security* [1] which is sold by the management company of a *unit trust* and which entitles its owners: (1) to demand *redemption* at any time at a price (called the 'bid price') which is related to the value of the securities held by the unit trust; and (2) to share in the income derived from the securities held by the unit trust.

unit costing. Synonym for *process costing*.

unitholder. Someone who owns one or more *units* of a *unit trust*.

unit of account. A unit used for measuring monetary values. For most purposes a particular country's unit of currency is used as the unit of account in that country; for many international purposes artificial units of account are defined (e.g. the unit of account of the European Communities, which was originally defined as 0.88867088 grammes of fine gold).

unit price. The price charged for goods expressed as a price per unit of measurement.

unit pricing. An instance or the activity of quoting *unit prices*.

unit trust. A *collective investment institution* in which the fund of money for investment comes from the sale of *units* and in which decisions about buying and selling securities, and about the sale of units, are made by a 'management company' which makes out a *trust deed* nominating a second company (usually a bank) to act as *trustee*. The trustee company controls the work of the management company for the benefit of the unitholders and acts as guardian of their interests. A characteristic feature of most modern unit trusts is that they are 'open-ended'—i.e. the management company promises to buy back (*redeem*) units at any time and can obtain more money for its investment at any time by selling new units. The management company receives an initial service charge, which is a percentage of the selling price of each unit, plus a half-yearly management fee which is a percentage of the total value of the securities held by the fund.

unlimited company. A *registered company*, the *members* of which are liable to pay all the company's debts without limit if it is *wound up*. An unlimited company may or may not have *shares* and may even issue *no-par shares*.

unlimited liability. Liability to pay all the debts of a firm.

unliquidated damages. *Damages* of an amount that must be decided by a court because no *liquidated damages* were fixed.

unlisted company. A *company* that is not a *listed company*. (Also called an 'unquoted company'.)

unmonitored control system. Synonym for *open-loop control system*.

unofficial strike. A strike that does not have the support of a trade union. (Cf. *official strike*.)

unquoted company. Synonym for *unlisted company*.

unsecured loan stock. *Stock* [4] issued by a *public company* [1] which gives no *security* [2] (e.g. in the form of a *floating charge*) that interest will be paid.

unskilled work. Work that consists of simple manual operations that can be learned in a short time and which requires the exercise of little or no independent judgment.

unskilled worker. Someone who performs, or can only perform, *unskilled work*.

updating training. Training that is intended to acquaint trainees with recent developments—e.g. new materials, tools or processes—and hence improve their performance in their occupations.

upgrading. Improving something without making major changes. Especially, giving an employee more money and/or status and/or responsibility and usually a different title without significantly changing his job.

usage value. In *stock control*, the total cost of the quantity of stock of a particular *stock-keeping unit* used during a period (typically one year—see *annual usage value*).

usage-value classification. Classification of *stocks* [1], for the purposes of *stock control*, according to their *usage value*. Often called 'ABC analysis' or 'ABC classification' because it is common to have three classes with A representing the items with highest usage value on which most of the effort of stock control should be concentrated.

usance. A customary period of time; especially a customary period from the date of making a *bill of exchange* to the date when it is due for payment.

utilities. Facilities for the supply of power and disposal of waste.

utility. 1. The satisfaction, or fulfilment of needs, that a person derives from the consumption of a good or of a specific quantity of a good. 2. Usefulness; ability to satisfy needs. 3. A *public utility*. 4. An organization providing a *public utility*.

utility function. A mathematical *function* [2] which assigns, to each value of the quantity of a good, a number representing the *utility* [1] of that quantity to a specified consumer.

utility program. A *program* [1] of instructions to a computer for performing routine tasks (such as transferring data from one type of store to another or testing programs for errors); the term also includes *translating routines*.

V

VAT. Abbreviation of *value added tax*.

valuation. Act or process of estimating the *value* (especially the *market value*) of something. *Also* the estimate of value arrived at by this process.

value. 1. The amount of money for which something could be sold. 2. Something given in exchange; a *quid pro quo*. Especially in the phrase 'for value received' traditionally written on *bills of exchange* that represent payment for goods.

value added. Difference between the *sales revenue* that a firm gets from selling its *products* [2] and the cost to it of the materials used in those products. (Also known as 'added value'.)

value added tax (VAT). A tax charged on the *value added* by an enterprise over a period.

In the UK the tax is charged on the supply of goods or service by 'taxable persons'—roughly, all individuals or firms with a *sales revenue* of more than £5000 a year—apart from certain supplies (e.g. of insurance and education) that are exempt. When a taxable person supplies goods or services he charges VAT to his customer and this is known as 'output tax'. The VAT that a taxable person pays when buying goods for use in his enterprise is called 'input tax'. At quarterly intervals, a taxable person pays, to the *Commissioners of Customs and Excise*, the difference between the total output tax charged by him and the total input

431

tax paid by him. If he has made only *zero-rated* supplies then all his input tax is refunded.

value analysis. Consideration of the function of all parts of the design of one of a firm's products to see whether any changes in materials, manufacturing methods or design will increase the product's value to the firm. The increase in value may arise because the product can be improved and its sale increased or because the cost of producing it can be reduced or both.

value date. 1. The date by which a deal on the *foreign-exchange market* must be complete—i.e. each party must have transferred money to the other party. 2. The date by which the amount of a loan made on the *external currency market* must be transferred to the borrower.

value envelope. A graph derived from the calculations used in *project network techniques*. The value envelope of a *project* [4] consists of two graphs of value of work done against time. One represents work that would be done if all *activities* were completed at their *earliest finish times;* the second represents work that would be done if all activities were completed at their *latest finish times*. Actual value of work done is then plotted week by week and if the line goes outside the value envelope, corrective action must be taken.

variable cost. A *cost* [2] associated with the production of something by a firm which is directly proportional to the quantity produced for a wide range of quantities.

variable costing. Computation of the *cost* [2] of a unit of production as the total of all *variable costs* associated with the manufacture of the unit. (Also known as 'marginal costing'.)

variable direct expense. A *direct expense* that is a *variable expense*.

variable expense. An *expense* [4] associated with the production of something by a firm and which is directly proportional to the quantity produced for a wide range of quantities.

variance. 1. The difference between actual performance and forecast, budgeted or standard performance. Especially, a difference between actual and budgeted cost or *standard cost*.

2. A measure of the extent to which the *probability distribu-*

tion of a *random variable* is dispersed about its *mean* [1]. If X is the random variable and μ is its mean then its variance is:

$$\text{Var}(X) = \text{E}\{(X - \mu)^2\}$$

where E represents *expectation*. (Also called 'population variance'.)

3. The square of a *standard deviation* [1] denoted by s^2. (Also called a 'sample variance'.)

4. The square of a *standard deviation* [3], denoted by k_2. (Also called 'sample variance', or 'second k-statistic'.)

variance analysis. Process or activity of calculating and explaining *variances* between actual costs and *standard costs*.

variance ratio. The ratio of one sample *variance* [3] to another sample variance when both samples are taken from a *normal population*. The ratio is usually denoted by F (see F *distribution*).

variate. Synonym for *random variable*.

venture capital. Funds provided to a firm by outsiders as *capital* [2] for the firm and on the basis that the providers of the funds will share in the profits of the firm. *Also* funds which a person or firm has available for investment in this way.

verge-perforated card. Synonym for *verge-punched card*.

verge-punched card. A card in which holes are punched in a strip near one edge to represent data. (Also known as an 'edge-punched card' or a 'verge-perforated card'.)

vertex. A point at the end of an *edge* in a *graph* [2]. (Also known as a 'node'.)

vertical merger. A *merger* between a firm and one of its suppliers (e.g. between a manufacturer and a supplier of its materials, or between a manufacturer and a wholesaler).

vest. To be placed in the possession or ownership of someone or of a *corporation*. (E.g., 'the assets are vested in the company'.)

visible (or visible transaction). A sale, by a resident of one country to a nonresident, of goods (rather than services). For the buyer's country, such a transaction is a 'visible import'; for the seller's country it is a 'visible export'.

visible-edge card. A card used for recording data and intended to be filed in a specially constructed drawer which holds cards so that they overlap and one edge of each is visible. The visible edge is used for identification purposes.

vocation. An *occupation* [1] that a person has chosen to follow for most of his life, especially one to which he is deeply committed.

volenti non fit injuria. The legal principle that a person who freely and voluntarily does something which he knows entails a risk of injury to him has no right to claim *damages* if he is in fact injured.

voluntary group. A number of retailers of similar goods who are associated with a single wholesaler and adopt a common policy of *promotion* [1]. The initiative for formation of the group may come from a wholesaler who wishes to have a secure market or from retailers who wish to form a cooperative buying organization to cut costs.

Vorstand. The *board of directors* of a German public company (an *Aktiengesellschaft* [1]). Members of the board (*Vorstandsmitglieder*) are appointed by the *Aufsichtsrat* of the company for a fixed term of up to 5 years. The *Aufsichtsrat* fixes directors' salaries and has power to dismiss directors for serious misconduct. (See also *two-tier board*.)

voucher. A document which explains why a payment was made.

voucher copy. Synonym for *checking copy*.

W

WCL. Abbreviation of *World Confederation of Labour*.

WFTU. Abbreviation of *World Federation of Trade Unions*.

wage (often used in plural). Regular payment to an employee for services or work done. Especially payment in cash for manual work paid at weekly intervals. *Also* the amount paid to someone as wages. See *remuneration*.

wage administration. Activities concerned with fixing and, sometimes, paying *wages* in an organization.

wage audit. A regular review, conducted by consultants, of all forms of payment to employees within a company.

wage drift. The rate of increase of the gap between actual average hourly earnings in an *industry* [2] and the nationally negotiated hourly rate for workers in that industry. It is usual to exclude payments for overtime when calculating wage drift.

wage-push inflation. See *cost-push inflation*.

wage rate. Payment to employees expressed as a sum per unit of time worked (*time rate*) or per unit of output produced (*piece rate*).

wages council. A body of people appointed by the Secretary of State for Employment to submit proposals for *wages regulation orders* to him. Each council covers a particular *industry* [2] and consists of up to three independent persons (one of whom acts as chairman) plus equal numbers of representatives of employers and employees in the industry covered. Wages councils are intended to operate only in industries where *collective bargaining* is not practised—usually because there are no effective *trade unions* [1]. There are about 50 councils but the number is being reduced as quickly as possible.

Wages Councils Act 1959. UK statute which consolidated all the previous law on *wages councils*.

wages regulation order. A *Statutory Instrument* stating: (1) the minimum wages to be paid to a particular type of worker; and/or (2) the holidays and holiday pay to be given. Orders are made by the Secretary of State for Employment and confirm proposals made by a *wages council*. Failure to pay at least the minimum wage when it is due is an offence.

wage stablization. Attempting to prevent a general rise in the level of wages; especially by governments, as was done, for example, in the USA between January 1951 and April 1953.

waiting line. Synonym for *queue*.

waiting-line theory. Synonym for *queuing theory*.

Wall Street. The street where the New York Stock Exchange is situated. Used as a synonym for the New York Stock Exchange and also for US financial interests generally.

warehouse company/warehouseman. An enterprise that stores other people's goods for a fee.

warehouse receipt (or warehouse-keeper's certificate). A document, issued by someone who regularly stores goods for others for a fee, which states that he is storing specified goods, how much he will charge for storing them and the conditions under which he will release them from his store.

warrant (noun). 1. Synonym for *subscription warrant*. 2. A *draft*—especially one drawn by a government official that instructs a government department to make a payment to a specified person. 3. A document that contains an authorization of some action—specifically one giving a court's authorization for the apprehension of someone. 4. A *warehouse receipt* which is used as evidence of ownership of the goods warehoused so that one person can transfer ownership of the goods to another by giving him the warrent. (Also called a 'negotiable warehouse receipt' and, sometimes, a 'dock warrant'.)

warrant (verb). To give a *warranty*.

warranty. 1. A promise that is included in a *contract* but is subsidiary, or additional, to the main purpose of the contract. 2. A guarantee given by a manufacturer of the quality of his product with a promise to repair or replace defective parts. 3. A promise given, by the *assured*, in a *contract of insurance* and which the assured must comply with in order to make a claim.

wash sale. A fictitious transaction at an artificially high price on a *commodity exchange* set up to create an impression that prices are rising.

wasting asset. A *fixed asset* that does not have an indefinite useful life (for UK tax purposes one that has a life of less than 50 years). Nearly all fixed assets except land (with the exception of mines) are wasting assets.

waybill. A document prepared by a carrier of goods (or his *agent*) stating the nature of the goods, the names of shipper and consignee and the charges for carriage. The conditions of the contract of carriage are usually included in the document.

weight. Synonym for *weighting factor*.

weighted arithmetic mean. The weighted arithmetic mean of n numbers $x_1, \ldots, x_n$ is:

$$\sum_{i=1}^{n} w_i x_i \bigg/ \sum_{i=1}^{n} w_i$$

where $w_1, \ldots, w_n$ are numbers (called 'weights' or 'weighting factors') that represent the significance or importance attached to each of the xs. (Also known as 'weighted average' or 'weighted mean'.)

weighted average. Synonym for *weighted arithmetic mean*.

weighted mean. Synonym for *weighted arithmetic mean*.

weighting factor. A number by which another number (such as a measurement, estimate or observation) is multiplied and which represents the significance, reliance or importance attached to the measurement, etc., compared to others which are given different weighting factors. (Also called a 'weight'—see also *weighted arithmetic mean*.)

whipsaw. A phenomenon in wage bargaining in multi-plant enterprises: workers at one plant strike for and achieve *parity* [4] of pay with workers at another plant who then demand a restoration of their former *differential* which sets off another demand for parity and so on.

white-collar. Of, relating to, or performing clerical or supervisory work (cf. *blue-collar*). (Presumably derives from the idea that clerical work is cleaner than manual work so that a shirt with a white collar can be worn and that clerical work is more respectable, or has higher status, so that a white collar is required.)

white paper. A publication of the British government with a white cover—usually a statement of policy.

wholesale (adjective). Of, relating to, or engaged in *wholesaling*.

wholesale (verb). To act as a *wholesaler*.

wholesale banking. Aspect of a banking business that is concerned with making loans to companies on a large scale (cf. *retail banking*).

wholesale price index. 1. (US.) An *index number* computed monthly by the US Bureau of Labor Statistics and reflecting the changes in prices that are paid for goods when they are sold by their producers. The index was first published in 1902 and its current base period is 1967. 2. (UK.) Used, loosely, to refer to any of the series of *index numbers* of wholesale prices computed by the Department of Industry and published in the *Monthly Digest of Statistics*.

wholesaler. A person or firm that buys goods and resells them to buyers who will either: (1) resell the goods for profit; or (2) use the goods to facilitate the production of other goods, or incorporate them in other goods they produce; or (3) use them for personal consumption but not in a household (e.g., in a hotel or hospital). *Also* a firm that acts as a *broker* in arranging sales of this type.

wholesaling. Secretly building up a large *shareholding* in a company knowing that a *takeover bid* for the company is likely and making a profit by selling out to the takeover bidder.

wildcat strike. Strike of workers, especially a small but

438

important section of a factory's workforce, that lasts for a short time, is not backed by a union and of which the employer is given very short notice.

winding-up order. An order made by a court that a *registered company* is to be *wound up* in accordance with the *Companies Act 1948.*

wind up. To arrange the affairs of a *company* [1, 2] or other *corporation* so that its *dissolution* can take place. In the UK, the process starts either with an application (by the company itself or by its *creditors* [1]) to a court for a *winding-up order,* or with a *special resolution* that the company be wound up (known as a 'voluntary winding up'). The *assets* [1] of the company are sold and the proceeds distributed to its creditors and the owners of its *equity* [4], and the company is finally dissolved.

'Wind-up', 'dissolve', and 'liquidate' all refer to ending the existence of a corporation. Wind up is commonly used in the UK but 'liquidate' is preferred in the USA. Sometimes 'liquidate' is used to refer only to the process of selling the corporation's property and 'wind up' is used for the legal formalities including dissolution.

wink. An interval of 0.0005 minute (0.03 second) employed in *method study.*

wink counter. A timing device, graduated in *winks,* which is photographed by a movie camera at the same time as the performance of a task for purposes of *method study.* A wink counter gives a digital display (cf. *microchronometer*).

work. Purposeful activity.

work centre (spelt work center in USA). A group of production facilities which, for administrative purposes, are treated as one unit.

work content. See *standard time* [1].

work cycle. 1. A pattern of movements that is repeated, with negligible variations, each time a worker (or a machine) produces a unit of output of a specified item. 2. A succession of operations or processes that is repeated, with negligible variation, each time a production system produces a unit of output of a specified item.

worker director. A member of a *board of directors* of a *company* [1] who is appointed to represent the interests of the employees of the company.

workers' control. An arrangement by which the employees of a firm appoint and have direct control over the management of the firm. See also, *employee participation*.

work-factor system. A *predetermined motion-time system* originally devised in the 1930s. The most important users of the system are an international group of management consultants (in the UK, the Wofac Company) founded by the devisers of the system. A full description of the system has been published in J. H. Quick, J. H. Duncan and J. A. Malcolm, Jr, *Work-Factor Time Standards: Measurement of Manual and Mental Work* (New York: McGraw-Hill, 1962).

work group. A *group* [1] of people who work closely together.

work-in. Occupation of a workplace, the owners of which have tried to close it, by employees who have been made redundant with the object of taking over management of the enterprise.

working capital. The difference between the values of a firm's *current assets* and its *current liabilities*. (This is sometimes called 'net' working capital, when 'gross' working capital means the total value of current assets.)

working conditions. The physical environment in which a worker performs his work—including space available, heating, lighting, ventilation and standards of hygiene and safety. (Also known as 'physical working conditions'.)

working practice. The way in which a particular kind of work is normally arranged: especially, the number of workers usually engaged on the work or their qualifications.

work-in-process. (US.) Synonym for *work-in-progress* [2].

work-in-progress. 1 A project, e.g. of a contractor or a writer, that is not yet complete. 2. Goods which a manufacturer has started to convert into manufactured products but which are not yet *finished goods*. (Also called 'work-in-process' or 'goods-in-process'.)

work measurement. (UK). Determination of the time required, under specified conditions, for the performance of tasks involving human activity. (In the USA, usually called 'time study'.)

workmen's compensation. US scheme for providing cash benefits and medical attention for employees who are injured at work. The benefits are paid by the employer of a person who is injured at work; all employers must be insured to cover such costs or convince the authorities that they have sufficient funds to pay any compensation. The scheme is administered by commissions in each state and benefits vary from state to state.

work sampling. Synonym for *activity sampling*.

works council (or works committee). A formally constituted committee of representatives of workers and management covering a whole workplace (a factory, shop or office) and established for purposes of *joint consultation*.

work sharing. Reduction by a group of workers of the amount of work each of them does in order to avoid laying off some workers. Hence when work is short, everyone suffers a loss of earnings to the same extent.

work simplification. A programme for improving methods of working based on involving all workers in a firm in a search for better methods of doing their jobs and applying common sense rather than sophisticated techniques of *method study*. The idea was developed chiefly by the American industrial engineer, Allan H. Mogensen.

work station. A point or location at which a particular operation or other productive activity is performed in a factory.

work study. (UK.) Activity or process of systematically examining, analysing and measuring methods of performing work that involves human activity in order to improve those methods. (In the USA, usually called 'motion and time study'. Also called 'methods engineering' or 'time-and-motion engineering' or 'time-and-motion study'.)

work ticket. Synonym for *job ticket*.

work-to-rule. A form of *industrial action* in which employees remain at work but apply any regulations relating to their work strictly or interpret regulations in such a way that the amount of work done is limited.

World Bank. Popular name for the *International Bank for Reconstruction and Development*.

World Confederation of Labour (WCL). An international association of national confederations of trade unions. WCL was founded in 1920 originally as an international federation of Christian trade unions. It now devotes its action to studying, promoting, representing and defending the material, moral and spiritual interests of the workers. The WCL condemns all forms of capitalism as well as Marxist 'state socialism' (i.e. an economic system with limited socialist characteristics) because they prevent the achievement of a humane economic system.

A congress of delegates from affiliated organizations is held every four years, decides policy and elects a 22-member Confederal Board which is responsible for general leadership. Day-to-day management is carried out by a permanent secretariat headed by a General Secretary.

International trade federations are organized under the auspices of the WCL.

Address: 50 rue Joseph II, B 1040 Bruxelles, Belgium (217.63.87).

World Federation of Trade Unions (WFTU). An international association of more than 60 national confederations of trade unions formed in 1945. In conformity with its constitution, the WFTU struggles for the improvement of the working and living conditions of the working class, for the interests of the workers at international level, for the right of peoples to self-determination and national independence, against colonialism, neo-colonialism and racism, paying also constant attention to consolidating world peace.

The policy of the WFTU is determined by a World Trade Union Congress held every 4 years. At a congress each affiliated confederation has a number of delegates proportional to its affiliated membership. Each country has one delegate to a General Council which meets annually to approve programmes of work. The General Council elects officers who form a bureau which meets twice a year. A permanent secretariat headed by a General Secretary elected by the General Council is in charge of executive tasks. *Trade union internationals* (TUIs) are formed within the federation.

Address: Nám. Curieových 1, Prague 1, Czechoslovakia (67.856).

writ. A written document containing a command from the Crown to a person to take some specified action.

write down. To decrease the value of a *fixed asset* as recorded in an account by deducting an amount for *depreciation* [2].

writing-down allowance. An amount that a person or company may deduct from taxable trading profits to represent *depreciation* [2] of *fixed assets* or *amortization* [3] of *intangible assets*.

X

xd. Abbreviation of 'ex dividend' (see *ex* [1]).

xerography. A method of making copies of documents. The original document to be copied is exposed to a bright light. White areas of the original reflect the light while dark areas (i.e. the printing or writing on the document) absorb it. The reflected light therefore outlines an image of the printing or writing on the original. This image is received on a metal plate that is coated with selenium powder. The plate has been electrically charged and has been kept in the dark before the projection of the document. Selenium becomes a good conductor of electricity when exposed to light and therefore during projection the electric charge is conducted away by the metal plate everywhere except the lines that were black on the original document. The uncharged selenium powder is no longer attracted to the metal plate and is brushed away. Copy paper is laid on the plate and electrically charged so that the remaining selenium powder, in the form of an image of the document, is transferred to the paper. The paper is then heated so that the image fuses to it. (The name is derived from the Greek xeros = dry and graphein = to write.)

y

yearling. A *security* [1] that is to be *redeemed* one year after issue.

year of assessment. A period of 12 months commencing on 6 April in one calendar year and ending on 5 April in the next calendar year over which an individual's income is measured in order to calculate UK *income tax*. (Also known as a 'fiscal year'.)

yellow-dog contract. A contract of employment that includes a promise by the employee that he will not join a union. (Also known as an 'ironclad'.)

yield. 1. Synonym for *rate of return*. 'Yield' is usually used with reference to investments in *securities* [1] while 'rate of return' is used when referring to investments in *capital goods* or *fixed assets*. 2. (Now infrequent.) Synonym for *internal rate of return*.

yield rate. Synonym for *internal rate of return*.

Z

Z chart. A *graph* [1] in which a *time series* over a specified period is represented by three lines: one represents the actual observations, one represents cumulative totals from the beginning of the chosen period and one represents a moving total (i.e. the total of the observations for a period of fixed length immediately preceding the time at which the moving total is calculated). At the end of the period the three lines form a shape like a capital Z.

zero defects. A programme for persuading employees to produce no faulty products at all. Originally developed in the US armaments industry as a reaction against what was thought to be a complacent attitude induced by *statistical quality control* in which a certain proportion of defects is set as an *acceptable quality level*. Programmes usually attempt to *motivate* employees by emphasizing pride in performance and craftsmanship and by providing rewards for defect-free performance. See J. F. Halpin, *Zero Defects : A New Dimension in Quality Assurance* (New York : McGraw-Hill, 1966).

zero-rated. Incurring UK *value added tax* at a rate of 0%. Supplies in this category include the supply of most kinds of food (except in the course of catering), books, newspapers and power. The effect is that a taxable person who makes zero-rated supplies can have his input tax refunded to him, whereas one who makes exempt supplies cannot have input tax refunded.

446

zero-sum game. In *game theory*, a game in which, for each outcome the sum of the payoffs for all players is always zero—in other words, a player only gains what other players lose.
zero-time activity. Synonym for *dummy*.

Peter Drucker

'Peter Drucker's fascination lies in combining sharp analysis with acute cynicism' THE TIMES

The New Markets 60p

A stimulating collection of essays on the economic, social and political environment in which executives and institutions operate. Among the most revealing are three essays on Japanese industry, culminating in 'What we Can Learn from Japanese Management'.

The Effective Executive 80p

'I can conscientiously recommend that this book be given the very highest priority for executive reading, and even re-reading' THE DIRECTOR

The Practice of Management £1.50

'Peter Drucker has three outstanding gifts as a writer on business – acute perception, brilliant skill as a reporter and unlimited self-confidence' NEW STATESMAN

Managing for Results 75p

'A guide to do-it-yourself management . . . contains many first-class suggestions that have the great virtue that they are likely to be widely and easily applicable to almost every business' TIMES REVIEW OF INDUSTRY

Also available
Technology, Management and Society 45p

Edited by S. E. Stiegeler BSc and Glyn Thomas BSc
A Dictionary of Economics and Commerce £1.50

An authoritative A–Z of the terms used internationally in the overlapping fields of theoretical economics and practical commerce.

A team of expert contributors provides a formal definition of each word or term, followed by an explanation of its underlying concepts and accompanied by appropriate illustrations. Special attention is paid to such new and rapidly expanding subjects as cost-benefit analysis and welfare economics.

In the field of commerce, the vocabularies of banking, accounting, insurance, stock exchanges, commodity dealing, shipping, transport and commercial law are all included.

With a Foreword by James A. Newman
The Universal Encyclopedia of Mathematics £1.50

A lucidly written and sensibly arranged mathematical reference book by the compilers of *How Things Work* (The Universal Encyclopedia of Machines).

With over two hundred pages of formulae and tables, it will be of the utmost value to parents, teachers, students, engineers, technicians and research workers, as well as to the intelligent layman for whom mathematics retains its fascination.

'The definitions are clear and the treatment just right'
TIMES LITERARY SUPPLEMENT

'Parents blackmailed into helping with the homework, as well as more professional calculators, should find the work invaluable'
DAILY TELEGRAPH

Rosemary Stewart
The Reality of Management 80p

'Not just another manual for executives, it is rather more like a set of
compass bearings to help the manager plot his course in his career and
his social life' NEW SOCIETY

The Reality of Organizations 80p

'Addressed to managers whether in industry, commerce, hospitals,
public administration or elsewhere and includes examples from these
latter fields . . . its style is excellent, concise and free of jargon'
PUBLIC ADMINISTRATION

Desmond Goch
Finance and Accounts for Managers 50p

The art of accountancy is now the most important instrument of
control in the management armoury. This comprehensive guide will
enable managers — even those without formal training in business
finance — to formulate trading policies, forecast future trends and
effectively administer their departments.

You can buy these and other Pan books from booksellers and
newsagents; or direct from the following address:
Pan Books, Cavaye Place, London SW10 9PG
Send purchase price plus 15p for the first book and 5p for
each additional book, to allow for postage and packing
Prices quoted are applicable in UK

While every effort is made to keep prices low, it is sometimes
necessary to increase prices at short notice. Pan Books reserve the
right to show on covers new retail prices which may differ
from those advertised in the text or elsewhere